The life of
John Berryman

The life of
John Berryman

John Haffenden

Routledge & Kegan Paul
Boston, London, Melbourne and Henley

First published in 1982
by Routledge & Kegan Paul Ltd
9 Park Street, Boston, Mass. 02108, USA,
39 Store Street, London WC1E 7DD,
296 Beaconsfield Parade, Middle Park
Melbourne 3206, Australia and
Broadway House, Newtown Road,
Henley-on-Thames, Oxon RG9 1EN
Set in Linotron Bembo by
Rowland Phototypesetting Ltd, Bury St Edmunds, Suffolk
and printed in the United States of America
© John Haffenden 1982

Library of Congress Cataloging in Publication Data

Haffenden, John
The life of John Berryman
Bibliography p.
Includes index
1. Berryman, John, 1914–1972 – Biography.
2. Poets, American – 20th century – Biography.
I. Title.
PS3503.E744Z59   811'.54(B)   81-23501
ISBN 0-7100-9216-4   AACR2

Contents

A note on spelling and punctuation

From the time of his arrival in England in 1936 (shortly before his twenty-second birthday), Berryman adopted the English spelling of all words which have American variants, and retained that convention for the rest of his life – in letters and journals, and in publications. Accordingly, all quotations given from Berryman's published works, and transcriptions from his unpublished writings and letters, follow his own form. By the same token, all quotations from his writings which predate his arrival in England in 1936 follow the originals. Likewise, the punctuation is in all cases Berryman's own, apart from any unintentional slips which are my responsibility.

Chronology

1914   Born, 25 October, the son of John Allyn Smith and Martha (Little) Smith, in McAlester, Oklahoma, where father works in a bank.

1919   Birth of Robert Jefferson, Berryman's brother.

1920/21   The Smith family moves to Anadarko, Oklahoma, where father works in the First State Bank and John attends West Grade school.

1924   John Allyn Smith resigns his post at the bank and is appointed Assistant Game and Fish Warden.

1925   Parents make a reconnaissance trip to Florida, while John and his brother become boarders at St Joseph's Academy in Chickasha, Oklahoma.

1926   The Smith family takes up residence in Tampa, Oklahoma, where John Angus McAlpin Berryman becomes their friend; John Allyn Smith commits suicide; Martha marries John Angus McAlpin Berryman, whose adoptive sons presently take his surname; the Berryman family moves to New York City, where John attends Public School 69, Jackson Heights.

1928   John enters South Kent School in Connecticut; bullied and unhappy, he none the less makes good academic progress.

1931   Attempts suicide.

1932   Enters Columbia College, New York, where, under the influence of his mother and of Mark Van Doren, he eventually makes the grade as a scholar.

1936   Graduates Phi Beta Kappa, and wins the Euretta J. Kellett scholarship to study in England; takes up residence at

ix

Clare College, Cambridge, where his tutor is George
Rylands; attends a talk by T. S. Eliot; meets W. H.
Auden.

1937   Befriends Brian Boydell; meets Dylan Thomas; also
meets W. B. Yeats at the Athenaeum Club; meets
Beatrice, who becomes his first fiancée, and takes a
summer holiday with her in Germany; wins Oldham
Shakespeare Scholarship.

1938   Returns home to New York, where Beatrice later visits
him; meets Bhain Campbell, and becomes part-time
poetry editor for the *Nation*.

1939   Meets Delmore Schwartz; is appointed Instructor in
English at Wayne State University, Detroit, where he
begins to suffer from a state of nervous collapse which is
diagnosed as *petit mal*.

1940   Berryman is appointed Instructor in English (for four
months) at Harvard University; publishes 'Twenty
Poems' in *Five Young American Poets*; Bhain Campbell
dies.

1941   Berryman meets Eileen Patricia Mulligan.

1942   Publishes *Poems*; marries Eileen.

1943   Ends appointment at Harvard; grubs for jobs and tackles
some temporary appointments, including three weeks'
teaching at the Iona School, New Rochelle, and is finally
appointed Instructor in English for one year at Princeton
University, where he works with Richard Blackmur;
meets Erich Kahler and Christian Gauss.

1944   Meets Robert Lowell; lectures for three weeks at
Briarcliff College, New York, and is then awarded a
Foundation research fellowship by the Rockefeller
Foundation; works on an edition of *King Lear*; meets
Dwight Macdonald, Paul Goodman, and Edmund
Wilson.

1945   Records his poetry for the Library of Congress; his
Rockefeller Fellowship is renewed for a further year;
commissioned to write a book on Stephen Crane; writes
'The Imaginary Jew', which wins first prize in *Kenyon
Review*–Doubleday Doran contest.

1946   Becomes Associate in Creative Writing at Princeton
University (1946–7), where his students include W. S.
Merwin, Bruce Berlind, Sidney Monas, and William
Arrowsmith.

1947   Meets and falls in love with 'Lise', and writes a sequence
of sonnets later published (1967) as *Berryman's Sonnets*;

meets T. S. Eliot and Ben Shahn; begins psychiatric treatment.

1948   Starts work on 'Homage to Mistress Bradstreet'; has other love affairs; publishes *The Dispossessed*; meets Saul Bellow and Ezra Pound; is appointed Resident Fellow in Creative Writing at Princeton University (1948–9).

1949   Works on an unfinished sequence of poems, *The Black Book*, and on his study of Stephen Crane; wins Guarantors Prize (*Poetry*) and Shelley Memorial Award (Poetry Society of America); is appointed Alfred Hodder Fellow at Princeton University (1950–1).

1950   Teaches one semester at the University of Washington, Seattle; wins Levinson Prize (*Poetry*); publishes *Stephen Crane* (critical biography); lectures for two weeks at the University of Vermont; meets Randall Jarrell.

1952   Spends spring semester as Elliston Professor of Poetry at the University of Cincinnati; undertakes more intensive work on 'Homage to Mistress Bradstreet'; awarded Guggenheim Fellowship (1952–3) for critical study of Shakespeare and for creative writing.

1953   Completes 'Homage to Mistress Bradstreet' (first published in *Partisan Review*); John and Eileen Berryman spend the summer months in Europe, where they meet Theodore Roethke and Louis MacNeice; they visit the MacNeices in London, where Eileen is hospitalised for a back injury; Berryman is separated from Eileen and spends the latter part of the year in New York City.

1954   Teaches one semester of creative writing at the University of Iowa (where he also begins to study Hebrew); his students include W. D. Snodgrass and Donald Justice; teaches a summer school at Harvard, where his students include Edward Hoagland; returns to teach at Iowa in the fall, but is dismissed after a drunken altercation; at Allen Tate's suggestion, moves to Minneapolis; begins a long period of dream-analysis.

1955   Starts teaching in Humanities at the University of Minnesota, where his chairman is Ralph Ross; at work on *The Dream Songs*.

1956   Translates Paul Claudel's 'Le Chemin de la croix' for Antal Dorati; divorced from Eileen; marries Elizabeth Ann Levine; publishes *Homage to Mistress Bradstreet*; awarded Rockefeller Fellowship in poetry by *Partisan Review*.

1957   Awarded Harriet Monroe Poetry Prize; son, Paul, is

born; Berryman is awarded a tenured appointment in Humanities and English at the University of Minnesota; visits Japan; lectures for two months in India under the auspices of the United States Information Service; spends last weeks of the year with his family vacationing in Spain.

1958   Appointed Associate Profesor of Interdisciplinary Studies at the University of Minnesota, but is aggrieved when a Special Faculty Meeting votes to disestablish the Department of Interdisciplinary Studies; publishes *His Thought Made Pockets & The Plane Buckt*.

1959   Divorced from Ann; awarded the Brandeis University Creative Arts Award; teaches for two weeks in June at the University of Utah.

1960   Teaches one semester in the Department of Speech at the University of California, Berkeley; publishes (with Ralph Ross and Allen Tate) *The Arts of Reading*, an anthology with commentary.

1961   Spends eight weeks teaching at the School of Letters, Indiana University; marries Kathleen (Kate) Donahue, his third and last wife.

1962   Teaches at Bread Load School of English, Middlebury, Vermont; meets Robert Frost; becomes visiting professor (1962–3) at Brown University, Providence, Rhode Island; participates in National Poetry Festival, Washington, DC; his first daughter, Martha, is born.

1963   Family spends summer weeks in rural Rhode Island; Berryman receives an award from the Ingram Merrill Foundation; family resides for some weeks (1963–4) in Washington, DC.

1964   Publishes *77 Dream Songs* (the first volume of *The Dream Songs*); wins Russell Loines Award (National Institute of Arts and Letters); buys house at 33 Arthur Avenue S.E., Minneapolis.

1965   Awarded Pulitzer Prize for *77 Dream Songs*; awarded Guggenheim Fellowship for 1966–7.

1966   The family lives in Dublin (1966–7).

1967   Awarded 5,000 dollars by the Academy of American Poets; receives 10,000-dollar award from the National Endowment for the Arts; publishes *Berryman's Sonnets* and *Short Poems*.

1968   Publishes *His Toy, His Dream, His Rest* (the conclusion of *The Dream Songs*).

1969   *His Toy, His Dream, His Rest* wins the National Book

Award and the Bollingen Prize; publishes *The Dream Songs* (complete edition); appointed Regents' Professor of Humanities at the University of Minnesota; admitted for treatment at Hazelden, an alcoholic rehabilitation centre.

1970   Treated for alcoholism at Abbott Hospital, Minneapolis; then at the Intensive Alcohol Treatment Center, St Mary's Hospital, Minneapolis; joins Alcoholics Anonymous; publishes *Love & Fame*.

1971   Works on a novel, *Recovery*, and on poems later collected in *Delusions, Etc.*; birth of Sarah Rebecca, second daughter; is awarded a Senior Fellowship by the National Endowment for the Humanities.

1972   Commits suicide, 7 January.

POSTHUMOUS PUBLICATIONS

1972   *Delusions, Etc.*
1973   *Recovery*, a novel
1976   *The Freedom of the Poet*, essays and stories
1977   *Henry's Fate & Other Poems, 1967–1972* (edited with an introduction by John Haffenden)

1

Introductory

My engagement with John Berryman began in 1970, at a time when I was reading for a research degree under the supervision of Professor Richard Ellmann at Oxford University. My topic was a study of the modern American long poem, taking into consideration texts by Ezra Pound, William Carlos Williams, and Charles Olson. After some months of failing to discover the significant lines of my proposed comparison, I turned dizzily to Berryman's *Dream Songs* with a naive view to including them under the same rubric. I had first read the *Songs* in the late 1960s, when they left me decidedly interested but baffled. Reading them again in 1970 and 1971, I found myself perhaps a little less baffled but stimulated beyond belief and compelled to understand more. I wrote a preliminary essay on Berryman and sent it to Berryman's London publisher. When I was invited to Faber & Faber in January 1972, I missed the day's newspaper on my journey and only learned on arrival that Berryman had just committed suicide.

I had recently read Berryman's latest volume, *Love & Fame*, which excited me as an entirely accessible book, teeming with idiomatic and moral risks and raising fascinating problems of form. Berryman seemed to have taken his real life on board in a new way. One poem, 'Friendless', for example, begins

> Friendless in Clare, except Brian Boydell
> a Dubliner with no hair
> an expressive tenor speaking voice

– lines which readily conjured up the Professor of Music I had met while an undergraduate at Trinity College, Dublin. Unable to control my curiosity, I contacted Professor Boydell, and from that point on my eagerness to comprehend the life of John Berryman would not be checked. With considerable lack of tact I wrote to Mrs Kate Berryman after only a few months, and she properly met my importunate queries by politely temporising. Eventually, at Easter 1974, while teaching at the University of Exeter, I made my first visit to Minneapolis: my search for John Berryman had truly begun.

Berryman belongs to what has become known as the Middle Generation of American poets, a group that includes Delmore Schwartz, Robert Lowell, Randall Jarrell, and Theodore Roethke. It is a critical convenience to call much of their work 'Confessional', a classification to which Berryman himself responded with 'rage and contempt'. 'The word doesn't mean anything,' he protested. Such a label may produce a sweet theory, but it might turn out – just as another theory turned out for those who attempted to use flamingoes as croquet-mallets in *Alice in Wonderland* – to be limp in application. Certainly the individual writers of that generation (it may be worth recalling that W. H. Auden was only eight years older than Berryman) either knew each other personally or had affinities with one another's work, but the question of literary affiliation cannot be glossed in terms of an easy succession. In popular opinion, as my own students sometimes tell me, Robert Lowell's *Life Studies*, published in 1959, instigated a new fashion of opening poems nakedly to the personal life which was followed by Sylvia Plath and her imitators. Even if that facile view were partly true, we need to reckon with the fact that Berryman began writing his *Dream Songs* in 1955 (not to mention *Berryman's Sonnets* from 1947) without knowing of Lowell's *Life Studies*: so the matter of borrowing or influence immediately runs up against an awkwardly anachronistic hitch. Anyway, influence runs in many directions. In the late 1960s, after the publication of *The Dream Songs*, Lowell wrote to Berryman, 'I think I am in your debt – at least I say so in my preface. I've just completed a long poem, *Notebook of a Year*. . . . It's considerably shorter than yours, and very different.' Evidently cautious of the possibility that critics might pan him for directly imitating Berryman, Lowell wrote him again in September 1969, 'I think anyone who cared for your book would for mine. Anyway, we're accomplished beyond jealousy. Without you, I would find writing more puzzling.' Whether he derived more from Berryman as a person or from his writing is a question which must be left to critics at large to assess and interpret, but I don't think it snide to point out that a Freudian slip on Lowell's part betrayed his feeling that he had actually gained much from Berryman's literary example: that last sentence originally read, 'Without your book, I would find writing more puzzling.' Furthermore, indebtedness is not confined to a reciprocity between one poet and another. Berryman publicly acknowledged that he took a certain charge off at least one novelist, Saul Bellow. 'In the Bradstreet poem, as I seized inspiration from *Augie March*, I sort of seized inspiration, I think, from Lowell, rather than imitated him.' When Bellow finished his novel *Herzog*, Berryman wrote him this fan-letter: 'Nobody has ever sat down & wallowed to this extent in his own life, *with* full art – I mean, novelists. I don't know of anything to compare it to, except you. . . . Go to heaven.' The fact that Berryman limited his praise to Bellow's achievement in the genre of the novel may imply that he reserved a like success to his own work in verse.

What I mean to say is that it requires another book altogether – and *many* books will come – to analyse Berryman's proper place in the literary culture of his historical epoch. The present book is the story of one life; it certainly draws on Berryman's friendships and associations, but I have not attempted to explore the entire literary milieu, only the psychology of one man. Time and study should tell us, for example, how much Lowell's work speaks to a sense of cultural and social history, and how much Berryman's is a function of moral and spiritual preoccupations.

Literary success and critical acclaim came late to Berryman. In retrospect he could announce with some wry satisfaction, 'early fame is very dangerous indeed, and my situation, which was so painful to me for many years, was really in a way beneficial.' The irony of that pronouncement is a sad one to investigate, since Berryman was a middle-aged man before he did his best work, and he lived only to the age of fifty-seven. Although what is arguably his greatest achievement, *Homage to Mistress Bradstreet* (which cost him untold anguish of spirit and energy in the early 1950s), earned intense praise – Edmund Wilson called it 'the most distinguished long poem by an American since *The Waste Land*' – it captured no quick public, and the poet had to labour into his last decade of life before his masterpiece, *The Dream Songs*, would be widely acknowledged as the product of someone quite other than a literary minimus. The course of his life runs the whole gamut from personal degradation to artistic ecstasy. It is, to say the least, distinguished for energy and intensity: he suffered the early suicide of his father, the dominance of his mother, poverty and professional setbacks, alcoholism and spiritual vexation. On one level, his story is that of an obsessional neurotic; but if he was cranky, he was also vibrant and entertaining, an electrifying and fearful teacher, loving and silly, occasionally unkind but far more often overwhelmingly generous toward his friends, lovers, colleagues and students.

Berryman's most severe critics have held him to be egocentric, self-indulgent and obscurantist, but Berryman's work nowhere rehearses the vanity denounced by such views. Fame, or the fact that he was not what Hemingway called a good drunk, Berryman sometimes took as his privilege for bad behaviour, but such conduct puts a scandal only on the man, not on his work. Whatever his subject, the poet imagines and composes it. While I relish the poet Douglas Dunn's belief that 'poems should come on as strong as they can', I would need persuading beyond reason to believe that Berryman belongs to what he has called 'the tradition of the crazed exposure of the American ego'. With respect to the hero of what he once termed the 'Tragical History' of *The Dream Songs*, Berryman observed, 'Henry both is and is not me, obviously. We touch at certain points. But I am an actual human being; he is nothing but a series of conceptions – my conceptions.' I see no reason to quarrel with that definition, and it is not a contradiction to say that his work draws on his life for subject-matter.

In what way, then, if at all, does the life throw light on the work? Although, as some critics believe, the imagination has no biography, biographical information can assuredly illuminate and provide an aid to analysis of the poems, even if it cannot explain them. To take one notable example: the poem *Homage to Mistress Bradstreet* is centrally concerned with childbirth, motherhood, adultery and alienation. Berryman declared that several factors contributed to his feeling of being ready to write the poem in 1952–3. One was his tremendously strong sense of guilt over the fact that his wife Eileen had not had a child, for which he blamed himself far more even than for his affairs. Throughout the marriage he had felt deeply ambivalent at the prospect of fatherhood, and had compounded it after 1947 through his adulteries, heavy drinking, and staying up all too often through the night. In a late interview with the *Paris Review* he made the misleadingly simple assertion that 'we very much wanted a child', but it comes much nearer to the truth of his experience to say that he always had dreadfully divided feelings about the possibility of becoming a father, feelings which pervaded the writing of the poem (see also note to Chapter 10).

That is a pointed example, but it does underline the need for us to discriminate the truths of Berryman's life from the sometimes unreliable constructions he himself put upon it, and from the conclusions critics might otherwise draw from unstable or improper evidence. It obliges us to be generously wary of the poet's own developing sense of his identity and history, and indeed to spell out all the biographical facts, of which any number gloss the vivid work which is Berryman's legacy. My study of Berryman's major poems, *John Berryman: A Critical Commentary* (Macmillan and New York University Press, 1980), will I hope complement this book.

In a very informative and useful work, *John Berryman: An Introduction to the Poetry* (New York: Columbia University Press, 1977), Joel Conarroe saliently remarks,

> The details of artists' lives have a strong attraction for us; this is especially true of a writer as brilliant, as troubled, and as flamboyant as Berryman. We are compelled to ask questions, some of which are probably unanswerable, about his erratic behavior and about the sources of his art. Did he, with the death of his father, suffer an irreversible loss, one that was to be the source of the guilt and despair that dominated his adult life? Can a man mourn a loss for nearly fifty years, or is such mourning merely an excuse for heavy drinking? Was it his loss of faith, following his father's suicide, that was in fact responsible for his lifelong anxiety? Was it his mother after all, as his posthumous novel suggests, who was the dominant person in his life? Was his preoccupation with fame a product of his insecurity? Were his classes and poetry readings, at times spellbinding and at times incoherent, an essential form of reinforcement? Did his sense of personal debasement also require reinforcement, thereby contributing to his behavior? Was he, as he suggests here and there in his work, latently homosexual? Are his *Dream Songs*, as Lewis Hyde insists, to be explained away as the self-pitying indulgences of a resentful alcoholic? Would he have survived in a city with an intellectual climate different from that of Minneapolis? Is there anything anyone could have done to rescue him from himself? Was his suicide a deliberate act? Was it impulsive? Was it, like that of Hemingway, a response to physical and intellectual deterioration?

I hope that the following pages provide the evidence, if not all the answers.

I have tried to trace the process of one man's life, both the dignity and the distress. Writing such a book within a relatively short period of Berryman's death, I have encountered and attempted to come to terms with the problems of historical perspective. While sentimentality should perhaps be avoided in writing about the recently dead, affection and irritation, for example, may have a place. As I discovered at an early stage of research Berryman's life story is not available to a synthetic view: the interstices of his complex career tell us as much as the achievements and prominent deeds, the high or the hot spots. I have been partial less to explanation than to information, in the conviction that greater knowledge might lead to deeper appreciation. In reading other lives, I have been struck, for example, at how infrequently biographers give details of the bank balances of their subjects. And yet the state of one's pocket is more than a material matter, it is a moral and spiritual condition, and I have accordingly included a number of facts about Berryman's earnings. I have often felt that determinative interpretations of a biography are postulated on the supposition that the dense pattern of a real life should yield to meanings as simple as a rhumb; they sell the reader short by trimming texture to a thesis. Biography is an art, but it owes a primary obligation to truth. To that end I have taken it as my brief to relate all the necessary facts of Berryman's life. To avoid offence to persons still living, I have omitted some facts, but I have done my best to avoid falsehood. In certain instances I have consented or chosen to employ pseudonyms in preference to specifically identifying persons. The name 'Beatrice' is used by agreement, and I have taken the convenient course of retaining the name 'Lise' (a pseudonym invented and used by Berryman in *Berryman's Sonnets*) for the woman who figured in his life during 1947 (chapter 9). Likewise, in a very few other passages where identification would serve no useful purpose, I have reduced two proper names to their initials – 'J' and 'S' – and two others (in a brief passage from Berryman's journal quoted in chapter 3) to random initials, 'Y' and 'Z'.

Although I have felt grave qualms over the radical issue of warts, there is some consolation in knowing that Berryman reckoned his life story would be written, and that he felt sanguine at the prospect. While examining his papers, I experienced a gratifying *frisson* when I read a passage from a Paris letter of December 1936 which describes an evening stroll to the aptly named Rue de la Lune, where he 'looked up and lo! it was the moon – right large & white & round in a purple sky.' Describing the phenomenon, young Berryman knowingly added in parentheses, 'Note to my biographer – leave that out, it's true but it ain't convincin'.' In later years he was occasionally heard to account for his behaviour with a remark such as, 'It's all part of my biography, that's all!' The years brought him spells of deep personal joy and artistic fulfilment, but all too heavy a hand of terrible suffering. Towards the end Berryman himself pinpointed the tragic irony of his life in these remarks to Peter Stitt:

> I have . . . a feeling that endowment is a very small part of
> achievement. I would rate it about fifteen or twenty percent.
> Then you have historical luck, personal luck, health, things like

that, then you have hard work, sweat. And you have
ambition. . . . I do feel strongly that among the greatest pieces
of luck for high achievement is ordeal. . . . My idea is this: the
artist is extremely lucky who is presented with the worst
possible ordeal which will not actually kill him ['The Art of
Poetry XVI', *Paris Review*, XIV, winter 1972].

2
Beginnings:
boyhood and father's
suicide

John Berryman believed that his life of trials was patterned from the age of eleven, when his father committed suicide, but his mother had first and long dominated his destiny. A troubled and powerful woman, she herself inherited a famous grandfather and parents who were divided too soon after her birth. Although her lineage was entirely a southern one, Martha was born on Sunday, 8 July 1894 in Du Quoin, Illinois, where her mother had chosen an ill-judged time to visit friends; Martha's kin sometimes teased her for being born a 'Yankee'. Except for the fact that her father, Alvin B. Little, gave her a bound edition of Shakespeare as a consolation present during an early bout of typhoid, he lacks a positive showing during her childhood: by the time she was five, he had deserted the family. As a possible consequence, Martha May, his wife, seems always to have disliked or distrusted most men, and lived a proud forsakenness for several decades.

There seems little reason to doubt that her mother was duly, if unlavishly, attentive to her upbringing, but Martha believed that she had gone unloved. Having no siblings, she apparently failed for not being a boy, and displeased her mother even further by bearing too great a resemblance to her father, which was especially a fault when she behaved badly. As years advanced she could no longer remember her father for herself, but – as she put it – 'entirely through my mother's eyes and tongue'. She felt badly deprived of her father, in fact, and longed for paternal love, doubly so when her mother blamed her for being his child. When she grew up, she consecrated her young maturity to a passionate love for her own offspring, and always burdened John Berryman with an impossibly great responsibility for her state of heart. In her sixty-fifth year, for example, she wrote him this piteous picture of her early deprivation:

I . . . loved my mother only in the family sense . . . liked her only rarely . . . knew that she cared for me only as an extension of herself, resented me for my youth and difference, hated me for the child of my father whom she despised and perhaps rightly, envied me the sons she lacked – I, who longed for her love and have love-groped my way through life for the need of it.

But during her girlhood she did find native grounds for believing herself to be special and socially superior. She basked in the prestige won for the family by that famous warrior General Robert Glenn Shaver (see Appendix), her valiant and kindly grandfather, whom she always regarded in terms of 'adoration'. He clearly loved the child in return, and gave her the indulgence she lacked from her mother. Mrs Little kept her in a close childhood which excluded the society of other children, and until the age of eleven Martha was taught by a tutoress and gave herself airs. All too taken with the selectness of her family background, she liked to retain a certain degree of disdainfulness throughout life, embodying in her own manner the eminence won by her grandfather.

As a single parent, Mrs Little was exposed to a good deal of small-town gossip, which added to make her jealous of privacy and exclusive in friendships. Martha always remembered the pain of ostracism and the isolation of her childhood.

I [was] the child of a broken marriage in the days when even a woman who divorced a man for just cause was regarded as declassee and her child little better than a bastard. You can have no idea what it was like at the end of the last century and the beginning of this; perhaps not everywhere, I don't know, I only know St Louis and Arkansas, and then Oklahoma. I was not quite twelve when we moved to Oklahoma, my mother and I, after seven years of pity and scorn. It is the children who peck at the stranger; my mother, an Episcopalian, oddly enough, went to my hated father's church, the Christian Church – not oddly, I suppose, the Episcopal Church was strongly opposed to divorces and divorcees then – and made friends and seemed to enjoy herself. I was never more than on the fringes, always subject to someone saying, you know she has no father, well, where is he, ohhhh . . .

Martha was twelve when her mother took her from St Louis, Missouri, to McAlester, Oklahoma, where she at last went to school with other children, but on first arrival must have struck her

classmates as precocious, snobbish, and fit for bullying, as this piece
of autobiography from among her papers suggests.

> Martha Little stood at bay, pressed flat against the wall of the
> school entry-way, hands outstretched against the rough brick,
> all of her sucked tight against that wall as if there only lay
> sanctuary. The desperate, wide gold-flecked eyes which had
> first flickered from one face to another in that semicircle of
> excited, scornful girls, clung now in a duel of gazes to the black
> eyes of the girl directly in front of her. This was dreadful, why,
> these girls were only a little older than she was, about twelve or
> thirteen, and they looked as if they wanted to tear her to pieces!
> *She* couldn't help it because her clothes weren't like theirs,
> perhaps if they knew that she'd *love* to be just like them – but
> this faint hope died as she listened to the jeers and hateful
> phrases pouring like toads from their mouths. It wasn't *her* fault
> that Katie brought her to school each morning and waited for
> her each evening – she'd *love* to come and go just like they did.
> The golden-bronze braids quivered as she thought of how she
> hoped she was going to be such happy friends with all of these
> girls; she'd never had a real friend, and – she'd have to do
> something right away or she'd cry and they'd laugh at her.

Because of her early tutoring she was higher in school than her
peers, and at fifteen entered Christian College, a Junior College for
Young Women, in Columbia, Missouri. After two years, she
graduated as valedictorian in 1911. According to her own account
from much later in life, she was then due to enter the University of
Oklahoma (with a job in the library to meet her expenses) to major
in philology, but her mother had no time for idle aspirations and
found her a post as schoolteacher in nearby Sasakwa, then a town of
fewer than five hundred inhabitants in a region of bleak sand-hills
and scrub-oak. Much later, on 17 January 1971, in a letter to her
son's third wife, Kate Berryman, she rehearsed the situation that
had been thrust upon her.

> I was 17 in July and started teaching the first of September, the
> fourth, fifth and sixth grades, only twenty-three in all, ranging
> in age from ten to a giant of 18 who hadn't had much time for
> schooling because he was needed at the farm. . . . In October I
> went over, on a weekend, and took my examination for the
> post and got the only 100 I ever had. And when I resigned in
> November, effective at the Christmas holiday, the
> Superintendent of Schools for the state wrote me that my classes

were the best in the state, in all areas, and I wept – I remember
because I never cried; that was my only defence, and it wasn't
kind of me because my mother would have comforted me, I
think, if I had sobbed and 'taken on' but I had only my pride and
my abilities, and they were mine and I would not do them
down.

Because her mother had shown her neither love nor confidence,
Martha had learned to harden in defiance of her, to commit her
activities to personal pride and not to any family feeling. The move
to McAlester allowed her professional independence and freedom
of association, and it was not long before the pleasant and unassum-
ing young bank manager, John Allyn Smith, began to court her.
John Berryman rather exaggerated the situation in which his
parents became acquainted when he told the *Harvard Advocate* in a
1969 interview, 'they were the only people who could read and
write for hundreds of miles around.'

Born and raised in the northern state of Minnesota, John Allyn
Smith was a comparative newcomer to the south. His father,
Jefferson Leonard Smith, had been born in Maine on 6 September
1838 of an old-established family. During the Civil War he was
severely wounded at the Battle of the Wilderness (it is possible that
his leg was amputated or maimed, since he walked with a limp for
the rest of his life), and consequently discharged from service. He
re-enlisted after recovering from his wounds, however, and served
out the remainder of the War. In 1866 he migrated to Minnesota
where he took up land in the western part of the state, but –
according to family tradition – was forced to withdraw because of
Indian troubles. He then settled in the town of South Stillwater
(about ten miles from Minneapolis), where he was for thirty years a
foreman for the St Croix Lumber Company.
   A tall, rugged man with enormous square shoulders, he married
in Minneapolis a handsome, forceful young woman of twenty-
two, Mary Kanar (variously Kenna or Kemrar in official documents), on 30 October 1869. Born in Indian Town, New Bruns-
wick, Canada, Mary was a stern, domineering, stubborn, illogical
woman of Irish Catholic ancestry from County Cork; she spoke
with a brogue, and had inherited a· flashing Irish wit from her
parents.
   In 1872, shortly before the birth of their third child, Jefferson
Leonard and Mary Smith took up their residence in South Stillwater
and built a fine wooden-frame family house, which they occupied
until their deaths. Altogether Mary bore her husband ten children

(six girls and four boys, at regular two-yearly intervals), of whom the last born – 'the spoiled baby of the family', Martha later called him – was John Allyn, on 21 March 1887.

Nothing is known of John Allyn Smith's childhood education, but from September 1905 he attended a course in Commerce for some months at the Globe College of Business in St Paul, Minnesota. It is not possible to discover whether or not he gained any qualification from his studies, but he subsequently spent two years as a relief man at the different yards of the Inter-State Lumber Company, Stillwater: 'a model young man, with no bad habits,' wrote his boss, W. B. Thorp, in a reference. His brother, James William (the Smiths' second child, John Allyn's senior by almost sixteen years), had at some time moved south to Holdenville, Oklahoma, where he made so good as to own a bank. John Allyn and another brother went down to work with him, but Will (as he was always called) died of pneumonia in 1911, probably before John Allyn Smith took up his duties at the branch bank in Sasakwa. (The career of the other brother is lost in mystery, since he disappeared from the bank and was possibly made the scapegoat for certain peculations.)

Stuck in what Berryman himself later called the 'little hole' of Sasakwa, Smith earnestly courted Martha, who apparently resisted him. She later claimed that, in consequence of her strict upbringing, she had been 'totally ignorant of sex' and that Smith 'raped me when I refused to marry him and said he would tell my mother if I didn't agree. I knew she would blame me, so I agreed.' She wrote that brief, unfinished account late in life, and we cannot now know the truth of the situation, but there is a ring of authenticity in the claim that Smith might have blackmailed her into marriage with the threat of her mother's astringent and uncompassionate response. (They lived in the same boarding-house, and – in order to gain entrance to her room – he apparently rapped on her door and said there was a fire downstairs.) Her account is blunt, and perhaps the situation was more complicated, but nothing is known in mitigation except that he did marry her.

The couple were regularly married on 25 July 1912. Martha was just eighteen years of age, Smith twenty-five. It seems characteristic of Mrs Little's nature that she refused Martha a wedding-dress on the grounds that the couple would barely have time to catch their train to Minnesota, where Smith took his bride to visit his family straight after the wedding.

Apart from the forbidding prospect of meeting several of Smith's brothers and sisters, the young Martha had to encounter the stalwart parents. She found Mary Smith 'a most commanding

woman' who instantly disliked her, most especially for her southern airs and for coming from the state of Oklahoma where one of
her sons had died and another been lost. Her mother-in-law's
dislike was made perfectly evident when Martha found herself, the
new bride and member of the family, served last at the table.
Looking critically at the girl, the domineering Mrs Smith had
finally asked, 'What part would you like?' Adopting a southern
convention in reply, Martha said bravely, 'Anything will be fine,
thank you, Lady Smith.' Mrs Smith scornfully responded, 'I don't
want to hear any of that southern nonsense – you can just call me
Mrs Smith until it comes natural when you have a child to call me
Gran'ma'.' Smith asked his blanching bride if she would like to be
excused from the table, but she stuck proudly by the board.

Leonard Jefferson Smith, who clearly reminded her of her grandfather, she thought 'a wonderful figure of an old man . . . stooped
somewhat, dried flesh holding a big bonerack together, quiet,
silent, interesting.' He too, it appears, had been appalled by his
wife's affront to their daughter-in-law, to the extent that Mrs Smith
asked why he was not eating? 'I am just waiting till everyone
finishes so I can leave,' he replied, 'and I notice that I am not the only
person whose appetite you took.' Then he stood up, said 'God
damn it, woman', and walked out. The next morning John Allyn
and Martha went off to the Chisaco Lakes for their honeymoon.
When they returned, no one showed any more rudeness, and on
their departure for Oklahoma, Jefferson Smith came to the porch of
his house, patted Martha on the back, hesitated, and kissed her on
the cheek. She put a hand on his arm and said, 'Thank you, Father,
for everything.' Though she never saw him again, she remained
loyal to his taciturn and solid worth. From her mother-in-law, as
from her own mother, she had received coldness in answer to her
appeals for love; after years of living with blunted affection, she was
more than ready to shower love on her own children, especially as it
was already apparent that she had been mistaken in her husband.

What Martha managed with Smith was less love than a sensible
participation. Above all else, she strove to keep up appearances.
From the beginning, honour came before passion and set the
pattern of their years together. She wrote to Berryman in 1959:

> You couldn't know that marriage was so sacred to me that
> when you were nine and I fell desperately, instantly, totally,
> forever in love with a man who wanted a wife not a mistress I
> refused to break up my marriage and my home, and lost the
> only chance in my life for a real marriage?

It had shocked Martha to learn from Mrs Smith that John Allyn, although the baby of the family, had been neither a planned nor a welcomed child: 'in his presence, at the full dinner table, his mother said that for an unwelcome child, the third unwelcome child, he had gone very well.' For Martha, this revelation in some way accounted for Smith's self-centred behaviour: because he himself had not been loved, she reasoned, he was unable to show or feel warmth in his own relationships.

After their return to Oklahoma, Smith was employed for a while in the bank at McAlester. Martha became pregnant after one-and-a-half years of marriage, a span which had given her grave worries, as she later told Berryman:

> No child was ever more wanted than you, I feared so after a year and a half of marriage that I was barren – then when you were put in my arms, it was you I loved, not the child I had wanted desperately but you, with your wrinkled forehead – my heart leaped out upon you.

What exactly she meant by 'the child I wanted' is not known, but her phrase seems to imply that she would have preferred a girl. For some months before the child was born, however, he was known as Billy, a name that stuck until John was three years old.

After eight months of pregnancy, Martha was rushed to hospital where Dr W. C. Graves delivered the eight-pound baby at eleven o'clock in the morning of Sunday, 25 October. 'No one ever had easier carriage of a child, I was never sick or in pain, just full of happiness and joy.' The child was born by Caesarian section, but the surgeon had never performed the operation before, and made a low fourteen-inch incision. Even so, all was safe, except that Martha suffered for a while almost pathological fears that her parturition had been improper, 'that I had been guilty of some sin or fault that I could not bear my sons in agony,' as she later curiously told Berryman himself, 'and by that agony have earned them, that they were gifts to which I was not entitled.' It seems, in fact, that someone (possibly her mother) suggested this guilt to her after she recovered from the anaesthetic, insinuating the cruel notion that she might not love the child enough because she had not borne him 'in travail and agony, fearful that the post-operative pain would be unavailing because it was sterile, futile, non-productive, not us but me. I was twenty, and alone; I didn't know how to think and I knew nothing.' From her account, written forty-five years later, it is quite reasonable to infer that Smith had not made himself available to give moral support and comfort, or even that he had been excluded by her mother. Whatever the facts of that matter, it is evident that at the time of writing to her son, she was appealing to him with her expressions of pathos.

If Martha's accounts of early years are to be believed, her mother had for too long suppressed her own feelings and checked her daughter's. 'To have a loving heart and to be unloved so that your love went underground,' she lamented. The consequence was that Martha felt at her son's birth – like Thackeray's Amelia at her Georgy's – this child was her being. She allowed no sense of proportion in loving her son, since she had waited all her life for such a channel of emotion. She swaddled him with feelings so intense that he could never reciprocate her insistent love, and grew to be burdened by it. In later life, when she was separated from him by school, university, and even by marriage, her letters to him fanned feelings to an artificial heat. She enunciated her love in a manner by turns elaborate, plaintive, and pettish, and protested it with such inveterate lavishness that any possible discrepancy between the felt and the feigned did not occur to her. Berryman could allow himself to recognise this only infrequently, and then with such a measure of self-reproach that he came to feel easier avoiding the truth. Martha seemed to construe any hint that his love for her was less than all as something more nearly approaching sacrilege than as the natural process of development and reaction. Her conduct none the less gives a sorry index of her own insecurity.

John Allyn was christened for his father (the real family name, Allen, had earlier been corrupted).

Berryman himself had a notion that the family soon moved to Wagoner, where they briefly occupied a large yellow house. He kept an Airedale dog which was poisoned, possibly by a black-haired girl he dubbed a 'swart bitch'. The incident probably occurred later, however, during years in Anadarko. In December 1915, the family may have been temporarily resident in Lamar. Leonard Jefferson Smith died within a month, and Smith travelled north to his father's funeral. He brought back stories of the intense cold of the Minnesota winter, which Martha had never experienced and found hard to believe.

They were still living in McAlester when their second child, Robert Jefferson, was born on 1 September 1919. During the early stages of that pregnancy, Smith and his mother-in-law joined unholy forces to impress upon Martha what they considered her need for a 'therapeutic abortion': since her first child had been a Caesarean, it was felt for some reason that a second could kill her. Smith harboured the more selfish consideration that he did not feel able to afford another child. Quite sure of her own wishes, Martha delayed the decision until it was too late for an abortion. Resisting the demands of both her husband and her mother, she had felt, as she later rehearsed it, 'better I die than my child not have a chance for life, how can you save your life at the cost of another's? And the child I had and the one to come were all I had; it was selfish, too, no doubt, I was dazzled by having someone else to love.' What the episode indicates is how soon and gravely Martha had lost confidence in her husband, as already in her mother. Mrs Little did not like any men who were not her blood relations and never approved of Smith. The fact that he leagued together with his mother-in-law in urging his wife to abort her second child must have alienated Martha and caused her great grief.

Late in 1920 or early in 1921, the family moved to Anadarko, a city (smaller by half than McAlester) where oil-field development boomed in the early 1920s. For four years the Smiths lived in a small white five-room frame house at 516 West Kentucky. Smith took up the post of Acting Vice-President and Loan Officer of the First State Bank on 26 January 1921. During his tenure he was to have complete charge of the bank, a small one with assets under 500,000 dollars.

The boy grew to the age of eleven in Anadarko, of which he kept few but vivid memories. As he recalled in a Dream Song fragment, he climbed the oil derricks whose stark frames were jutting forth in increasing numbers. He would walk out of town to fetch buttermilk when it was needed, and on one occasion earned about fifty cents, which he boastfully paraded, for picking cotton. On Saturday afternoons his mother often allowed him to take his brother downtown by the hand, to have their hair cut and to pay twenty cents to see Hoot Gibson and William S. Hart in one of the two cinemas on Main Street and Broadway. Real cowhands and Indians walked the streets.

It was from this time that, guided by his mother, he began to take an interest in books. Martha herself had always fostered her own writing ambitions; she seems in fact to have been the only one of his forebears who took any interest in literature at all. She passed on to Berryman her love for the written word, and his writings later provided a vicarious satisfaction for her frustrated ambitions. As a boy at least, however, John preferred for a while to pore over the illustrations in borrowed books, as he recalled in this verse fragment:

> Deep blue picture-books
> Of birds I kept months, eager to return
> And shameful from return, O kept so long.

On one occasion he showed his mother a reproduction of the *Laocöon* in the *Encyclopaedia Britannica*, but she had an archetypal horror of snakes and severely and unjustifiably punished him for confronting her with the picture.

He attended a school called West Grade, just a block from home, and attained consistently high grades in a usual range of subjects. He was never, in the official term, 'tardy'.

His best friend was Richard Dutcher, whose older sister Dolly Massingale worked as a teller in Smith's Bank. Mrs Smith seemed nice 'but aloof' to Dolly Massingale. Martha was indeed snobbish and took care to select her children's friends (she did not like the children who lived closest to their home), but thought so highly of Mrs Dutcher that she had no hesitation in letting their boys play together. She was none the less so protective of her offspring that, at least for a time, she always walked them the six short blocks to the Dutchers' house (Richard rarely went to theirs). If Mrs Smith thought that John Allyn and Robert were good company, she was mistaken, since the boys ganged together with two others, Henry, the son of a neighbourhood grocer, and John Leroy Jones, the son of the Dutchers' black maid and washerwoman, and managed a great many pranks, including playing doctor with two girls from down the street. Once only, John Allyn and Richard crept round to the Dutchers' back porch and called Mrs Jones (who was doing the washing) an 'old, black nigger'. 'My mother, who was in the kitchen, heard us,' Richard Dutcher recalls:

> I haven't the slightest idea as to what happened to John Allyn but my mother took me upstairs and gave me the damnedest licking I ever got in my life. I remember Mrs Jones standing at the door crying and telling my mother that 'they're just kids, they didn't mean anything by it'. I'm sure John got that licking secondhand just by listening to my screams (mother used her quirt). I'm also sure that John's mother was told but I have no idea what she did.

When another close friend, F. J. Callahan, died, John was early initiated to the reality of mourning for an older boy he had worshipped. Awed and terrified, he secretly managed to touch his friend's dead hand.

> . . . the dead friend's hand at ten he toucht, as cork
> yieldless, odd-textured, with nobody looking
> [unpublished Dream Song fragment].

He suffered nightmares from remembering that touch, and would run screaming to his mother in the living room. For some time afterwards he would cross the street from the undertaker's parlour.

Since her husband was a Catholic, Martha had been converted to the Catholic Church on her marriage, and John was brought up devoutly, serving the six o'clock Mass every morning throughout the year, from the age of eight until the family left Anadarko. Torturing himself if he was late, he assisted a Belgian priest named Father Boniface, whom Berryman later claimed had influenced him as a child only less than his father. 'He was a squat man, good, stern, friendly,' Berryman recalled, and resembled physically the later 'interim' Pope, John XXIII. 'I believed in God & my Guardian Angel to the hilt.' Such was the boy's absolute and ingenuous religiosity that, his mother remembered, he got out of bed one evening and asked her – 'from the depths of what childish sin it would have been indecent to probe into' – whether he would go to hell if he died? Mother and son said an Act of Perfect Contrition together, and when she had explained the prayer to him he smiled serenely as she tucked him back into bed. The grave sin that had troubled him is probably the one recorded in this Dream Song fragment.

> Once after midnight he did sneak downstairs
> and drank a drink of water!
> and took Communion anyway – while roll
> himward the grand fires yet. He gave hisself airs;
> thought him a great matter.

With increasing financial security, the family together with a maid took a holiday cottage at the popular summer resort of Medicine Park high in the Wichita Mountains. The region is composed of small, rugged mountains, streams, plentiful leafy trees, and oddly-shaped lakes. Berryman remembered sliding down a chute into a pool, going duck-hunting, and fishing with his father from a sixty-foot-high dam. One incident at Medicine Park remained to shock Berryman's memory; while wrestling with Robert to pass one another on a wall, John shoved and gave his brother a bloody fall. The image of Robert Jefferson covered with blood stuck in his mind as a ghastly totem for at least thirty years.

In September 1923 Smith was appointed a Notary Public in Caddo County, Oklahoma. He also joined the Oklahoma National Guard, which operated from Fort Sill, and by 8 July 1924 became Captain of Battery 'E', 160th Field Artillery. Berryman keenly remembered one rainy day when his father took him on a visit to

Fort Sill: he was exhilarated by visions of men with field-glasses, gun manoeuvres, his father in puttees moving away to give orders, and the firing of field guns.

At work, however, Smith ran into difficulties which obliged him to resign his post on 10 March 1924: the record is written in his own hand. There were two reasons for his leaving: one, his own, the jealousy of a rival, who seems to have discredited him to the woman who had a controlling interest in the bank; the other, his wife's, was his truancy from work, as she explained in a letter which she wrote but did not send to Berryman in 1970.

> Allyn is the only person I ever knew who was totally self-centered: he was kind in general; amiable, pleasant, courteous; no close friends; he never, as far as I knew, ever inconvenienced himself for any one – example: while very important matters were pending at the bank in Anadarko and Allyn should have been there to handle them, he went off on a fishing trip to Colorado, despite the bank's owner insisting that he stay and despite all the arguments I put up . . . he came back to find that he was no longer at the bank, and that is why we went to Florida.

If her account is to be trusted, her husband's position was quite unsupportable, but it must be mentioned in his favour that, over a year later, on 9 September 1925, Ben Mills, President of the Oklahoma National Bank, gave Smith an unqualifiedly clean reference for his fifteen years in the banking business within the state: 'He is honest, sober and industrious and strictly reliable and a gentleman in every sense of the word.' Richard Dutcher recalls that his own father, despite losing his farms through a bankruptcy which may have been Smith's responsibility, relied unreservedly both before and afterwards on Smith's financial advice.

In private life, perhaps because he felt emotionally dispossessed by his wife's strong, exclusive love for the children, Smith had become fickle. According to Martha, he had at least one affair with a friend of hers; when he made a trip to Chicago in order to float a bond issue for the Anadarko gas company, the woman had apparently gone with him. Smith had been otherwise unexceptionable as a member of society; he played baseball at Sasakwa, swam, and enjoyed the occasional hunting and fishing trip. In Anadarko he played a good hand at bridge when they visited with a local doctor and his wife (Berryman considered later in life that the doctor had in fact shown too much interest in his mother). Not even Martha disputed the fact that he was a pleasant and courteous man, though

he made no close friends and perhaps did not want any. What is
evident is that he was too self-contained and unassertive a personality to please his vivacious and striving wife. While she developed
social and intellectual interests, and joined the local Philomathic
Study Club, Smith had no interest in reading books and did not
share her energy for climbing in society and disdaining ordinary
folk. A shrewd, witty, wily woman, her snobbish and managerial
nature had underscored the incompatibility of their backgrounds
and expectations of life. It seems likely that if he was negligent at
work, the veering path of his emotions contributed strongly to
distract him; rather than tackle his headstrong wife, he had begun to
secede from what was increasingly their vacuous and painful relationship.

Smith did not despair of himself, nor become idle and diffident,
after resigning from the bank. Within eleven days he was appointed
assistant game and fish warden of Oklahoma. By the middle of the
next year, however, he felt stale and restless for a new departure.
Years before, his mother-in-law had bought some land in Florida,
at that time worthless, for a very low price, and had given half the
property to Smith and Martha for a wedding present. He went to
McAlester and talked matters over with his mother-in-law, an
otherwise ambiguous partner, and they decided together to try
their fortunes in Florida. Their resolve went much against Martha
who did not want the children to be uprooted, especially as Robert
was just about to enter school. When Smith and his mother-in-law
determined that only the three adults should make a reconnaissance
trip, Martha insisted that she would stay behind with the boys, but
her objections were overruled because they needed her to drive the
car.
    Martha chose the boys a boarding-school called St Joseph's
Academy in Chickasha, the centre for a prosperous farm and ranch
region, and arranged for them to spend weekends with Mrs Dutcher in Anadarko. The parents began their trip in September 1925.
    John was approaching his eleventh birthday as the term began;
Robert was just six. The school routine consisted of rising at 6.15,
Holy Communion in Chapel at 6.30, breakfast and a brief playtime
followed by Mass at 8.15, and an otherwise usual school day ended
with bed at 8 p.m. Both boys badly missed their mother, but John
wrote her many letters and tried to conceal his misery. 'I love you
too much to talk about,' he told her bravely. As the term progressed, he said he was 'getting along fine' at the school, which
meticulously awarded grades for every aspect of the daily routine:
he achieved As (95–100) in application, catechism, arithmetic,

hygiene, geography, composition, spelling, and homework, a B
(90–5) for politeness, Cs (80–90) for deportment, order, neatness,
reading, penmanship, and grammar, and slipped to D (70–80) only
in history. Although the routine went relatively unrelieved, there
were small pleasures such as buying corn candy in town and
drinking chocolate at recess. Because he was not allowed to take
books from the school library, John complained that he had been
unable to read anything since arriving at the school, and asked his
mother to send in magazines, especially *Adventure* and *Cosmopolitan*
and *Hearst International*, when she had finished with them.

Although John made a number of friends, both he and his brother
were bullied by the other boys. Later in life Berryman reflected on
that time and feared that he had not been as valiant in defending
Robert as he should have been. 'I protected Bob, or I think I did –
how horrible for Bob if I didn't – how we longed for mother to
come.' 'The worst bully,' he remembered,

> was a bow-legged boy. He had organized, I think, half the boys
> in the dormitory. Hair fell over his forehead. He was taller –
> tho' short, & hump-shouldered – than I was, and he respected
> me because I once made him shout with pain; I forget how; he &
> one Lieutenant were torturing Bob when I came on them.
> However . . . he beat me senseless one day to show me where I
> stood.

The priests inflicted other stiff punishments.

> My impression of myself then is Peter Rabbit – Burgess was my
> sole author. I was docile, I think. But my image is of the school
> room deserted in the afternoon except by one or two other
> malefactors and me, always me, writing 'I must not throw
> chalk in geography' or '*I must bring my missal to Sacred Studies*'
> 500 or 1000 or 1500 times. I got very good. To use two pencils
> held in the right hand is an obvious device. Until, tho' you get
> good, the effort slows you down worse than one. I could use
> four.

When Mrs Dutcher reported to Martha that the boys were
unhappy and might like it better to stay with her and attend school
in Anadarko, Martha defied both her husband and her mother and
immediately took the train back to fetch her sons from Chickasha.
Waiting with paper bags in an office near the headmistress's, the
boys felt 'unspeakable relief'.

In Florida they sold half the property originally purchased by Mrs Little and bought a restaurant in Tampa, where they employed two cooks and divided the other labours. Mrs Little supervised the kitchen, Smith did the buying and kept the books; Martha made chocolate sodas and other drinks behind the counter, acted as cashier, kept an eye on the waitresses and periodically waited on the tables herself. Profits accumulated, and when Smith was offered a good price for the parcel of remaining land, he sold it against his mother-in-law's wishes. According to the Tampa City Directory for both 1925 and 1926, moreover, Smith seems also to have worked from home, 725 South Boulevard, as president of Bay Realty and Insurance Company, but the venture has otherwise gone unrecorded. The boys were put to school.

On the failure of the Florida boom, suicide became common, as Berryman wrote later in a verse fragment.

> In Tampa, where my friends died, '26
> . . . .
> And they were my parents' friends, none of them mine,
> But every day somebody shot himself.

Smith sold the restaurant for cash, but at only a third of the price they had paid for it. School was out for the summer, and the family took an apartment, early in June 1926, in the Kipling Arms, a building owned and occupied by a man in his late forties named John Angus Berryman (who originally hailed from Georgia) and his wife Ethel. The house was situated right on the beach on Clearwater Isle, across the bay from the city of Tampa itself. Enjoying the summer holidays, young John played golf in the hall of the Kipling Arms and went swimming in the Gulf, as he recalled in a fragmentary poem of much later date.

> We went to bed with colds, but more the burn
> One broiling morning I remember now.
> The blisters rose & broke, & more were born
> Beneath them. One day in a hopeless row
>
> I put a spear from twenty feet so near
> My brother's eye my heart stopped.

'Those lovely beach parties,' he recalled. 'I had no idea what was wrong, of course, but a child picks up atmosphere.' He was unaware that the adults in his life were acting out a bizarre drama.

In a letter of Thanksgiving 1970, Martha Berryman set the scene for her son. 'The first signs of the death of the boom came in summer, early summer, and everything went like snow in the sun: there was a miasma, a weight beyond enduring, the city reeked of failure.' It is typical of the extent to which Berryman accepted his mother as gospeller that he took her account almost without emendation as the text for this stanza from a late poem 'Tampa Stomp' (*Delusions, Etc.*):

The first signs of the death of the boom came in the summer,
early, and everything went like snow in the sun.
Out of their office windows. There was miasma,
a weight beyond enduring, the city reeked of failure.

John Angus Berryman and his wife became the only friends the Smiths made in the locality, as Martha recalled:

John Angus lunched at our place every day . . . he got out of the
real estate business in time to keep part of his profits; his wife
wanted to go back to New York and he did not, there may have
been other reasons, I don't know, but he gave her the car, half
his take, and his blessing, she divorced him, and left.

Her account seems to suggest that this sequence of events – the growing friendship with John Angus and Ethel, the divorce and settlement – all happened within the span of their acquaintance, but (perhaps for her son's benefit) she is clearly conflating the time-scheme, and omits to mention the fact that part of these events must have happened after Smith's death. Smith himself became bitterly unhappy when his career and resources crumbled, sullen in his conduct, and had an affair with a Cuban woman, but it is possible that his own waywardness may have been incited by the obvious fact that Martha and Berryman were much taken with each other. It is ironic that in the beginning Mrs Little (and for a while Smith and Martha herself) believed that John Angus, who was sixteen years older than Martha, proposed to pay court to herself as the dowager of the family. 'As it turned out,' the future Martha Berryman wryly observed, 'it was just southern courtesy, and she never forgave him.'

Registering an inevitable sense of disengagement, Smith's state of mind rapidly deteriorated. He had felt 'out of context without us', Martha told her son, 'and rendered monstrous by the fiendish strain and depression of the boom-break in Florida.' Smith asked her for a divorce in order to marry the Cuban woman with whom he seemed besotted. After consulting with the doctors who had been brought in to advise on his mental health, she 'agreed to sue him for divorce and the custody of the children and half of our joint funds.' That Berryman shared his mother's point of view is indicated by the way in which this stanza from 'Tampa Stomp' slights his father's relationship.

> The Lord fled that forlorn peninsula
> of fine sunlight and millions of fishes & moccasins
> & Spanish moss & the Cuban bit my father
> bedded & would abandon Mother for.

Martha apparently tried to dissuade her husband from divorce because of the Catholicism they all shared (even, she supposed, the Cuban woman), since the Church would not recognise a second marriage, and because of the effect it could have on the children: all to no avail. 'He said he couldn't think of anything else he wanted to do. Then I told him that he could, of course, see his sons whenever he wanted to, but in their home; and he said that would be all right, and that of course the furniture etc. stored in Anadarko I could have.' (When she eventually inquired after those goods, she discovered that Smith had not been paying the rent of six dollars a month, and that all their possessions had been sold.)

If Martha's tales are to be trusted, a swimming incident took place in which Smith may have tried to kill himself and Robert Jefferson. In a letter of October 1954 she gave an absolute and uncircumstantial account of the incident: 'it was Bob that he took out in the Gulf at Clearwater, meaning to drown Bob and himself. . . . Allyn told me what he had meant to do but couldn't.' On the other hand, in letters from 1970 (which she never actually sent to Berryman), she wrote two accounts which qualify the incident to an extent that redresses the blame attached to Smith. Written on 23 November 1970, the first letter seems to suggest, in fact, that Smith had no execrable intentions.

> When I came out to say lunch was ready, I asked where Bob was and you said your father had taken him down the beach. I went down the beach, which was shallow there, past some people sitting around, and then saw Allyn swimming out, and called to him asking where Bob was . . . and then I saw that Bob was out there by him and I screamed and several people came, John Angus among them but by that time Allyn had turned around and was holding Bob up – then they reached us. . . . It was your grandmother, my mother, who, later, told

you that your father had tried to drown your brother: she told me this, long afterward, when berating me for not telling you the truth, as she put it – she never liked Allyn, or any man, for that matter, except her blood kin.

Allyn was in a very disturbed state of mind (I had taken him to every good psychiatrist in Tampa) but I have never believed that he would, when it came to it, have drowned or allowed to drown, Bob or anyone including himself.

In her last account, she does actually state that Smith had taken Robert into the water, but avoids giving her own opinion of his intentions.

Allyn was pretty far out and I couldn't see Bob at all. I was terrified and screamed but he didn't seem to hear, so John Angus tore off his shoes and swam out to where Allyn was, and I screamed and screamed, and evidently Allyn heard me, and turned round – he had had Bob in front of him held by a cord around under his arms. When they got back to the beach Mother went into hysterics and accused Allyn of meaning to drown Bob when he got far enough out, and had hysterics – very bad for Allyn. I asked Allyn, later, why he didn't take you, too, and he said he didn't know, he just thought he'd take Bob and swim out into the Bay.

My mother hated all men except her blood kin, and she may well have told you that your father tried to drown your brother.

It is certainly possible that advancing years had dulled her memory and that she sincerely believed each of her accounts as she wrote it, and yet the last two accounts were written within days of one another and contain manifest contradictions which must be intentional. Her specific motive seems to be twofold: to mitigate her son's opinion of his father (which her letters of earlier years had incited to scorn) and to cast her own mother as the villain (rather than herself, as her son did from time to time) for so heartlessly and perhaps groundlessly calumniating Smith. In any event, if the incident took place at all, it was a terribly irresponsible adventure or the act of a deranged mind, but the contradictions in Martha's accounts must cast doubt on the forensic value of her evidence.

Certain of Berryman's Dream Songs, working with the little and often partial knowledge he had gleaned from his mother, work to compose his ambivalent feelings towards his father's actions, but at least one – number 145 – urges a mitigating pathos. (The persona 'Henry' stands more or less for Berryman himself.)

> Also I love him: me he's done no wrong
> for going on forty years – forgiveness time –
> I touch now his despair,
> he felt as bad as Whitman on his tower
> but he did not swim out with me or my brother
> as he threatened –
>
> a powerful swimmer, to   take one of us along
> as company in the defeat sublime,
> freezing my helpless mother:
> he only, very early in the morning,
> rose with his gun and went outdoors by my window
> and did what was needed.
>
> I cannot read that wretched mind, so strong
> & so undone. I've always tried. I – I'm
> trying to forgive
> whose frantic passage, when he could not live
> an instant longer, in the summer dawn
> left Henry to live on.

The period leading up to Smith's suicide brought threatening behaviour and long, dour conferences between Smith, John Angus, and Martha. On one occasion, she alleged, Smith tried to choke her. She considered that he was a remote being, that 'nothing was deeply important to him', and that he felt lost. The bulk of what she says depicts a man deeply alienated, at a point of existential crisis, and irremediably selfish. Her versions variously allow pity or scorn for a man who cannot change his inveterately self-centred nature. As far as Berryman was concerned, his mother had likely contributed in some part to the sense of rejection Smith experienced. In notes dating from 1954, Berryman recorded (as his mother must some time have told him) that his father felt 'small' after returning from the swimming venture with Robert Jefferson (especially when she specified that she no longer felt 'love' but only 'affection' for him), and that he consequently felt furious and unreal.

The most alarming aspect of Smith's last days was that he could be seen walking up and down the beach with a gun in his hand. Occasionally, Martha said, someone would take it away from him. When she consulted doctors, they apparently advised that

> it might be the thing that made him feel strong and powerful
> and all agreed that it should not be taken from him, it was an
> assertion of self and was an affirmation of strength and even
> responsibility that he, alone of the men around, had a gun.

Although she took the precaution of burying five of the bullets way down the beach where he might not find them, she gives no account in letters to her son of the sixth bullet – the one with which Smith shot himself.

As far as she was concerned, she felt convinced – a belief which she energetically and consistently professed – that Smith had killed himself by chance. She often inspected the magazine and never discovered a bullet, and believed that Smith did not know the gun was loaded when he pulled the trigger. She searched the house and car daily for hiding places, 'so the only possible solution is that Allyn did put that sixth bullet in and forgot it, and when clicked often enough would bring that sixth bullet into the firing chamber.'

There are three immediate and apparent reasons for Smith's suicide. The first might have been that the divorce proceedings were apparently to be finalised on the very day of his death – Saturday 26 June – or, more likely, the following Monday. The second, as Martha told me personally in her eightieth year, was that Smith had given the Cuban woman 'every nickel he had'. Third, moreover, that very woman (Martha told Berryman) 'with whom he was either totally in love or who was an image of everything different (and hence safe from all the failure and despair) and hence safety to him, had gone back to Cuba without any warning, farewell, and explanation.'

On the night of Friday, 25 June, as Martha related to her son, she had offered to withdraw the suit 'and continue to share a household with him', both for the sake of the children and in hopes of his recovery if they moved to another environment. Smith declined. (A further contradiction figures in her accounts of this matter, however, since in one of her uncompleted draft letters of 1970, she tells how Smith 'didn't really want the divorce, he didn't know what he wanted, maybe nothing, maybe back home he'd feel different, he didn't know. So I didn't withdraw the suit for divorce which was filed only so that he could marry this woman, thinking he might change his mind again.' The later account differs so radically, in fact, as to suggest the possibility that one of Smith's immediate motives for suicide might have been that she had rejected his confused overture of reconciliation.) Smith talked for a long while to John Angus in Martha's presence until she fell asleep, she said. When they left the room at about 1 a.m., she woke up but stayed dressed and dozed on the couch.

> I looked into Allyn's room once, and he was asleep. Very early, around dawn, I woke again and looked into his room, and he was not there. I had not undressed, so I went down

immediately, and there he lay, with the gun fallen from his right hand. I ran upstairs and knocked on John Angus's door and I can still see his eyes rheumed together – when I told him, he said to wait, shut the door, pulled on trousers over his night-shirt, and went down with me – when he touched the gun, the muzzle was warm, probably the shot woke me from dozing. I stayed with him, after bringing a sheet to put over him, while John Angus called the police; the Chief came, at once. I could not believe that he would kill himself, he had seemed quite cheerful about making a new life for himself with no obligations, with freedom to do what he liked, etc. But there were only his prints on the gun and it was the gun used (the police tested that, as well as everything else), and when they (the police) learned from all the people staying there how he would walk the beach and pull out the gun and say he was going to shoot himself

That account, written on 23 November 1970, breaks off, and although addressed to her son, the letter was never sent.

Smith died early in the morning of 26 June. The coroner's investigation was held the same day and concluded that he had died through a self-inflicted wound from a .32 calibre special automatic. The newspaper report of the hearing includes these remarks:

According to testimony given at the trial by Mrs. Smith, her husband has for several weeks been suffering from insomnia, which she believes caused despondency and was the reason for his committing suicide. She stated that she awoke about 6:15 o'clock Saturday morning and found her husband gone, but thought she saw him sitting in their car which was parked near the apartment. She went down and upon finding that she was apparently mistaken, returned for the keys to the car, intending to drive around the island to look for him.

On the dresser, Mrs. Smith reported, she found a note from her husband, weighted down by pocket articles. The note read:

'Dear Peggy: Again I am not able to sleep – three nights now and the terrible headaches.'

There was no signature.

Mrs. Smith descended again and at the rear of the apartment building found the lifeless body of her husband lying in a spreadeagle fashion. There were blood stains on his shirt, though investigation has revealed no trace of powder burns. A .32 calibre automatic pistol, which Mrs. Smith testified her husband gave her about four years ago, was found lying near his head.

The jury was unable to find any substantiation for what the newspaper calls 'several points' in the case which might have interfered with the theory of suicide. If the newspaper report is competent, it is curious that no mention was made of a pending divorce, and that the coroner did not pursue the question of powder burns, which are unavoidable in such a case. But any theory must remain conjectural. The death certificate, signed by Dr W. H. Groves, reveals no other circumstantial particulars except that, shot through the left chest, Smith died instantly.

They hied the body (probably because of the heat) back to Holdenville, Oklahoma, to bury Smith alongside his brother Will. Martha took the children for a duty visit to Smith's family in Minnesota. She recalled that 'the sister just older than Allyn did kill herself which is probably why his family accepted his death as suicide immediately.' Martha herself never thought it suicide, but always maintained her belief that Smith had accidentally shot himself. Her mother, who was 'a very strong woman with views', she said, and perhaps one of her sisters-in-law, filled her elder son 'full of lies and insinuations'.

In an unfinished draft story called 'Little Me', Berryman wrote, 'I take it therefore that my desolation and rage over his death persisted, although for years I thought it purely grief.' He believed he had gone through an agony of grief after his father's death, but it seems probable that his mother and other kin grievously agitated and confused his natural feelings. Berryman could never actually recall his immediate sensations about his father's death, only the ride to Tampa and the darkened funeral-home room. He could remember curiously little even of the man himself, except for his dark hair cut short, the fact that he smoked Camels, and the mistaken notion that he resembled King George VI.

Later in life Berryman believed that he had been stunned by his loss, and took it as the *point d'appui* of his psychological problems. Convinced that his father's self-serving action had broken his own peace of mind, he swung between compassion and loathing for the man. From time to time he sought to resolve his tormenting ambivalence by asking about the circumstances surrounding his father's suicide, but he never looked beyond his mother, who was partial and severely prejudiced his judgment of the situation, to documentary or other sources of evidence. In the 1940s he was to write a biography of Stephen Crane, and from that work and from further research on Shakespeare he learned biographical procedures and lines of inquiry. What may reasonably be inferred from his deliberate restriction of research about his father is that he wanted to comprehend the situation from his mother's point of view, and to avoid any contradictions and ambiguities which might accrue from alternative evidence. Since his mother showed a reluctance to witness to a worth she had rejected, however, it confused and goaded Berryman's sense of guilt and responsibility to learn, when he asked her if his father had preferred him to Robert Jefferson, first that 'Your father did not show any marked partiality, I know, as that would have registered,' and then, 'I believe now, seeing then as clearly as I can, that Allyn preferred you.' In the same letter she added, 'You will, I know, rejoice to learn that my devotions in the present and future are daily offered for Allyn.' Berryman could meet his duty to his mother only by disallowing the claims of affection owed to his father, her antagonist.

Late in 1954, when Berryman first went to Minneapolis, he undertook a period of rigorous self-analysis, and included among his notes the wishful, if strictly untrue, observation that 'I came here to Minnesota to tear him to pieces, to get square, to even the score with him! *expose* him,' and hectically construed a dream of 7 September that year with the comment, 'So dream is my bloody father looking down at me, whom he's just fucked by killing himself, making me into shit: and taunting me before he flushes me away.'

He set about to pattern his life on a bias, and later shaped his poetry in the same spirit. '*So few memories!!*' he lamented in 1970, while conceding that he retained 'enough *feelings* to dominate' the *Dream Songs*. His work served to focus and confirm the partial truth to which the balance of his mind clung, and to perpetuate self-deception. In hospital in 1970, he took notes on what he saw as a 'new problem' (though it was no such thing).

> Did I myself feel any *guilt* perhaps – long-repressed if so & this is mere speculation (*defense here*) *about Daddy's death*? (I certainly pickt up enough of Mother's self-blame to accuse her once, drunk & raging, of having actually *murdered* him & staged a suicide.) . . . Can't seem to remember his *ever* getting angry at me . . . BLANK, probably *odd*. . . .
> Such a vacant relationship compared to the (horrible) *richness* of mine with Mother! ODD . . .
> How do I actually now see him? limited, weak, unfaithful, not a success, not a soldier (fake soldier) & do I feel guilt about this rather *contemptuous* view? Were we, in fact, close Father-son as I tell myself; (Mother said he was rather *cold*.)

He chose to live by a negative and distanced moment of fixation, and to repress too much of his continuing disaffection for his mother. Berryman's rationalisation of his troubles as father-fixation (whence his preoccupation with suicide, fatherhood, and godhead, concepts which became major themes of the *Dream Songs*) was an attempt to be decisive about his malaise, rather than the malaise itself. His creative output may be accounted for (to some extent) as the product of dwelling on himself: a self, he felt, intruded on by the outside world. His cast of mind construed affliction as a creative stimulant. Song 384, which may be interpreted strictly according to Freudian theories of love and anger, is an important and characteristic expression of Berryman's prevalent attitude towards his father's suicide.

> The marker slants, flowerless, day's almost done,
> I stand above my father's grave with rage,
> often, often before
> I've made this awful pilgrimage to one
> who cannot visit me, who tore his page
> out: I come back for more,
>
> I spit upon this dreadful banker's grave
> who shot his heart out in a Florida dawn
> O ho alas alas
> When will indifference come, I moan & rave
> I'd like to scrabble till I got right down
> away down under the grass
>
> and ax the casket open ha to see
> just how he's taking it, which he sought so hard
> we'll tear apart
> the mouldering grave clothes ha & then Henry
> will heft the ax once more, his final card,
> and fell it on the start.

(His return to the graveside is metaphorical, since he never actually went there.)

Late in life, on 21 November 1970, in a letter which Martha actually refrained from sending to her son, she wrote of Smith as 'an inner gazer, one who saw and respected and required his own way, one to whom he and his desires and concerns came first and there was no second,' and a letter of 1954, which Berryman did receive, depicts Smith as naturally but not deliberately selfish, introverted, and detached from reality:

he was remote and not by choice nor was he conscious of this: it
was *natural* for him not to comprehend the aims, wishes,
feelings of others . . . he did not *feel* that they existed . . . he
stood further from the fire of life and needed or wanted to come
no nearer . . . he felt lost in a world which somehow seemed to
see him as other than he saw himself.

The effect of that letter was to make Berryman despise his father –
'suicide is all *self-pity* & *aggression*', he wrote on one page of her letter
– and to convince him that his mother had 'the most *fantastically*
over-develop sense of responsibility I think I ever encountered.'

   To her son's delight and occasional embarrassment she looked
for a long time like his sister, and took pains to exploit all her natural
talents, a strong personality and youthful looks. Even in her
sixty-fifth year she could safely risk writing a *curriculum vitae* which
gave her age as fifty-three.

   It was in that very year, 1959, that Berryman correctly acknowledged to himself that his 'unspeakably powerful possessive adoring' mother still centred her emotional life on him. Burdened by her
influence and dominance, he continually worried in his breast and
brain the neurotic conflict he believed his father's suicide had
triggered. He had to plot what amounted to a therapeutic strategy,
but his strivings foundered on the ration of prejudice, half-truth,
self-contradiction, and misinformation that his mother supplied
over the years. Confronted by her own purposes, his state of
unknowing and psychological dislocation persisted. This abortive
essay, which he wrote even as late as the age of forty-eight in 1962,
illustrates the sorry limitations of knowledge and understanding on
which he had to base his perceptions and judgment:

   He left no note, and this is unusual. Moreover he was not a
   suicidal type, not moody, not very sensitive, in good health,
   about forty, making money, loving his wife and children. But
   he was immensely disturbed. He had not only threatened
   suicide, repeatedly, but murder. He had threatened to swim out
   into the Gulf – he was a strong swimmer – taking either my
   brother or me with him. This not to us but to my mother,
   whom I imagine he scared blue. . . .
      In one sense it is usually idle to enquire into the motives for
   suicide: the criminal (let's call him) may not even know himself,
   he simply feels his act is *necessary*, who knows whether the
   reason he gives himself in the final instant is the same one he
   wrote down? On the other hand this aggressive action, always
   accompanied by hatred and despair, must always also, I think,

be over-determined: serve, that is, more purposes than one. So, here my father's self-murder seems readily explained by the fact that my mother had fallen in love with another man and wanted a divorce. He restores his pride (suicide takes courage) and at the same time punishes her. But matters are rarely that simple.

My father was not a very competitive man, perhaps, and he had been double thrust into battle. First he had switched from banking, a safe profession (if it is a profession), to business, a cutthroat business in a frantic time at a frantic place, and next he had been brought into rivalry with an older man, a close friend, of better position and stronger personality, my 'Uncle Jack'. My mother, though the target of the shot, was only part of the picture.

Naturally I cannot know what was in my father's mind.

As late as 1970 he seems to have found it a surprise when he penetrated to this apparently novel recognition:

Have I been wrong all these years, and it was *not* Daddy's death that blocked my development for so long? . . . *Did I in fact take his death in stride*, and succumb over a year later to something else? or is a *delayed* reaction possible? . . .

So maybe my long self-pity has been based on an *error*, and there has been no (hero-) villain (Father) ruling my life, but only an unspeakably powerful possessive adoring MOTHER, whose life at 75 is still centered wholly on *me*. And my (omnipotent) feeling that I can *get away with anything* . . . has been based on the knowledge that she will *always* forgive me, always come to the rescue. . . . And my vanity based on *her* uncritical passionate admiration . . . rendering me invulnerable ('indifferent' – a *fact* too) to all criticism, and impatient with anything less than total prostration before the products of my genius. . . .

My debts to her immeasurable: ambition, stamina, resourcefulness, taste . . . faith, originality, her sacrifices for my schooling . . . blind confidence in me. But she helped destroy my father & Uncle Jack; affairs . . . intermittent heavy drinking; horribly weakened my brother; would never, & *still* hasn't, let go of me in *any* degree – e.g. *in*terminable letters, clippings, incessant talk SEDUCTIVE – 'beautiful', forcible but v. feminine (Saul's amazement) vanity (even now), self-pity (tho' great courage), frustrated writer.

Within a few weeks of Smith's death – on 8 September 1926 – Martha married their landlord, John Angus Berryman, whose adoptive sons took his name. He was forty-eight years of age, she was thirty-two. The family presently took up residence in New York, where John Angus was a bond salesman, but after the Depression his income and health considerably declined, to the point where he was virtually dependent on his wife. She began to realise bold dimensions to her character and abilities and in due time won a high reputation in business.

It seems that she married again so fleetly for the sake of her sons. 'Did you never wonder why I remarried so soon?' she asked John in 1959; 'my sons should never have to say they were fatherless, never.' The extent to which she cared for her husband as a person must remain in doubt. She saw the marriage as a useful alliance, and probably supposed him to be a more financially promising *parti* than he turned out to be. The boys certainly respected their stepfather, but Martha seems to have been ambivalent in her feelings for the older man. In February 1959 she told her son, 'I lived with John Angus for thirteen years pretending to return his love and when I could literally not go on another day, supported him and his sister for almost two years while I tried to whip myself into a resumption of the marriage.' It was another twelve years before she mellowed enough to give him proper credit: 'We, all three of us, owe so much of our happiness in those years to John Angus, who loved me with all his heart and in you and your brother found the sons he had not had.'

3

A monkey among kings, 1927-32

After Martha Smith married John Angus Berryman, the family briefly lived at 89 Bedford Street, and subsequently at 75 83rd Street, Jackson Heights, New York. John Berryman attended Public School 69, Jackson Heights, where he studied hard and made some good friends, in particular Charlotte Coquet – outside whose house he would skate up and down in pubescent rapture – and Helen Justice, who became so devoted to his budding literariness that she transcribed in her fine hand a science fiction novel he was writing about the planet Neptune. He found much to excite him: the girl who sat over on the right aisle of the classroom who was, as he put it later in life, 'supposed to fuck', or the Museum of Natural History, where he marvelled at the whale. He also took typing lessons. At home, the boys' stepfather was benevolent but firm; he would concoct hashed-potatoes-in-cream, and querulously shake his head as the boys devoured their copies of *Amazing Stories* full of impossible subjects like atomic weapons.

Towards the end of the academic year in mid-1928, Berryman entered the annual spelling bee sponsored by the Lions Club at Bryant High School, Long Island City, where he won third place, being beaten by a girl who could negotiate the word 'syzygy'. A week later he won the gold medal in a composition contest sponsored by the American Society for the Prevention of Cruelty to Animals, worsting hundreds of competitors from the city schools on the subject of 'humane practices'. His brief, earnest essay contrasted the respect formerly shown to animals with the neglect and indignity they had lately suffered. Warming to the topic of inhuman practices such as branding and vivisection, he let his grammar go awry with one sentence, 'In the western states, another and more gentle method of identifying cattle is now in progress,

and let us all hope that this will be legally forbidden.' Words follow
about just how useful and compatible animals are to man, 'Milk,
one of our foremost foods, comes from cows; eggs, another
necessity, come from an animal; all of our meat is obtained from
them. They were the only means of inland locomotion in the early
days,' and the essay concludes with suitable admonitions against
urban cruelty to animals. His essay was printed in the school
magazine, the *Blue and Gold*, of which he was an associate editor.

On 6 June 1928, he applied to South Kent School, which lies on the
west slope of a small, beautiful valley, partly wooded, partly open
fields, which feeds a stream into the Housatonic River. During
Berryman's schooldays the outside world could only be reached by
dirt roads, the village was no more than a few houses and a general
store, and just two trains a day passed each way on the New Haven
Railroad. The school was founded in 1923 at the instigation and
with the co-operation of Father Frederick H. Sill, of the Episcopalian Order of the Holy Cross, whose own school, Kent, had proved
so successful in its icy rigour that it became necessary to calve a
similar, but independent, foundation.
    According to D. Pierre G. Cameron, who was one of Berry-
man's masters, the school offered 'unfancy living with a job-system
of self-help which included dish-washing, shovelling snow, freez-
ing the rink on a nearby lake, and leading a rugged and pretty much
monastic life.' Berryman was lodged with nineteen other boys in a
barracks-type dormitory on the third floor of a clapboard building
known as the 'Old Building'. Among his contemporaries, snobbery was apparent but not marked, as one of his classmates,
Theodore Jones, recalls. 'We were scions of the fading society of the
cities and children of the first generation of suburban commuters.
We were well-scrubbed, bought our clothes at Brooks Brothers,
and a credit to our Junior League mothers and banker fathers.' Most
of the boys came from fairly affluent homes in Baltimore, Philadelphia, or Boston, or from newer places such as Cos Cob, Old
Saybrook, and Darien. The modish young man of the second form
turned out in knickers and a matching coat, and was presently
initiated into the school's credo of self-reliance and directness of
purpose, in accord with the precepts of Anglican Episcopalianism.
    Henry Kurtz remembers Berryman as 'rather gawky and clum-
sy, very studious', attributes which were utterly out of place in a
school which set the highest value by excellence in competitive
sports, much more than by academic accomplishment. It is not
known why his parents chose South Kent School for him (presumably its rigour appealed to John Angus, who was himself an

Episcopalian), but it is clear that Berryman was grievously misplaced. For four years he was subjected to an emotionally bam-
boozling existence which compelled him to fissure his natural
aptitudes from his pretended interests and ambitions. Although he
attained high academic success he had to do so while affecting
self-disparagement and in the face of what amounted to the school's
depreciation. Since no amount of effort could fully overcome his
disabilities, his experience at the school left him miserably trailing
in the esteem he had learned to covet and sometimes even hysterically frustrated by his failure at sports.

He was withdrawn, unaggressive, and wore glasses with lenses
so thick that they earned him the nickname 'Blears'. 'I remember,'
Frank Forester, Jr, writes, 'that his eye glasses were so thick you
could perform physics experiments with them.' Theodore Jones
recalls that

> He showed no sign of being in the least bit as we were and,
> what was worse, didn't seem to want to be. He was short and
> stocky with a shock of light brown hair that fell into his right
> eye. His voice came from somewhere down around his heels
> and he prefaced his remarks with a sort of rumbling ahhhr.

That characteristic merited him the alternative sobriquet of 'Burrs',
from his own pronunciation of 'Berryman' as 'Burrman'. At once
odd and ordinary, he was shy, introspective, and generally regarded as almost eccentric for his ineptitude at sports; being small,
unathletic, as well as brainy, he was the typical victim, and began to
be bullied soon after his arrival at the school. He did not help
matters by entrapping himself in solitary habits of bookish application and by betraying disdain for the school. If he exerted himself
socially, his efforts were far from ingratiating, but rather 'arrogant
and uncompromising', Durand Echeverria recalls. Despite the fact
that, according to Pierre Cameron, Berryman 'slowly won their
respect because of his brains', for some time the elite of the school
made him suffer for the success of his intelligence and returned him
scorn for scorn 'because of his appearance and his boorishness and
his excellent mind.'

It is ironic that his mother, ambitious for his success, urged him
to excel not only in his studies but equally in sports. Since even she
played her tune in time with the school, Berryman had no alternative but to dance. She unknowingly exacerbated his sense of
self-conflict by pushing him to work up an interest in field sports for
her sake as much as for the school's, and by heightening the degree
to which he grew at variance with any true standard for his real

disposition. By so doing, she helped to forge a divide between his genuine and his professed feelings, and indeed between herself and him – since he had in effect to lie even to her. The insincerity of his career at school disturbed the kilter of his moral and emotional development. It took Berryman six years – four at school and two at college – before he learned that the life of the mind could provide an honourable calling.

Outstanding in will and character, the headmaster, Samuel Bartlett, a man aged twenty-eight when Berryman arrived, personified the principles of South Kent School. Direct, intelligent without being intellectual, he resembled Daniel Chester French's idea of a Puritan, and gave an example of austerity with benevolence. Since his own legacy had been patrician, he had, according to Durand Echeverria, 'an unshakable faith in his religion and in an ethical code . . . capable of towering indignation and dogged intolerance of what he thought was wrong, but also warm and compassionate.' He inspired lasting and incomparable respect among many of his former students and friends, but an equal unease, if not fear, among an unlike sector of the student body who were accustomed neither to such a personality nor to the ordonnance that he practised. He showed concern above all for building character among the boys. Shortly after term began Berryman reported home,

> Mr. Bartlett gave the second formers a talk on how we were
> supposed to conduct ourselves. He said in substance just what
> Uncle Jack told me – that until we proved ourselves otherwise,
> he considered us all thoughtful, polite, courteous,
> sportsmanlike gentlemen. He also advised us not to try to be
> smart or to show off.

It was because Bartlett took by nature to the sporting life that the school earned its early reputation for being 'jock', while Berryman had to camouflage his natural aptitudes in a forced athleticism. When the 'old man' had been a sixth former at Kent School, his team had enjoyed an undefeated year, Berryman learned. 'Boy, the old man can certainly play football.' Just what curt credit Bartlett occasionally gave to academic success is shown by the fact that when Berryman topped the school with an average mark of 90.4 at the beginning of his fourth form year, the 'old man' commented disingenuously in his official report, 'John is doing good work at football. I imagine he is happier about that than his lessons.'

History lessons brought the esoteric, which Berryman relished, 'we are taking up Assyria, Chalea [*sic*] and the Medo-Persian

Empires. I know all about Hammurapi [*sic*], Sennacherib, Assurba-
nipal, Nebuchadnezzar and all the rest. It is very interesting.'
Shortly the class undertook 'ancient Palestine and the Hebrews. It's
all about Isiah [*sic*], Amos, Jeremiah, Solomon and bloody Elijah.'
The history master, known as 'Moose-jaw', was Samuel A. Woodward, a man whom Berryman numbered among the three teachers
who 'ever taught me anything there.' A compassionate man, dryly
humorous, 'Woody', as he was otherwise called, was, by one
account, a man of 'ingenuity, parsimoniousness, native cunning,
and natural bargaining ability.' Despite the fact that, when opening
the school in 1923, Bartlett had determined, 'I do not want to spank
any of the boys if I can possibly get at them in any other way,'
Samuel Woodward believed that corporal punishment hurt little.
As years wore on, Berryman too professed that 'paddling', whether
by a master or by one of the prefects, 'inspired more fear than pain,'
but without discriminating the pain of fear.

One of Woodward's disciplinary procedures for the second form
inspired a great deal more anguish, which Berryman remembered
so vividly over thirty years later that he wrote a memoir called 'It
Hurts to Learn Anything'.

One grey Saturday afternoon of my first year we assembled in
the second form classroom under our History master. Classes
on Saturday were over at 12.45, we had had lunch, it must have
been two. We had no idea what was going to happen except that
he had a paddle, and we wondered if he was going to paddle us
all.
 'Take out your history books,' he said, 'and close your
desks.'
 We did.
 'Now this first row here, get down in the aisle by your seats,
on your knees, and open the book in your left hand and read. I
want you to crawl out across the terrace and down the walk and
across the courtyard and around the flagpole and back, *reading*.
You can start now, and the second row get down, and so on.
Don't forget: Read. I want you brats to understand' – he went
on, while the procession began – 'that history is an important
and interesting subject to which you have to pay *close attention* –
as you have not done in class for two weeks.'
 Out we crawled.
 I was in the aisle next farthest from the door. In my quarter
we were not unduly alarmed, although the distance struck us as
considerable. As we lumbered into the hall and onto the terrace
we felt our mistake. The terrace of the New Building, which we

were to cross diagonally to the head of the walk down to the Main Building, was sharp gravel. We knew this, but it had never mattered. It was about a hundred feet long and 20 wide. The master walked up and down the line, assessing with his paddle the quality of our reading attention. The walk was smoother, though the old boards were full of splinters, but it was steep. The courtyard was flagstones, uneven and edgy. Far away, when I threw a quick glance up, was the flagpole.

Some of us were already dressed for the game that was to start in half an hour, football pants hitching, leaving our knees bare.

And then, as we came slowly up the walk, we learned that we had to do it all over again.

Such a discipline, though never to be forgotten, left a certain sentimental afterglow, as the *South Kent Year Book* for 1933 (Berryman's official graduating year) affectionately reflected,

Our chief memories . . . are the nightly paddlings by prefects, crawling on hands and knees over the school gravel reading history books all the while, bent over reading same, knowing that to straighten out was to receive a whack; these . . . leave us enjoyably reminiscing.

Woodward professes that the discipline was intended more as an 'exercise in concentration' than as a torture. He imposed a further discipline which Berryman well remembered.

It was the same master who late in the following winter again became dissatisfied with our attention. Again we mysteriously assembled after classes were over, this time at 3:30, and again he had a paddle. We trembled. But this time we were told to stand, not kneel. We filed upright out onto the terrace, for something much simpler and more nerve-wracking. Lined up along the concrete border and worshipped it [*sic*], with our hands holding our ankles. He walkt up and down behind us with the paddle, measuring our devotion. How long this went on I have no idea. He called it sun-worshipping and it was worse than our crawl.

When drafting a Dream Song fragment after a return visit to the school in 1962, Berryman remembered Woodward and Cameron, along with the mathematics master: Frank West had once been a 'dorm' master who, rumour had it, donned sneakers in order to creep out and catch boys up after hours, so earning himself the indelible nickname 'Sneaking'.

The headmaster just left. It all looks small.
Here's the stairway where Sneakin' Jesus got his name
Here's where Mr Cameron threw erasers
for goofing off in French.

Here's where Brown II goosed the Old Man,
and here's where Moose-jaw
sent us on hands & knees down the steep walk
to the flag-pole (now moved)
& around it & back up.
Brother, that hurt. Shins, too.

Berryman loved Latin, principally because it was taught by the engaging priest, Father Jasper Kemmis, an Englishman with, Pierre Cameron recalls,

> a droll but not overbearing manner, yet still a firm man of God, who wielded a fine influence on the students. He was warm, friendly, likable, but not pompous, though I guess we were all concerned with his clerical collar and his terse manner of speaking. But he was a great guy, far above the run of succeeding chaplains after Father 'Kemmy' returned to England.

Berryman's enthusiasm for any subject was directly proportionate to his interest in the personality of the pedagogue.

Probably as a result of the priest's happy influence, Berryman resolved to go to chapel every morning of the week and to take communion three times a week, and largely kept his resolution. He attended chapel on Easter Sunday 1929, he told his mother, 'for our whole family for this year. For a long time I didn't go to church at all and now I can't get enough.' The chapel, a long, narrow catacomb-like room in the basement under the old farmhouse, awed him with white linen, wax candles, silken vestments, and the language of the King James Version. Many of the boys related fervently to the poetry of the hymns, knew all the services by heart, and stared intensely as the wafer was elevated during the scented mysteries of the Mass. Martha had switched from the Catholic to the Episcopalian Churches after marrying John Angus, and Berryman smoothly assimilated the new faith. 'I find this church almost identical with the Roman Catholic Church – prayers and all; in some respects I like it even better.'

The one maternal influence at the school was the house-mother, Clara Christiane Dulon, an affiliate of the Order of St Anne, who commonly dispensed tea and cookies in immoderate amounts to boys on their birthdays and other high days. 'Garbed in her costume of grey cloth,' Pierre Cameron recalls, 'she was a diminutive person in size, but the love and respect (and devotion) that she carried in her large heart, was immediately observed and accepted by all the boys.' Decidedly drawn to the 'saintly mite', Berryman joined for her sake the 'Crafters', a branch of the 'Gardeners', a group or club which, as the name suggests, pursued gardening under her direction. 'Not,' he had to confess, 'that gardening appeals to me – nix!' It is not surprising that he was attracted to Miss Dulon: her tea-time ministrations had affinities with the religious services conjured by Father Kemmis, and Berryman received at her hands innumerable cups of 'South Kent Brew'.

Strictly regimented, the school day began with chapel bell at 6.15 (voluntary attendance), and the whole school assembled after 6.45 in Classroom B of the Old Building. Classes, athletics, showers, chores, and another assembly followed in short order. Jobs, which were constantly changed, had to be completed twice a day to the satisfaction of the prefects, who held sway over all matters of discipline with the masters only as a higher resort. The boys conducted themselves on an honour system, the punishment commonly being a paddling, but infractions might otherwise be punished with a sentence of certain 'Hours' which were worked off by tasks such as pulling weeds, or cutting the grass.

Meals were served by the boys themselves, who had to wear coats and not sweaters. Berryman seems to have suffered from an unappeasable hunger: during the freshman picnic, for example, he ate six sausage rolls, two enormous pieces of pumpkin pie, at least twelve roasted marshmallows, and drank seven cups of cocoa. At every meal he would drink from two to five glasses of milk, and urged his stepfather to make copious cheese-jabs and scrambled eggs for his arrival home at Christmas. Although he considered school desserts 'dandy', he felt hungry enough, he added, to 'eat a whole ton of piggies and a million tons of cheese-jabs right this minute.'

His 'especial chum', as he called him, at least for the first part of his school career, was a boy named Lester Wittenberg, perhaps because he was, like Berryman himself, awkward and gauche, though he had a marvellous sense of humour and was fascinated by the theatre. 'He IS *NOT* A HEBREW,' Berryman told his family, clearly aware that they would not approve if he made close friends with a Jew. 'He is not "dirty", but his mother has told him all about things, just as you have told me.'

Another of his classmates was a painfully thin boy named Alexander Hamilton, whose redeeming feature (Berryman claimed) was
a splendid stamp collection. Although Theodore Jones distinctly
recalls that Berryman himself rarely bathed, whether from shyness
or forgetfulness, Berryman looked on Hamilton as '*awful*' for going
without a shower for two months – by his reckoning. 'John and I
probably had the highest IQ's,' Hamilton remembers, 'so were
assigned together as roommates. We grated on each other more and
more and we did not live together again, partly because John was
maturing faster than myself.' Berryman despised Hamilton less
than wholeheartedly because in many respects he reflected his own
image; he was grateful for anyone else who could draw some of the
heat of his own oppression.

Within two months of starting school, Berryman encountered
another type of punishment which struck him ever after as vicious.

> The one alarming institutional cruelty was . . . chiefly mental,
> though it involved going without dinner. When no culprit
> could be discovered for something grave that had occurred, we
> had what was called a 'Who-done-it.' (I don't know who
> invented this, I have never heard of it elsewhere, but it was
> dreadful.) The whole school – some 75 boys – was assembled in
> the Schoolroom, generally after evening chapel but *before*
> dinner, and there we sat until somebody owned up. After an
> hour or so, the Council began ushering us in one by one before
> the Headmaster for inquisition, but this was only an added
> horror.

What he later referred to as the worst 'Who-done-it' of his school
career took place early in 1929, in consequence of someone's
sprinkling itching powder in a master's bed. 'We sat there, groggy,
ravenous, and frantic, till past eleven when the "old man" gave up.
Next day it turned out that the master's brother, a clown who was
visiting him at the school, was guilty. I never knew a wholly
successful Who-done-it. But at least its purpose was clear, and the
whole school underwent it together.'

Although the school certainly indulged the boys with occasional
jollifications, such as a Hallowe'en party which Berryman delight-
edly attended as a Jewish pawnbroker garbed in seedy clothing, or
another party which extravagantly aped the Hoover-Al Smith
presidential campaign (Mr Woodward mimicked the socialist
candidate, Norman Thomas, over the school relay system, while
Mr Bartlett – a Hooverite – composed a poem to Hoover), it

continually brought Berryman the gnawing anxiety of the sports field.

During the football season of 1929 he played right guard, being unable to pass or to kick well enough for the backfield. If his letters home are to be believed, his numerous injuries on the field might provide a negative index of valour, but he made so much of his injuries that, it must be seen, he was concealing constant unsuccess between the lines of martyrdom. After receiving what he calls a deep cut on his forehead one day, he was just recovering when 'somebody stepped on it in scrimmage . . . and ruined it'; the next Saturday, as he attempted to block a goal kick by the Heavy Kid Team, the ball hit him 'hard as a thunderbolt square in the face'. By 5 October, his face had much improved, but he twisted his knee in practice and had to be carried in from the field. He had managed none the less to execute one flying tackle, for which Mr West gave some encouragement. Two weeks later he was again indisposed with water on the knee, inflicted by 'one ordinary off-tackle play – ye gods!'

Of all sports he favoured tennis, and worked hard to conquer his lack of co-ordination, particularly in view of the example set by Allison and Ellsworth Vines (Vines was to win at Wimbledon in 1932). If his achievements were small, his aims were too high; he often condemned himself in terms of being 'utterly disgusted', and in fact the vehemence of his self-condemnation suggests that he had developed an inferiority complex towards both tennis and football. 'I judge bounces very poorly, my foot work is terrible, I don't watch the ball closely enough, I am late getting in position, my strokes are incorrectly produced, my service is a series of double-faults, etc. In fact, I'm ashamed to appear on the court.'

He did show a talent for running, however, a fact which he virtually 'discovered' at a track-meet early in June 1929, where he came third out of twenty-five in the fifty-yard dash – and made very good times in other races. 'This may not seem good to you,' he told his mother, 'but I'm proud of it. You know, I never have been very good at athletics, and when I can tie and beat all but two second formers, I think it's good for me. . . . Not a single one laughed at me when I ran yesterday.' (His contemporaries used to make fun of his peculiar loping gait.)

> You know, Mother, I want to be good in studies, but I've always wanted to be really *good* in some important sport. And I've found two in which I can be even better than average in – hockey at South Kent and track at Princeton.

The disparity of value he had learned at South Kent between studies and sport is clearly indicated in his use of 'good' and 'really *good*', but his suggestion that he could succeed in hockey is unaccountable since he fared as badly there as in football. He played defence, and took the puck only a couple of times each game. What really disabled him was his poor eyesight, which made him (to use his own word from a letter of January 1930) 'hate' the game because of his ignominious performance. He had also to wear an eye-glass protector. 'It's taken every bit of fun I got out of hockey away. If God created us in His image, I don't see why the devil He didn't give us a little better eyesight! I'd better take up Ping-pong as a year-round sport; all the others seem too rough for my delicate glasses.' Accordingly, his dire reports of being injured time after time must ring true, since the other boys – as spiteful as can be expected towards the weak of their number – tackled him all the more roughly for his disabilities.

Apart from his many small injuries, his general sickliness brought him often to the infirmary; his letters are full of instances of his being treated for what he called 'a bad pulse', and of reporting to have 'a cold repaired'. Self-consciousness heaped shame upon his illnesses, since he worried gravely about his build, his stamina, his eyesight, and increasingly his skin. His complexion and dandruff gave him great anxiety, undermining his self-confidence and cru-cially irritating a problem that surfaced all too infrequently, his resentment of his parents for putting such pressure upon him. (His anxiety over his maddeningly itchy scalp, and then over what he considered to be an alarmingly precipitate loss of hair, continued into his thirties.)

Because of his thankless face, his studiousness, his scornful demeanour, his small size, and his poor showing at sports, he became – a monkey among kings – a butt for bullying. At least during his early school career he was at the centre of a scrimmage every few days: once, for example, being bundled into a closet and locked in the dark where he broke his glasses. In another tussle his glasses were again knocked off, 'so I cut my knuckles on the wall. I'll take a ragging about that for a month, I guess. This school! To hell with it!' When his mother scolded him for scrapping with one boy, it became clear that the victim and the bully, like the worm and the bird, knew their own roles, since he whined with self-justification, 'He's as big as I am and much stronger – a regular tough! And maybe could clean on me, so don't feel sorry for *him*!' Even by his third year at the school matters had not significantly improved, since the bullies still beset him, as he wrote after tussling with another boy. 'He, as well as about 70 other guys around, gives me a pain,' he set down in his diary, which, mixing despondency with indignation, more reliably reports his state of mind than the special pleading of letters home. 'The older I get and the more I know about people, the less I like them. Boys are a cruel, selfish, dishonorable bunch, most of them.'

The most melodramatic incident of a series took place on 7 March 1931. That morning Berryman had ironically written for examination an essay on 'The Ideal Way of Living' (which he almost spoiled by spilling an ink bottle over his papers), and he set off after lunch for a jog of two miles by the railroad tracks. He encountered three boys, as Frank Forester, Jr, recalls.

> One of my companions made a snowball out of the vestiges of snow that were left alongside the tracks and threw it at John but missed him. John did, however, have to pass us on the way back and again he was missed the first time but the same fellow who had missed made another snowball and ran up behind John and hit him in the back of the head with it. This caused John to get very angry and he took a swing at the other fellow, missing him by about a foot. He got clipped alongside the chops for his trouble and was having well the worst of the battle when suddenly the 3:45 train came tearing around the bend by the ice house. At the sound of the train, which was then about a quarter of a mile away, my friend rose from John's chest and John started to get up saying 'Which track is the train on?' I replied 'That one' and with that John made a dash for the rail which he clung to as though for life. With the train bearing down on us, I took one arm, our third companion took the other arm and the fellow who had been battling him got him under the chin and threw him on the other track and sat on him as the old steam engine rushed past. I must say I was absolutely scared to death. After the train had passed we let John up. He looked at us with anger and tears and told us that we had saved him from despatching himself for the moment but he would get on with the job before another day had passed. This worried the three of us terribly and for 24 hours we didn't let John out of our sight. He finally promised that he would not do anything if only we would leave him alone.

Whether motivated by temper, exacerbation, or self-pity, Berryman's suicidal impulse (which, it is interesting to observe, he immediately used for the purposes of emotional blackmail against his persecutors) was clearly more than a melodramatic pretence: the other boys moved desperately to save his life. His own account of the incident, which he wrote in his diary that very night, shows an absence of emotion, rhetoric, or special pleading, which speaks for the seriousness of his purpose.

> Went for a run in the afternoon. X picked a fight on the tracks and gave me a hell of a beating. I threw myself in front of the train, but he, Forester and Y dragged me away. Didn't go to the movies, had a long talk with Forester and Y. They apologized.

Although self-destructive behaviour was to be a mainspring of his life, Berryman assumed in later years the mellowness of disinterested resignation; a fragmentary memoir, 'It Hurts to Learn Anything' (c. 1955) belies deeper feelings with this tone of wry self-detachment.

> Though we lived in terror of the prefects, the serious troubles of life for the weaker boys came from members of their own form – bullying flourished. I am not clear that this was a bad thing, since much of life for most people appears to consist of being bullied. One may as well get used to it early and in a dignified atmosphere. Few boys' spirits were broken, and even for this you could only fully blame them – or the other boys – if you knew, as we don't, what would have happened to them otherwise.

What the passage seems to suggest (perhaps ironically) is that an early dose of intimidation can build resourcefulness. All the same, he was not unaware that bullying would not always aid strength of character, but could heighten vulnerability even to a critical degree; though in his own case the passage of time brought him magnanimity enough to mitigate vengefulness, as he told in a verse fragment, 'Old memories meld, mild. I forgive my bullies'.

Memory also helped him to dissociate himself from the original experience: for the poem 'Drunks' in *Love & Fame* (1970) he wrote a stanza which appears to neutralise the experience, removing traces of its turbid suggestiveness.

> I wondered every day about suicide.
> Once at South Kent – maybe in the Third Form? –
> I lay down on the tracks before a train
> & had to be hauled off, the Headmaster was furious.

Such terseness seems entirely denotative, and holds sensation or mood in suspension.

For all his deficiencies in skin, health and sporting achievements, Berryman showed immense academic and literary promise. He soon became the foremost scholar of his class. The achievement could give him little cheer among his contemporaries at least, however, since he always suffered from the impression that his intellect was less a happy compensation than a terrible symptom of his physical puniness. Even within a few weeks of starting at the school he gained 90 in Latin and history, and although English was disappointing with 65, Mr Bartlett was justly impressed enough to reward him. 'John is one of but five boys relieved from afternoon study. He is doing well.' Only too conscious of the excessively high standards expected by his mother, Berryman spoke with regret, 'My marks aren't exactly anything to be proud of . . . but believe me I'm going to work in this next two weeks, and watch me average 90 next time marks are given out. . . . But don't feel ashamed of me, as 90 as an average in any subject is regarded as spectacular.' When his mother none the less made it known that she expected better of him, he had to remind her that he was one of five boys in 'the whole school' relieved from afternoon study. 'Does that make you feel any better?' Very soon his grades topped 90 in three subjects. 'Does that hit you below the belt?' he asked proudly. 'It is the first or second highest average in the whole school.'

During his second year he willed himself to achieve a term average of 90 and to lead the school again, and by 3 February, still first in his class, he stood 21.02 points above the school average. By 17 April, excelling all the while, he began to tire momentarily of the pressure exerted by his mother, and guardedly retaliated:

> Now there's one thing in your letter that I object to strenuously: I call 88 in Math good enough for any woman after I missed five days of stiff algebra which I haven't quite made up. And Mr Bartlett called me into the study yesterday and congratulated me on my fine average – so there!

Part of the credit for Berryman's academic enthusiasm and success is owed to a master named Albion Patterson, a thin, lanky, rather intense man whose hands made ample gestures as he talked. Although some boys thought him 'the effete among the faculty', as Aldis Butler explains, 'he had no prowess on the athletic field as a coach and therefore he was a classroom and tearoom personality, fascinating though he was.' Durand Echeverria clearly reflects Berryman's opinion in remembering him with different emphasis as 'a brilliant teacher, Shelleyish, bohemian, eccentric, fresh out of Princeton, who taught French and Spanish.' Berryman wholeheartedly responded to his subtle, intellectual mind, and was flattered when Patterson encouraged and favoured him.

A far larger part of his ambition and consequent success, however, must be laid to his mother's influence. While he was naturally intelligent – even at the time, he professed (in his own words) 'a natural love for study' – it was her devotion and psychological exploitation which drove him to excel, since she behaved as if her wishes were his. She assumed a role which was academically rewarding but psychologically damaging, and wrote numerous letters to encourage, wheedle, and upbraid him, directing him, for example, to leave Hugo 'severely alone' and to try Conrad. How many letters she wrote can be estimated from the fact that by 28 October 1928, when Berryman had passed just over a month at the school, she had sent him twenty-seven letters. At the time he did not find her importunacy enervating, his mind and talents harmonising splendidly with hers, and wrote her in return well over four hundred letters during his school career. So often and persuasively did she write, in fact, that she herself became wary of preaching, but he dismissed her fears and readily borrowed ideas from her conversation and tutoring. They would discuss literature by the hour, and rejoiced in each other's company well into Berryman's college days. Her blessings ironically helped only to delay his emotional development, since her love was cloying and often less that of a parent than of a girlfriend, as it is proper to infer from the topic and tone of this unexceptional letter he wrote her in January 1929 (though christened Martha, his mother had lately adopted the names Jill Angel, presumably to chime with her husband's – John Angus).

> I had the most horrible dream last night . . . I dreamed that you were suddenly taken ill with a fever and died before I could get there. And when I came you were lying on the bed, and you got up and chased me. Then we talked and you said you were sorry to have left me and that it was too bad I'd come too late. Your eyes were glassy and pitiful and you were pale and stiff. I must have cried for hours after I woke up and found that it was only a dream. If Jill Angel ever dies, I think I'd kill myself. But De Bebe Dirl isn't going to, is she?

When his brother attended the school for a year in 1931–2, he too was expected to match his mother's relentless demands for attainment, as Berryman reported: 'I have impressed on him that he must be on the honor roll this term (over 80) and that he is to lead the form if possible – there is no reason he can't.' Berryman's attitude betrayed elements of wanting Robert Jefferson to make his own way and of an unwillingness to be too closely associated with a second former, albeit a brother. Having been bullied so often himself, he was also careful to avoid involvement in Robert's troubles.

> Bob seems to be getting along well – better than I expected. The fellows up in the dorm all like him and respect his fighting ability – I hear that he beat up a brat . . . much larger and heavier than he. Of course if anyone in especial bullied him, I'd take it up, but I am very glad he is looking after himself. I believe he is rather homesick, but he conceals it well and behaves far better than I expected. He is doing well in all Third Form subjects except Latin, with which he is having a great deal of difficulty. Unfortunately, I find it impossible to coach him, due to my heavy schedule, but am trying to get someone to help him.

As time went on, he happily reported that Bob was improving all round and played a better game of football than he did, but he also had occasion to feel embarrassed at how 'obedient' Robert was (since he promptly said 'gladly' to any direction from his elder brother). In spite of that sort of awkwardness between them, Berryman developed a sincere fondness and respect for his brother, 'He's a peach of a kid – I wish I had more time to talk to him and go on walks and play chess with him,' but was too wrapped up in his own drives and problems to make less comment and more time.

In addition to his academic excellence, Berryman worked well at his own creative work and journalism; even by early 1929 he had penned an article called 'The Law Goes Pistol-Whipping' and sent it, presumably without success, to 'a western publication'. When he wrote to the *Kenyon Review* offering a story and an essay, John Crowe Ransom replied, on 6 January 1931, that he would like to see them, but there is no record that the items were ever submitted. Although Berryman's talent had scarcely stirred in the egg, he certainly felt ready at an early age to enter the market.

He wrote too for the *Pigtail*, the school paper so called because the town of South Kent had sported that name in the nineteenth century. By his third year, he was expertly reporting on school football matches and other matters of ephemeral interest, and became an associate editor of the paper. Exigencies of space and the factuality of his articles helped so well to tighten his prose style that he was soon called upon to write editorials, even if they were tendentious.

In May 1932 he wrote a three-page letter home explaining that he would like to be transferred to a high school rather than remain at South Kent for his sixth form year. The prep school insulation served to intensify his shyness, he said, and he could no longer tolerate the continual ridicule of his 'physical defects' which aggravated what he called his 'budding inferiority complex'. He wanted to undertake a harder standard of academic work than South Kent expected of its pupils, and to redress the sense of smugness that the school seemed to foster. He needed, he explained further, to have more practice in elocution and public speaking, to correct himself of habits of cursing and swearing, and – probably most important of all, though it figured low in his letter – to remove himself from a place where he was (to use his own understatement) 'not particularly well liked'. His plea to leave the school resulted from nearly four years of mental and emotional distress; he conceded that the school had taught him a lot, but it was often in the way of personal resourcefulness and of acquiescence with physical and psychological belittlement. Fortunately his cleverness at last worked to his good: he was the first boy in the history of the school to by-pass the sixth form and to go straight from the fifth into college.

Later in life Berryman claimed that he could not remember '*one book*' he read during his four prep school years, and tended most often to attribute what he called his 'prep school oblivion' to the traumatic shock he had experienced following his father's suicide. The facts speak otherwise of his reading at least, which he evidently enjoyed. Apart from his early eagerness for *Argosy*, *Weird Tales*, and *Amazing Stories*, he read items such as *The Idylls of the King*, Kipling's story 'The Maltese Cat', and Wells's *The History of Mr Polly*, in addition to prescribed works, and his diary for 16 February 1931 records, 'I hate to read the "Classics", but enjoy them hugely – Dickens, Eliot & Scott. They make a much deeper impression than any other reading, probably because they portray life more accurately.' But the evidence does confirm his sense (as he recorded it in his novel *Recovery*) that he had been 'thought a sissy' at school: '. . . have always seen myself ruined there by this, but is it likely? And the bullying? awful, but adequate to explain an almost-four-year-ambition-lacuna?' To cite another phrase from *Recovery*, he had been 'a completely uncharacteristic person' at school precisely because he could not cope with the disparity between his real bookish self and the boy of straw who pretended otherwise. His sporting inadequacies had thrust him into self-conflict and obliged him to become a moral chameleon, to conceal his studiousness and to endure painfully mixed feelings about the academic success he

did achieve because the other boys vilified him for it. It is a measure
of the generosity he attained in life that he could write this wry
Dream Song (369) as late as December 1966.

> I threw myself out helter-skelter-whiz
> as goalie to head off a lucky puck.
> Henry was tough on that day.
> Tricky Dick the coach was pleased, for a change.
> He returned the first offense, like a mountain range.
> We still lost to The Gunnery, hooray.
>
> At the tea afterward I askt him why
> he hadn't replaced me: he said we were lost,
> let the discredit go where it belongs.
> Thank you, I call back down the whiskey years –
> he came to hear me in   Chicago with both ears –
> god knows what he thought of them Songs.
>
> I have more respect for him than I have for me,
> and yet I said I headed for respect,
> I pickt the wrong field.

His 'prep school oblivion' must accordingly be laid least to his
father's death but most to his own unhappiness at being put to the
wrong school. The sorry image Berryman was left of himself is
illustrated from these fragmentary notes of self-analysis which date
from about 1954: 'I lurking as usual – shirking – with dirty thoughts
– always nervous of being found out – felt guilty with Old Man –
'sissy'. . . . a silly ignorant lazy dirty-minded little boy, no promise
of *anything* & *selfish* to the last degree – *took* everything done, & full
of self-pity – very bad to Bob who worshipped me . . . I can't
discover in myself *one trait* not contemptible then.'

South Kent School, with its spartan routine of sports and studies,
inhibited and humiliated him, but he took every opportunity to
compensate to himself by adopting a radically different pose during
the holidays. It seems altogether surprising for such a slight,
studious boy who felt demoralised and grey at school, but
altogether characteristic of the young Berryman, that at home he
pulsated to fashion and jumped at any chance offered to flirt his
person before numberless girls in the glittering promise of New
York City.
    He grew rapidly aware of all that was *à la mode*, and followed the
latest fads in dress, dance, Broadway shows and recording stars. He

collected pictures of Ramon Navarro, Douglas Fairbanks and
Maurice Chevalier, listened for hours on end to Lopez, Rudy
Vallée's Connecticut Yankees, Coon-Saunders, and Calloway and
Whiteman on Station WEAF, and disdained any girl who was not a
proficient dancer. Late in 1928 his family had moved to Great Neck,
Long Island, where they occupied a modest suburban house which
stood almost in the country and backed on to fields and woods, but
a fast electric train connected them in only thirty minutes to
Pennsylvania Station for big city fun. After less than three years, the
Berrymans moved back into New York City. During the Christmas vacation in 1931 his mother and stepfather took Berryman out
one evening to Petrushka's on 48th Street west of Broadway, where
they enjoyed a fine meal for ninety cents and danced to a balalaika
orchestra. Berryman studied the six chorus girls, especially 'one
very cute hussy with rolling eyes, a huge ass and plump breasts',
watched while his parents danced and then joined his mother on the
floor to the tune of 'Goodnight, Sweetheart'. Back at school he
stored up hopes as Mr Cameron talked about 'clubs, Yale, dancing,
femmes, college life, etc.' and commented with awe, 'He knows a
lot about that.'

Since school confined him to drabness and monotony, life at
home released him to follow every trend of fashion, a habit in which
he persisted for many years. He showed in fact enormous particu-
larity about sartorial elegance, as in this fussy letter written just
before his family moved back to the city:

> I don't quite know how one dresses in New York, or what
> clothes to bring home. I suppose one doesn't appear on the
> street without coat and tie, do they? or in a sweater? Are white
> shoes or my black-&-white Spaldings allowable around
> Christmas? How about my great spring coat and knickers?

and provided fastidious directions for his Christmas present:

> I want a pair of plain, pointed-toe, black and white,
> leather-soled sport oxfords, with either rubber or leather heels.
> I'd like them wing-tipped, like the ancient ones I had last year,
> with black front tips and black flanges and a black spot along the
> laces, not connected with black to any other black, if you know
> what I mean. I want them good-looking for dress wear, but not
> with fancy engraving and needle work. I like Regal's shoes very
> much – they are a swell make and around five dollars. I take
> about an 8½, width C.

If he could not star at school, he determined, he would elsewhere cut a spiffy figure for girls, dances and parties.

During the Easter vacation of 1931, when the family still resided at Great Neck, Berryman's typical day found him rising at noon and catching the 1.09 train into New York City, where he strolled up Broadway and took in a movie for seventy-five cents in the loges of the Globe; later in the afternoon he met up with his mother at the Hunt Club, a small, interesting speakeasy with 18,000 members, at 112½ West Forty-Fifth Street; the grown-ups had Martinis, Berryman a ginger ale, while a negro 'pianod [sic] and sang'; later still they had dinner at the Hollywood Restaurant while watching what Berryman described as 'the nakedest floor show I ever heard of' for one-and-a-half hours, and finished the evening in the front orchestra box at the Palace, where the bill starred such attractions as Burns and Allen, Murray, Dorothy Stone, and Vincent Lopez. It is hardly surprising that when, two days later, he returned to school (which no doubt appeared, as he had called it the previous term, 'black as sin when we arrived'), he felt homesick and misplaced. The contrast between the sophisticated New York world and the drab buildings and austere regimen of school shocked him, and deepened the fissure between the sterility and persecution of his school days and what seemed the full-blooded life miles beyond the ice rink and the football pitch. The occasional Fathers' Weekend would bring home life into a brief, synthetic relation to the school, but the strangeness of that intrusion would cause as much anxiety and tension as sympathetic understanding. When Berryman's stepfather visited the school in May 1931, for example, he carelessly departed in the middle of Sunday chapel – 'embarrassing me mightily,' Berryman grudged.

He took little interest in the family fortunes; like other children from families without apparent hardship, he never doubted that money would be sempiternally available. When the family first moved to New York, his mother tried to impress upon him that they could not afford much, but business opportunities opened up and their finances flourished for a while. His stepfather, who at first provided the main source of income (within a very few years, however, as John Angus's health declined, Martha became the chief provider by making her own more and more enterprising way in the world of fashion and advertising consultancy), was a bond salesman on Wall Street, and it gave Berryman singularly snobbish pleasure to patronise his stepfather's barber there. John Angus had a good year in 1929, but the Depression arrested his affairs. Towards the end of 1930 he joined a new firm, but the outlook did not change. Even Berryman had cause to notice that resources were running low; on 14 January 1930, he had written to his stepfather, 'I certainly hope that your business picks up and you can get results from your work again,' but business continued in a variable state through 1931. The family's financial position remained perilous into 1932, enough even to curb Berryman's adolescent egocentricity at moments; money was in general unreal to him. 'I guess things couldn't be as bad with me as they are with you and Uncle Jack, and this is *not* going to be a griping letter,' he wrote during the summer term of 1932, and went on to speak enthusiastically about New York theatre, tennis and friends. When at home he exposed himself to the illimitable world of entertainment, and remarked only the difference between what seemed to him the unsparing expense of life in New York and the primitive and humdrum face of South Kent School. It is probable that his indifference to the Depression, or his unawareness of its true character, set the pattern for his own later inability to handle money matters.

Throughout what has been called the elaborate era of the Depression, therefore, Berryman acted in two disparate worlds: the one, study under threat at school; the other, a lubricious round of chasing girls named Marie or Natalie ('some figure, I mean!'). Late in December 1931, for example, when his friend Jim Leonard came for a visit to his home, they went to a show at Minsky's Republic which consisted of what Berryman described as 'decent music, indecent chorus and swell strippers, with displayed figures. Very suggestive and filthy.' Later that evening the boys moved next door to see 'Palmy Days', and then went straight on to Honeymoon Lane, a cheap dance-hall at 50th Street and Broadway, where they found themselves being solicited for dances by buxom hostesses whose breasts hung out of their gowns. Berryman studied the prospect carefully, decided that two girls looked 'all right', and finally danced with a small girl named 'Kitty'. Compulsively gay, Berryman spent much of his middle and later teens seeking and mingling with the originals of the girl whom John O'Hara gave the name Gloria Wandrous in his novel *Butterfield 8*.

When Leonard returned home from that Christmas visit, after an extravagant whirl – which included being present in Times Square on New Year's Eve, and running up a bill for ten dollars to eat at the Roosevelt Grill, where Guy Lombardo performed – Martha scolded Berryman. Although his studiousness promised to fulfil her hard ambitions for him, he reacted so often and so extremely against scholarly straitness with soars of socialising that she had cause to fear for the continuation of his best endeavours. In any case, as far as she was concerned, bad behaviour brought to mind her dead, selfish husband. She gave Berryman 'Hell', he recounted, 'about a trait I've inherited from Dad.' Playing on his guilt towards her did not instantly trick him into sober behaviour, however, since he was to pass two years at university before discovering his responsible vocation in literature.

4

Scapegrace and spirited student, 1932-36

Berryman left his preparatory school after just five years. In the annual exams he had achieved an average grade of 78 and did not anticipate much difficulty in being admitted to Columbia College in the fall. Although he professed among his 'vocational experiences', a number of money-making odd jobs such as tutoring, chauffeuring, gardening, and selling magazines, he spent most of the summer of 1932 playing games and going to the movies. He persevered at contract bridge and chess, and spoiled himself by buying a bargain tennis racquet in order to emulate Ellsworth Vines, his hero of the season. At the cinema he marvelled at Jean Harlow (wearing 'stunning clothes, concealing nothing') in *Red-Headed Woman*, and sat through two consecutive performances of the Paul Muni film *Scarface*. He beguiled at least one long day in July with abstracting three-letter words from the slogan 'Get Phillips Magnesia Toothpaste' for a contest. His listless habits promised no better things to come. Intellectually he excelled, but lazy ways during his freshman years at Columbia culminated in his failing an exam, losing his scholarship, and dropping out of college for a while.

It was with great financial hardship that his family sent him to university at all. Early in 1930 his stepfather's income had been reduced to 6,000 dollars a year. John Angus Berryman's ventures in two or three stock exchange firms proved less and less rewarding, and by the beginning of 1932 he was virtually unemployed. Berryman's younger brother was withdrawn from South Kent School for lack of funds. By the time Berryman went up to college, the family was solely dependent on his mother's annual income of 1,620 dollars as a secretary at General Refractories Company on Lexington Avenue, New York City. Berryman lived at home for his first undergraduate year. In the spring he received a special grant of 150 dollars to assist him at college. In the interests of economy, his family were obliged to move house from East 60th Street to 119 East 24th Street.

Financial insecurity did not, however, stimulate any meritorious study in Berryman. 'I fell at school into slack habits of mind, in which I have continued here,' he admitted on his scholarship statement. In 'In & Out', a poem written much later in life,* Berryman characterised his attitude towards Columbia:

> After my dismal exile at my school
> I made at Columbia a point of being popular,
> by mid-November already I knew by name
> most of the nearly 500 men in my class,
>
> including commuters, touchingly pleased
> to have a soul recognize them.
> I liked them, a man of the world, I felt like them,
> barring my inordinate desire.

In reaction to his cloistral, diffident and repressed life at school, Berryman braved the new world of Columbia with a vengeance. He was a thin, medium tall young man, with a ghostly pallor and intense eyes that moved from side to side constantly because of what appeared to be a muscular defect, but he had a talent that gave him immense status: he was a superb dancer. In common with so many undergraduates of the period, he danced his way through college. Life seemed to be one continuous dance, including one or two dances every weekend in college halls, tea dances, coffee hours (which were really informal dances), and coming-out parties. When the college dances closed at 1.00 or 2.00 a.m., everyone poured out to carry on dancing wherever it could be afforded: sometimes at the Starlight Roof of the Waldorf, or at the Essex House.

The mark of outstanding dancing was 'smoothness' – a criterion which extended to clothes and personality and movement alike. Dancing was literally smooth: shoulders moved parallel to the floor, legs from the hip in long smooth dips and glides. Roselle Davenport remembers: 'Amongst all these really excellent dancers, Berryman was one of the best, brilliant, inventive, smooth, with marvelous control although he danced with the same almost tremb-

* Except where otherwise indicated, Berryman's verses quoted in Chapter 4 and 5 were written early in 1970, and are extracted (individual titles usually following in brackets) from *Love & Fame*, 1970.

ling muscular intensity with which he did everything else.' Berryman himself recorded:

I wore white buckskin shoes with tails sometimes
& was widely known on Morningside Heights,

a tireless & inventive dancing man   ['My Special Fate'].

He was certainly popular among the girls, not so much for his looks as for his dancing skills and a witty personality.

He also threw himself into other extracurricular activities for his first year at college, including running and rowing. Although he was affiliated with a fraternity – Phi Kappa Psi – he soon became tired of what he called 'the hegemony of the fraternities'. With his friends Tom McGovern and Paul McCutcheon, he founded the Freshman Independent Movement during his first year, but lost what he later referred to as the 'trivial' vice-presidency of the class to another candidate, 'a combed void', from Kent School, by just five votes. 'In two years,' he recalled in a poem, 'we had a majority on Student Council.'

In sum, almost all of Berryman's immediate interests lay outside the classroom, as listed on his scholarship statement: 'most sports (tennis in particular), driving, reading (almost any literary form), music, chess, the theater, dancing, bridge, museum exhibits, conversation and intelligent criticism, politics, etc.' His neglect of strictly academic pursuits resulted in a summons from the dean:

Our interview was friendly but stern: unless I cut down on my extracurricular activities and stopped cutting classes, Columbia was obviously not for me. The Dean seemed to be horribly well informed about those activities – how I don't know to this day.

During his first summer vacation he worked for a month at his old school, South Kent, receiving board, room, and laundry. Supported by a number of references, including one from the vice-president of his mother's firm, he was awarded a scholarship for the next academic year, enabling him to take a room on the seventh floor of John Jay Hall, on 114th Street, from where his social exploits intensified. His closest friend was Ernest Milton Halliday, commonly known as 'Milt', a tall, good-looking young man who measured up to Berryman's social vitality. Like Berryman, Halliday did not spare himself in the quest for prowess:

My intense friend was tall & strongly made,
almost too handsome – & he was afraid
his penis was too small.
We mooted it, we did everything but examine it
    ['Freshman Blues'].

On one occasion, in fact, spurred by their misgivings, Berryman
and Halliday repaired to their lodgings, measured themselves, and
compared sizes by telephone: they were immensely relieved to find
themselves not incomparable.

The object of Berryman's affections this year was Garnette
Snedeker, an attractive, full-bosomed girl from Savannah, Georgia, who had just entered neighbouring Barnard College, and
whose southern accent Berryman apostrophised as a 'slur hypno-
tic'. For some weeks she saw both Berryman and Halliday, often
together, occasionally in succession. Seventeen years old, Garnette
was more immediately impressed by Halliday's good looks, but she
soon entered into a closer relationship with Berryman. Their times
together were rarely calm, more often tumultuous or rapturous.
One source of friction was that Garnette insisted on dating other
boys. 'Dixie', as she was nicknamed (although Berryman always
called her Garnette), had just tasted freedom for the first time, and
resisted being tied down to one partner. When she and Berryman
met at dances with other partners, their encounters were painful and
would lead to reconciliations by telephone or letter or in person.
The inter-college phone system allowed long hours of conversation
at no cost. 'John's letters,' Garnette remembers,

> were beautiful and passionate. Often there was a poem
> included. Often the poem *was* the letter. Always after a quarrel
> there was a letter, sometimes two or three of them. He seemed
> to be able to release his pent-up emotions by writing.

Since money was so scarce, their dates often consisted of a walk in
Riverside Park, or a ride on the top deck of the Fifth Avenue bus.
When they could afford it, they would go to the cinema, or else play

Ping-pong at the Little Carnegie,
the cheapest firstrate date in the Depression city   ['Nowhere'].

Garnette's Aunt Amy, who lived on East 33rd Street, had been
deputed by Mrs Snedeker to keep an eye on Garnette's affairs, and
Aunt Amy did not much favour Berryman. While her family may
have disapproved of the association, Garnette herself felt that she

was getting a wonderful education in the company of a kind and gentle New Yorker. Their relationship was intimate but basically innocent: they exchanged a first kiss only after some weeks, and confined sexual contact thereafter to kissing and petting. 'I don't believe,' she recalls, 'he ever suggested we have sexual relations. I think my naivete intrigued him.' Nevertheless they tended often to lose control of themselves in the 'date parlors' of the dormitory.

> She set up a dazing clamour across this blood
> in one of Brooks Hall's little visiting rooms.
> In blunt view of whoever might pass by
> we fondled each other's wonders   ['Cadenza on Garnette'].

Once at least, since the rooms had no doors, they were surprised by the reproachful matron, Mrs Crook. 'I was so embarrassed,' Garnette wrote in her diary for 5 January. 'I wish I could make John understand that I feel terrible about it and am not going to do it anymore.'

Berryman was more wayward and calculating than Garnette; in spirit less faithful, but no less emotional. Their cross-currents of feeling resulted in some quarrels. Garnette's friend Louise often acted as arbiter, and after one particular row with Garnette, Berryman took Louise herself to a dance,

> to squirrel together inklings as to Garnette,
> any, no matter what, she did, said, was.
>
> O it flowed fuller than the girl herself,
> I feasted on Louise.
> I all but fell in love with her instead,
> so rich with news   ['Cadenza on Garnette'].

Berryman chose to remember that his behaviour towards Louise had been disinterested, but he actually took her out on a number of dates. He regarded the matter coolly, as his diary relates: 'Like her a lot – she may love me. Picture of me at midnight, disorderly, unstudied, thinking about women.' Berryman later told Garnette that Louise had been 'refreshing': when Garnette learned of the duplicity they quarrelled again, but all three promptly reaffirmed their friendship.

Berryman's diary does show a distinct self-consciousness about such sexual gambits: 'Didn't kiss Garnette for a long time in the evening – satisfactory reaction.' He would allow himself, from an unwitting sense of revenge, to be crudely dispassionate in the diary, but he was not nearly so detached in person. It is evident from many diary entries that his protestations of love were often directly proportionate to sexual arousal, and ingenuously confused, since sex was no less urgent and relentless for Berryman than for most teenagers. At least, for Berryman and Halliday it was not furtive but an open issue, the topic of frank vulgarity between themselves and a matter of honest gropes with current girlfriends.

Garnette recalls that the spring of 1934 was turbulent with quarrels, reconciliations, and her own gradual disenchantment with Berryman's possessiveness. 'He seemed desperately to need to be loved, and exclusively.' She was far more extroverted than Berryman, unwilling to cope long with his tormented behaviour, and the relationship came to an end. 'John was very tender and sweet to me. I was both sensitive to and often impatient with his capacity for hurt and depression.'

Berryman's habits of study in no way improved. After the fall term he received an examination grade of C+, and was called upon by Dean Hawkes to account for absenting himself twenty times from class. In February he submitted his explanation, concluding 'I regret my poor judgment and lack of foresight in not attending class, but I think I deserve full credit for the course.' In spite of apologising, he was not allowed credit. Other courses too suffered from neglect, and erratic work in English finally brought about a catastrophe. In 'English 64' (the eighteenth century), his work had been wide-ranging but cursory. He wrote many papers, most of them exiguous efforts of only one or two pages; the better ones extended to four or five pages (and, in one exceptional instance, on Pope, to seventeen pages). He acknowledged his actual lack of application when he came to sit the final examination:

> I wrote a strong exam, but since it was Mark
> a personal friend, I had to add a note
> saying that of the 42 books on the bloody course
> I'd only read 17.
>   He liked my candour
> (he wrote) & had enjoyed the exam
> but had no option except to give me F in the course –
>
> costing my scholarship. The Dean was nice
> but thought the college & I should part company
> at least for a term, to give me 'time to think'
> & regroup my forces (if I'd any left).
>
> A *jolt*. And almost worse, I had let Mark down.
> I set about to fix the second thing   ['Down & Back'].

Berryman told Mark Van Doren, 'It was a grand course, sorry I've been such a fool in it and in English 64 – I'd like to take them both over.' As 'Down & Back' states, his examination failure caused his scholarship to be suspended, which then *de facto* prevented his return to college purely for financial reasons.

Although the poem anachronistically connects his failure with his relationship with Jane Atherton (a girl he dated only the following year), it is important to observe that Berryman associated the crisis with the upsetting dissolution of his love for a girl – actually Garnette Snedeker. Immature and erratic, he had over-reacted to the end of their relationship, being not yet steady enough to regulate the apparently conflicting claims of social and sexual contact and of academic commitment.

After a summer vacation partly occupied with the job of typing for the author Clinton Dangerfield, Berryman himself applied for leave of absence 'until at least the Spring Semester.' He explained to the dean:

> After flunking English 64 last spring, thus losing my
> scholarship, I set to work in the summer to do the course and
> was occupied with it until I got this literary work – I am
> collaborating with a woman author who writes for magazines. I
> had expected to be able to save enough to return this fall, but
> unfortunately my father has been unable to make a connection
> of any value for well over a year. . . . If he is successful, I shall
> come in to see you regarding the possibility of my registering
> this fall, albeit late. . . . I have every intention of continuing and
> completing my college course at the earliest moment possible.

In 'Down & Back', Berryman misrepresents the situation for the purposes of dramatic effect with these lines:

> The Dean was nice
> but thought the college & I should part company
> at least for a term, to give me 'time to think'
> & regroup my forces (if I'd any left).

In fact, leave of absence was granted him at the beginning of October, when Dean Hawkes wrote: 'I regret to learn that you are obliged to drop out of college for a little while. I enclose a leave of absence as you request and hope that we may see you back in school before long.' The poem gives the situation a more wryly heroic cast than it actually took, being more precise as to art than as to history.

The last twelve lines of the poem return to verisimilitude,

including the facts that he kept what he calls 'an encyclopedic notebook' and that he made 'an abridgement of Locke's Essay' (which was even more concise than the 'hundred pages' he cited), but their effectiveness as a denouement relies heavily on the earlier implication that he had been rusticated – phrased euphemistically in the suggestion that the Dean 'thought the college & I should part company' – when his family's indigence alone had kept him from school. The dean had granted him a year's leave of absence, but Berryman was able to return to college the next spring when his stepfather managed for a while to make some money on the stock exchange. Berryman's reconstitution of historical fact in the poem is climaxed with this note of elation in the last two lines:

> My scholarship was restored, the Prodigal Son
> welcomed with crimson joy.

He completed his renewed study for 'English 64' by 12 February, and recorded in his diary Van Doren's response to his abridgment of Locke's *Essay Concerning Human Understanding*:

> *Van Doren is changing my mark!!!* I had a perfect interview with him at noon. He said he was proud of this – had spoken of it to several, especially Weaver and the Dean! He would have suggested changing the mark himself – is glad to do it, and knows that these conditions do not affect the spirit in which I did the work.

The exam failure and consequent need for application had shocked him into more regular patterns of work, and his growing personal respect for Mark Van Doren (fully reciprocated) sustained new habits of achievement for the next two years.

But one peg did not drive out another. In fact, Berryman's amorous adventures continued to gain momentum throughout his college career. Although he recognised that his new favourite Elspeth (whom he was soon to style 'The Vision'), was 'lovely, of course', she apparently lacked his expertise at dancing, a deficiency which did not weigh heavily for long: 'she is incredibly charming & sweet, wonder whether I love her.' On 14 March he decided that he was in love with her, and told her so. 'I do, gently, wildly, incessantly, finally. She was perfect, very kind, sweet, lovely – she doesn't love me now, but I think she may.' For some weeks he remained infatuated with her, and took every chance to extol her virtues. He dated her a few times during the summer of 1935, and was sometimes invited back to her home on Claremont Avenue, but he found it extremely difficult to assess her moods and emotions, and was only too eager to take a smile for a swoon. On 1 April Elspeth was elected secretary of the Barnard College Undergraduate Association. As Berryman noted in his poem 'My Special Fate', the appointment made her 'eminent at Barnard', and she could spare even less time for him. He was left in a state of acute uncertainty and frustration, and later referred to himself as 'Elspeth's haggard unsuccessful lover'. He was too bound up in the daily nervousness and excitement of his life to make adequate judgments of choice and value, and took too long to realise that she was unavailable. 'I know – I pray – the girl must be fond of me in some way,' he wrote. 'But I want her to love me completely, madly, as I do her – something says it can't be. My life's in it. . . . I hope for her!' Remote, reserved, and tantalising, Elspeth never lost her mystique for Berryman; he was always sensible of what he called 'fragile Elspeth's opinion', and continued to find her personality compelling and exotic.

Berryman's thoughts next centred on Jane Atherton, a slim, attractive young lady with curly brown hair and hazel eyes. She enjoyed an even, calm, optimistic disposition; although shy and modest, she was secure and confident in herself. 'I didn't enjoy arguments or disputes,' she recalls. 'Most of all I was in no way psychologically able to cope with scenes, theatrics, emotional complications, dramatic confrontations. . . . I was just the wrong girl for Berryman to fancy.'

Jane was a close friend of Dorothy Rockwell, who became her roommate at Smith College in Northampton, Massachusetts. Berryman and Halliday (types of Damon and Pythias), and Jane and Dorothy, formed the nucleus of a 'group' from the summer of 1935 into 1936. 'The group had no leader,' Dorothy remembers,

> unless it was Berryman, who needed people all the time. He was thin and gratingly intense – kind of grim-jawed but every now and then his face would split in a fiendish grin. He was going to be a poet and was Van Doren's protégé, and this put him a cut above the rest of us if we thought about it. We were all unusually intelligent, I think – kind of a golden crew though I don't believe we thought about ourselves that way. What I mainly remember is a lot of wit and laughter and a lot of thronging onto subways, buses or trolleys to go do something – down to the Village for a French film, or up to the Cloisters to go stand in the back of a night club to hear a new singer. What we had in common aside from extreme youth . . . was the great

love affair with literature, poetry, the arts, with . . . music to a
lesser extent, though we all liked to dance. I think we were *all*
self-centered, though it was most noticeable in Berryman. Most
of us were thoroughly neurotic and some were precocious;
Berryman certainly was both and so was I, and so was poor
Steve Aylward.
 . . . most of the time was spent in uproar and laughter.
Indeed that's my main memory of Berryman, or one of them.
We'd all be splitting our sides, gasping, falling down with
laughter – or he'd be sulking around Jane.

Berryman passed what he regarded as an idyllic and intimate
summer in Jane's company. Jane herself recalls:

We had a marvelous time junketing around together. Once as a
special treat we all three went to the Radio City Music Hall
which had recently opened and saw Fred Astaire in 'Top
Hat'. . . . We loved the picture so much that we sat through it
twice and from then on 'Dancing Cheek to Cheek' was our
theme song.
 Another time we all went to Jones Beach together in a car my
mother had acquired. . . . Berryman didn't think he should go
because he had a paper to write, but we assured him he could
start it on the way, so we installed him in the rumble seat
complete with typewriter. We all agreed that the paper should
start 'Obviously – comma'. . . .
 Toward the end of the summer it must have been that he
started to get more serious than I was prepared to be and our
relationship became somewhat intense and difficult. I was very
fond of him, but I could never have truly loved him.

He was delighted and excited by Jane – to his growing conviction
that they would eventually get married – even though she would
never allow an intimate sexual relationship.

Over Atherton I almost lost not only my mind

but my physical well-being!
night on night till 4 till 5 a.m.
intertangled breathless, sweating, on a verge
six or seven nerve-destroying hours

sometimes a foul dawn saw me totter home.
Mental my torment too all that fierce time

she 'loved' me; but she wouldn't quite sleep with me
although each instant brought a burning chance

she suddenly might!   ['Down & Back'].

In September she returned to Smith College, '& only wrote once or
twice a day/in that prize-winning penmanship.' Berryman confided to his mother that he wanted to marry Jane, but Jane could not
match his passion. Though her refusal was not open to misinter-
pretation, 'I'm afraid,' she recalls, 'that he just took it for granted
that whatever he wanted would be so.'

E. M. Halliday had a romantic crush on Dorothy Rockwell, but
Dorothy herself cared more for another close friend and contemporary of Berryman's at Columbia, Steve Aylward, a young man
who seemed to share Berryman's tension, according to Robert Lax:
'as friends they looked, seemed physically, a little more alike than
did Berryman and any of his other friends on campus.' Berryman
and Halliday had known Aylward since their first undergraduate
year, and delighted in his strange, provocative ways.

Dorothy Rockwell remembers Aylward (who came from an
Irish Catholic background and later took Holy Orders) as

> funny, melancholy, tortured and loving. I think he truly loved
> Berryman, to whom he felt inferior as a poet . . . and for whose
> soul and his own he would pray when he would pray. We
> would have the wildest Irish times and wind up in tears. Sex
> was evil, and Steve was sexy, and in this respect he and I were
> alike. I always thought, without surprise or any reaction except
> affection for Steve, that he was physically attracted to Berryman
> and fighting it.

On the occasion of Berryman's twenty-first birthday party, both
Jane and Dorothy came down from Smith College. Halliday had
transferred to Michigan in the autumn and was unable to attend.
Dressed in a new full-dress outfit (a present from his family),
Berryman took all his friends to a dance in John Jay Hall. The party
proceeded merrily until about eleven o'clock, when he became
aware that Aylward and Jane had disappeared. He presumed that
they had taken a bottle of whiskey given him by his brother. What
had happened, in fact, was that, during a dance with Aylward, Jane
had mentioned that she once attended a little primary school located
in a brownstone house just down the block:

The school later moved further downtown and the brownstone was now a Columbia fraternity. Steve asked me if I would like to see what it looked like now and I thought it was a splendid idea. (The idea of fresh air also appealed to me at this point.) We walked over – a one minute walk – and were greeted by the brothers who were at home with open arms and hospitality in the form of yet another drink. . . . Unfortunately, in the middle of the tour and the additional drink, I became terribly dizzy and ill and had to lie down. I went right to sleep and have no idea how long we were away from the dance. Later, Steve must have woken me up.

After what seemed like ages, during which Berryman's mood swung between panic and despair, he saw Aylward and Jane return for the last dance-numbers. To Berryman's jealous and prejudiced eyes, Jane looked drunk, Aylward sheepish and unkempt. He felt appalled and entered into a whirl of torment, jealousy and rage, which did not abate for some days. 'Unable to get to work,' he recorded, 'harried, torn, lonely, nauseated, anguished, hurt.' He took every opportunity to berate Jane's character, convinced that she was as false as Cressida, spurious and superficial in her sentiments. As far as Jane herself was concerned, the supposedly horrific 'betrayal' was 'a perfect soap bubble and farce. . . . The only thing that made it serious was Berryman's talk of suicide, something we all took seriously in view of his background which we respected.' Aylward was distraught at Berryman's reaction, and wrote him an apology two days later. A stiff reconciliation followed, but it did not last long; Berryman would not allow their friendship to be fully made up.

In spite of the rapprochement that followed, it was difficult for Jane to forget Berryman's frightening display of obsessional neurotic behaviour. He seemed unable to sustain a mean between despair and ecstasy, or to distinguish love-play from love. Callow projections of the inevitability of his marrying Jane, combined with melodramatic threats that few could challenge, betrayed a deeper insecurity than simple egotism. In the balance, however, the extremity of his response may have been partly the result of exhaustion: for some time before his birthday he had studied so intensively as to leave his physical and emotional reserves low enough to be dangerous.

Although they went out together intermittently through early 1936, Jane never again felt fully at ease with Berryman. He was capable of becoming so moody as to sit in dismal silence for a whole day. The relationship was fated to fizzle out.

As early as June 1935 Berryman dated another girl, Jean Bennett, an appealing, wistful, brown-eyed sixteen-year-old reading Political Science in her first year at Hunter College, New York. Jean became 'totally mesmerized' by Berryman's brilliance and dramatic appearance. From November onwards they went out together more exclusively.

Jean's family coincidentally came to occupy an apartment at 408 West 115th Street, a brownstone building where the Berrymans had the top floor above them. The apartments, known as 'railroad-flats', consisted of one long hall with a sitting-room in front and three bedrooms at the back. Even in those reduced conditions, Mrs Berryman managed, with good furniture and a sense of taste, to arrange a civilised environment. Jane Roman recalls that

> Mrs Berryman was a very unusual and dynamic person – the source of much of the drama and electricity when it wasn't emanating from John. She seemed very young to me for a mother – much younger than my mother. Her hair was dark reddish-gold done up in a fashionable coiffure of curls. She had a vivacious face with a slightly tip-tilted nose, and a very young figure.

Jean Bennett was 'terribly impressed' by Mrs Berryman's competence and intellect, and seemed to meet with approval as her son's belle. The Berryman family 'represented culture in a big way' for Jean. Mother and son would rival each other for learning and brilliance, leaping to the bookcase to check a quotation or arguing the merits of Schubert's *Unfinished Symphony*. Jean noticed that Berryman, who often adverted to Mark Van Doren, wanted 'always to be famous, he wanted to be, I felt, cleverer than his mother. For me he was literature, and music and romance.' Jean did not know that the ageing grey-haired man – a 'mass of grey' – who nursed a wracking cough in the corner of the room, was Berryman's stepfather. 'I didn't have the feeling that he fitted in at all.' Her own parents did not approve of her infatuation with the bright, spectacular young man who carried his head on one side, nor would they befriend his parents. Berryman seemed to them altogether 'too dramatic, too poetic, too odd'.

As the months of 1936 drew on, Berryman and Jean engaged in more and more heavy 'necking'. Although they could not sleep together, they once went so far as to undress on the stairs of the apartment building, where Jean's father discovered them and gave chase as they scrambled up to the roof to put their clothes on. Berryman immediately offered to marry Jean, but far from countenancing such an outrageous suggestion, her father would never forgive or forget their impropriety.

Initially Berryman had regarded Jean as the picture of youth and innocence, someone whom he might exploit if not seduce. By the following May, however, he admitted to having fallen in love with her. His affectedly blasé attitude had given way to a more sincere care for the young girl who flattered his ego with her devotion. Even when he moved to England for the next academic year, and fell in love with the girl who was to become his first fiancée, he was careful to protect Jean's feelings, although – ironically – Jean herself had meanwhile transferred her affections to another brilliant young man.

Despite the facetiousness of some of the entries in Berryman's diaries and letters from this period it is clear that, for the most part, his relationships found him vulnerable. It would be a misconception to take his self-scrutiny for self-conceit. Often he felt in command of a situation when, in truth, his command was merely notional. Even to admit love (as he did on a number of occasions) was to surrender his affected cynicism and vigilance, his defiant insecurity, and – most crucially – his chronic sense of responsibility toward his mother. The need to please and subserve his mother's wishes shadowed Berryman's days until he died, a necessity which it was as painful to conceal as to concede. Most of his significant responses have to be seen in that light for their full significance to be appreciated. Berryman himself was aware of the insidiousness of his mother's influence, and tended from time to time to distance his affairs from her, especially if his mother deemed them to detract in any way from the prospects which she had appointed for him. He was always to be reminded just how much he owed to his mother's selflessness, and how much his independence hurt her.

Although his love did not find a lasting match at Columbia, Berryman finally became alive to the wonder of literature and to the possibilities of his own creativity, being partly stimulated by his mother's stern warnings about his lax, self-indulgent behaviour. 'Long, serious, furious talk by Mother after breakfast,' he noted in his journal, 'releases all responsibility & serious implication in my affairs. Very ghastly. Resolutions – work, little play, punctuality, honesty.' Immediately he began to read and imitate Stephen Spender and W. H. Auden.

> I recognized Auden at once as a new master,
> I was by then a bit completely with it.
> My love for that odd man has never altered
> thro' some of his facile bodiless later books.

Berryman's poem 'Shirley & Auden' further records that

> When I flew through *The Orators* first
> I felt outstretched, like an archaeologist

The simile was peculiarly apt: in a Geology notebook dating from February 1935, Berryman had noted with relief 'And to think that I once wanted to be an archeologist.' He drafted poems almost daily, often inspired by his girlfriends – one a forty-two line poem in blank verse on 'that gnarled fantastic lava-land of love' – and numerous sonnets (including one addressed to Milton Halliday) with first lines such as 'If you think that I shall buckle' and 'Let me not reconcile to thorn of flower.' (To Elspeth he wrote 'From your indifference I could not tell'.)

As early as February 1935, he became involved with establishing a short-lived poetry society in protest against the long-established Philolexian Society of Columbia College. The other two members of the new foundation were the wiry, witty Thomas Merton (later a Trappist monk and distinguished author) and the writer Robert Lax, a tall, lanky, dark-haired young man whom Berryman thought a 'well-bred' fellow. Together they felt 'that there should be this smaller and less formal group whose activity would be purely creative; that is, we'd write poems, read them to each other and discuss them; nothing more.' So far, so good; but at the first meeting Berryman read a poem which silenced discussion because his audience could not understand it. 'Berryman then led off with a commentary of his own, which helped somewhat but didn't loosen our tongues,' Lax remembers; 'the meeting then ended, & I think the society did, too.' (For a while, in 1936, Berryman was himself president of the Philolexian Society.)

In late February Berryman wrote what he called an '80-line epic poem' to enter in a contest called the Barnard Bimbo. His rhyming doggerel (shortened by six lines) was printed in the *Barnard Bulletin* on 27 February, and accordingly takes its place as Berryman's first published work. The next month *Columbia Review* took 'Essential', a poem to which Berryman referred as his 'first publication', though he recorded 'no thrill' on seeing it in print. In April, *Columbia Review* published five of his poems, two of which ('Ars Poetica' and 'Blake') won second prize, and another two ('Lead Out the Weary Dancers' and 'Apostrophe') third prize, in the Boar's Head Poetry Contest. Four poems published in *Columbia Poetry* 1935 won him the Mariana Griswold Van Rensselaer Prize of fifty dollars. One of the prize poems, 'Note on E. A. Robinson' (Berryman wrote a number of poems in a Robinsonian vein during 1935) was reprinted two months later in the *Nation*.

Berryman's mother played an enormously influential part in fostering the poetic talent that Berryman showed, and it is symptomatic of her influence that he wrote a poem called 'Genius' after what he described as a 'very excellent talk' with her. Even as early as mid-February they discussed what he called his mother's 'marvellous idea for my first book of poems'. The same day he wrote 'Time Does Not Engulf', a poem which celebrates the durability of true talent and ends with these lines:

> With a grief which may be personal
> I recognize lesser lines:
> Which falter into the void and are mute.
> But Time contains in absolute
> No silence for greatness.

The other fundamentally important influence on Berryman's development at the time came from Mark Van Doren, to whom he gave every credit as 'the presiding genius of all my work until my second year, when I fell under the influence of W. B. Yeats.' Awed by his mentor's constant and unfeigned guidance, Berryman characterised his teaching as 'strongly structured, lit with wit, leaving ample play for grace and charm. . . . It stuck steadily to its subject and was highly disciplined. . . . If during my stay at Columbia I had met only Mark Van Doren and his work, it would have been worth the trouble. It was the force of his example, for instance, that made me a poet.'[*] Van Doren reciprocated Berryman's respect and fondness, remembering him as 'first and last a literary youth: all of his thought sank into poetry, which he studied and wrote as if there were no other exercise for the human brain. Slender, abstracted, courteous, he lived one life alone, and walked with verse as in a trance.' In April Berryman took the bold opportunity to review Van Doren's volume of poetry, *A Winter Diary and Other Poems*, for the *Columbia Review*.

Mark Van Doren was alone among the teachers then at Columbia to have exercised a significant influence upon Berryman, principally because Berryman did not avail himself of all the opportunities: he himself remembered, 'as proof of definite idiocy on my part, that I never took anything from either Meyer Schapiro or Lionel Trilling.' Lionel Trilling was not unaware of Berryman at the time: 'I met him once, heard about him often, and didn't like him. As I

[*] 'Three and a Half Years at Columbia', in Wesley First (ed.), *University on the Heights*, New York: Doubleday & Co., 1969

recall my judgment, it was a response to what I took to be an affected manner.'

By mid-year Berryman was regularly submitting poems to magazines, most of which were promptly rejected. 'We recognize the quality here,' *Poetry* commented on one group, 'but I think you have strained too hard for your effects.' Berryman related the remark to Mark Van Doren, who scrutinised the poems in question (which included 'Elegy: Hart Crane', drafted early in June), made some marginal notes, and wrote encouragingly:

> I can tell you, though, not to mind what *Poetry* says. Go on and strain. Naturalness will come later. It would be shocking for you to be natural now, as it would for you to know everything about death and women. This is the time to strain – i.e. to pull at yourself until you assume the shape which is to be yours uniquely and permanently. Only God knows what that is. I don't want to know, even if Delphic Harriet [Monroe, editor of *Poetry*] does.

Berryman shortly sent 'Elegy: Hart Crane' to the *New Republic*, where Malcolm Cowley responded: 'Your poem to Hart Crane is a fine piece of workmanship in which the thought is less distinguished than the imagery.' Eventually *Columbia Review*, which Berryman's friend Robert Giroux ably modelled on *Hound & Horn*, published the poem.

His reviews also appeared in *Columbia Review* (where, for instance, he placed an excited and informed piece about Auden and Isherwood's *The Dog Beneath the Skin*). Through Mark Van Doren, Berryman gained an introduction to Joseph Wood Krutch at the *Nation*, where he published a critical notice of three novels under the title 'Types of Pedantry', written with the assistance of Robert Giroux, who later became Berryman's publisher.

One of the highlights of Berryman's undergraduate career was his discovery of R. P. Blackmur's criticism, published in *Hound & Horn*, as he later recorded in the poem 'Olympus'.

> I had all 28 numbers
> & had fired my followers at Philolexian & Boar's Head
> with the merits of this prophet.
>
> My girls suffered during this month or so,
> so did my seminars & lectures &
> my poetry even. To be a *critic*, ah,
> how deeper & more scientific.

> I wrote & printed an essay on Yeats's plays
> re-deploying all of Blackmur's key terms
> & even his sentence-structure wherever I could.

In April 1936 Berryman enjoyed the splendid honour of seeing four of his poems published in *Columbia Review* alongside 'A Critic's Job of Work' – a review by Mark Van Doren of Blackmur's *The Double Agent* – and 'The Experience of Ideas', a review by Blackmur himself of Allen Tate's collection *Reactionary Essays*. He invited Blackmur to be guest of honour at the annual poetry reading of the Boar's Head Poetry Society, and thrilled to sit with his idol in the Harkness Academic Theater on 30 April 1936 as Mark Van Doren gave an address on Blackmur's criticism.

From early 1935 until the middle of 1936, when he graduated from Columbia, Berryman mastered a considerable body of literature and critical thought. He would study to excess for days and weeks at a time, often staying up all night, since his enthusiasm could not be contained by the regularity of a discipline.

Shortly after his lamentable twenty-first birthday Berryman's exhaustion and distress were lifted by a unique incentive. Mark Van Doren unexpectedly mentioned that he was in the running for an academic fellowship, the Euretta J. Kellett, a prestigious award which enabled the recipient to study at Cambridge in England. (The scholarship had originally been offered to Robert Giroux, but he decided not to take it up.) The hint was enough for Berryman to apply himself wholeheartedly, and he became a conspicuous scholar as the academic wheels slowly turned. The English department notified Dean Herbert E. Hawkes that Berryman was front-runner for the fellowship (with Robert Krapp, who had graduated the year before, as an alternative). Asked for a statement of his aims and worthiness to meet the appointment, Berryman affirmed that he was committed to poetry, drama, and literary criticism, and expressed his interest in writing a book-length critical and biographical study of Hart Crane.

In the event, he almost failed to graduate because of his antipathy towards one professor, Emery Neff, who (as Berryman put it) 'mouthed' Wordsworth at the class – 'holding up my appreciation of that great poet' – and squandered his attention on Carlyle and Swinburne. Berryman showed such ardent dislike for Neff throughout the year that the professor (repaying his animosity, Berryman believed) gave him a C in the examination, and promptly took off abroad. Since Berryman needed a grade of B, the consequences were frantic.

They held unhappy meetings for two days.
To change the mark of a colleague in his absence?

Finally, a command decision:
they'd give me a second exam, invented by themselves,
& judge it, & if my paper justified,
they'd elevate the highly irrational mark.

I took it – it was fair, hard – & I killed it.
I never knew what I got, but the course-grade
cranked upward to a B. I graduated   ['Crisis'].

But Berryman also ran close to failure for other than academic
reasons. Early in 1936 he began suffering from strain and fatigue
which was further complicated by a dangerous ear infection. He
was in such pain that he underwent an emergency operation to open
an abscess, and the doctor advised Mrs Berryman to withdraw her
son from college at once, 'as the boy was on the edge of complete
breakdown'. The English department began to think again about
appointing Robert Krapp to the Kellett Fellowship, but Berryman
laboured on without knowing the danger he was in. Late in May his
mother justified her questionable course of action to Berryman's
adviser, Dr Gutmann:

I am not able to do anything for him that could replace the
fellowship and I could not find it in my heart to allow him to
lose it. I fought it out with myself, and let him go on,
depending on his lack of strength to prevent overwork while
reserves were being built up again.

In the event, Berryman survived his exams on the brink of collapse,
and never did become aware of the dangerous calculated risk that
his mother had taken in allowing him to persevere.

His future offered nothing but great promise, a radical change
from the outlook of his first years at college when he had seemed
destined for no more than social success. It is remarkable that,
within a period of less than two years, he had reformed himself so
thoroughly as to be called by H. R. Steeves 'conspicuously qualified . . . for academic distinction.'

5
Distinction and first fiancée, 1936-39

Berryman graduated Phi Beta Kappa in 1936 and looked to England as his oyster; not many months earlier he would have been amazed to find himself in such an illustrious position, but he could now take a just pride in his accomplishment. At Cambridge, he had to learn, he needed to build solidly on success before a larger world would echo his acclaim.

Assuring Van Doren that he would 'work like a canine and not dishonour thee', Berryman

> mounted to the *Britannic's* topmost deck
> O a young American poet, not yet good,
> off to the strange Old World to pick their brains
> & visit by hook or crook with W. B. Yeats   ['Recovery'].

Later in life he described feeling then, as the ship slipped away from the pier, like 'Jacob with his father's blessing'.

His supervisor at Cambridge was George Rylands, then a man in his early thirties who had written a book called *Words and Poetry*. Berryman found him able and delightful, and considered that his book was 'generally sound' and that it contained some excellent notes on Shakespeare's style. Rylands saw him once a week 'in his posh rooms at King's' ('Transit'). Years later, Rylands himself remembers that Berryman 'was strange and wayward and original and much loved and admired by his friends who believed in his future.' He found him also 'exceedingly interested in all the problems and potentialities of verse composition.' Although Rylands thought highly of Mark Van Doren's book on Dryden, Berryman wrote at the time, he did not know of him as a poet, nor of Hart Crane and John Crowe Ransom. Berryman learned a great deal from Rylands, including a sense of perspective. They read much American poetry together, Rylands's exegeses and opinions acting as a corrective to Berryman's enthusiasms, and determined that poets such as Robinson, Jeffers, and MacLeish were pleasant, though not significant. Major writers emerged triumphant from close inspection, although Berryman came gradually to feel that America lacked a real verse tradition, and that its sensibilities were raw.

Berryman avidly read Yeats and Blake, and much French poetry, including Ronsard, Mallarmé, Rimbaud, Laforgue, Verlaine, and two Romantics, Vigny and Lamartine – 'to keep', as he put it, 'my sense of values straight.' He thought more of Hugo and less of Gautier than was current, and felt strongly that Henry James had misjudged Baudelaire. He also read Chaucer, seventeenth-century verse, and Shakespeare above all, in addition to Montaigne, Joyce, Auden, and exactly '2½' novels. He was immensely excited by Donne's poetry, especially a line like 'Hither with christall vyals lovers come': 'I want,' he exclaimed, 'to get down and bite a large piece from the poker when I see that.' He upbraided Allen Tate 'incidentally' for dismissing Donne's prose: 'I love the stuff.' He began too to study Dryden with some care (using Van Doren's *Dryden*), and was spry, intelligent, and grateful in his praise and questioning: 'I wish to suggest,' he told Van Doren boldly, 'in Mac-Flecknoe that A—— Hall, which, 1682, says Oxford, read Aston, should be Arsehole Hall in line with Pissing-Alley above. What say you, admirable man?' Van Doren liked the gloss.

But Berryman was nervous and agitated for his first weeks in Cambridge, mostly from loneliness which seemed to find no relief. His craving for congenial company grew so intense that he claimed, after a period of hours in his rooms, to have dashed outside and insulted everyone he met. In time he would display an almost morbid dependence on the marriage of true minds: friendship became an addiction. He could also be implacable towards his foes, and it was around this aspect of his temperament that his energies found an occasion to crystallise. By his own account, he resolved one particular bout of 'nervousness and vast loneliness' by writing a poem. Fresh with the memory that Emery Neff had almost cost him his scholarship, Berryman wrote a vitriolic poem about him. Other forms of refuge were provided by the cinema, and by his own attempts to write poetic drama. Although he knew it might be five or ten years before he could write well, he affirmed that he would one day write superb plays. For the moment, his personality and life-style denied him the power. He felt that he was lazy and acquisitive, dissipating his energies, lost for love, and balked at the apparent dichotomy between the ordinary man and the artist. High art seemed foreclosed to him for his lack of a discipline, an intellectual mask, an order through style which might function as a 'moral defense'. Control of his natural energies and personality might serve to make them effective in the order of art. 'I detest,' he said, 'appearing a kind of Hart Crane – he had nothing but talent, not moral integrity nor intelligence nor discipline – even Rimbaud whom I've been reading had more, and how much greater than either is Baudelaire, magnificent vitality through control.' In harmony with his own version of poetic etiology, he complained that he could make little advance with his own play, 'I get too excited and am continually writing poems.'

When he was not devouring his books, Berryman mooned around Cambridge and ferreted in bookshops, especially 'sparkling Gordon Fraser's in Portugal Place' ('The Other Cambridge'). Browsing one day, he fell into talk with Gordon Fraser himself. Much to Berryman's delight, he learned that Fraser had published in England not only Van Doren's *Dryden* but also a work by Richard Blackmur, *Dirty Hands*. He told Van Doren that Fraser was a 'very nice fellow and with knowledge and taste.' He also met Katharine Fraser, 'a dark, charming young' woman from Chicago whose mother's name happened to be Berriman. To Berryman the Frasers seemed, in brief, 'young, pleasant and remarkably interesting, he brilliant as the devil but rather insane and she a dark Beatrice Lillie, oddly charming.' The Frasers enjoyed the nervous, intense bookworm, and invited him (for the first time on 7 November) to tea at their house, 274A Mill Road.

It was the beginning of a close friendship. The Frasers readily absorbed the excitable, temperamental young poet into their home. Their drawing-room was large, and furnished with comfortable chairs and sofas, a dartboard, a gramophone, and Fraser's extensive collection of books, which were useful for arming an argument. Berryman played dance music non-stop on the gramophone during darts sessions, but sometimes out of boredom with a conversation. Katharine Fraser recalls how serious Berryman was about himself, 'his chief interest and main worry. He had three moods – hysterical joy, deep depression and obvious boredom.' He would become extremely animated during a discussion, his voice climbing to a shrill pitch. Unable to suppress his excitement, he would jump up from his chair, walk about waving his arms, and cut in shrilly on the person who was speaking. At evening gatherings, the Frasers would have to shout at him, 'Shut up, John' – 'Sit down and shut up.' In return he would dismiss argument – 'Don't argue with me.

I've taken a course' – and was absolutely serious that he was right for having studied the subject.

'John's joy was always very noisy.' Katharine Fraser recalls:

> He loved it when someone was really witty. It was the idea that someone was so clever that pleased him, almost more than what the person had said. He let out this same 'joy shout' when he thought a meal table looked particularly pleasant, or when someone was looking chic or attractive. I well remember when John screamed 'Gordon!! you look marvellous. Gosh I love your suit!' My husband was appalled. 'Men don't say things like that to other men' – but John did. One was never in doubt about John's moods or his likes and dislikes. He was lavish and extremely voluble. When it came to the depressions one had to dig a bit and then try to wheedle him out of them.

Berryman was very keen on darts, played to win, and was annoyed with himself when he lost. He played, as Katharine Fraser remembers, in absolute solemn silence, and would polish his glasses for a very long time if he anticipated losing or before playing any opponent whom he recognised as an expert. One such expert was another new friend, Patrick, who shared Berryman's enthusiasm for chess. Pat (as he seems always to have been called) was a strange, complex figure: well-built and good-looking, he stood over six feet, with a pallid complexion and straight, smooth blond hair with one lock that flopped down into his eyes. His voice was soft and sometimes difficult to catch, and he commonly spoke either very quickly or in such a hesitant manner that he almost stuttered. Shy, arrogant, a fatalist, Pat loved chatting about books and could be disarming with his literary opinions. Brought up in an orphanage, he later took a variety of lowly jobs (at one time, a paid partner in a ballroom), but then inherited an unexpected fortune and got married. He never went to university but, after living for a while in London, he insisted on taking up residence in Cambridge, where – apparently to his wife's displeasure – he attended open lectures and studied independently. He frequented the Gordon Fraser bookshop and chatted without check. Pat and his wife rented a furnished house in Hills Road, to which they invited the Frasers for tea, calling for them in a lush Buick or Chrysler.

When Pat and his wife split up, the Frasers took him into their home for a few weeks, where Berryman first met him. Much to the chagrin of the Frasers' daily help, Pat slept late and was messy. He conducted himself so uncertainly that he had difficulty deciding which of his beautiful and expensive clothes to wear each day, and

often stayed out most of the night. His maudlin, expressive character and bizarre history and habits held great appeal for Berryman,
whom he engrossed both as a spectacle with a big, soft manner and
as a man licensed by temperament and fortune to investigate books
and ideas.

> Pat's reading Conrad through for the second time
> 'to see if I was right', my new companion,
> with 35/- a week from his solicitors.
> I buy him *breakfast* at the Dorothy
>
> & we dawdle over it discussing suicide.
> He has only two things left (his wife *took* him),
> a carmine sports car & a large-paper set of Conrad.
> Maybe I better add
>
> an all but preternatural ability at darts
> which keeps him in drink.
> He is sleeping with both his landlady & his landlady's daughter,
> one on the ground floor & one upstairs,
>
> he hates to go on across there back at night.
> And I think in my unwilling monkhood *I* have problems!
> He's studying with Wittgenstein & borrowing Kafka.
> A hulking sly depressed attractive talker   ['Monkhood'].

In view of Berryman's use of the word 'companion', it is
interesting to learn from a letter he wrote to his mother on 15 March
1937 (shortly after meeting Pat) that he was in fact utterly fascinated
with the man.

> 22 but very wise. . . . Extraordinary modesty and the most
> destructive mind I've ever encountered; idea that no one is of
> the slightest value, but he is worth a little less than anyone
> else. . . . I liked him extremely from the first, but very strange
> and uncannily silent in company he is. Constant delusions,
> terror of strangers and people: all, he thinks, believe him
> mad. . . . He will unquestionably be insane in a few months if
> all continues, but I think it won't. . . . Fantastic theories he has
> and devastating, some of them . . . one day a complete plan for
> criticism of the novel . . . the next the most profound despair.
> He was not at the university here but knew Witkenstein [*sic*],
> the metaphysician, well, and has been greatly influenced by
> him. . . . There is a total lack of both conviction and pretension

in all that he does. But I am certain that if his balance can be restored in the next year he may do great work. If not, he will infallibly kill himself. I would do all I can even if we were not, as we already are, close friends.

Pat's curious and engaging demeanour clearly complemented Berryman's intense and striving disposition, and helped him to define the limits of his own waywardness: he could identify in himself scope for a similar errantry.

Another, younger friend was Anthony Godwin, 'a bright charming kid of 16', who was working as an apprentice to Gordon Fraser's business. Godwin, who later earned an international reputation as a literary editor, had been unhappy at school. His mother sought out the help of her old friend Mansfield Forbes, a life fellow of Clare College, who arranged for the boy to work with Gordon Fraser. Berryman came to regard Godwin as full of promise, if precocious, and was bored and annoyed when Pat started taking the boy along on pub crawls. He was amazed that Pat should ask Godwin for his views on creative or critical works, but he was irritated not only by Pat's delight in relating Godwin's pompous remarks but also by his irresponsibility in permitting the boy to drink. He felt perhaps even more impatient with Godwin just because of what he considered Pat's bad influence, but he evidently showed signs of being jealous of Pat's companionship.

Berryman himself alienated a number of people during his period in Cambridge, mostly from arrogance and a set of affectations. He seemed to regard himself, for a time at least, as being like Carlyle's character Diogenes Teufelsdröckh – a cinnamon-tree choking among pumpkins and reed-grass. The misery of his solitude during the Michaelmas Term was sometimes so acute that he almost turned, like Sir Hudibras's sword, to eat himself with rust. It was in fact a comparatively short period before he met the Frasers and his circle began to grow, but it felt like a lengthy spell of loneliness.

By 14 November he was railing against England and 'its clammy inhabitants' for forcing upon him his 'solitary damnation'. He liked to discriminate between the dreary English character and the 'passion' of the American. 'The English by god I largely detest,' he said, barely disguising self-pity, 'a smug and passionless people of ugly women and remote men.' During October he often walked to nearby Fenland villages before Hall at 7.30, and was very taken with the spectral fogs, thatched houses under moonlight, and even the notion of being 'a Nature poet (prior problem, to be a poet)'. He would not venture as far as Ely because that would necessitate bicycling: he could not face the prospect of gears and handbrakes, besides the real danger of looking 'infinitely silly'. When his former schoolmate John Ward showed up, however, they explored Cambridge together and later cycled to Ely.

Far more of Berryman's time was spent with brooding on 'heroic possibilities and tragic dimensions everywhere'. He used letter-writing, like Rilke, as an intense and perhaps excessive means of association. He was a rhapsode before becoming a scholiast, and would speak lengthily to his exultation at reading Vaughan.

> I don't show my work to anybody, I am quite alone.
> The only souls I feel toward are Henry Vaughan &
>   Wordsworth   ['Monkhood'].

At other times he would fire off literary tirades, and then lapse for periods, after Rilke's manner, into a *sécheresse d'âme*.

Berryman did ponder the worsening political situation in Europe, the foment and the violence: 'I think Italy, Germany and Russia will be at war by January, grave trouble over riddled Spain. France can't stay out, and neither, probably, can anyone else. I shall not, so far as I can tell, go under any conditions.'

On 13 November, T. S. Eliot gave a talk on 'The Idiom of Modern Verse' to the English Club in Mill Lane. Berryman found it interesting – 'for I expected nothing.' Rylands had advised him that Eliot had been suffering interminable nervous stress from his wife for years, and Berryman observed for himself 'a very shy, neurotic man . . . tall and fairly solid, dark glasses, monotonous and humorless delivery.' Eliot looked undistinguished, like an American executive, but had (as Berryman conceded rhetorically) 'some force of brow and a justice of glance'.

Berryman regarded Eliot as an *éminence grise* that he had to surmount. He felt envious of Eliot's fame, and of an achievement from which he himself could not draw, and was constantly in the act of (to borrow a phrase from Carlyle) trampling on a thistle because it yielded no figs. He relieved his stress and resentment by a sentiment approaching *Schadenfreude*, and by belittling Eliot's appearance and manner. When Macmillan later turned down a manuscript by Mark Van Doren, Berryman took the occasion to suggest that he should bear a copy to Eliot and beat him into publishing it: 'the beating idea occurred to me because I should like to beat Eliot on my own account.' He had recently discovered that Eliot's line, 'The army of unalterable law,' had been borrowed from Meredith's poem 'Lucifer in Starlight'. He was cross and disillusioned with Eliot for appropriating a line to which he himself was so attached as to allude to it in the line, 'Compulsion and inexorable

law,' of his own poem 'Ritual'. He criticised Eliot as an anthologis-
er, a role that may have been legitimate in *The Waste Land* but was
less so in the religious poems, and inadmissible in a 'straight poem'
– 'But there are limits to decency, he screamed.' Berryman had
detected too that Eliot had elsewhere borrowed extensively from
Van Doren's *Dryden*, even to the affronting extent of quoting, just
as Van Doren had done, the entire Oldham poem – with the same
comment and without acknowledgment. He determined to follow
the line of Johnson and Coleridge (even Dryden, though a sketchy
critic), rather than that of Hazlitt and Arnold and Eliot.

Berryman later commented on himself at the time,

> I suffered a little from shyness, which was just arrogance not
>   even inverted.
> I refused to meet Eliot, on two occasions,
>
> I knew I wasn't with it yet
> & would not meet my superiors. Screw them   ['Monkhood'].

But Berryman certainly met and spoke with W. H. Auden at this
time. Later in life he remembered that George Rylands

>   was kind to me stranded, & even to an evening party
> he invited me, where Keynes & Auden
> sat on the floor in the hubbub trading stories
> out of their Oxbridge wealth of folklore   ['Transit'].

Auden came to a meeting of the Spenser Society on Sunday, 15
November, and read two stories by Edward Upward. Afterwards
Berryman took the chance to talk with him at a party in Rylands's
rooms. He reported that Auden had sandy, unruly hair, 'with oddly
light eyes and an indetermined face, although his manner of talking
and what he says are compact of decision.' The young, slim Auden
lounged about, at once easy and awkward, wearing one brown sock
and one black. He told Berryman that his generation at Oxford had
read Yeats hardly at all. They talked about John Crowe Ransom
(whom Auden admired), about *The Ascent of F6*, the second play
that Auden had written in collaboration with Christopher Isherwood, and about Iceland, which Auden had visited with MacNeice
the previous summer. They also chatted about poetry in general, as
well as another constant topic, the English neglect of American
literature.

Keynes, who had been at Cambridge with Lytton Strachey,
quoted his phrase, 'Two kisses are too many, one too few,' to

which Auden responded with a gesture, commenting, 'Rather obscure sentiment, that.' They gossiped about Eliot (whom Berryman was surprised to hear referred to as 'Tom') and his practical jokes. Eliot had apparently discovered a shop which supplied him with exploding sugar for sabotaging tea parties with Virginia Woolf and John Hayward.

Most of the poetry that Berryman himself wrote during this period was full of high sentence, abstract, and nearly incomprehensible in grammar and idea. One poem written on his twenty-second birthday sounded a note of agonised resignation, 'the love and the long failure / Likewise are caught in the strict wheel and turn,' and concluded with this sentiment:

> What breaks about my head next year or next
> Let it be intolerable, let it be
> Agony's discipline, let it not be strange.

He resolved to adopt the mantle of the suffering life, to live intensively and to use his life as discipline. He was choosing, in other words, to make art of his life. It was characteristic that he should have spoken of his most recent work in bodily terms: 'Several of these poems . . . have doubtless been torn and membered, polished since.' When Mark Van Doren complained of his introspection, Berryman was quick to agree: 'I deplore my recent writing, but it's probably better than nothing – relieves me, purgative, & keeps what hand I have technically "in".' Although he spoke of his work in terms of therapy, he did not strictly expect others to appreciate what amounted to a private literary version of an enema.

At the same time he corrected himself on another point: 'To hell, by the way, with the mask: I daresay I've written and thought more rot to the square inch than ever anyone – but the more out, the less fester; nothing was ever accomplished by sitting tight; and other homilies.' Maudlin sentiments were shuffled off with self-deprecation. The irony was forced: beneath it roosted arrogance, impatience, and ambition, but the better part was just loneliness, shyness, and a little learning with a bigger show. What seemed pretentiousness was often the public face of a sound, if over-extended ambition. Complaining still of 'loneliness intensified through misfortunes here', his hopes for himself were hopes for the progress of art: 'People have forgotten what tragic literature is – but they'll remember. Gigantic, unspeakable but articulate disaster. Perhaps I can.' It was evident to almost anyone but himself that, at twenty-two, he lacked experience for such consummate undertakings. What was not so clear was that, in arrogating to himself fundamental exercises in tragic art, he was in a way courting disaster in his personal life. His determination to play the suffering role was sustained by one hapless event after another.

Berryman's mother was equally ambiguous in her directives. On the one hand, she would try to deflate his poses, to stabilise flights and neurotic fancies:

> But the strength to be gained by the standing alone should be worth more than all the pangs to you, if you will forego self-dramatization about them. You really, you know, John, aren't the worst-off fellow in the world. . . . If you don't write a good poem now, you will next month or week or year or tomorrow – after all, son, you aren't precisely aged yet.

On the other hand, she often turned to support his dreams and exertions which had yet to prove themselves viable as a career. 'How can you say,' she asked,

> that the disinterested, passionate intellect of Swift, of Vaughan, is vanished, spent irretrievable: while *you* live and breathe, are they dead? Man has two immortalities: the flesh and the spirit, and the second is often the gift of the artist to one whom he perpetuates.

As Berryman's second term gathered momentum, he read an enormous number of plays and worked to establish the text and chronology of *Twelfth Night*. He conceived a love for textual analysis that was to find issue, within a few years, in his critical and textual work on *King Lear*, and later still in biographical research. 'It's awfully silly, I think,' he decided in February 1937, 'ever to do anything but read Shakespeare – particularly when we've only one lifetime.'

His other current literary passion received a boost when Andrew Chiappe asked him to speak about W. B. Yeats to the Dilettante Society, the Clare College literary society, on 11 February. Excited, if diffident, at the prospect, he decided to concentrate on the lyric poetry, and to analyse and comment on Yeats's symbolism. In the event, he managed to control his nerves and spoke with some assurance and at such length that his talk, scheduled to last one hour, took more than two.

Out of the depth of his inquiries came the sudden notion that perhaps he could write a biography of Yeats. He made plans to tour Ireland by bicycle, to meet Yeats and his friends, and even to spend time in the master's library. While wary of over-estimating the

importance of Yeats's life to his work, he did think that all biographical data were not only relevant, but also invaluable for him as a
critic. 'Many of the symbols in his poems,' he wrote, 'are personal
symbols, to be understood in terms of his history, and only when
understood can they be appraised.' His enthusiasm for the project
was reinforced by the conviction that no worthwhile criticism had
yet been written about Yeats, not even Edmund Wilson's account
in *Axel's Castle* which he found 'contemptible'.

For the moment, he was well pleased to have researched various
influences on Yeats's work, from Spenser, Shelley, Rossetti, French
Symbolist and English Metaphysical poetry, to the versification of
Ezra Pound and stanzaic tightening by comparison with good
speech. He was the first critic to be aware of the drastic lengths to
which Yeats took revision of his poems. He had also discovered
something that was to help support and contain his own creative
drift, the importance of Yeats's personal symbols, Pollexfen,
Taylor, Synge, and Lady Gregory, and two others above all:
'Parnell, as tragic hero, and Swift, as tragic ironist, both, lonely,
passionate, ambitious, proud and bitter men.'

During this period of intensive study, he became so possessed by
Yeats and so exhausted from overwork that he experienced an
hallucination.

> Wednesday evening while I was reading here [10 February],
> suddenly my attention wandered, as if forcibly; I shut my eyes
> and an image rose before them, not clear but strong: I saw that it
> was the figure of Yeats, white-haired and tall, struggling
> laboriously to lift something dark which was on his right side
> and below the level on which he stood; as it came into view, he
> lifting it with difficulty, I saw that it was a great piece of coal,
> irregular, black. He raised it high above his head, hair flying and
> with a set expression, brilliant eyes, and dashed it to the ground
> at his feet, a polished ground that might have been a floor: the
> pieces rolled away silver.

The symbolic vision of a Yeats purging Ireland, striking silver out
of coal, was the product of heroic identification.

Berryman learned much about his own sensibilities from his
study of Yeats. A poem such as 'That the Night Come' (in
Responsibilities) could inspire him with the blinding force of perfect
austerity, every word contributing to its dynamic meaning. He
decided that he could never be a scholar, his mind being too
unsystematic and impatient, but preened himself on possessing a

fine aesthetic sense. For Berryman, Yeats *united* action and contem-
plation as a complete man. Against such an example ranged the
modern forces of cant and popular journalism, of half-education
and spurious emotion. He resolved:

> To read no reviews, to avoid rather than taunt stupidity, to keep
> free from any struggle for an 'American literature', or a 'new
> state', such as that which exhausted Yeats for twenty years,
> never to borrow the opinion of an inferior, and to recognize no
> superior, to work. Never to be competent, never to be satisfied.
> To form a style which will present what is actual and
> passionate. To tolerate no compromise with this unfortunate
> time.

During his talk to the Dilettante Society, Berryman looked up at
one point and 'saw among the inane faces one sharp intelligent face,
and thereafter talked to him, as concisely and ably as I could.' Later,
over coffee, Andrew Chiappe introduced Brian Boydell, a young
Irishman in his final year at Clare College. Berryman had heard
Boydell give a piano recital during the Michaelmas Term, and
wanted to meet him. Boydell was reading Natural Sciences, he told
Berryman, because he wanted information beyond the music
which would be his work (he later became Professor of Music at
Trinity College, Dublin). They liked each other instantly, and
Berryman decided to join the Psychical Research Society, of which
Boydell was already a member. When several members of the
audience later asked to borrow Berryman's various editions of
Yeats, Boydell took the music for the dance plays.

For a time, Berryman became closely involved with what
Boydell has called their 'frightfully aesthetic/intellectual group'.
Boydell had digs on Midsummer Common, looking out towards
Jesus College, the seat of the boat club which wrecked the rooms of
undergraduates who, like Boydell himself, collected modern pictures and gramophone records. Later in February, Boydell played
and sang from his own setting of Yeats's 'Red Hanrahan's Song
About Ireland' (which Berryman thought superb), and then several
songs from the dance plays to Dulac's music. Berryman was
impressed with Boydell's singing and speaking voice, and described him years later as

> a Dubliner with no hair
> an expressive tenor speaking voice
> who introduced me to the music of Peter Warlock

who had just knocked himself off, fearing the return
of his other personality, Philip Heseltine.
Brian used to play *The Curlew* with the lights out,
voice of a lost soul moving   ['Friendless'].

Boydell played the five records of *The Curlew*, Peter Warlock's
melancholy settings for four of Yeats's early poems, which convinced Berryman that music had to be heard in the dark. Berryman
liked Warlock's music because of its melancholy aestheticism, and
because of what he took to be a bizarre and maudlin pose, a mask –
an extreme, but amenable, aesthetic device. '"The Curlew",'
Berryman said, 'is beautiful but utterly despairing, the most desolate art I know.'

Boydell asked Berryman if he would write him a cradle song to
set to music. Berryman doubted his ability for the job, but went
home at midnight and wrote a rather ordinary one (in imitation, as
Kevin Barry has pointed out, of Warlock's 'Cradle Song') with no
great trouble.

> Let you now sleep, my dear.
> After the time of play
> Your head is drowsy and far away
> And all is darkness here.
> Let you now sleep.
>
> Let you now sleep, and where
> Your cradle is, let white
> Fabulous angels watch tonight
> Until the dawn come clear.
> Let you now sleep.

Boydell later incorporated his setting into a series of three songs for
soprano and string quartet.

At the time, Berryman's ignorance of music was almost complete. He had gained real pleasure and understanding from playing
the Kreutzer Sonata over and over again while staying with the
Frasers in December, as from some Bach, Sibelius, Beethoven and
Tchaikovsky, and that was about all. As the years wore on, he grew
fiercely percipient about music; for the moment, he was just fierce.
He argued that 'since years are short enough for one art, I think it
better to keep clear,' but he was momentarily lurking from the
effort needed to acquire knowledge and taste.

At the beginning of March, his friend Pat fetched Berryman out
to the Frasers' house, where he became immersed in a tumbling

round of happy excess with 'a mad group of people who chanted poetry and drank and argued till all hours.' The party was prompted by a visit by Dylan Thomas, who had come to give a reading at the Nashe Society in St John's College. Disciples gathered about Thomas and celebrated with a binge at Mill Road that lasted literally for a week. (Thomas stayed with Gordon Fraser during Katharine's absence.) Andrews Wanning, who was among the celebrants, remembers one moment when Berryman, referring to Thomas, addressed him, 'Hush, the poet's asleep!' Berryman imitated Thomas to some extent – at least on this occasion – by getting heavily drunk.

In reaction to that week's revelry, Berryman entered a period of despondency lasting at least another week, worrying his sense of incompetency and unfulfilled ambition. On Monday, 15 March, he claimed to have destroyed several hundred poems, 'the room was littered with crumpled pages, I fed the fire for an hour or two.' His state of mind was real, if short-lived, yet he tended to arrogate the entire fate of the world of letters to his own troubled soul. 'I begin to believe that my accomplishment will be as fragmentary as Crane's, except that it will not see print; one poem by Marvell is worth a hundred Cranes.' He felt for the most part that his verses had lacked style and strength and beauty, as well as voice and matter. On 9 March he wrote a poem, 'Last Days of the City', expressing his discontent.

The rest of term sped by busily. He completed twenty-five poems and despatched them to Robert Penn Warren at the *Southern Review*. Then he gave another talk on Yeats – to the Nashe Society. Ian Watt was then president of the society, and remembers that 'it was not so much a lecture as a reading, and I don't think it was regarded as very successful.' Watt recalls too that Berryman was particularly enthusiastic about Yeats's 'poems of memory and friendship, rather than the more abstract ones like "Byzantium" or "The Gyres".' He found Berryman shy but friendly and generous-spirited.

In early April, Berryman went to Ireland to see if he could meet Yeats, but the trip was fruitless – for Yeats was in London. Returning to London, he applied for an interview with his master, and Yeats promptly responded with the ingenuous question, 'What did you want to see me about?'

Berryman's major ambition on crossing the Atlantic had been to visit Yeats. As early as 9 October 1936, he had sent a fan letter and a poem.

> A glory there is over Ireland now:
> . . . .
> An aged man there is in Ireland now
> Alone who is the honour of that praise,
> Craftsman intense and disciplined, a man
> Who set luxuriance aside and ran,
> A creature of bone and heart and rigid brow,
> The race that wears the rest, eternal ways,
> That solitary man.

Berryman could not later recall which of Yeats's poems he had singled out for praise – except for 'The Second Coming', the poems in 'Words to Music Perhaps', 'Sailing to Byzantium', 'Among School Children', and 'In Memory of Major Robert Gregory'. Yeats had replied exactly a month later with special thanks both for the fact that Berryman had cited the poems which he too favoured and for what he called the 'eloquent compliment' of his verse. Berryman was exhilarated by the response: the myth was a man after all, and even wrote a crabbed hand. 'The man writes a quite illegible and characterless scrawl – in fact the worst I've ever seen – and it took me an hour to make the few lines out.'

Friday, 16 April, was the day fixed for the historic meeting. Beforehand, Berryman had met up again with Dylan Thomas, as he described in a *Paris Review* interview (Winter, 1972):

> All I can say is that my mouth was dry and my heart was in my mouth. Thomas had very nearly succeeded in getting me drunk earlier in the day. He was full of scorn for Yeats, as he was for Eliot, Pound, Auden. He thought my admiration for Yeats was the funniest thing in that part of London. It wasn't until about three o'clock that I realized that he and I were drinking more than usual. I didn't drink much at that time; Thomas drank much more than I did. I had the sense to leave. I . . . just made it for the appointment. I remember the taxi ride over. The taxi was left over from the First World War, and when we arrived in Pall Mall – we could see the Athenaeum – the driver said he didn't feel he could get in. Finally I decided to abandon ship and take off on my own. So I went in and asked for Mr. Yeats. Very much like asking, 'Is Mr. Ben Jonson here?' And he came down. He was much taller than I expected, and haggard. Big though, big head, rather wonderful looking in a sort of blunt, patrician kind of way, but there was something shrunken also. He told me he was just recovering from an illness. He was very courteous, and we went in to tea.

Immediately afterwards, Berryman wrote notes about his august encounter. Yeats had been left very weak from an illness which had almost killed him the year before. He talked about writing 'The Great Herne's Egg' and other recent lyrics. They agreed that literary criticism seemed poor compared to music and art criticism. They discussed Swift and Parnell; Abbey finances and the Peacock Theatre; Spengler; Indian thought; and what Yeats called 'artistic pessimism'. Yeats mentioned too his *Autobiography*, his family, croquet, a broadcasting scheme that he was hatching, 'Leda and the Swan' and 'Demon and Beast', his dance plays and *The Player Queen* recently written, and Auden and Aldous Huxley. He professed to have a very bad memory. Berryman thought him curiously humourless, except for quoting an inscription cut on glass,

> Mary Carmichael, very young,
> Ugly of face & pleasant of tongue.

They spoke further about Peter Warlock and *The Curlew*, Ninette de Valois at the Cambridge Festival, and the characters of Robartes and Owen Aherne that Yeats himself had raised. Berryman asked about his work-habits, and Yeats told him: 'I never revise now except in the interests of a more passionate syntax, a more natural.' In connection with his bad health, Yeats said he had to stick to a rigid diet and regimen, and that he was limited to two cigarettes a day.

> At a certain point, I had a cigarette, and I asked him if he would like one. To my great surprise he said yes. So I gave him a Craven-A and then lit it for him, and I thought, 'Immortality is mine! From now on it's just a question of reaping the fruits of my effort!'

Yeats left Berryman, as he related at the time, with 'an impression of tremendous but querulous force, a wandering intensely personal mind which resists natural bent (formal metaphysics by intuition, responsible vision) to its own exhaustion.'

Always the watch-dog of his career, his mother felt that he had lately been frittering his time in Cambridge. When she admonished him by post, he tried to excuse himself.

> While accusing me of complete and vicious inactivity, you in the same letter ignored the long poem I had but sent you – a poem which, I suggest, is absolutely first-rate and of

considerable dimension. These items out, the substance of the
indictment is right and is welcome, though its terms are at times
so unwarrantedly harsh that I doubt my acceptance of it had I
not come during the past week in London to similar conclusions
and already begun relentless work, which I do not intend shall
be interrupted until June.

About a month earlier he had lamented, 'God knows what I need is
someone to keep me sane', and although his American girlfriend
Jean Bennett had written to the effect that she loved him until she
herself told him otherwise, it had become clear that neither of them
could last the course.

He found fresh love at a party thrown by Andrews Wanning, a
sociable, good-looking fellow-American who was up at Magdalene.

> One luncheon party in Andy's rooms in Magdalene
> was dominated by a sort of beauty of a queen
> whose charm the company kept enchanted to centre on
> whose voice & carriage seemed perhaps those of an actress
>
> Indeed I caught on: the most passionate & versatile actress
>   in Cambridge   ['Meeting'].

Beatrice had beauty, charm and intelligence; dark straight hair, a
broad face and forehead with delicate eyebrows and huge dark eyes,
a generous mouth, fine and creamy white skin. Her good looks and
a fine voice matched her sociability, and more particularly her keen
interest in acting on the stage.

> I couldn't drink my sherry, I couldn't eat.
> I looked; I listened.
> I don't know how I made it home to Memorial Court.
> I never expected to meet her again   ['Meeting'].

Berryman rushed to tell Katharine Fraser, 'I've met the most
beautiful, stunning and brilliant girl.'

In spite of his abashment, he invited her to tea; she came, he was
conquered. Since they shared a passionate love for the theatre, he
felt inspired to write a dramatic poem – a version of Cleopatra – as a
vehicle for her. 'Shakespeare,' he asserted, 'was magnificent (and
wrong), I hope to be interesting as well as right.' He found himself
wonderfully energised, hardly stopping to think because, as he

affirmed naively, 'I ruined a fine poem recently by thinking,' and prepared even to display her for the sake of his art:

> she ought really to be nude, but Proctors being proctors, the alternative is such a gown as Cleopatra wore at the council in Tarsus: a robe of transparent gauze fastened beneath the breasts. Fetching, eh? And *might* help the box office, for Beatrice is superbly made.

While he tried to play down his interest in her – calling her coolly, 'lovely and able' – it is clear that he had become rapidly intoxicated with her. But when he asked her for some commitment without teasing, she was not ready to flop into love and scrupulously temporised. 'As for my teasing you,' she wrote, 'Fie! Do you refer to self-dramatization? It's my fatal leaning towards honesty, – most misguided no doubt, but there you are.' She excused herself from clarifying her feelings, saying that she was unsure of herself and was in any case not a playful person. Berryman told his mother that he could not return to New York for the summer because the passage was too dear at £35 and because he needed to study for the Oldham Shakespeare Scholarship later in the year, but Beatrice presumably provided his most compelling reason for staying in England.

When George Rylands took him over the Oldham Shakespeare papers for the year 1931, Berryman felt breathless at how hard they seemed. Rylands had himself won the scholarship in his youth, at a time when (he explained) he could identify any three-line gobbet from the entire Folio. Other examinations were already in progress: Berryman began his preliminary exams on 4 June, while Beatrice had her own papers to tackle. At an official sherry party on 4 June she took the opportunity of consulting with Rylands, and relayed her information to Berryman.

> This is what he said. You absorb things like a sponge, but you can't squeeze them out in a stream, & he doubts your powers of coordination & organization – if you can write an essay. He says you may get a first or a third. If a third, he'll get into a hell of a row, and you will have to do an essay & time paper per week . . . if you play the fool in your exams. He seemed rather perturbed about your fooling around with them. Just thought you might like to know. Do your best tomorrow. Don't come out early. I'll be around at 12
> All love, B.

In a supplementary note that night she told him, 'It's one-thirty, my dearest, and I love. . . . Dearest heart, don't be black or cynical. I love you. I still need time to know how deeply, for what reason, with certainty.' Given the circumstance of his impending examination, such an admission showed how deeply and generously she felt for him, but her course was in any case set. While Berryman had followed his impulses, she had taken proper time to assess her feelings.

He gained a high second in the examination; Beatrice turned twenty-one years of age on 7 June, celebrating with a strawberries-and-hock party in the grounds of the Garden House Hotel.

They planned to take a trip together to Heidelberg in Germany, but beforehand Berryman had to work tenaciously for the Harness Prize, to be awarded for an essay on Shakespeare. Worth £70 to the winner, the prize essay would also be published. With only ten days to go before the deadline on 30 June, he embarked on the topic of 'The Character and Role of the Heroine in Shakespearian Comedy'. On 23 June he moved into 34 Bridge Street, where he took a little bedroom on the ground floor with a study on the first floor only slightly smaller than his old room at M4. He felt sorry to leave his bedmaker, Mrs Mizzen, but the new accommodation had distinct advantages: the house stood on the main street near to Magdalene, and the rent was only £14 a term instead of £20. Nevertheless, although the doorkey hung behind the letter-slot, available for use at all hours, he would not budge outdoors until his task was done – 'my brain buzzes with theory & reference more satisfactorily than it has ever done before,' he claimed. Totalling seventy-seven pages in six days, Berryman delivered his essay and turned his attention wholly to Beatrice. 'The fact of her being directs, makes full & significant my life as no relationship except yours and mine has ever done before,' he declared to his mother in a brave and conciliatory spirit. 'She is 21, physically beautiful and vigorous and graceful, with a strong, direct, skeptical intelligence, no sentimentality, but a powerful emotional nature held rigidly by will and self-examination.'

Their summer jaunt brought them to Heidelberg, where they found rooms in Friedrichstrasse. German nationalism was heavy in the air, flags and troops everywhere, and boys who looked hardly older than fourteen bore rifles with bayonets on their bicycles. Berryman began to feel as Rilke had in 1919, when he lamented the loss of that humility he discerned in Dürer's drawings. Taking full advantage of the Reichsfestspiele, the official festival for which Goebbels had assembled all the best actors in Germany, Berryman and Beatrice attended several drama productions including *Romeo and Juliet* at the Castle on 21 July – a massive and magnificent spectacle: 'several hundred actors storming in from four angles, brilliant lighting, fireworks at the banquet,' Berryman related, 'drums & swords & dances & a 20-minute wordless procession to lay Juliet in the tomb – it was very exciting.' When they later chanced to meet one of the principal actors and entertained him to tea, Berryman could not contain his hero-worship: 'possibly the most satisfying human being I've ever seen, large, powerful, open, brilliantly alive, laughing, magnificent.' Another day they went for a ten-hour hike up the Heiligenberg, just across the river from Heidelberg, and observed the massive new Nazi stadium.

Back in London, they engaged to be married. 'I am very happy,' Berryman wrote, 'and more hopeful of value, human and creative, for my life than I think I have ever been. Several brilliant poems done.' The last remark was one to propitiate his mother, who had shown her resentment at being superseded in her son's affections by a young girl whose quality she could not know for herself. Jealous of Berryman, she thought he might be selling himself cheap and squandering energies which she urged him to channel into literary activity. She argued that creativity and personal happiness invariably stood at odds, and that he should not surrender too easily to what might prove an illusion. 'Passionately as I desire not to,' he responded,

> I agree with you all but unconditionally about creation and happiness. But I have not a mind that is easily or long satisfied, and I do not expect ever to lack torment. And on my honour, I *cannot* let go by what may be my one chance for a full and rich and permanent (if, necessarily, desperately partial) human happiness. I find capacities I [had] not dreamed of, never admitted the existence of, and derided in art.

He satisfied himself that life with Beatrice should work to complement rather than to compromise his art: 'delight and pain, comedy and tragedy, exist inseparable on a *moral* plane when the love has been tested and accepted by two acute sensibilities.' Since Berryman often let language flirt with life, his mother must have sensed that his eloquence embroidered a comparatively untested experience.

Beatrice set off at the end of August for a Scandinavian tour with the Cambridge Amateur Dramatic Company, during which she wrote him several fine letters candidly probing her affections and motives – she regretted what she called her 'hellish temper' and 'boring tirades' – and expressing her love with exquisitely moving felicity. From Oslo she told him,

> No one can love more, or use their love to greater advantage than I do. . . . You shall be great & I may help. . . . Blessed blessed John. Were anything to happen to us now, nothing could detract from the infinite good you have given me

and counteracted whatever might seem too earnest in her letters with comments like, 'You'd love Norway. All kings are kongs.' At other times she showed an adult unwillingness to humour all his moods. 'Read some,' she answered one of his plaints, '& try to get out of this trivial superficiality of outlook.'

During her absence Berryman prepared himself for the Oldham Shakespeare Scholarship (he had failed to win the Harness Prize). As an appropriate prelude he treated himself to some theatre-going at Stratford-on-Avon, where among other plays he saw *King Lear* done by Komisarjevsky, a famous production he thought a butchery. He scrutinised such a vast number of commentaries that it is surprising that his own creative efforts had not halted. The examination he tackled with a certain qualified satisfaction, 'I am still bursting with information I'd no opportunity to use, but it was with great relief that I turned in the final paper, and I've had since such a sense of leisure as never before. It depends on what the other ten or so did, of course; I find it very difficult to believe that anyone wrote a better examination, but I am by no means hopeful about the prize.' Beatrice received his news in London. Although fearful that her being, as she put it, 'frivolous and partyfied' might put a strain on their marriage, she overflowed with devotion and respect for Berryman, and felt confident of his achievement because of his application and will. What she called her 'blessed vanity' should prevent her from feeling his inferior, and her hopes were in any case his: 'your achievement seems irretrievably, hopelessly & blessedly tied to mine for mine is yours.' When Berryman learned the news on 23 November that he had won the prize, valued at £83, it is characteristic that he chose to exercise a curiously self-belittling trick by dubbing the judges, Enid Welsford and F. P. Wilson, 'nonentities both, well-known and ignorant'. He called his inverted feeling, 'my unhappily persistent capacity for self-pity'. (Arnold Kettle, who later became a distinguished literary critic, was *proxime accessit*.)

With the beginning of the new academic year in 1937 he again entered what he called 'the Cambridge round, and hell'. He told his mother self-doubtingly that he would marry Beatrice on condition that he gained employment for the next year – 'If I've any prospect for livelihood, we'll marry next year' – but from the evidence of his journal there is no doubt that his feelings were fast. In addition to renewing his own contacts, he had to extend his friendship to Beatrice's circle, but increased sociability became a trial to his confidence and sense of self-worth. He often masked his intense nervousness in a compensatory braggadocio, and could scarcely hide the tics and stresses of his disposition. One of their friends, Diana Crutchley, remembers Beatrice as 'somewhat tensed up, so was John – he was thin and pale then, no beard. They both had restless, enquiring minds.' Driven by a desperate need to prove himself and to overcome his querulousness, Berryman often made assertive conversation, barracking his listeners and scorning whatever he considered mediocre. He watched himself warily: 'my tact and rhetorical organization improve, I'm glad to find. I am, at once, intensely and not at all dogmatic.' Being himself inclined to tendentiousness, he hated the same fault in others; jealous of those who seemed more at ease with themselves and their ideas, he displayed a certain antipathy which evidently stemmed from his own sense of inadequacy and competitiveness. Proud of his own brain, he set up absolute standards, felt galled to fall short of them, and tried incessantly to rationalise his arrogance. 'Dogma is never true – but it is nearly always necessary; chaos otherwise. . . . I cannot slack care, to achieve triviality; nor do I regret conscience.' One of the more searching of the entries in his journal figures on his birthday, when he laboured under a sense of time passing and the hopelessness of ever realising his potential. 'I had last night a profound conviction that my whole last year of life was ending. Cf. my plans, my traditional inability to admit a future. Uneasy. . . . Again and again, the meaning of life and its negation. I must go deeper before I leave.'

It seems typical of his attitude that when he heard Christopher Isherwood speak at Tulliver's on 7 November, he dismissed as 'Damned nonsense mostly' what he considered to be Isherwood's dogmatic discussions of modern drama, politics, symbols, expressionism, realistic drama, the radio, and Freud. Among his own friends and disputants he reminded himself, 'I must stop telling people who are of no sensibility what I think, and my useless rages must stop. They exhaust me. The point is communication with the few who matter to me, discovery of faith, and work – three points. Years are not long enough.' After taking tea with one of the best-known figures in Cambridge. F. R. Leavis, he found reasons for reviling the famous critic as 'a vacant popularizer, vacant and impudent'. Writing to his mother, he told only part of his turbid self-conflict: 'The pleasant aimless optimism you have so often justly censured is at last falling to pieces.'

In general his work and writing proceeded smoothly in the new academic year. Robert Penn Warren rewarded his efforts by accepting some poems for publication in *Southern Review* (they eventually appeared in the Summer of 1938) with the comment, 'I like your stuff very, very much.' Berryman took his commitment to poetry most seriously. 'Given life and tenacity in discipline,' he wrote, 'I shall be a great poet.'

His mother's communications served to exacerbate his personal qualms and tensions. On 22 October, for example, he received two letters from her, one of which – pointedly analysing the distresses of her life – caused what he described as 'the greatest and purest grief I can remember – unable to weep, but long dry sobs tore me to pieces; I vow to achieve her happiness by all ways open to me. Pray these prizes give me a start.' As always, her psychological manipulations caused him to feel hysterically guilty and responsible for her well-being. Although her letters have not survived, it seems likely that – jealous of the love he had wholeheartedly given over to Beatrice – she tried to play his affections back in her own favour. What would appear to have been her calculating letters – indeed, if Berryman's sometimes insipid replies were in kind, they must often have been cloying – took sharp effect. (In the mid-1940s Berryman reread with distaste the letters he had written his mother from England – she had recently returned them – 'how desperately then, almost obscenely,' he wrote in his diary, 'I was bound to Mother.') His agonies on her behalf compounded the melodrama of his own temperament and struggles. 'When I consider your life as it has been till now,' he responded to one of her letters, for instance, on 15 December, 'I feel a dignity and pride such as nothing else can give me. I see much fortitude and understanding flowering into beauty absolute on earth. It is my love that sees truth.'

Although he kept busy, Berryman felt emotionally drubbed. Even the letters of congratulation he received after the Oldham Prize gave him the impression that 'all my acquaintances are illiterate, insincere and extravagant.' Profoundly impatient of his literary unfulfilment and of a world that would not yet yield to him, he wrote to his mother at length,

my habitual condition is rage. Blind unprofitable anger, with Leavis and all literary fashion, all parasites, all the spurious and the touted, all vague, all worthless thought, all pretension, all politics, all novelty, all sham, all fools, all greed, all insolence.

He perceived in America only

> The love of theory and generalization, the superficial, the
> displaced, the raw. That baffling competence, that shabby
> vanity, that sentimental rhetoric. . . . England is a well-fed, a
> disagreeable corpse. . . .
>   The central difficulty is that of being certain one will be able
> to write well. More than ever before, the world is full of men
> who have given their lives to literature and have achieved
> nothing: humiliation to eternity. I have only contempt for such
> men, they clutter the horizon. . . . Before me continually is the
> danger that I may be wrong, that my conviction of talent and
> great talent may be an act of will, that I am being deluded to
> betray my years. . . . My dissatisfaction with what I have done,
> the increasing excellence of my verse, and my steady work, are
> documenting that conviction to a certainty. I shall build a
> powerful and subtle instrument, given time. . . .
>   I believe I had never told you how deeply I am grateful for all
> your relationship with my verse. You neither discouraged nor
> unduly encouraged, but bore with patience and great wisdom
> my drivel, directing very quietly indeed my inclinations. Your
> insistence on the traditional and the plain kept me from sterile
> obscurity and formlessness. It is certainly most to you, perhaps
> to you entirely, that I owe what I have done and will do.

It is hardly surprising that all the while Berryman worked to
reassure his mother, he neglected Beatrice. A friend told her that
Berryman had 'been contemplating': 'apparently from time to time
I must be alone,' he is reported to have said. Not unnaturally
inferring that his behaviour implied criticism of herself, she wrote,
'You should have told me in the past when my presence was a
curse.' Yet she was in no way at fault; it was all a question of virulent
family games. When Berryman's mother told him that she held him
up as an example to his brother, Berryman was shocked into a true
self-appraisal which at once bilked her flattery and flattered back.

> A few things must be cleared up. First, I am no person to be
> held up as an example to anyone or quoted by him as a
> 'successful relation'. I am sure I have as little acquaintance with
> that difficult virtue humility as anyone now living; but certain
> facts are patent: . . . my character is a disagreeable compound of
> arrogance, selfishness and impatience, scarcely relieved by
> dashes of courtesy and honesty and a certain amount of
> industry; I have been, I believe, thoroughly disliked by most of

the people whom I have not known intimately. . . . I suggest
that he look at you, on whose justice and brilliant generosity I
have, with little success, endeavoured to model my moral
being.

It was in large part Beatrice's firm love which gave Berryman the
moral strength to return his mother small change in the form of
elegant and obsequious letters rather than the substance of his
feelings.

With the new year Beatrice tried to initiate a programme of
physical distance between herself and Berryman, not because she
loved him less, but only because they seemed to absorb each other's
time and energy to the exclusion of numerous other duties.
'Through my own foolishness and weakness I find seeing as much
of you as I did last term rather exhausting,' she wrote. 'I imagine I
live on my nerves too much and am inefficient at slackening
emotional tension.' In spite of her best intentions, however, she had
to allow that loving him meant being able to see him.

The necessity for Berryman to find a job for the next year became
pressing; having gained some confidence in public speaking from
his talks on Yeats, and from a poetry reading for the Cambridge
Poetry Society, he decided that he could at last countenance a career
in teaching, which he had previously regarded as 'an unpleasant
necessity'. Although he felt that 'my nervous system may do a
tarantella when first I face a classroom', he had found firm grounds
for entering the profession.

> I have become convinced of the value of teaching people to
> read, which is what education comes to, so far as literature is
> concerned. . . . I certainly don't feel confident of my
> qualifications, but I'm willing to do a great deal of work, and
> though I regret my lacunae I don't see that erudition is as
> necessary as knowledge of and interest in the method and ends
> of teaching.

He asked Mark Van Doren to help him find a teaching position at
his alma mater, Columbia College, but the gates there were closed.
Always the firmest and most selfless of friends, Van Doren zealous-
ly advanced Berryman's cause with an ally, Scott Buchanan, Dean
of St John's College, Annapolis, which had lately begun an exciting
and integrated liberal arts programme; he felt that holding a post in
such an institution might help Berryman to better his poetry. 'I
think it might make all the difference between your becoming a
good poet and your becoming a great one: a wise one, I mean.'

Berryman had to confess that he had no Greek and small mathematics but welcomed the chance to get them up.

For unknown reasons he had to change his rooms on 17 March, and moved to 32 Thompson's Lane. On an Easter trip to Paris he took a squalid room in the Hotel de l'univers, Rue Monsieur-le-Prince, in the centre of the Quartier Latin. Beatrice lodged with friends near the Place Victor Hugo. Perhaps under the influence of reading Laforgue and Kierkegaard – particularly in the knowledge that Laforgue had died at the age of 27 – Berryman fell into another depression, glazed by the prospect of what seemed to him his own unpromising future. 'I think,' he wrote, 'we shall all very soon be dead – and nothing lost. . . . I cannot think I shall attain animal maturity, I have not prepared, the attack will come before my rooks are developed. In ill thoughts again, but this is a city of death.' He languished in Paris for just over two weeks, before returning to Cambridge to discover a disappointment that partly realised his rhetoric.

Earlier in the year he had submitted a group of poems to T. S. Eliot at the *Criterion*: they were rejected on 1 April. It was not an absolute failure, however, for Eliot had taken the trouble to pencil in some comments and small suggestions on the manuscript. One poem, 'On a Portrait in Dublin', he called 'almost good'. In recompense for that disappointment, Berryman heard from Scott Buchanan the consoling news, 'I think I can say definitely we want you here.'

The next month Berryman visited the Lake District – 'This is an absolute Paradise. I think I have never in my life so enjoyed a time. Superb, intoxicating air, total peace' – but the idyll was brief, for his last term at Cambridge began late in April.

In the English tripos he felt confident that he could gain a First Class degree; when he came out with an upper second, he felt dismayed only because, as he told Van Doren, 'I set to at the last minute and wrote excellent papers.' The day before he left for home in New York, he wrote to his mother in terms that seem curiously treacherous to his feelings for Beatrice, 'I shall begin to live again, better equipped, when I get off the boat and kiss you.' *Ile-de-France* sailed on 15 June 1938, bearing him from a life which had supplied him with love and ambition to a world where the crabbier exigencies of employment and money would inflict harsh lessons and gradually worry away his relationship with Beatrice. He must in a way have feared returning to his mother. Formerly he had shared with her before anyone else all the intimate fulfilments of his life; they had seemed her triumphs as much as his. Never before had he faced her with an attachment so deep as his love for Beatrice, which radically threatened her status and power in his heart. Vulnerable and in many respects immature, he could not be sure whether he would demonstrate firmness of purpose before his mother. Nor could he be sure that – committed to Beatrice by love and as a gentleman – he would find means to support her as his wife. In at least one recent letter home, he had called his plans for marriage 'vague'.

For her part, Beatrice showed integrity, candour and strength; if anything could have done so, her selflessness would have set his feet firm. Yet she also managed to be studiously realistic and even prophetic.

> As for my feelings about your tripos, they no longer exist. . . . Your lack of discipline shocks me profoundly, and more, your perhaps unconscious conviction that it needs someone other than yourself to remedy this lack . . .
>
> I too love you devotedly and believe you love me. And I too think that we have been happier than most men seem to have any right to expect. . . . When I wrote to your mother I said among other things, the following: 'John is my dearest blessing; he shall have all I can give, for my happiness lies in his.' And that is the truth as it is known to God. . . .
>
> A few points. By all I hold most dear, I would rather live poor with you than in easy circumstances without you. . . .
>
> As for the artist in you, you are as you are, and I shall love you as long as I am not hurt beyond your dealing. . . . I have no desire, no hope or expectation of living happily; life and happiness contradict each other as I understand them. But I have a most passionate desire to live *fully*. To do the work I must do, I must live, and sweet or bitter, the taste must be strong. . . .
>
> You must say too where I am more of a hindrance than any human being loved and loving is of necessity. More, does that very love hamper you? . . . I am not considering what stress I might suffer were I to stay with you. I choose to do so if it pleases you. I am convinced that what I have been granted in knowing you is more valuable to me than all of which I have knowledge or conception. Finally, do you wish to marry at all? and is marriage of vast importance anyhow?

Berryman felt confused by conflicting priorities. Ambitious both for what could seem the selfish ends of his artistic career and for his proposed marriage, he made things painfully difficult for himself by regarding his desires as alternatives rather than as options which could be taken up equally. He seemed to think it more or less a law that personal relationships told against a life in art, a dichotomy in which his mother evidently encouraged him to believe. Beatrice, who seems to have matured faster than Berryman, needed all her strength of character in the months to come.

After an absence of two years, Berryman arrived back in New York on 21 June 1938, and took up residence at his mother's apartment, 408 West 115th Street. New York seemed rude and unaccommodating to the talent he brought to the test; it also swung him away from his hopes for marriage, back into his mother's influence. In the forefront of his mind was the knowledge that he would have to find some way of supporting his future wife. His mother was more deeply engaged with her own work and contacts than he could possibly have anticipated. In fact, he was shocked by what had taken place in his absence, the professional realisation of his mother's abilities and drives; she had become a shrewd, absorbed, wholly sufficient businesswoman. Starting in 1935 she had worked her way through a number of positions, mostly in advertising and sales promotions. (Later still – from 1951 through 1959 – she became the boss of her own business, Berryman & O'Leary, earning at her peak almost forty thousand dollars a year.)

Within two weeks of his return home, Berryman telephoned Scott Buchanan at St John's College, Annapolis, to ask further about the possibility of a job; Buchanan told him the appointment was 'quite certain'. Still, agitated and apprehensive, Berryman started writing fiercely, salving his raw feelings, missing his fiancée. The machinery of life put him so much on edge that he decided to take up Mark Van Doren's offer of a weekend in the country, at Falls Village, Connecticut. His hand shook as he wrote a note accepting the offer, 'The city is killing me, heat, strain, anxiety, loneliness'; he described himself as being 'at absolute ebb', and had indeed suffered an hysterical fit the night before. In Connecticut, Allen and Caroline Tate stayed nearby, inviting friendly meetings, and Van Doren took time, as always, to go through Berryman's work and suggest improvements.

Life brought a spate of checks and shocks. The *New Yorker* rejected five of Berryman's poems; *New York Herald Tribune* reported that it could not offer him any reviewing; and Princeton and Queen's Colleges (to which he had applied in case St John's failed him) reported no staff vacancies. To carry the resonance of his sorry situation to those who should listen, Berryman lamented

the whole complicated business of my return: mental
adjustment, a terrible strain, which was unavoidable but which

I had in no way foreseen. For days nothing but nervous agony. Also the weather has been exhausting, I've been seeing various people about a position for next year, and I've been writing steadily. And for a year now I've been engaged to an English girl . . . in Italy now, she won't be over for several more months. Add that separation to my other troubles, and you enter pathology. But the worst of it is now probably past, and in any case I should be thankful: the energy released has given me half a dozen poems.

Mark Van Doren had slipped Berryman a cheque for cash against the day of crisis. James Laughlin, whom Berryman had met briefly in Cambridge, provided further consolation by selecting a few of his poems for publication in *New Directions*, but even that success seemed a mixed blessing: the three poems were already at press by the beginning of August, too late for Berryman to learn that the proofs were 'full of errors', and that two of the poems had been mistitled. Since he already felt wrought by what he considered desperate circumstances, the publishing mishap distressed him all the more. 'I've no readers,' he admitted paradoxically, 'but I feel as if I'd betrayed them all.'

He began casting about anxiously, quite sure that he would be given a job if the right persons took a moment's notice, and momentarily pondered a plan to offer his services to Orson Welles. His designs did not pass further muster before Scott Buchanan wrote him a carefully worded letter on 19 August to say that St John's had no place for him. It is probable that Berryman fell ill from strain at a time coinciding with Buchanan's letter. No specific details survive, but it may reasonably be inferred that he had a form of nervous breakdown. Allen Tate intervened between Berryman and his troubles, and invited him to stay until the end of the month with his wife Caroline at West Cornwall, Connecticut, while Tate himself went fishing with his brother on Lake Ontario. Berryman was grateful for a ten days' rest in a locale of lakes and small mountains, where the agenda consisted of nothing more taxing than swimming, drinking, and talking. Mark and Dorothy Van Doren often called, the Malcolm Cowleys came to dinner one evening, James Laughlin another. Berryman avidly read Tate's novel *The Fathers*, which had just appeared, and thought it 'brilliant, scrupulously done and very rich'. The Tates' daughter Nancy, then aged twelve, together with a friend on a visit, considered for a time that Berryman was 'the most awful fink that ever lived', and would imitate his Anglicised and mannered behaviour. Exasperated, Berryman asked for them to be fed separately.

In September he wrote six short poems and one of 120 lines, trying all the while to break away from the influence of Yeats on what he called 'the compositional base' of his verses. Malcolm Cowley, to whom he submitted certain poems at the *New Republic*, thought them 'very skilful exercises, based on the very best models', and although he rejected them he did repose enough faith in Berryman's talent to recommend him early the next year for a visit to Yaddo, the artists' colony in upstate New York (Berryman never actually took up the offer).

When Berryman returned home from his visit with the Tates, his family had just moved house, to 41 Park Avenue. Though he liked the new double apartment (as it was known), where he had a good workroom, his personal upset, as he described it, was still acute, 'living here with my family, no income, unable so far to get any sort of position for this year; terrible gloom; B coming this month, and when I'll be able to support her I don't know. The political world in crazy pieces, and moral order a matter of toothpicks.' On 5 October he shaved off his beard, which he had grown in a spirit of neglect in England, but then kept because he disliked shaving. On his return from England to New York, however, he grimly believed that the beard served the function of distinguishing him from 'the shining, empty young fools this time breeds in such numbers,' but in due course had to admit to himself that such an attitude was affected, the beard an 'emblem of stage-disappointment and horror'. Wounded vanity understandably coloured much of his thinking. The interviews to which he was invited brought him no success, and he considered his interviewers 'stupid'. Stung by their indifference, he castigated his potential employers for what he called their 'practical shrewdness and self-absorption hideous to see'. When Time, Inc. interviewed him for a post and turned him down, for instance, the experience left him feeling 'quite ill'. His thoughts took maundering and melodramatic postures: 'life is only a progressive disingenuousness to the point in sensibility when the brain breaks and the man, his sentence up, can die.' While writing poetry gave him an activity in which he could sublimate his feelings, he also cared deeply that the art should flourish in itself. He determined to write well, and worked doggedly to craft his best.

Berryman's immediate concern (as he told Mark Van Doren) was 'to live with as little loss of self-respect as soon as possible until I can support myself and B. and we can marry. Peace is impossible until then.' His mother saw the robust truth that he was leaning on his fiancée's affection – in one way at least – for consolation; such an imbalance could topple their relationship. Berryman commented that

Mother says B. and I cling so together because there are no
respectable certainties anywhere else. This is true and is part of
it. More and more, with the decay of the family as a social unit,
and the world what it contemptibly is, love and friendship must
take on the burdens that the Church and State and general
hopefulness once bore and bear no more. Personal relationships
and, for some, work – are all. Honour in defeat, perhaps, 'a
dignity to be dumb'.

He characteristically identified himself with the type of Othryadas,
a hero who refused to survive in disrepute; refusing to be van-
quished by circumstances, Othryadas had anticipated that contingency by honourably killing himself. The pattern of Othryadas'
'precarious nobility' provided Berryman with the subject for a
poem he called 'Survivor'.

Berryman's fiancée, Beatrice, had meanwhile spent the summer
in Europe, feeling distinct doubts about their relationship. She was
probably most distressed by his apparent lack of seriousness, and
though she reiterated her feelings for him, she did so with a measure
of self-detachment. Back in England by October, she prepared to
depart for the USA, and wrote – with a candour buttressed by dark
apprehensions – that she felt subject to severe doubts.

She arrived in New York on 25 October, just in time for
Berryman's birthday celebrations. The day was also notable because, that very morning, he began work on a play to be called *The
Architect*, a project for which she could share his enthusiasm since
she had been working on a play of her own.

Beatrice displaced her doubts and recriminations, and they
reaffirmed their deep affection for one another. Once introduced to
the double household at 41 Park Avenue, her intelligence, charm,
and attractiveness at first smoothed any wrinkles, and only Robert
Jefferson, Berryman's brother, felt a little disgruntled at being
ousted from his bedroom by the guest. It was a rule of the
apartment that Berryman worked in his room during the day, but
clearly Beatrice was a distraction to which he eagerly yielded; she
was vitally interested in the people, places and museums, and
Berryman was more than willing to oblige her keenness. They
went to a few films, sometimes accompanied by Milton Halliday,
worried their theatrical ambitions, and once or twice dined with
Mark and Dorothy Van Doren. Otherwise, Berryman bent dutiful-
ly to his literary tasks. Since it had become clear that he would have
to support the year innocent of academic employment – and indeed
without any job – he disciplined himself to forge his reputation by
writing.

He found a kindred spirit in a new friend, Bhain Campbell, a young man whose life was soon to be cut tragically short by cancer. Good-looking, charismatic, slightly narcissistic, Campbell had attended the University of Michigan with Milton Halliday, and showed promise as well as accomplishment (at Michigan he had won two of the coveted Avery and Julia Hopwood Awards for poetry). He was well travelled, had even visited the USSR, and was radical in politics. Milton Halliday had spent nine months living in the same room with Campbell and what he called – for Berryman's benefit – 'his peculiar foibles'. In later years Berryman himself remembered Campbell as 'an attractive man' who 'made no use of it; absolutely candid; considerate, & gay; uncontentious – indeed, innocent, for all his political wishes; loyal; I am obliged to say: virtuous; I never knew him do an ill action; devoted to verse; brave.' Campbell came to reciprocate Berryman's feelings of intimacy and fellowship: 'I cannot remember parting from any other mind, except Florence [his wife], with as much regret.'

As a Marxist, Campbell urged Berryman to commit his talent to the struggle for reorganisation of social and personal life, but Berryman's turn of mind and literary endeavours did not really bend Campbell's way; Campbell was unsettled by his failure to envision a new society, future perfect. Although he felt deeply concerned at the world's political situation as 1939 drew on, Berryman's terms of reference were still largely literary, and urgent with personal rather than social energy. A poem called 'Heritage' (written on 27 November) is a typical effort.

> The pitiless American
> Looked down into the hollow past,
> Despising what he saw; he ran
> Nevertheless from the shade cast
> Across his country by the past
> As if it were a thing alive
> And monstrous. . . .
> . . . .
> He sat there silent, with no friend.

He preoccupied himself with the craft of poetry – the dynamics of style, form, metrics – to the extent of neglecting content. While he wrote a good many poems at this time, including '1938' and 'Winter Landscape' (certainly one of the most accomplished of his early poems, written on 9 January 1939), he worked with more excitement on yet another new play called *Dictator*, which he began on 18 December. 'I thought for a while of doing something foolish &

final,' he told Mark Van Doren in his anxiety for the play's welfare, 'I know better now. . . . All my former troubles, which continue, are nothing to what I face now.' *Dictator* failed his purposes, but he turned out yet more poems: in one day, for example – 27 February 1939 – he wrote 'Prospect', '1939' (eight stanzas), completely remodelled 'Conversation', revised another poem, 'Councillors', for the last time, made some revisions to '1938', 'Night and the City', and yet other poems, and finally studied the idea of putting out a pamphlet to be called 'The Dangerous Year'.

When the *Nation* asked him to write a 300-word obituary piece on W. B. Yeats at the end of January, he paced about like a madman, and completed his notice only by four o'clock the next day. Being profoundly disturbed by what he called 'the alteration of a permanent symbol', he then planned to compile a memorial volume (a book of essays by various hands), to which Mark Van Doren, Allen Tate, Richard Blackmur, and Cleanth Brooks all expressed a willingness to contribute. After sounding out Macmillan in New York, he had an initially favourable interview with the editor James Putnam, but the project unaccountably foundered.

Beatrice's visit drew to an end on 1 April, when she sailed from New York. Her visit had lasted just over five months, an intense and loving period, though the undertow was dense with emotional snarls. Her beauty and charm had appealed to her prospective mother-in-law, but mother and son generated unspoken conflicts between themselves. Protective and dominant, Mrs Berryman aimed to channel her son's energies, and after a while disapproved of his making himself so available to Beatrice. Berryman himself was happy to entertain Beatrice, resisted his mother's counsel, and became angry when she tried to restrain him. She was shocked at his deteriorating state of health. Beatrice saw the sorry drift of things; for her, all had been well in the beginning, but she felt a deep unhappiness underlying the genuine joy of her love. Although he worked extremely hard at writing poetry and plays, he completely shied away from the truth that such writings would not earn a living wage. The pattern of his life and unstable behaviour sadly undermined the reality of the life they had planned together as husband and wife. She was prepared to wait for him until the summer of 1941, but against that time she could only formulate her misgivings.

Although Beatrice wanted to get married and to have children in good time, she also professed her need – 'my almost passionate desire' – to retain her independence of mind and interests, and she questioned Berryman's apparent self-involvement. Within three months of returning home, she categorised their differences, and felt distressed by the fact that he seemed to prefer only solitude, meditation and peace, to her own involvement in life. In the event, circumstances were to keep their lives apart, but differences of temperament and interest might otherwise have done so.

Although Berryman did in fact care deeply for other people, he felt his importunate internal conflicts and drives so gravely that sometimes he could hardly resist venting his frustration in displays of unsociable sulking or childish assaults. He would feel driven to make quick, sharp, sometimes too readily critical judgments of his elders, even of his heroes, as on the occasion when he attended a public reading on 6 April by W. H. Auden, Louis MacNeice, and Christopher Isherwood. While Auden struck him as being completely unaffected and at his ease, wearing a dilapidated suit and reading in a slightly thick voice, Berryman thought MacNeice a vain and nervous man with no timbre to his voice, and disapproved of the way he read Housman, Graves, Lawrence, and even his own poetry. Isherwood he considered a personable and engaging man, bright and distinguished, in spite of the fact that he read 'at tedious length' from his China diary and propounded what Berryman regarded as a great deal of twaddle.

Towards the end of April Berryman had made forty poems ready for publication, but his feelings towards the project alternated between boredom and arrogance. Just at the moment when he acknowledged to himself that he needed a disinterested and severe critic, one opportunely showed up in the person of the young Jewish poet Delmore Schwartz, who first visited him to discuss some verse that Berryman had submitted to *Partisan Review*. They liked each other immediately, Berryman being particularly struck by Schwartz's 'calm and modesty and good sense'. Impressed by Schwartz both as a person and as a fellow poet ready with debate and springing questions, Berryman promptly developed what he called 'a shameless and barbaric enthusiasm about Delmore Schwartz's book [*In Dreams Begin Responsibilities*], which I finally bought and have been absorbing.'

Columbia University at length offered Berryman the post of assistant in English, with a stipend of 1,000 dollars, on 20 March, the appointment to end on 30 June 1940. By 11 April Berryman had accepted the position, and felt content enough to spend some time at Fountain Valley, a farm in Reisterstown, Maryland, owned by his 'Aunt' Ethel, his stepfather's sister. Between 1 April, the day that Beatrice left, and 25 May, he wrote fifteen poems: all of them, he professed, brought on by a feeling of excited loneliness. At the end of May more luck turned up: the *Nation* accepted his offer to become their part-time poetry editor, and he at once began to compile a two-page collection for the July issue. His first selection, slowly and conscientiously put together, eventually appeared on 30 September, with contributions by Wallace Stevens, John Peale Bishop. W. H. Auden, W. R. Moses, and Bhain Campbell.

He returned home for a few days; then, instead of spending time, as he had planned, with Delmore and Gertrude Schwartz at Yaddo, he moved on to visit Bhain and Florence Campbell in Grand Marais, Michigan, a small, decayed lumbering town (with five taverns) on Lake Superior. Immersed in dunes and woods, fog and sun, he found the visit exhilarating.

In June, Bhain Campbell had applied to Dr C. B. Hilberry for a position in the English department of Wayne State University, Detroit, and gained a job in spite of uncompromisingly submitting that he would need to subordinate any teaching to his own writing, currently a book on Shelley, a novel, and a book of verse. As the summer wore on, he told Dr Hilberry that his accomplished friend John Berryman would make a very useful addition to the staff. Berryman made his own formal application on 20 August, justifying his release from the position he had already accepted at Columbia on the grounds that his work there would consist merely of consultation with students in composition. Mark Van Doren backed him with a glowing reference: 'He is to my certain knowledge both brilliant and promising: a fine poet, a fully equipped critic, and insatiable reader, and – though you must know this – an engaging person. I have no doubt as to his future, or as to his great usefulness in an English department.' Since the size of registration was to determine the numbers of the English staff, Berryman had to wait for news, and impatiently told Scott Buchanan in the meanwhile, 'Wayne is I think a poor place and Detroit a worse one, but when the difference in living expense is considered I'd be paid about twice as much as Columbia now pays me. I could pay most of my debts during the year, and probably could send for B. at once, so this is very important to me.'

He had an affair during the summer, despite being still very much in love with Beatrice, who was distressed by the news but took it in a forgiving spirit. She had lately taken a more realistic and philosophical view of Berryman's state. Although she consistently told Berryman her love for him, her letters were acute with questions and doubts. In August, for example, she asked pertinently if he had formed any decision about the direction of his life. For his part, Berryman fully reciprocated her love, and in fact she represented the chief motive in his eagerness to gain employment in a city that he considered otherwise unappetising. Forces moved hurriedly between Berryman and Beatrice, however, and her own brave decisiveness was to hasten the eventual dissolution of their relationship. She had returned home in April just in time to hear Hitler's speech following the introduction of conscription in England. When Europe exploded into war, she wrote to Berryman – ironically just at the time when he won the appointment at Wayne State University that he hoped would ensure their future life together – that, all the while she could usefully serve her country, she would stay in England for the duration. Berryman entered his own arena alone.

6

First teaching and another loss, 1939-40

While his hope of marrying his English fiancée endured, Berryman could entertain exile; as that hope diminished, he sank into a slough of alienation, bouts of work and crazy habits of living including literal starvation and social withdrawal, which brought about physical and mental breakdown. It was a self-punishing year of increasing psychological dislocation. From the start, his loneliness was sublimated in strenuous work; exhaustion took over, then a number of uncanny 'attacks' which doctors found hard to diagnose. Even throughout 1940, when he at last gained the chance to have some poems printed in a volume, a relentless drive towards self-punishment led him to criticise the policy of the publisher, James Laughlin, and to stall until he was almost dropped from the project. In April 1940, Berryman was to write, 'All my sins have their ugly roots in my decision last fall to leave Columbia and accept an instructorship here; that is to say, OUT HERE. This was, from any viewpoint, an insane mistake, and I am paying – in health, in temper, in *time*.' The time factor seemed so crucial because he felt that his real gifts, as a poet, were being wasted, languishing in the sterile hours of teaching and assessing themes.

The Department of English, in the college of liberal arts, formed the largest in the university, with 35–40 teachers. The new chairman was Clarence B. Hilberry – 'a very able, perceptive person who cultivated cordial acquaintance with everybody' – while Dr Leslie Hanawalt, then an associate professor of forty-three, a little older than Hilberry and his closest friend, bore the new title of Chairman of Basic Courses. Berryman's post – he called himself 'special instructor' on his nomination blank – was decidedly a temporary appointment.

Berryman boldly faced the rigours of his work, but soon reported to Mark Van Doren that he was 'monstrously overloaded' with 135 freshman students. 'I think I am a good teacher and I know I like it,' he said. 'It is mainly the fatigue, and the terrible sense of waste I have, that makes me a spectre and a sad spectre.' After two months he felt he had aged ten years. 'Certainly,' as he himself granted, 'no-one could be more conscientious.' One of his colleagues, George Peck, remembers a midnight stroll with his wife when they discovered Berryman marking student papers at his attic desk.

> He had been at it since eight that morning, without stopping for meals, and on the floor in the corner next to him stood a pile at least two feet high, still unread, of research papers. . . . We urged John to call it a day, but he insisted that he had to go on, because until he had read these papers he could not give attention to his own writing nor to his duties as poetry editor of the *Nation*, which, he said, was getting impatient because he had not been able all year to do the job. But he felt his students came first. The papers, I knew, were not a neglected backlog, but an end of semester pile-up inevitable in John's unrealistic notion that he should assign (and read and comment on) as many papers as he could get his students to write.

Peck and his wife persuaded Berryman to take a short break in their apartment:

> My wife cajoled him into accepting a bowl of tomato soup and some crackers. The effect was startling. Starved without knowing it, once the soup got to him he began to talk in a stream very like a genial drunk, a case of logorrhea. We had, neither of us, ever seen anybody respond so dramatically to a little nourishment. He talked brilliantly, of course, but when he ran down and got sleepy we walked him home to his door.

In addition to his own teaching, Berryman signed on for two courses in the Horace H. Rackham School of Graduate Studies, an extension division of the University of Michigan.

While he complained mightily to his friends, Berryman was rather more diplomatic in addressing H. R. Steeves of Columbia University, and made light of his work-load and ability:

> The teaching itself, I can say without reservation, I like immensely, I find I am perfectly at ease in the classroom, and most of the students are endlessly interesting, particularly those

in my night classes who are mature men and women working during the day at regular jobs. I lecture only occasionally; the materials of the course (elementary logic, the projection and organization of opinion, and a good deal of reading) can be handled much more satisfactorily in discussion; I simply initiate, direct and summarize.

There is no doubt that Berryman was very well disposed towards his students, ready to help, never inconvenienced by their demands. One close student, Michael Jacobs, took Berryman's night class in English composition.

My most vivid impression of John was his propensity for superlatives. Nothing was ever average or just 'so-so'. Everything seemed 'incredible', or 'fantastic', or 'utterly ridiculous'. His reactions in addition to being intense always seemed full of wide-eyed wonder and surprise. He had a perpetual look of open-mouthed surprise. It had a certain owlish charm and naivete which I found both amusing and appealing.

Another student, Calvin Shubow, developed a tremendous fondness for Berryman, who made a 'great impression' on him. Berryman was devoted to his students, he remembers, and paid them individual attention, trying to enlarge their reading, especially in the classics and Shakespeare, which he would quote at length from memory. He often adverted to the superiority of the educational system in England, which traditionally studied the classics, whereas the upstart American colleges had departed from the way. He did not mention that this concern for England, coupled with a pessimism about current events in Europe, derived as much force from his anguished care for the safety of his fiancée. In addition to the impermanence of his job, Berryman had to reckon with the terrible possibility that all his personal hopes of love and marriage might any day be annihilated in the European theatre of war. In general, Berryman seemed to Shubow often depressed and always nervous; he showed 'no sense of humor, and took himself very seriously'.

In gear with his nervous intensity, Berryman always drank coffee black, and chain-smoked cigarettes: his fingers were stained with nicotine and tar. He was thin and gaunt, and sported a very bushy moustache at a time when they were not common among younger men. Across the avenue from his office stood Webster Hall, a residential hotel with a barber shop, 'and it was generally understood that John went there daily to be shaved.' George Peck recalls that this expensive habit was thought as unusual luxury by other members of staff.

Berryman's affectation (which, he felt, gave him some distinction – even if only for folly) was not the only thing that set him apart from his colleagues. He tended more and more to scorn and avoid them – not necessarily on account of their faults, but because his own estrangement and misery took little account of other persons. Through a self-imposed social and spiritual exile, Berryman made his own state worse and sustained his colleagues' case for finding him odd and rebarbative. Even among his students, to whom he would generally show warmth, Berryman never spoke of his earlier life, shied away from questions about his background, school, and father, voiced a contempt for most of his colleagues, and evinced what Shubow called a 'passion for privacy'. When a colleague, Alva Gay, and his wife Virginia, invited Berryman to dinner, 'he refused the invitation saying that he would rather spend his time with non-university people than with faculty members.' Even Alexander Rose, who shared Berryman's office, found him 'extremely unpleasant': 'he seemed completely wrapped up in his own interior world and was barely civil.'

> His general response to 'Good morning' or 'Hi' was a rather surly growl – or even nothing. My recollection is that most of us came gradually to ignore him, since that was the treatment he seemed to want. I might say that most of us had a rather poor opinion of him – mainly, I suppose – because we all had the feeling that he was very contemptuous of us. In one other respect, he was not a joy to have as an office mate: his baths and changes of clothing were all too infrequent, and all too often a very 'gamey' odor seemed to be coming from his corner of the office.

Since Berryman did so little to ease his own lot, but continually indulged in anti-social behaviour, it was only too easy for his colleagues to take his revulsion at face value, despite the fact that his apparent contempt was not directed at any individuals. Along with his sense of 'otherness', which was often taken for superiority, went the pain of shyness and self-commiseration. Berryman felt that his specialness was wasted in a role which any average teacher could fulfil. His ability to be misunderstood is illuminated by George Peck's reflections on his behaviour at a party given by the Pecks themselves:

He was very shy, and had no small talk. Two things stand out in my memory of him at that party. One is that he sat at the end of a couch, with book shelves next to him, from which he pulled out a dictionary . . . and read in apparent absorption and pleasure while the party talk swirled around him. We were all (or almost all) a little in awe of him, a published poet and poetry editor of the *Nation* . . . so nobody would readily disturb him. This same tinge of deference was involved in the other characteristic situation that I recall about this party, though it was repeated on other occasions. In retrospect I believe our deference and John's profound shyness produced an unintended cruel trap for him. When he stood with a small group and brought himself to speak, he would utter a strong opinion or make an extreme assertion. Most of us were reared in the tradition that it is unmannerly to take exception unnecessarily, and that it is rude to be contentious. So John's assertion would get polite acknowledgement; nobody, I think, was so rude – or so baffled – as to simply ignore the remark. But in retrospect I have realized that John was trying to get a discussion going, to start a rubbing of brains as well as of elbows. When he got no opposition he would swing his shoulders a bit and wade in with a still wilder statement, and so on, producing increasing astonishment in the group, until at last John had given it so many whirls that his position had become entirely untenable and figuratively he whirled until he fell on his face, as we used to say then. None of us had the wit to find a way out for him on the spot, so the group would dissolve – what is there left to say? – and it is easy to see (now) that John's shyness and withdrawal were increased.

Apart from a brief acquaintance with a colleague named Theodore Miles commemorated in his poem 'Farewell to Miles' *(Short Poems)*, Berryman had only Bhain and Florence Campbell for kindred spirits. At the beginning of the academic year, he and the Campbells took an apartment together about four blocks from the university at 261 East Ferry. (The accommodation was tight, with one bedroom off a large living–dining–room–kitchen.) Berryman and Campbell had the most tremendous liking and respect for each other, and assuredly complemented one another in personality. Campbell was always sweet and good-natured, charming and outgoing, whereas Berryman seemed mostly to display contemptuous behaviour.

Between their classes, Berryman and Campbell worked hard at writing poetry, and submitted their efforts to detailed discussion and analysis. After critical sessions together, both men revised their drafts. Their poetic predilections also tended to complement one another, Berryman being private and inward in his verse, Campbell public and social. 'On the other hand,' Florence Campbell (now Mrs Morton Miller) remembers, 'John had the stronger mastery of structure,' and according to John Malcolm Brinnin, a good friend, Campbell's poetry 'picked up under Berryman'. For Berryman's part, he was 'so involved with Bhain's stuff,' as he told James Dickey long after, 'that I should as soon think of beating a drum for my own.'

When not working, the two men played handball or chess. 'For a brief time things went along smoothly, though even at best John was subject to abrupt and seemingly uncaused swings of mood.' Florence Miller remembers one particular occasion:

In the early, good days of our ménage à trois, on a very hot September afternoon when Bhain and John had just begun their teaching at Wayne, John did a very sweet thing, at considerable labor. The University library was getting rid of some of its older books, for lack of space, and John learned that one discarded item was a complete set of the Encyclopedia Britannica, a desirable edition for literary matters. Determined to get it for Bhain, he spent that whole scorching afternoon lugging it, a few volumes at a time, from the library, along the 4 or 5 blocks to our apartment, and up the two steep flights of stairs.

The pressures of his life and working situation soon began to tell on Berryman. His teaching, to which (in itself) he did not feel committed, became tedious and exhausting. His sense of attachment to his fiancée in England – he sometimes referred to her as 'my wife' – confused and sorrowed him, since he still looked to their eventual (although, month by month, less likely) marriage. Florence found it 'inconceivably painful' to witness his 'intrinsic state of acute sensibility':

as Bhain and I watched him become more and more moody, quick to lash out, unpredictable and obviously unhappy, we both thought that one element of the strain upon him was the inevitable one of a young, single man living closely with a young, happily married and loving couple, and the contrast between our relatedness and his lack of it.

There was certainly no question of Berryman's being improperly attracted to Florence: partly from a concept of honourable behaviour ('To John, the wife of a dear friend was something so utterly out of bounds that one doesn't think of it at all'), but more because, as Berryman let his brother know, he affected to despise Florence. What is perhaps most evident is that Berryman felt so close to Campbell as to be jealous of him, resentful of the love and attention he gave his wife. Being so attached to Campbell, Berryman indeed showed every sign of possessiveness. 'He was impersonally kind and friendly toward me when he was in a good mood,' Florence Miller remembers, 'and deliberately rude in a bad one, but there was no man–woman component in it.' In fact, it was Berryman's very disinterestedness towards Florence that enabled the household to run smoothly for as long as some months, in addition to the love shared by the men.

Berryman's tension, and the intensity of his work-habits, eventually reached a crisis, as Florence Miller relates:

> As autumn went on, John showed signs of being under great pressure. More and more of the time he was sullen, angry, withdrawn, and might not speak a word for days. He lost weight, and his color was bad. In these moods he would go out and walk all night, stopping at a bar occasionally, but drinking wasn't a big thing with him, and so far as we could make out he mostly just walked, with his private anguish. He would somehow get to his classes next day, without having been home, and come straggling back in the late afternoon, 'feeling like death', he often said. Then began a series of 'attacks': he would walk in the door without speaking, go rigid, and crash to the floor unconscious. We had seen him through one such attack in the summer at Grand Marais, but it had been one isolated episode with no after-effects, so we had thought no more about it. Now they became frequent. . . . They were also followed, after consciousness returned, by a day or two of exhaustion and prostration. On one appalling occasion, after we had got him into his bed, he insisted that I sit all night by his bedside and hold his hand, in order, he said, to keep away the 'little creatures' which were in his bed and were tormenting him.

Alexander Rose remembers Berryman's behaviour as so atypical that, one day when he discovered him stretched out on the floor of their office with his eyes closed, he disregarded the matter 'and merely stepped cautiously around him. Only later did I discover that he was ill and had fainted!'

On 5 December, Berryman's worsening state of health and continual over-work brought on a most severe collapse just before an afternoon faculty meeting. He had been reading papers steadily for four days. The day before his collapse, he had sustained a twelve-hour non-stop stint of papers, conferences, and classes. He did not recover as quickly as on earlier occasions, and fell down again after a few minutes. The university doctor and a private nerve specialist agreed it was a case of 'nervous exhaustion'. The specialist recommended heavy reading before going to bed – such as *Redbook*, *Gone With The Wind*, or some Dickens. After a few days, Berryman was able to walk languidly with the Campbells to view an art gallery. At this time Berryman himself confessed, 'I would like to scream and smash things, I will be responsible for nothing I say.'

He flew to New York in mid-December, to recuperate – with little success – for immediately he met up with Delmore Schwartz, and then visited William Phillips at his apartment until 1 a.m. On returning to his address at 11 East 30th Street, Berryman was unable to get in and walked about all night. That day he went to a Picasso exhibition at the Museum of Modern Art in company with Delmore and Gertrude Schwartz, and at two o'clock the next morning he at last got to bed. Unaware of Berryman's ill-advised activity, Campbell wrote, 'I was happy, even though your note contained no news of sleep, to know that Delmore had turned up. He's a pillar, I think.' The next day, Berryman dealt with some poetry manuscripts at the offices of the *Nation*, called on Dwight Macdonald (to collect some books to review for a poetry chronicle which he was in fact unable to write), returned home to write a number of letters, read *Tess of the D'Urbervilles*, and worked on a poem about Hardy. It was not a regimen to aid recovery. By 26 December he reported, 'I am worse – crazily weak and irritable, and I nearly broke my head last night. I have let Mother bring a Bellevue man in, and he seems not to be a complete fool, so I am doing as he says, even to continual sedatives.' Campbell responded, 'With your last letter I began to feel sadly certain that you would not be returning. . . . Sometimes I thought I could not bear to watch your suffering another moment.' Allen Tate took Berryman down to Princeton for the last weekend of the month. It was a short-lived respite, however, since Berryman proposed to return to Detroit the following Tuesday. 'My malady is in the headache–dizziness–insomnia stage,' he explained, 'and how I will feel from day to day I simply cannot tell; if it improves, I can teach – if not, I may as well be there as here, for a time.'

He resumed his teaching for about three weeks. Towards the end of that period he endured a phase of bad insomnia, ate little, and again collapsed. Bhain Campbell realised that the collapse was markedly different from earlier attacks and called in a doctor, Eugene Shafarman. For about two hours after his fall, Berryman paced about or sat in a chair, but seemed unable to communicate anything. Dr Shafarman made a tentative diagnosis of 'post-epileptic confusion', and recommended a psychiatrist. The doctor arrived with the psychiatrist, Dr David Leach, two nights later, at which time Berryman could speak only in a strained, unnatural voice. The psychiatrist notified Campbell that Berryman was suffering from some form of psycho-neurotic maladjustment, and feared the onset of schizophrenia. Berryman appeared to be in a serious stage of total retreat from the real world into an inner obsessive or disintegrating mental life. Dr Leach was sufficiently alarmed by Berryman's developing instability of mind as to advise that he should leave Detroit as soon as possible.

The Campbells themselves were in a state of consternation. Berryman seemed unconscious of his environment or those about him, and they were forced, from love and a sense of acute responsibility, to oblige his whims and indissuadable moods to the point of denying their own lives. Campbell found it difficult to fulfil his duties at the university, and both he and Florence were approaching a state of collapse. 'John's behavior,' Florence recalls, 'became so harrowing to us that we began to fear he might do us some harm; there was a brief period when we always braced the back of a straight chair under our doorknob before going to sleep.' To aid Berryman's health, Campbell dissuaded colleagues from calling at the apartment.

Campbell took Berryman's classes at need in addition to his own, as well as urging patience on Dr Hilberry during Berryman's temporary illness. Taking all the advice he could, Campbell put into operation a plan to forestall Berryman's complete divorce from real life. The first extremely painful step was to refuse Berryman a refuge from himself, in order that he should face up to his own life. Allen Tate generously offered Berryman his home, but even that recourse had to be avoided. It seemed better for Berryman to take leave of absence – or even to resign outright – from Wayne, to move to Ann Arbor (a more clement and calm city than Detroit), and to register at the University of Michigan in order to compete for one of the fairly lucrative Hopwood Awards. (Milton Halliday, who was then studying at Ann Arbor, would keep an eye on Berryman.) Since the start of the year, Berryman had been totally unaware of what Campbell had done for him, a factor which was more vexing for Campbell because Berryman would have to be 'tricked' into the expedients proposed. To Berryman, even the intercession of the doctors seemed accidental. His precarious state of mind would have been even more endangered if he had reacted by rebelling against being 'managed' by those he deemed his inferiors. Campbell thought it imperative that Berryman's 'hopeless arrogance and blind selfishness' – what he later referred to as his 'ball of hate' – should be dispelled by his being forced to acknowledge the real world of human beings (which, in Campbell's experience, he had never before come to terms with).

Berryman's mother briefly visited Detroit and had a talk with Dr Hilberry which seems further to have smoothed the professional path. On the domestic front, the frazzled situation between Berryman and the Campbells reached a climax. Convinced that to destroy his friendship with Berryman (even against all his instincts of fondness) was a salutary step, Campbell gradually succeeded so well that Berryman despised and treated him as a scapegoat – the 'locus of all evil and stupidity.' On 16 February, Berryman learned that he was suffering from a variant form of *petit mal* epilepsy (not severe, and without signs of deterioration). 'I think I kept quite calm' Berryman recorded,

> but small things all day sent my spirits to ebb. Epilepsy – it is nothing but a word, and the condition seems slight. On the score of imagery, as Derbyshire [a doctor] says, I suppose I should be glad. It is the abnormality creates us – only the freak endures. . . . Today the knowledge has somehow brought me back to life: I read with absorption for the first time in weeks. . . . Resolution: to scorn or ignore any honour, any fame, my poems may get during my life. Expect nothing, distrust what comes, work.

Such terms clearly mark Berryman's dangerously delusional state of mind. Whether or not he was really suffering from epilepsy, it is evident that his mental breakdown had passed through a severe stage in January, and through other degrees in the weeks following.

For some time he frequented bars in the evenings, probably to avoid the company of the Campbells. At home, his rudeness to Florence Campbell intensified, to the point where he would shrink from her presence. When he spoke with Campbell, he would not allow her to enter the conversation. By mid-February, his conduct reached such a bizarre pitch that whenever the phone rang, for example, he would bang the receiver up and down until the caller gave up.

It was clear that they would have to disband the household. Florence had lost over ten pounds in weight. But Campbell could not bring himself to ask Berryman to leave; he had no heart for the task. Eventually Florence just began to pack while the Campbells themselves hunted for another apartment. After two days, Berryman absently observed that they must be moving, and decided to keep the apartment for himself. Campbell offered him the use of the living-room furniture, but Berryman asked only to keep a shabby old dresser. Leaving the room, Berryman fell headlong down the stairs in a faint, but collected himself and carried on without speaking. Four days passed, and he and Campbell exchanged no more than two sentences. The Campbells finally moved on 20 February, leaving Berryman to himself in what he called 'this horror', the dirty apartment. 'Their conduct for some weeks now,' he noted with disdain stemming from delusion, 'has been unspeakable.' He took to having some meals in an unpleasantly greasy restaurant on Third Avenue, while Campbell, who had to watch from a pitying distance, asked the waitresses to ensure that Berryman got the best. Berryman entered a period of sleeplessness followed by 'horrible dreams' from which he would wake 'retching with grief.'

He began slowly to recover health. He resumed his teaching, became reconciled with the Campbells, and presently moved to another apartment across from Old Main, at 4827 Cass Avenue. 'He has devoted himself,' Clarence Hilberry told Professor Theodore Morrison at Harvard (where Berryman was applying for a job by mid-year),

> whole-heartedly to his students and has become strongly interested in many of them and their individual writing problems. They have, in turn, responded well to his teaching. In fact, I have had more students come to me to praise his work than that of any other young man in the department. He seems to claim the loyalty (almost devotion) of his students.

In the meantime, Berryman registered again at the University of Michigan, mainly with a view to gaining a Hopwood Prize. John Malcolm Brinnin, who was then running a bookshop in Ann Arbor to pay his way through college, also entered for the Hopwood Prize in poetry. Berryman made it known to him that he did not intend to be worsted in the competition, but Brinnin went ahead and won the prize. Berryman reported to his mother, 'I feel little anger or disappointment. But I am more generally bitter than I have ever been in my life.

'My students have helped me, or have kept me alive. In the year that ended today I take no pleasure except in thinking of some of them. Error and waste, betrayal, loneliness, disease, war, failure.'

By May Berryman felt his health giving out again – 'mainly', he told Delmore Schwartz, 'violent headaches, insomnia and fatigue.' Dr Shafarman gave him a thorough examination, and attributed the current trouble to malnutrition. With a substantial diet Berryman began to recover. The future looked momentarily bleak in terms of money and employment, since the Wayne contract lapsed, but his hopes revived when Theodore Morrison asked him to an interview at Harvard early in June. Berryman made a good impression, and was consequently offered an appointment.

Relief seemed possible, but not enthusiasm. What absolutely darkened the future was the sudden deterioration of Bhain Campbell's health. Berryman was appalled that his friend's cancer had advanced so rapidly; a growth was active in Campbell's left side, and very painful. 'I see it my duty,' Berryman wrote, 'to be as useful to Campbell as I can for as long as I can, and I believe he would be very depressed to see me go permanently now . . . also, we have begun work on a volume of translations from Corbière, to be done jointly.' Campbell went into hospital, where Berryman visited him daily. Subsequently, the Campbells moved to a summer cottage owned by his parents on the shore of Union Lake, about twenty-five miles north-west of downtown Detroit. Berryman visited them at the Lake, and spent the last week of July nursing Campbell while Florence was in Canada. When he returned to town, Berryman was prostrated from the heat, and began to faint with exhaustion. 'I am also afraid, frankly,' he wrote, 'of the return of my disorder' – meaning a recurrence of nervous breakdown.

As August drew on, Campbell became even more ill, with fever and paroxysms, and he and Florence moved back to Detroit, taking an apartment at 25 East Palmer, to be near the doctors and the hospitals. 'John was most solicitous,' Florence Miller recalls. 'He increased his visits, affectionately bolstering Bhain's morale, encouraging him to keep up his writing, entertaining him with good conversation, gaiety and wit, and bringing him little things for his physical comfort, such as on one occasion a comfortable padded back-rest to aid him in sitting up in bed.' Campbell was admitted to hospital, where a tumour was removed, but the cancer had spread to his right thigh, abdomen, and chest. Back at home, Florence had to administer codeine by injection. In spite of getting much thinner, having transfusions, and then developing pleurisy, Campbell carried on writing, and even started an autobiography which he continued by dictation to within a short while of his death.

Bound by his contract to Harvard, Berryman had to leave Detroit by 20 September, but he continued to solace and chivvy his friend by letter, suggesting that he try 'fixing the growth with a baleful stare'. He was also very positive and constructive in his comments on Campbell's writing. 'Take care of yourself,' he wrote, 'husband your strength for its best use, be as happy as you can in a work going brilliantly on and in a life far far better lived than most lives are.' Unhappy and overworked at Harvard, Berryman suffered for Campbell:

> Dearest Bhain, [he told him] I hope you are better than you were, in particular that your breathing improves and that those sores disappear – if I could take them from you, I would. The worst is that everyone suffers and a time comes when no one can do another one good. I wish merely that the great good you have done me could return for you. In a way it does, and my love always does.

In late November Berryman took the train to Detroit to see his friend once more, a visit which, Florence Miller explains, 'gave Bhain great pleasure, and must have been a severe emotional strain on John, though he took good care not to let that appear.' Berryman was in fact aghast at what he saw; seventeen years later he remembered vividly that Campbell 'was saffron-coloured, his eyes danced, his teeth shot from retreating gums like a madman's, and dying he was full of the senseless hopes (encouraged by his mother who sought quack remedies) that tubercular patients have at the end.' Berryman returned to Cambridge. Just a few days later, Campbell became delirious with cerebral anaemia and severe cerebral irritation, his condition worsened by water in the lungs. He went into a coma and died in the afternoon of 3 December. 'I thought life would bring me nothing like this again,' Berryman sorrowed.

> Bhain Campbell was extracted from me
> in dolour, yellow as a second sheet
> & I have not since tried to resume the same
> ['Relations', *Love & Fame*].

Berryman could never recover from his grief. Campbell's death – premature, hasty and hideous – came to be associated in his mind with his own father's death. The recrudescence of that pain was also inextricably bound up with the harrowing experience of his first year of teaching. After some years, on 12 April 1947, he began to sketch a story called 'Vain Surmise' (published, for the first time, only in 1975 as 'Wash Far Away', later included in *The Freedom of the Poet*), which turns on a professor's decision to teach Milton's

'Lycidas' with conviction and love, since 'His earliest ambition depends, his dead friend who initiated him. He must be worthy!' In the story Berryman remembers that Campbell (who figures as 'Hugh')

> lay on a couch in the August sun, his short beard glinting, saying, 'It's just as well. I could never have got done what I wanted to.' Later, when he had got very weak and was chiefly teeth and eyes, his wandering mind wanted pathetically to live, certain he would. But the professor clung still to the resignation, the judgement on the couch; he himself had done nothing he wanted, and he had come to believe that Hugh was right. He had come to believe this after his grief had dimmed.

Campbell's death at the age of twenty-nine confirmed Berryman's own sense of fatalism; but it was a delusion for Berryman to have felt acquiescent with day-to-day tribulations and regrets. 'Wash Far Away' conveys the attitude of triumphing over reversals and misgivings with passion and affirmation, but, for Berryman, that posture was more a policy decision that a statement of faith. Earlier he had recorded, 'Ah I am not fortified against the death of anyone. The marks of the only deaths I have undergone, my father's and Bhain's, I will carry always.'

One of Bhain Campbell's students became a girlfriend to Berryman for a while, and she accompanied him when he visited the Campbells at Union Lake during the summer of 1940. (She also typed out much of Campbell's autobiography.) When he departed for Cambridge, she was tempted to follow and to get work near him. He did have other girlfriends during the period at Wayne, but – presumably because he already felt so strongly attached to his far-distant fiancée – did not form 'any regular relation with any other woman', Florence Miller remembers, 'though he was strongly attracted to them in general. As he once exclaimed in mock anger, "After all, a man is nothing but an ambulatory penis!"' It was rumoured, however, that he was having sexual relations with one or more of his students; one of them, according to Alexander Rose, 'had confided to a male student (who rather angrily and jealously passed the tale on to me) that John was an incredibly great lover, capable of prolonging the ecstatic moment almost indefinitely!'

Berryman derived little joy from writing poetry during 1939 and 1940. For one matter, he was too busy and sick for creative thought; for another, the times, both personal and political, had fallen out of joint. With one eye to the cataclysm approaching in Europe, he wrote '1st September 1939', which laments the immediate effects of the Russo-German pact. With another eye to the influential presence of Bhain Campbell – an avowed Communist – he wrote 'Thanksgiving: Detroit', which treats, as from Campbell's point of view, the sociopolitical theme of a workers' strike at the Highland Park Ford motor plant in Detroit. With both eyes open, he turned a critical poem, 'Communist', on the 'honest young man', Bhain Campbell, who had espoused delusive ideals. In 'A Point of Age' (begun in February 1940), Berryman took (as Joseph Warren Beach once pointed out) 'a very discouraged view of our hopeful political prophecies.'

> In the city of the stranger I discovered
> Strike and corruption: cars sat on the bench
> To horn their justice at the citizen's head
> And deafen the citizen alive or dead.
> . . . .
> In storm and gloom, before it is too late
> I make my testament: I bequeath my heart
> To the disappointed few who have wished me well;
> My vision I leave to one who has the will
> To master it, and the consuming art;
> What else, the sorrow, the disease, the hate
> I scatter; and I am prepared to start.

It is perhaps Berryman's most personal utterance from this period, dispiritedly aligning his own apostasy with the earlier political rebelliousness of Ethan Allen (from whom Berryman believed himself to be descended):

> Ethan Allen, father, in the rebel wood
> Teach trust and disobedience to the son
> Who neither obeys nor can disobey One
> Never, in the reaches of his longing, known.

Berryman called the poem 'the best trophy I have of the worst year I have spent on earth,' a statement which dates from 3 June 1940.

In November 1939, Berryman estimated that he had written seventy poems worth publishing (of which about twenty had already appeared), but expressed no interest in publishing any more at the time. When his poem 'Auden Landscape' appeared in the *New Republic* (8 July 1940), he noted that 'Auden has an article on Rilke in the same number; I am depressed when I recall how glad I would once have been to appear with him.' The sentiment had no pretence about it.

A potentially more exciting project was started by James Laughlin towards the end of 1939 – to publish in a single volume a group of
young poets including Randall Jarrell, W. R. Moses, George
Marion O'Donnell, and Elizabeth Bishop. Inhibited and self-
punitive, Berryman immediately took a dislike to what he called
'the machinery' – photographs, facsimiles, and an introduction by
each poet – that Laughlin planned for the volume. At Christmas
1939, Delmore Schwartz, Allen Tate, and Mark Van Doren were all
of a mind that Berryman should accede to the idea. (Schwartz even
volunteered to write Berryman's introduction, to relieve him of
that scruple.) At some point Tate generously wrote to Berryman,
'It seems to me that you and Jarrell are the best of your generation,
and I want to see you both published. . . . You would be in the
company of your peers, and the group exhibit would strengthen
your claims to individual attention later on.'

By early 1940, Elizabeth Bishop had for some reason dropped out
of the group, but Laughlin was particularly insistent on including a
woman, and sounded out opinions on Emma Swan, Mary Barnard,
and others. Berryman was opposed to the principle of including a
woman, not necessarily because of sexual discrimination but because he could see no argument for including a female poet if there
were no obviously meritorious candidates; the poet's sex seemed
immaterial. Laughlin decided to take votes on which poetess to
include and, by 8 August, Mary Barnard was elected.

Another development took place now that Robert Giroux,
Berryman's contemporary and friend at Columbia, started working as an editor for Harcourt, Brace & Co., Inc., and expressed an
interest in publishing a Berryman volume. Berryman submitted a
group of poems, grateful for Giroux's assistance and acknowledging that 'you were one of the first persons to take any intelligent
interest in the verse.' For his part, Giroux was wary of Berryman's
sense of haste and emergency about gaining acceptance for the
volume, but he was not the less enthusiastic: 'I'm ready to battle for
you to the bitter end. I'm delighted to; it will be the first occasion
since I've been here that I really want to see a book published.'
Berryman was evidently in a hurry to put out his separate volume in
order to excuse himself from James Laughlin's project. Taking
account of that, Giroux hung on for a decision from his superiors
until late in the year, and in the meantime judiciously recommended
Berryman to proceed with Laughlin's proposals.

The publication date of *Five Young American Poets* drew on, but
still Berryman prevaricated. He felt disabled from writing an
introduction; diffident and lacking conviction, he could not speak
about his own beliefs and practices in poetry. He eventually drafted

at least seven prefaces, and sent the last to Laughlin late in August. Laughlin disliked the effort, his patience wearing thin: 'I must ask you to write a decent preface. It is perfect fiddlesticks that a person of your mentality can't say what he thinks about poetry.' But Berryman had not yet worked out a cogent theory or rationale, and saw no reason to do so, believing that poetry was not a matter for categorical thinking. Also, suffering from nervous exhaustion, he was barely equipped to deal with the matter.

Berryman's trouble lay deeper than the simple irritation of being expected to write an essay he did not believe in. Something more than professional steadfastness was at stake. That he should grope to write at least seven entirely different prefaces showed confusion of mind more than meticulousness. At heart he felt disturbed and unreal. Berryman had to brave his insecurity until – if ever – he could find his own poetic voice and the nervous poise to cope with the inner life which provoked him to poetry. Eventually, in mid-October, Laughlin accepted 'A Note on Poetry' (substantially a paraphrase of the poem 'On the London Train', with an argument against paraphrase as a useful exercise in criticism), which begins, 'None of the extant definitions of poetry is very useful; certainly none is adequate; and I do not propose to invent a new one. I should like to suggest what I understand the nature and working of poetry to be by studying one of the poems in this selection' (*Five Young American Poets*, Norfolk, Conn.: New Directions, 1940). In propounding the view that the technical devices of verse enable a writer to discover something 'coherent, directed, intelligible' out of 'an experience in itself usually vague,' Berryman in effect conceded that he had as yet little sense of subject-matter, but only of a 'mere' feeling or a phrase.

Many of Berryman's poems from this period, it is widely agreed, rely more on the organisation of syntax and image than on the substantial pressure of something to be said. They avoid the figure for the contours and the colours, the subject for the style. Gradually, with the help of Bhain Campbell, he had been emerging towards social consciousness and a shared content in his poems, but his personal incoherence and fear often acted as a barrier to communicable expression. To learn to write well was to construct his personality. Aware of the weaknesses in many of his 'Twenty Poems', and of the inadequacy of his 'Note', Berryman was hardly happy about his part in the volume. The rewards were few (financially, in addition to an advance of 25 dollars, the book earned him a royalty of only 6.25 dollars after nearly a year); the reviews were mixed; and Bhain Campbell's death and the rigours of Berryman's new career at Harvard allowed for little rejoicing.

7
Harvard and marriage,
1940-43

Berryman did not settle happily to work at Harvard University in 1940. He was appointed instructor in English on an annual basis at a salary of 2,500 dollars, but his duties differed little from those that had oppressed him at Wayne State University the previous year. English A, the composition section of the English department headed by Theodore Morrison, provided considerable drudgery for the teachers.

Berryman considered himself 'plainly too indulgent' with his students, who both irritated and charmed him with their 'illiterate urbanity', but many of them grew fond of his ingenious and sometimes tyrannical teaching. He responded enthusiastically to genuineness and sensitivity. One aspect of his behaviour was his edginess with other members of staff. He appeared always to carry a chip on his shoulder. His colleagues at Harvard included Harry Levin, Mark Schorer, Andrews Wanning, Wallace Stegner, and Delmore Schwartz, a group of singular talents from most of whom Berryman set himself apart. Wallace Stegner recalls that he was 'recessive and difficult to know . . . I remember one somewhat bibulous party of the English A staff in which he got illuminated and became, unexpectedly, funny and somewhat loud and willing to go on all night. Somebody remarked that the Century Plant had bloomed.' Although Berryman was often to be heard arguing the demerits of Harvard, even his colleagues came to respect him as a teacher. By March 1941, he recorded, 'My reading & such writing as I do aside, I find little outside myself to interest me here.'

On his birthday some months before, he had divulged another distress, his long absence from his English fiancée:

Twenty-six years ago I was born, at what cost of distress and hope, and how little glad I am, how little reason anyone has to

129

be glad. I work and work and postpone my disappointments, delay my terrors – if she comes, I think forever. If not, they come and they will be more than I can bear.

– This was a day of leisure and the acute unhappiness which only continual senseless activity can keep off now. I read verse also, a gate for the enemy, and if it were not for her I would wish that I were dead.

The morbidity was overstated, but the sense of deprivation lasted throughout his years at Harvard. In January 1941, for example, he wrote what he thought an 'exceedingly and complexly ironic' eighty-line poem ending:

> Go with the tide. . . .
>
> . . . .
> And all life moves from drink to drink, the stream
> Moves, and under the stream we join a happy ghost.

On first arrival at Harvard, Berryman took a house, 10½ Appian Way, with his brother Robert Jefferson, who had just transferred from Columbia College to Boston University. The house, which lies within easy walking distance of the Harvard campus, was 'so flimsy built', Robert Jefferson Berryman recalls, that, if the blinds were pulled down during the daytime, 'you could look out through the walls. . . . We were heating the neighborhood.' In order to furnish the house, the brothers withdrew most of their mother's possessions from a warehouse. When Mrs Berryman discovered their sly action, she called by telephone, 'My sons, I am not one to let veracity interfere with invective: you damned sons of bitches, where the hell is my furniture?'

On 19 October, Robert Jefferson married his first wife, Barbara, and the trio shared a fairly equable household well into 1941. In spite of the apparently good relationship that obtained between Berryman and his brother, however, their mother felt obliged to comment on subliminal tensions; after a visit in January she remarked to Berryman, 'One thing troubles me seriously . . . I believe you are quite unconscious of it but your manner to Bob [Jefferson] is such as to lead me to believe you hold him to be without much worth.' Although he was indeed unaware of it, Berryman's attitude towards his brother was more characteristic of his response to life in general.

For the next academic year – 1941–2 – Berryman took an apartment at 49 Grove Street in Boston. The dull demands of his teaching did not ease up, nor did he take many steps to enliven the routine by socialising with his colleagues. For conversation he turned to the highly acclaimed young poet Delmore Schwartz, a man – dynamic and depressive by turns – whom Berryman always found a treat to talk to. Both men had little respect for their tasks at Harvard, and shared the pains and ardours of writing poetry. Although Schwartz's best friend, William Barrett, remembers the years 1940–2 as 'most calm and secure' in Schwartz's life – 'His academic chores were light, and teaching was a new and enjoyable experience into which he threw himself with enthusiasm' – both Schwartz and Berryman constantly strained their nerves and doubted their aptitude and knowledge for teaching. Gertrude Buckman, who was then married to Schwartz, recalls of her husband:

> His looks: as he had a spinal curvature, S-fashion, he walked badly, with a shambling short step. He didn't stride at all. But he played tennis rather strongly despite his awkwardness. He had an oatmealy kind of complexion, a thick skin that had been acned earlier, no colour in it, and even less colour when he was choleric which was often. He had dirty blond hair, a noticeable bit of scar tissue in the middle of his forehead, a thick sensual mouth. Compared with John, he was a messy dresser, had no interest in clothes in any way – though he did have an awareness of his appearance otherwise. That is to say he took on a different expression when he looked into a mirror or posed for a photograph – and he was marvelously photogenic, with his tartarish bone structure. He had a slight speech defect – just a kind of thickening of enunciation. . . .
>
> I think John's esteem for Delmore was not matched by a responsive esteem. . . . I don't believe he had the same kind of academic ambition that John did, though they shared an *intense* poetic, intellectual ambition.
>
> Delmore was very gregarious when he wasn't working. At his desk he concentrated, wrote endlessly, chewed on a much bitten pipe stem, took on an absent expression. He was unable or unwilling to do anything for himself, but was demanding, with a powerful will. He loved an audience, and his social personality was rambunctious, noisy, argumentative, laughing. He loved shouting arguments.

Berryman was highly stimulated by Schwartz's company, and seemed often to identify with him in the role of *poète maudit*. At times he would discern in Schwartz a certain constraint, a terror of betrayal, and tremendous curiosity, attributes which matched

Berryman's own. Berryman wrote to Bhain Campbell: 'one's emotions exist to be used, not to be suppressed. Cambridge is especially glacial in this; Delmore & I have decided to buy a remote & warm island, where we invite you to come & stay. . . . More pretentious than Wayne and nearly as stupid, Harvard is a haven for the boring and the foolish.' After his move from Cambridge to the apartment in Boston, however, Berryman was occasionally struck by what he called 'most grievous nostalgia' for Cambridge:

> I hated Cambridge, mostly, while I was there, but the image of the place delights and saddens me . . . what sickens me is that the intelligent boys each year . . . are at once caught into the cliques and the pretenses. . . . An intelligent sensitive boy quickly becomes a fraud. . . . Harvard has not fathered a serious writer for many years, and this is the reason.

When depressed by his abused students, Berryman could always find consolation from Schwartz, whose warmth of personality and incisive mind gave him a type to emulate: 'I have Machiavelli's grandson, Delmore, for model,' he wrote in March 1943. On another occasion, as they strolled together from the Charles River up to Harvard Yard, Schwartz praised and commiserated with Berryman:

> Delmore told me plainly this afternoon what he suggested, and I did not credit, last fall. 'No one else in the country is doing such work. Stevens – but never in single poems like The Disciple and A Point of Age. No poem of yours is without merit, but these are the peaks. The richness and complexity.' I felt like weeping. He made, actually, the comparison which I have hardly dared allow in my mind, and made it for me. One word is worth it all. The sick waiting, and letting the poems go out despised, the insufferable reviewers, the silence from whatever readers; the arrogance and the sick doubt; the terrible hours of probing as at a wound, looking, looking, for what may not be there; the conscience and the dry throat, the dry eyes; the piercing hope.

Berryman's other lasting consolation was provided by Eileen Mulligan, whom he met at a New Year's party in 1941. An orphan, and a practising Catholic, Eileen had been a contemporary of Jean Bennett's at Hunter College; from time to time she had shared the letters Berryman wrote Jean from England. Eileen and her married sister, Marie, to whom she was particularly close, had been brought up by an aunt. Emotionally susceptible and diffident of her abilities, Eileen felt that life had been good to her, even though she was disappointed in her achievements so far.

While his relationship with Eileen developed over the next eighteen months, Berryman still retained hopes of marrying Beatrice. At one point he proposed to visit England by clipper in June 1941. Both he and Beatrice regretted the great sea between them. Wistful and often guilt-ridden, he knew that their relationship now rested more and more on memory and imagination. Each in turn lapsed from letter-writing, arousing pleas for honesty and straight dealing. Both harked back to times when, in spite of quarrels and differences, they had been quite happy. An instance of his failure to confide in Beatrice is that she learned of his epilepsy only more than a year after his attacks had first been diagnosed. For the seven months ending in August 1942, Berryman heard nothing from England, even as his love for Eileen grew. In March of that year, Delmore Schwartz gave Mark Van Doren his opinion:

My own impression, whatever it is worth, is that the only thing wrong with John is some kind of hysteria. The fainting fits he has occur when he is spoken to sternly or contradicted; I don't think they're sheer frauds, but if they spring from his secret disease, the disease is an open secret, and besides the fainting, there is no sign of anything wrong with him.

However, if B's inquiry means that she is thinking of coming to America, and if you are going to advise her about John's general circumstances, I think that her coming to America and marrying him would do him an immense amount of good, for what he needs in the most obvious way is some kind of situation to cope with besides his own feelings. Living alone as he does, in Boston not Cambridge, and seeing no one at all for days at a time, he is really not well off; and being improvident, he sometimes spends all his money and then tries to feed himself on chocolate bars until the first of the month. Gertrude and I do what we can when we know what is going on, but usually we don't.

Beatrice herself had meanwhile undertaken a secret job at the Foreign Office in London. After periods of illness, and of absorption in her job, she had to acknowledge a sense of radical withdrawal from what Berryman called their 'hopeless & terrible engagement'.

Berryman had begun to involve himself with Eileen as early as April 1941. Eileen had derived her image of him from reading his poetry and his letters to Jean Bennett. It came as a shock for her to learn that he liked dancing, especially Boogie-Woogie, and that he had altogether a good many other sides to his personality. She herself was tied to New York by her work for Resco Inc. on Broadway, but as the months wore on she snatched weekends away from her lodging at 109 West 12th Street. They saw each other intermittently throughout 1941, and so on into 1942; but, as with Beatrice, a large part of the courtship had to be conducted by letter. In the long lapses of time between intense interludes together they exchanged passionate letters. 'At times I want you torturingly – I do now,' he wrote, for example, at the end of September. His urgings earned not only her response, but her deeper commitment.

By October she was very doubtful about going on with Berryman, however, most acutely because of the fatigue of living from one visit to the next, and because she knew that he was always thinking of Beatrice. She felt, in fact, that she was much too vulnerable to the tyranny of his moods, and that the impetuousness of her own feelings was naive. He did not try to protect her feelings, but exploited her sense of compassion; he told her on one occasion, 'I'm exhausted', 'I am not sleeping well, for one thing, & I eat irregularly. I had a magnificent dinner in Cambridge tonight & almost it upset me. The novelty. . . . Nothing seems to me at this moment to possess the slightest importance. If Michael appeared & told me Christ were waiting outside in the hall I don't believe I should feel any interest.' When he was ill or merely in his own phrase, 'spiritless as a fog', just to tell Eileen so was to excite her sympathies.

It was eventually a vast relief for her to spend a whole evening in confidential talk with Mrs Berryman. Eileen was particularly excited and flattered when Mrs Berryman offered to employ her as an assistant, even though she had fundamental doubts about her ability to meet the challenge. As it turned out, the job did not materialise, and Eileen went to work for the Canadian Aviation Bureau in the Waldorf Astoria Hotel. Yet she was impressed by the fact that Mrs Berryman seemed to offer a real kindness, and that, for the first time, she could envisage the possibility of a friendship between two people of different generations. Eileen also perceived the paradox that while Mrs Berryman loved her sons consumingly she seemed to lack a really affectionate nature. More to the point of her discomfiture in loving Berryman, Eileen learned from his mother that his feelings for Beatrice were likely to abate before too long, even though she had been a fine, beautiful and talented person. Mrs Berryman acutely understood the fact that Berryman now and then reserved some of his deepest feelings for what was past, accommodating idealistic regrets more readily than present joys.

Eileen's growing respect and admiration for Mrs Berryman answered well to what Berryman himself would have wished, especially as he managed constantly to suppress his own bursts of resentment. But Eileen's happy responsiveness to Mrs Berryman made little difference when she next visited Boston at the beginning of November, to find Berryman gaunt and exhausted. For hours, he sat idly in a chair.

December 1941 brought the Japanese attack on Pearl Harbor: America was at war. Berryman was pained at the state of the world, but more immediately disturbed about capturing Eileen's love. He felt remorse and an uncommon sense of self-abnegation. To allow her love, and his own, was to accept responsibility. What appeared to be the imposition and manipulation of feelings rightly occurred to him as often monstrous.

> I'm ashamed to say that the fact of our being finally openly at war has upset me a good deal, although I recognize what I call its necessity & actually I am glad or ought to be. . . . Forgive me if I don't make you happy, little Broom [they often called each other 'Broom', though Berryman also nicknamed Eileen 'Rusty'] – I know I don't now. What good are intentions? I ought to say again that if you *want* to cut free, *do it*. I hate the notion of your being tied to me except by your love. And your feelings are more important than mine. I love you & I do not want to be the source, more than I can, of your being hurt or held to your hurt. This may all be insane.

It may be understood from the passage that Berryman was frightened at the compelling state of their relationship; but, although unwilling to remit a breath of it, he did want to make an adjustment of the object to the force. He hoped that Eileen would square her expressed wishes with his; by announcing reciprocity, she would relieve him of his sense of blame for winning her. Insecure at heart, he felt afflicted with perhaps more obligations than triumphant rights. After a few days, on 14 December 1941, he wrote her another letter:

> The ironical falseness of that conversation we had comes to me again & again, one of many things that sicken me tonight. All a lie: it is you who give to me, give freely & sustain me, and it is I who can give you nothing. And I want so to give to you, Broom, to cherish you & to make & keep you happy. If my will were free, or if it still existed – I don't know whether it does or

not – I tell you I think at times I have lost my power of mind & choice – the ability to *steady* – I feel as if I were shaking, loose, control gone. I am not a good one to know. My bitterness I cannot long keep in – it is terrible to me to see it touch you – your religion, your ways of mind, your whole life. Anywhere I turn I see or imagine unhappiness for you. Where is the worst of it? I wish I knew. Let me tell you a truth: I will do anything in my power for your happiness. I don't know what to say, because anything may bind you to me or drive you from me, and the first may be what should not happen for you and the second is a kind of suicide for me, to lose you, even for you to withdraw as perhaps you ought. Devils in the mind moving about: nothing that I say here may be right. I can tell you one thing plainly without harm because you know it already: I love you in all possible sizes & qualities of the notion of love, with every tenderness, every wish, every desire, and it is simple hell not to have you with me – not, I won't pretend, my only hell, but hell certainly & constantly.

In December 1941, Jean Bennett, his old flame from Columbia days, became engaged to Edwin Webster. Berryman was delighted and amused by an invitation 'to meet' Miss Bennett at an opulent engagement party, and Jean herself was grateful when he came: he was her only friend in attendance. He did not go to the wedding in New York because of poverty, an incipient cold, and the necessity of preparing a new book-manuscript for James Laughlin at New Directions.

Feeling dreary, sick, and often angry at having so many papers and examinations to read – to the detriment of his creative work – he dragged through the winter weeks. The manuscript of his poems was finished by 19 January, when he decided 'to let God (i.e. Delmore) look at it' before sending it to Laughlin. The possibility that Theodore Morrison might want him to teach during the summer months at first irritated him, but his mood lifted when he learned that the rate of payment under discussion was 500 dollars, a sum he needed to defray the expense of buying a gramophone owned by the well-known musicologist B. H. Haggin. He began work on an abortive short story, and then, in February, on what he called 'the finest poem I ever planned'. When that poem, 'Boston Common', stalled in mid-March, he became bad-tempered and gloomy with Eileen, and completed a first version only by the end of June.

It is possible that Berryman had mentioned to Eileen that they might become engaged at this time, but postponed doing so because of moodiness: 'I've not talked yet with a priest,' he told her on 22 March, 'my mind is not free and my temper poor.'

Apart from the uncertain state of his relationship with Beatrice, one significant barrier to getting engaged was that he might well have been indigent within a few months if his appointment were not renewed: Delmore Schwartz took the consoling view that unemployment would do wonders for Berryman's poetry. More money-difficulties cropped up as the summer months drew on. In July, Eileen took a temporary job in an advertising agency, Charles W. Hoyt Co. Inc., but the job was finished just over a month later.

Both he and Eileen were overdue for some joy together: it was ironically provided when Berryman's fiancée wrote to renounce her engagement in July. 'I am three-quarters in pieces,' he told Mark Van Doren. Shortly afterwards Eileen accepted his proposal of marriage; Berryman felt rewarded 'with a second chance – a chance at health & work, life even so far as the War will permit it.'

Their problems were not at once resolved. New Directions had agreed to publish Berryman's *Poems* in October or November. When James Laughlin brought out the slim volume early – in August – Berryman felt outraged because one poem, 'A Point of Age', could no longer appear in the September issue of *Kenyon Review*. On her side, Eileen felt worried and nervous about their forthcoming marriage; she hated to think of him torturing himself by rereading Beatrice's last letter. Their engagement seemed unreal to her, at least until 20 August, when she had lunch at the Claremont Hotel with Mrs Berryman, who gave her a ring to wear on her engagement finger. It was not until 16 October that Berryman himself called on Tiffany's in New York to have a ring engraved – 'J. B. to E. M. – NOW AND THEN ONE – 24 October 1942', the date fixed for their wedding.

By late August Eileen was at work again, in fashion and advertising, for Eastman Kodak Company on East 40th Street. Because of Berryman's fecklessness, she was obliged to make all the material arrangements for the wedding. In December 1941, the Local Army Board in Boston had classified him 4-F, a rebuff – presumably on grounds of poor eyesight or of a medical history of epilepsy and psychiatric treatment – which harassed both of them as a possible impediment to their marriage. Berryman's declaration that he would be married as an atheist was a matter of personal hurt for Eileen. Her grand-uncle, Charles Tully, arranged for them to be married in St Patrick's Cathedral, but the expense of the service and music amounting to 35 dollars seemed almost prohibitive when Eileen left her job with Kodak at the end of September. For two weeks she took a clerical job at 50 cents an hour. Jean Webster relieved one of their headaches by making arrangements to provide the reception at her home on East 52nd Street. 'Do you waltz?' Eileen asked her fiancé, apprehensive for him about the grandness of the gathering.

In the final weeks before the wedding Berryman was tormented by doubts. He purported that the sacrament of marriage seemed a 'farce' which made him impatient and angry, and formulated all his misgivings on 5 September:

> I wonder whether this wedding will come off. I am afraid on some point or other, or on none, we will quarrel to the bone, and kick away – I desire even that we should, and yet I am willing, very willing, to marry, however we marry even thus; perhaps I will destroy myself if we break. Is it right to go ahead? Do I wrong her in submitting when I abhor to this degree the pretense and vacancy of the ceremony? How much *can* it mean to her? What means most? *Is* she a Christian? Ah the empty sky, how it tricks men. There is not a shred of reason for believing Anything or Anyone is there. Have I any real patience with the belief that there is? Little! little! And how much joy do I get from my knowledge? O exactly none, yet in marrying her I expose her to the desolate chance that she will lose that hope of hers which comforts men. Is anything worse? And can I live with *anyone* for long, be with them always, be responsible, bc open? But can I live alone? SO FAR, NOT WELL. Can she? What grief will it be to her if we break? Have I unfitted her for life with anyone else? I cannot answer any of these questions. I have the wit to ask them, and I am tormented by a mind which knows that they cannot be answered. Or you, Spirit, sitting in the empty sky, Master of lies and hatred and sorrow and death, Your faithful daughter Eileen Mulligan, Your *good* daughter who believes in You. Bring her happiness and peace, Who have tortured and destroyed since the beginning of time the best of men and the worst of men and all men, according to Your Will, I defy You.

Despite the fact that his accustomed self-pity tended to reduce even genuine feeling to rhetoric, it must be seen that the state of mind expressed here really hurt him. A little later, on 11 October, he reckoned up another inauspicious factor, the meagreness of his income and resources. Since 1937, for example, he had earned only 300 dollars from his poetry, and only scant critical attention for it.

Robert Giroux was to be best man at the wedding, but he could not get leave from his naval posting at Norfolk, Virginia. Instead,

Mark Van Doren stood up with Berryman, and dealt admirably with the proceedings. On the day itself, Berryman felt 'terror' at the long waiting, and noted that Eileen looked 'frightened and faint under the veil'; then, 'The simultaneous casualness and concentration, transfiguration, indifference and fright, unity with her and last desperate solitude.' On her side, Eileen was afraid that Berryman might faint, and took his arm to steady him at the altar. The clarity of their responses surprised her; the dignity of the occasion calmed them both. 'God was not there,' Berryman noted. 'I watched for Him.'

They spent the wedding-night at the Murray Hill Hotel, and returned to his flat in Boston the next day. Eileen's photograph appeared in the *New York Herald Tribune*. Berryman felt a 'strange double sense, in her being here, of our being together, of transience and permanence.' Within a few weeks he wrote a memorial poem 'For His Marriage':

> Lilies of the valley
> And the face of the priest.
> The pushing eyes
> Upon my back of guest and guest.
> Music, and crush of fear
> I never felt before.
>
> . . . .
>
> Resist, resist, pressed Heart,
> In the breast be still.
> If you can still and stay
> Perhaps I will
> Until comes lover to my side
> The terrifying Bride.

Their first days together were spent in quiet and seclusion, 'talking about all the numberless violent calm remarkable familiar absorbing things we talk about always.' He felt 'very tired, very happy – I am, I am, I hope she is.' Berryman felt suddenly so exhausted one day soon after their marriage that he almost collapsed. Eileen failed to understand the incident – 'Why so nervous?' – which deeply disturbed her. Berryman hid his own dread of a recurrence of *petit mal*. 'This October,' he wrote at the end of the month, 'I think was the most racking month of my life. Inexpressibly painful . . . has been my inability even to try to conceal from Rusty my state . . . I am afraid it has upset her badly, as I am afraid she has grave reason for uneasiness.' The sense he always retained of himself as *maudit* led him to reflect by association on doomed figures like Peter Warlock, Hart Crane, Nijinsky, Bix Beiderbecke, and his friend Bhain Campbell – 'as a group or in some combination, linked, desperate, brilliant, a dying movement'. Since peace of mind never created high art, he felt, one alternative was to dramatise a self-image of suffering. He told Eileen the plangent tale of his unsuccessful bid for the Hopwood Award during his term at Wayne State University.

Eileen presently took a job as an endorsement clerk in the Home Office legal department of Liberty Mutual Insurance Company, at a wage of 22 dollars a week. Although Eileen's day was long and dull, Berryman took care of the household chores, and they were able to entertain company – his remarkable students Anthony Clark, Frederick Boyden, and Claude Fredericks, or his colleagues Eddie Weismiller and Mark Schorer and their wives. Berryman's health remained unsteady, and he spent at least one day of November in a state of illness and apathy. Such days, which occurred periodically in the following weeks and months, induced his most grave bouts of self-pity.

Delmore Schwartz remained Berryman's best companion. In December Berryman helped him read the page-proofs of his new poem, *Genesis*. 'You are the greatest writer on sex in modern times,' he told him. 'It's the strength of non-participation,' Schwartz quipped in reply.

Schwartz gave a great deal of praise to Berryman's own poems, particularly the line, 'We must travel in the direction of our fear,' in which, he felt, 'every reading discovers more. . . . It takes the largest view.' Later they spoke again about Berryman's refusal to grub for jobs, an attitude which Schwartz both respected and deplored because 'at the bottom of it all,' he told Berryman, 'if you'll forgive me, is your demonic pride.' Berryman himself never forgot the imputation, which he liked to regard as complimentary.

At Christmas Eileen spent a few days in New York. Berryman resolved to keep himself busy, but he could scarcely quell his fretfulness. As always, his self-searching habit of mind led him to make New Year resolutions:

> To keep my temper, and to preserve an even manner; to feign self-possession if I can't achieve it.
> Not to exaggerate unless my irony is perfectly clear. To keep my opinions to myself.
> To try to bring my humility and my arrogance together. Is a more regular current of feeling *impossible*?
> To be a better husband altogether.
> And a better friend: to allow, to have faith, to answer letters, to be kind.

To keep the Journal and to make it continually more useful to me.
To learn to know Christ.

With the New Year, the balance of his friendship with Delmore
Schwartz shifted: Schwartz entered a depressive and paranoid phase
of mind which led him to estrange himself from his closest friends,
including Dwight Macdonald and William Barrett. Berryman
feared for a while that Schwartz's depression might lead to suicide.
Yet, in view of the vulnerability of both their jobs at Harvard, he
shared much of the misery. Eileen's gentle sympathy, when she
heard of their despondency, left Berryman weeping. Schwartz's
periods of depression and exaltation put such a strain on both his
professional and private life that, within a few weeks, he and
Gertrude separated. The spectacle of Schwartz's apathy and alienation was reflected in Berryman's tendency to dwell dourly on the
stresses of his own personal life, and on the frustrations of his work
at Harvard.

Berryman found himself unable to talk about his work. He was
made uneasy by his own silence, his preference for not publishing
anything, and what he pretended to be his induration to obscurity.
He felt that his neuroses and conversational difficulties ran deep,
despite Eileen's aid. He worried obsessively about his falling hair
and consulted a clinic. He also lived in fear of being unemployed
before many months were out. He was gratified, however, when
Theodore Spencer asked him to give one of the select Morris Gray
Poetry Readings; pressed by Eileen and by Delmore Schwartz, he
accepted. In mid-February, buoyed up by that recognition of his
talent, he conceived a cycle of poems that was to become *The
Nervous Songs*. Nervous and restless in himself, he found that his
body itched, and his stomach throbbed, from thought and frustration. Racked by the difficulties of his idea, he spoke out angrily to
Eileen about what he called 'my frenzied desire to get away, to be
alone, to sink into myself and into the Songs. I never felt so helpless,
so wild, bound to the insufferable University and this stifling
apartment.' Berating Eileen – sometimes outspokenly, sometimes
tacitly – for complicating and confusing his life with domesticity
and responsibility, and for distracting him from the writing of
poetry, he did not realise that he was using her as a scapegoat for his
own emotional and creative consternations. He continued to persuade himself that real life was secondary to art, since, as he
expressed it, 'what day of mere living presents so rich & complicated an experience' as the life of literature? That such a priority
might be mistaken was a possibility that certainly troubled him,
but, having relied for so long on the supreme value of poetic

utterance, he dared not confess it. Although he solved the immediate problems of *The Nervous Songs*, part of his mind stayed restless at being bound and restricted by his marriage. In fact, as he well knew, he placed immense faith in Eileen's love and support. Even when most tranquil and content, however, his journal suggests scruples:

> R[usty] called in from the kitchen, 'Put down in your Journal that I love you.' She is my dear little Broom and I put down that I love her too. In four months of marriage, under galling conditions of debt & work & war, she says we have done very well together & I think we have. How I lived unmarried I hardly know – except that now I have written that, suddenly, in a corner of my brain, I know very well.

From staff meetings, neither he nor Delmore Schwartz gained any satisfaction about the future of their jobs. Instead, Berryman learned, Theodore Morrison was entitled to use his discretion in reappointing staff. In any case, if retained, his teaching would be considerably increased, to perhaps as much as forty-eight weeks a year. When he gave Eileen the news, they went out to dinner in a state of 'savage gloom': 'Rusty sad & tired, . . . with such grace. . . . Bless her.'

There is no doubt that Berryman loved Eileen deeply. He was happy when she spoke out in company, but hurt if ever she deprecated herself or her seriousness and piety. He was sensible of her fears for his health and peace of mind. In spite of being loving and solicitous for Eileen's well-being, and enjoying their many good times together, Berryman brooded always as much about himself. He worried the claims of poetry over marriage, and could not find them compatible. Insecure and over-anxious by nature, there was probably no state of affairs in life which he would not have found exacting and perilous. If such a state seemed about to prevail, his impulse was to exasperate it, to engineer self-disruptive situations or ideas. This diary-entry, from 22 April, is typical of his recurrent frame of mind:

> Solitude? Is it necessary for Me . . .

> What sort of conscience could I have in asking Rusty to be separated from me for weeks, or longer, *on the chance . . . ?*

> When Rusty tells me that she is happy with me, as she does very often, I feel more guilt than pleasure: I wish she were so much *more* happy. But that she is at all works my heart.

Her expressions. She is twenty women.

Her view of me: tadpole (in bath), Broom, my cat-yawning,
Mr. Broom, our heights together, my thinness, my
sitting-down-to-think-it-over-and-have-a-cigarette, as a boy,
as an old man.

I wonder if, in spite of all, I have been happier ever than I am
now, have been this year. What the hell is 'happy'?

When he at last learned that he was not to be reappointed at
Harvard, Berryman felt resentful towards Theodore Morrison. In
May he suffered another blow when Frank Morley, of Harcourt,
Brace & Company, rejected a book of poems that Delmore
Schwartz had urged him to submit. There was no alternative but to
enter the job market in earnest; he went to New York in June to try
every possible opening, and stayed with Eileen's sister at 511 East
82nd Street. Eileen followed after a few days and managed to obtain
a temporary job. Berryman himself went to work briefly for the
Publishers Service Company, where he had to help write an
encyclopedia.

By mid-July he had applied to more than fifty schools and
colleges as well as to the State Department in Washington, and had
no success in placing himself. Eileen was unwell, and Berryman
grew increasingly nervous and irritable. On 11 July he placed a
desperate advertisement in the *New York Times*:

POET, 28, married, 4F, educated here and abroad, critic,
editor, an experienced and competent university instructor,
would like to continue living and writing if possible.

The sardonic tone fetched no response.

They moved next to take temporary occupation of a Bronx
apartment, 272 East 163rd Street, which belonged to Eileen's aunt.
From there, Berryman pestered James Agee at *Time* magazine; but
Agee, a friend of Delmore Schwartz's, was elusive, and Berryman
was able to locate him only after several days' telephoning. At
length Agee agreed to talk to his supervisor about him. Meanwhile,
Berryman joined the junior sales staff of the *Encyclopaedia Britannica*. For several hours each day he tramped the streets of New York's
East Side without reward; he felt hopeless and degraded, and
resigned the job after a week.

When he declared to Eileen that he hated life, she argued that
people who do so should not get married.

Aggrieved, after eight weeks of job-hunting in New York, exhausted, and terrified, Berryman took stock of their hopeless situation. Undernourished, he was sleeping very badly and suffering from indigestion, and the burning and itching of his scalp depressed him. It horrified him that going bald should seem so 'irrecoverable & defacing'. He also feared another onset of what he called 'my special malady' – *petit mal* – as a result of 'nervous fatigue & laceration, weakness & impatience & irritability.' He alternated between feelings of listlessness and rage:

> Hysteria flows in me like blood at such times – frantic *rejection* of anyone present, of the world. This is precisely & horribly the Dog-feeling which I had first in the summer of 1938 and 408 East 115th: hiding in closets & snarling. . . .
>
> Central in this – morbid or not – is *the sense of guilt*: that I cannot make money, that I cannot write, that I cannot care for Eileen's health or prevent her unhappiness. These three, and my indescribably horrible conviction that she does not believe in my illness – thinks I could control it if I would, or even thinks, as Allen Tate did, as Mother has, that I *stimulated it*, – are the greatest sources of my guilt-sense. But it seizes me as undifferentiated terror, inadequacy, weakness. I grovel. And it is partly this feeling, and partly by blind resentment and bitterness against Fate, Humanity – which can find no proper object – that produces the self-destroying hysterical rage which a hundred times I have conquered and twice I didn't but slapped and beat myself. This would have brought me irresistibly to suicide long ago if I had not my absolute promise to Eileen to keep. It never will.

It may have been, as he himself tended to recognise, that many of his ills were psychosomatic, the physical manifestations of a hysterical disposition. What rightly worried him beyond his symptoms, however, was the very fact that he reacted so acutely and painfully to bad luck. Poetry, he declared, had been the strongest passion of his life; now, he felt indifferent towards it, his imagination balked. For the summer weeks of 1943 his constant feeling was one of unreality and shame, a state of mind highly coloured, it should be seen, by the nature of the assaults made on his temperament and pride. The act of selling himself injured and nauseated him, just as his stint of selling encyclopedias left him feeling 'remorse, self-hatred, *contempt*, execration'. In was during July and August 1943 also that he first considered taking refuge from life in drunkenness, at a time when (until 1947) he was in general abstemious:

Liquor might have helped me – and might have helped us both in New York. Drinking, I can even talk, I think. But liquor is one of the things which most painfully we have not money to buy. . . . The necessity, at such times, of some drug, I have only come to see this summer. . . . Our isolation, our *exhaustion*, dictate the forms. Everything is temporary, nothing has weight or substance or love – time must be got *through*.

On 6 August, he was granted an interview with Whittaker Chambers of *Time* magazine. Among other questions, Chambers irrelevantly asked if he had ever blown up a bridge. At the end, Berryman was sent away to write a review – to test his merit in *Time*-style. Four days later, Chambers criticised Berryman's piece heavily, and promptly dismissed him. He said that he would keep him 'definitely in mind, when an opening occurs – and they occur all the time.' Berryman volunteered to write another review, and left the office. Sick at heart, he went back and protested that he had a right to know more before continuing to work for nothing. Chambers quite agreed; Berryman had no further dealings with *Time* until 1968, when he was commissioned to write a poem about the Apollo spacecraft. At that time, Berryman sat in front of his television and wrote an 18-line poem, 'Apollo 8', in *Dream Song* style. Although *Time* paid him several hundred dollars, the poem was not printed. (Nevertheless, Berryman invariably read *Time* week by week – in something of a vengeful spirit.)

August dragged on and other applications, including those to the CBS and the Guggenheim Foundation, bore no fruit. Towards the end of the month they returned to Boston to pack up the apartment in Grove Street. Before departing, they again saw Delmore Schwartz, who poured forth a self-absorbed account of his academic woes. Berryman felt so desolate, hot, and exhausted during the journey back to New York that, after the walk across town, he wept on arrival at his sister-in-law's apartment.

Early in September, during a visit to his brother at Brattleboro in Vermont, Berryman was appointed to a job at the Iona School, New Rochelle. For a salary of 2,400 dollars, he was to teach English and Latin six hours every day. For three days before his work began on 13 September, he studied Latin for twelve hours at a stretch, and departed for New Rochelle as though he were preparing himself for death. The job seems to have been as taxing as Berryman had anticipated; after three weeks he resigned, complaining that he had been the victim of 'inhuman conditions. They have two-thirds wrecked my health; now the school must find another goat. Please do not speak to anyone of my having taught there,' he told his

mother, 'or in such a place. It has been grotesque, horrible, from
start to end, – the end, Laus Deo, soon, this week.' During his time
at the school, he recorded these remarks:

> Little has happened save terror.
>   *The first week*:
>   dead mad work – papers & preparations & rush, hatred of
>   my two hundred students – incredulity – rage against the
>   stupid fools I sit at luncheon with . . . sleeplessness –
>   despair. . . .
>   *The second week*:
>   much the same:–
>   all accord lost under the ferocious strains of my work. . . .

What saved him from despair was a letter, dated 7 October 1943,
from Richard Blackmur, advising him that Princeton University
was about to offer him a four-month appointment as instructor. He
would teach some Army or Navy courses; the novel; nineteenth-
century poetry; a combined composition, literature, and public
speaking course for engineers; or, as Blackmur put it bluffly, 'some
other damned course of which I forget the name.' It was back in
mid-June that Blackmur had first shown Berryman's dossier to
Gordon Hall Gerould, the head of English at Princeton; now he was
delighted at the prospect of working with Berryman, whom he had
first met in 1936, and encouraged him to accept the appointment.
Under his present circumstances, Berryman needed little persuading, in spite of the fact that he was to be engaged only on a
term-to-term basis at a salary of 225 dollars a month. The appointment was timely, for, in addition to the rent still owed on his
apartment in Boston, he was still indebted to Columbia for student
loans amounting to nearly 500 dollars. Early in October he had
borrowed a large sum from Gertrude Schwartz.

Within a week, Blackmur had found Berryman a small apartment at 36 Vandeventer Avenue. The Berrymans gaily celebrated
their first wedding anniversary in anticipation of better prospects
and peace of mind. When Berryman started teaching at Princeton,
he wrote with renewed hope on 5 November: 'Not only have I
got to live (how far away the notion of suicide seems now, & two
weeks ago I would have died gladly – rushing) but I have got to
move & work in life.' But, at the age of twenty-nine, he had found life
to be bitter and adverse, and within another week, on 11 November, he resumed what was by now his customarily morose self-
appraisal.

Thinking of the terrible night – tonight two weeks ago, my last
in New York – when she walked in the wet wind along the river
& I followed her. She said that night again *how little she wanted* to
make her happy, & how she wanted mainly to *do someone good* &
had felt always that she could do *me* good – & that satisfied her –
but how she did not know . . . she knows with what intensity
& ultimateness I need her. But that night SHOOK me with the
force of the summer concentrated. . . Is she doomed only to
stand & watch? She has seen me grow bitter & hopeless. . . .
She knows that I have lost self-confidence, but even she does
not know how utterly. When she speaks of my hopes, of my
being or becoming a 'great man', I wince and want to hide.
When she speaks of me as a writer, I feel a fraud, I want to cry
out. . . . For I want her to be happy! . . .

That such things are possible! . . .

Can she be happy, or happier, with someone else?

Could I bear her leaving? . . .

True that I must do my work . . . alone, but to *be* alone. I lost
B[eatrice], I lost Bhain, if I lost her I would never try again.
Could I work at all? Could I love? *Would* I?

Quoi faire? 1939!

Yes I would try to live. But what would be the motive of
kindness, of control, what would be the object of love? . . .
even the nervous *paralysis* to which I have been subject, except
for intervals, all my life, & from which I have suffered especially
this year. *Most* of it is *fear*. I am afraid that I will meet someone
to whom I must talk.

I fear even the mails. . . . I hope for nothing good. I hope – as in
meeting people, in conversation – only not to disgrace myself or
to be disgraced, only not to be abused or exposed, only not to
offend (to have offended, in letters) anyone. This is true fear.

8

Princeton and the pains of scholarship, 1943-46

Lying within short range of Manhattan Island in New York, Princeton provided a peaceful, genteel, small-town life (still with whiffs of a curiously southern decadence), centred on the dignified and scholarly ambience of the university itself. In spite of the precariously brief start to his career there, Princeton was to become Berryman's home for the next decade. His circle of friends expanded markedly during that time. After his initial period of teaching, he undertook a stretch of independent research in Shakespearean textual criticism which lasted for two-and-a-half years, before he was again appointed to the teaching faculty. During that intervening stint of full-time study, he succumbed to phases of guilt, insecurity, and self-exaction. For three years already – at Harvard University from 1940 until 1943 – he had suffered a more oppressive and bitching intellectual climate, from much of which (unlike his colleague Delmore Schwartz) he had shielded himself – only to indulge in increasingly morbid and paralysing habits of self-appraisal. Subsequently, at Princeton, long hours of isolated study drew him more and more into patterns of brooding. His tolerance for setbacks both personal and professional became lower than ever before. By the time he returned to teaching in 1946, he had assumed something of a second nature, a guise in which to outface what he felt to be the frightful demands of his work and society. His public role became one which many of his acquaintances took to be eccentric, a combination of the braggart, the womaniser, the unpredictable drinker, and the formidable – often savagely assertive or dismissive – intellectual. His endearing or intimidating behaviour was often just the superficial aspect of a temperament given over almost entirely to feelings of acute insecurity and self-recrimination. As years passed, Berryman began to hide his fears in drink, but it is surprising that his gross experience of frustration and shame did not give rise to even more frequent nervous crises. Berryman's diaries from the 1940s give all too little evidence of happy times with his wife, more of a man stricken by neurosis and self-analysis, but paradoxically sustaining himself by a programme of greater self-demand. In time, his outrageous, drunken antics became legion; but whatever the show, beneath it Berryman found himself hateful, unworthy, pitiable.

In November 1943, as he began teaching at Princeton, Berryman felt a renewed sense of purpose. Although cautioning himself against intensity and too much self-expectation – '*Don't take things too much at the top*' – he derived curious satisfaction from the weeks of summer horror passed: 'I have the authority of suffering; – extraordinary suffering I think.' According to his journal, Eileen chaffed him on one occasion, 'You talk like a damned school-teacher!' Berryman tried to allay disaffection by outbursts of pre-ceptual thinking, such as this from 16 November:

> *Walden!* Is it not possible that this whole intolerable summer & experience of despair was given me as a penitence – a *good* – to clear my soul: immured at Harvard for years in sloth & possessions & selfishness? Yes! to teach me my despair, force me to work & wonder, hunger, doubt – force me to keep from being crushed. I have not done it well, but I have come through. Perhaps I can learn to live independently not in the sense I did – in a new sense – to work – to love. To be *content* with little; rich & various in mind & in work done. To be free.

His efforts at self-persuasion were often hysterical. Although tense in himself, however, he reported an absence of strain in returning to teaching,

> My work is heavy and unrewarding, but it is so pleasant to live, simply, that I have no thought of complaint. The boys, all soldiers and Marines, are agreeable, unspeakably ignorant and overworked. The programme is confused and I am afraid not very intelligent; a hodgepodge of the liberal and the technical from which they learn almost nothing. Still they do what they can, and everyone indeed blunders forward, tired and hopeful.

His social contacts increased by many times; among his new acquaintances were Erich Kahler, the historian, and his friend

Herman Broch who then lived in his house at work on the epic novel, *The Death of Virgil*; Carlos Baker (later biographer of Ernest Hemingway); Cy Black, an historian whom he found 'polished' and 'wonderful'; and the wise, beneficent dean, Christian Gauss, a man equally at home with football and with Byron, whom Berryman supported in liberal ideals such as his antipathy to the notion of a separable department of English literature. Berryman frequented the Parnassus Bookshop, where he associated with the proprietors, Keene and Anne Fleck, and their distinguished patrons. Anne Fleck recalls that 'Once he said to me in the bookshop that when he was in certain groups he would deliberately do most of the talking because he was bored with others' conversation. I sensed a type of "secrecy" about him and a certain "pain".' When Erich Kahler began to hold gatherings at 1 Evelyn Place for conversation among prestigious guests from both the arts and the sciences, Berryman was naturally included. Anne Fleck was impressed by 'the enthusiastic unpretentiousness of the group . . . the humility of great men. I always supposed that is why these men were admired by John Berryman. He seemed to be able to cover up a deep humility by certain outward trimmings.' That was true, but it was also true that Berryman often felt inferior and ill-informed, lacking in aplomb and presence of mind; 'I was silent as usual,' he wrote after one of his first encounters with certain eminent figures, 'the age of these men presses on me.' What passed for reserve or humility in early days often masked an acute sense of inferiority and chronic nervousness, later fronted by arrogance and bombast.

It was also in Princeton, in 1944, that Berryman first met Robert Lowell, who remembered the 'casual intensity, the almost intimate mumble of a don':

> From the first, John was humorous, learned, thrustingly vehement in liking . . . more adolescent than boyish. He and I preferred critics who were writers to critics who were not writers. We hated literary discussions animated by jealousy and pushed by caution. John's own criticism, mostly spoken, had a poetry. Hyperenthusiasms made him a hot friend, and could also make him wearing to friends – one of his dearest, Delmore Schwartz, used to say no one had John's loyalty, but you liked him to live in another city ['For John Berryman', the *New York Review of Books*, 6 April 1972].

Above all, Berryman admired his mentor Richard Blackmur, whom he styled

your Educated Person, – more perfectly so than anybody I ever
saw, one man [Mark Van Doren] excepted. His intelligence and
moderation and wisdom, displayed endlessly in charming and
spacious conversation, have astonished me every day since I
came here.

Edmund Keeley, who was for a time Blackmur's assistant and close
personal friend (later translator of Seferis and Cavafy), remembers a
complicated genius:

[Blackmur] was without doubt a kind of genius, almost totally
self-educated (he didn't earn even a high-school diploma), a
brilliant talker who managed to express himself in casual
circumstances much as he does in his published essays. . . .
Though an essentially kind man, he always pressed his listeners
to think beyond their normal means and to match the quality of
his own discourse. Few could achieve this; but John Berryman
was among the very few who apparently did, and Blackmur
therefore regarded him as among his most stimulating
intellectual companions. He once told me that he considered
Berryman the best critic of Shakespeare in American letters, and
it dismayed him that Berryman never received what Blackmur
thought he ought to receive, in recognition and professional
opportunity, from American academic circles. He also
considered Berryman an entertaining eccentric, though what
amused Blackmur set others on edge sometimes (for example,
Berryman's excessive drinking, his megalomania, his relentless
pursuit of women, married or not). Blackmur also recognized
Berryman's potential in poetry at a very early stage.

Frederick Buechner remembers that Berryman showed great respect and affection for Blackmur, 'whom he always called Richard,
never Dick. Blackmur seemed much older, quieter, more guarded,
sounder, with his clear blue eyes and wispy little moustache. Blackmur seemed an old gull drying his wise wings in the sun, Berryman
a sandpiper skittering along the edge of the tide.'
   Although he found the Princeton ethos and society invigorating,
Berryman's sense of inadequacy persisted. He very much needed to
contain the excesses of his temperament, and determined in his
New Year resolutions:

To endure patiently.
To desire what is good – to fix my thought there.
Without indulging myself, to try to be *sincere*: to be more

naturally & continuously myself – not to defer, not to
conform, no 'thanks' & 'sorry'.
To fulfil duties (as, books to review, letters, university work) *at
once*.
To keep my End – my work – always in full view.
To be a better husband.

His wish to be more sincere stemmed from a feeling of falsehood,
which he determined to check by behaving more naturally – as true
to his own nature. Yet it was his nature to feel blistered by outrage
and neglect, the very feelings which he needed to take in his stride.
    Early in January 1944, his brother, Robert Jefferson, was em-
ployed to write a column called 'Milestones' for *Time* magazine.
Berryman felt immediately happy at the news, but later depressed
at the limited prospects offered by his own future. As the month
drew on, he became obsessed with what he regarded as his failure as
a poet, and his nervousness intensified. When Eileen delighted in
James Agee's *Let Us Now Praise Famous Men*, Berryman reflected
that he felt hopelessly fraudulent as a writer by the standard
conjured up by Agee. Desperation led him to suffer more bouts of
insomnia, and then nightmares in which he dreamed that Eileen
produced 'from my right side & chest a monster'. At the end of
February 1944, his appointment at Princeton ended, the cue to a
more intense phase of despondency at unemployment. 'Each year,'
he wrote,

> I hope that next year will find me dead, and so far I have been
> disappointed, but I do not lose that hope, which is almost my
> only one. I despair, placed as I am, of making anyone very
> happy, my own griefs are deep, ineradicable, and my hope of
> writing something of value, while it has not vanished,
> dwindles. In the lake of the heart, storm, the fragments of the
> houses of my youth.

He became so accustomed to self-pity that the fatalism of such
statements took on a disinterested air, as if spoken of a third person.
It was characteristic of his attitude that he should have espoused the
poetry of Aragon, especially in *Le Crève-Coeur*, where a bitter
sentimentality and personal defeatism vis-à-vis the War in Europe
harmonised with Berryman's own sense of affairs. Many of the
poems that Berryman was to write for a while – later included in
The Dispossessed (1948) – followed Aragon's example and tone. He
tended to see the conflicts of his own soul mirrored in the European
holocaust.

In December 1943, Eileen had taken a job in the economics section of the League of Nations, at the Institute for Advanced Study in Princeton, a position which earned her just over 140 dollars a month Although her income was small, Eileen's employment probably intensified Berryman's guilt at idleness, and he falsely accused her of neglecting him.

Reckoning up his prospects – which included writing fiction, and applications to the Rockefeller Foundation, and to the Guggenheim Foundation (in which he placed most hope) – Berryman felt his depression worsen. Exhaustion and headache incapacitated him from work, he alleged. Dwelling on his illness, he could not resist associating himself with other epileptics such as Dostoievsky, St Paul, Flaubert, Handel, and Molière, and derived perverse satisfaction from the reflection that genius was a condition of atypical persons. 'I do not want to become involved,' he told his mother on 6 March, 'to the exclusion of something firstrate, in anything secondary.'

The cramped, gloomy apartment on the first floor of 120 Prospect Avenue, some quiet tree-lined blocks from the main university buildings, Berryman found frustrated his work. Soon he was able to borrow Helen Blackmur's studio high on the other side of what he called the 'foolish building where we live'. This change of working environment instantly lifted his spirits as he sat down amid her paintings, with paper and a yellow pencil at a green table, 'and wrote a crude lyric at once in my excitement over the light & colour & height & air & solitude. Poetry there only.' For days in mid-March, Berryman was tormented by waiting for the Guggenheim announcement. In the afternoon of 20 March, two letters arrived for him. The one, a registered envelope, he snatched open eagerly, only to find it a letter from Columbia University pressing for repayment of student debts; the other, from the Guggenheim Foundation, informed him of failure. 'Stupor for hours,' he wrote, 'I did not come out of it that night.' After a few days, Lewis Jones, President of Bennington College (whom Berryman had consulted at great length), told him that a position might be open in August. If Berryman found that news consoling, he did not betray it; guilt-feelings again beset him for his failure. He spoke bitterly to Eileen once more, for which shame succeeded sorrow. So intense was his guilt, he felt for a while that his only hope of recovering himself was to write a book about it. It is not at all surprising that, on 1 May, Berryman's former student Frederick Boyden should have dubbed him 'a completely despairing human being if ever I saw one'. By way of respite from his self-engrossed study, Berryman went to New York a number of times during March and April, but he found his visits to his brother's family, or to his sister-in-law's, confusing and constricting.

The situation was retrieved when the Rockefeller Foundation, referred by Douglas Southall Freeman to Berryman's review of W. W. Greg's *The Editorial Problem in Shakespeare: A Survey of the Foundations of the Text* ('Shakespeare's Text', in the *Nation*, 21 August 1943, p. 218), took keen stock of his proposals to undertake Shakespearean textual study. After a preliminary exchange of letters and further inquiries, he was interviewed by David H. Stevens, director of the Rockefeller Foundation, and John Marshall, associate director. Berryman recorded that he felt 'throughout an imposter [*sic*] & a beggar, – unwilling frantic commitment – lying about health. Every nerve leaping.' In the meantime, he was invited by Mrs Ordway Tead to give three weeks' lectures on contemporary literature at Briarcliff Junior College, near New York.

Early in May he was posted good news by the Rockefeller Foundation, which awarded him 'a Foundation research fellowship for study at Princeton, Folger, Widener, and New York Public Libraries, for a period not to exceed twelve months, beginning approximately June 1, 1944.' The fellowship carried a remuneration of 200 dollars a month, with an additional 200 dollars for travel and other expenses: 'No great sum of money – less than half, indeed,' Berryman told Mark Van Doren, 'what my brother receives for his sufferings at *Time* – but enough for us who are used to nothing. . . . Being numb I felt little, but Eileen after an hour of shock was like a bird singing.'

The fellowship did little to alter the self-consuming pattern of Berryman's days. He became upset with his falling hair to the point of pathology; a year later, he spent two months visiting Philadelphia for scalp treatment. At night he endured nightmares which contained all his 'symbols of horror' – including 'houselessness . . . academic life . . . the government, having my library & papers always inaccessible, uncertainty, exposure, restraint, dependence.' He identified his malaise with Baudelaire's, who had suffered like areas of gloom, depression, silence, and apathy, an extent of misery which was, Berryman felt, strikingly reproduced in his own:

> in debts & oppressive awareness of hopeless obligation, in
> poverty & homelessness, in his father's death, his mother's
> failure to understand, alienation from his brother, in violent
> temper & razor sensibility to disgrace, in passion for privacy, in
> avoidance of talk of what he did, in procrastination alternating
> with furious absorption, in his hero-worship . . . (mine:

Aragon, Kierkegaard, Picasso, Mozart), in the shocks of his conversation, in his fear of madness, in his contempt & savage self-contempt which is brother to mine.

In consequence, on 11 June, he wrote a verse-quatrain addressed to Baudelaire:

> Brother of silences, vacancy & anguish,
> Incapable & pure, proud, – every crime is new,
> Tosses & humiliation fresh, –
> Turn, turn to me: I recognize you!

Ironically, although he suffered no less than abject misery from his temperamental indisposition, Berryman gratified himself by such associations with literary genius, and found a perverse refuge from pain in this type of supercilious utterance: 'I am always the victim of indiscretion & malice: WHY? Because I am fitted to suffer more acutely thus than others.' His outlook had radically changed from that of his late adolescence at Columbia, for example, when he had dismissed subtlety and compromise in favour of the one truth of every relation. Dogmatic, impatient with hesitation and ignorance, he had read Plato's *Dialogues* with the professor he described as 'that tepid rodent Edman' without realising that he was himself a Platonist. For the young Berryman, everything seemed ranged and eternal, with immortality near at hand; now he felt that knowledge and experience were contingent and flawed.

In mid-June, the Berrymans moved to another apartment (M–1) in the same building. Although the accommodation was slightly larger, Berryman was depressed at their lack of privacy, since people on the lawn outside seemed to be almost in the living room. In spite of the fact that he no longer maintained direct contact with teaching colleagues, social life was sustained, with many joyful dinner-parties and picnics, and canoeing outings with Richard Blackmur.

Berryman failed to maintain system and consistency in his working life. All sorts of pressures and influences disturbed his well-being. Though obsessed with his own psychology, he constantly apprised himself of developments in Europe – of the fall of Rome; the invasion of France; the Russian northern drive; the British counteraction to German V-bombs; and the plot against Hitler – all of which took place during June and July. 'The suffocation of the War one realises only as it is intermitted,' he noted, 'in great incredulous joy as bulletins come over the radio punctuating the tedious nomination of Roosevelt.' Quite often, however, he worked passionately, and made gradual headway with his study of the Quartos for an edition of *King Lear*, and with verse-composition and stories – most notably at least two gruelling weeks on 'The Lovers', a story which John Crowe Ransom at *Kenyon Review* considered 'brilliant'. Eileen was 'overjoyed' at that news; Berryman, as he himself recorded, 'all but ill in reaction to uncertainty; could not work.'

In August the Berrymans spent two weeks with a friend on Cape Cod, where they saw Dwight and Nancy Macdonald, Paul Goodman, Polly Boyden, and Edmund Wilson, who seemed 'grander' than he had been at an earlier encounter; his wife, Mary, more glamorous. One evening they met Hart Crane's closest friend, Slater Brown (who was also the 'B' of e. e. cummings's *The Enormous Room*), a charming man who described bicycling with cummings from Nice to Rome in 1922. 'The hills are full of writers & radicals, to Eileen's delight,' Berryman told his mother. On return to Princeton, he realised that the vacation had changed his perspective:

> The whole experience in short stood as Anti-Princeton in 50 ways, & I feel it in frightful depression after hours with Cy Black & the Persons today.
> – Academic, suburban, parasitic.
> Eileen is depressed also. Did we do right in determining to live here this year?

He returned to his studies, but not without wishing for release from what he called 'pedant-reading', for a return to the life of the imagination. As the weeks advanced, he did indeed work again at stories and poems, most notably 'Canto Eileen', a poem in terza rima (later published as 'Canto Amor') which he finished only the next year. Other work included a poem temporarily called 'Rock-Study and Wanderer', as well as extensive reading – in Homer, Dante, the Elizabethans, Shakespeare, aesthetics, Jefferson, James, Adams, the New Testament, Golding's Ovid, Montaigne, Eliot's criticism, and Villon. For all his industriousness, however, he considered himself only a dilettante and wastrel:

> Extreme gloom. The end of my 30th year. I may do something hereafter, or later something something [*sic*] already done may show as worth while, – but it does not appear so. My talent lost, like my hair, sex crumbling like my scalp. Disappointment & horror. And the collapse of will: self-distrust, contempt, sloth, & paralysis. Everything begun . . . everything abandoned. Every day I wish to die.

In spite of all his misgivings, his professional work made good progress; he wrote a number of reviews for the *New York Times* in the early part of 1945, and an omnibus review on Henry James for *Sewanee Review*. In March, he was gratified when Robert Penn Warren asked him to record his poetry for the Library of Congress.

By VE Day, 8 May 1945, Berryman had made such substantial progress with his work on *King Lear* that he completed the text and commentary in a first form. 'The whole air of the world feels a little changed. *Hope a little.*' On 11 May, after submitting his 'Report on Progress' to the Rockefeller Foundation, his fellowship was renewed for another year. Shortly before, Bard College, at Annandale-on-Hudson, had asked him to join their staff for the next academic year, but the fellowship seemed the more propitious option. At the same time, Richard Blackmur mentioned that the Hodder Fellowship, an award administered by Princeton University itself, would certainly have been offered to him if his Rockefeller fellowship had not been renewed; Berryman found the news a gratifying statement of faith in his solitary strivings.

He reckoned up his and Eileen's expenses, and decided that they could manage. Although still enduring periods of anxiety and frustration with his creative work, his general improvement in circumstances and confidence is best summarised in a diary-entry dating from 1 June 1945: 'For another whole year I can see our having a place and way to live. Eileen will have a child we hope and will stop working in six months from now. We love each other.'

He received another boost to his morale in June. In a letter congratulating Mark Van Doren for undertaking to write a volume on Hawthorne for the *American Men of Letters* series published by Holt and Company, he expressed casual interest in Stephen Crane, whom he had read the year before. Van Doren recommended his interest to the publishers, in consequence of which Margaret Marshall presently offered the Crane volume to Berryman. He enthusiastically accepted, proposing a completion date of 1 June 1947, but postponed drawing an advance on royalties until 1946.

Another piece of writing successfully accomplished in 1945 was 'The Imaginary Jew', an autobiographical story based on an incident that occurred in Union Square, New York, in 1941, when Berryman – mistaken for a Jew – had been accosted by an Irishman. (He first tried a version in verse, but the tale fell more naturally into prose.) He even returned to the scene to refresh his memory before writing.

Eileen underwent an emergency appendectomy during the summer; while she convalesced, Berryman doggedly did the housework. As in 1944, they took their summer vacation on Cape Cod. While in Truro, they heard of the dropping of the atomic bomb on Japan, and Berryman immediately wrote an editorial for *Politics*, at Dwight Macdonald's suggestion.

> We suggest that no clear responsibility can ever be determined in any individual or group either for this atrocious action or for the use which will be made hereafter of U-235 to exterminate populations and cultures. We think this guilt is general. . . .
>
> We do not dream of a world in which atomic fission will produce benefits for the mass of men and women working for a few men and women under existing systems of economy. The new energy is political, rather, as a gun is political. The new energy, like the existing energies, will be at the service of the powers which possess and control; it will change their strength but not their aims. Until their aims have been forcibly changed, or until they have been dispossessed by the people, the people should regard the owners' new weapon with the interest of victims.
>
> We stare with interest and fear upon the terror which in our name has been wrought.

On return to Princeton, Berryman discovered not only that John Crowe Ransom had accepted 'The Imaginary Jew' for publication but also that the story had won the *Kenyon Review* – Doubleday Doran first prize of 500 dollars. Later in the year, Erich Kahler paid him the compliment of translating the story for *Die Neue Rundschau*.

The one disappointment of the time was that Harcourt, Brace & Co. again rejected a volume of poems he had called *A Point of Age*. But his work on *King Lear* thrived in the span from 1945 into the new year. In one week of March 1946 alone, for example, he collated 24 copies of the First Folio in Washington.

Charles Bell remembers Berryman well from this period.

> I went to Princeton towards the end of the war, doing electronics research in Palmer Lab; but my main aim, pursued in off hours of making temperature tests on telemetering equipment, was a Renaissance and Promethean one, to comprehend and write about the cultural history of the West, introducing the study with a new organic philosophy, closing it with a fictional presentation of our own times, its tensions and currents; and finally expressing the whole – refined and extracted – in a series of poems converging ultimately towards a

Lucretian epic. I met John Berryman early, I guess at the
Parnassus Bookshop. . . . He was delighted to find anyone in
physics with such a mad project – especially delighted when I
presented the philosophical and cultural side of my work in a
paper to the English Department. For I had moved into the
English Department as soon as the war was over . . . and saw
quite a bit of John Berryman.

In August, Berryman recommended Bell to the Rockefeller Foundation, in consequence of which Bell was awarded a fellowship to
travel to Europe the following year. Berryman had remarked of
him,

> I am not sure that I have known anyone whose ability promised
> more for the integration, educational and philosophical, of the
> areas of thought. During a Rhodes Scholarship, and since, he
> appears quietly to have picked up enough exact and ranging
> knowledge of half a dozen arts and sciences and philosophy to
> suffice most specialists. . . . He bristles with ideas.

Nevertheless, when he came to a fuller understanding of Bell's
poetic ambitions, Berryman's enthusiasm cooled markedly. 'When
I made the mistake,' Bell recalls,

> of showing him some of my poetry, which was moving (rather
> feebly) in a different direction than anything he wished to write,
> I think he got upset. He wrote me anyway a sharp letter . . .
> saying that nothing was more miserable than to go through life
> writing sloppy poetry and that I should give it up. I have never
> been able to take his advice. . . . But of course, he was a
> difficult man for a long-term relationship and I was probably
> incapable of sustaining a friendship that he maybe could have
> used. His ironic power was considerable. . . . He was a strange
> man, when he wasn't himself in a literary or personal or other
> hostility he could certainly be generous and always a moving
> friend. I guess the trouble really between us was that there was a
> literary feud going on, perhaps it came to a focus most once in
> his house, when he was revising a poem for a magazine and he
> asked me to try to choose between two revisions, and I told him
> I didn't think anything of either one of them, and I didn't even
> like the poem. In fact, his early poems, I found precious and
> unnecessarily so.

In March 1946 – a time when, anticipating the expiry of his fellowship, Berryman would otherwise have begun to worry frantically about his future – a succession of job-opportunities fell his way. The Women's College of Greensboro, North Carolina, notified him of an opening among their staff. After a few days, he visited the college, and was either unimpressed or made a bad impression; in either case, the writer Peter Taylor got the job. Later, in April, the University of Rochester offered him a position as instructor, but Allen Tate had in the meantime brought up a more compelling offer – the editorship of the *Sewanee Review*, at a salary of 4,100 dollars – which Berryman discussed with Dr Alexander Guerry, the Vice-Chancellor of the University of the South at Sewanee. Although he found the idea of being editor attractive, he did not relish what he considered the notion of being exiled in Tennessee. After a short delay for consideration, he was saved more worry by a timely offer from Princeton itself; without hesitation, he accepted the appointment as associate in creative writing, at a salary of 3,750 dollars for the academic year 1946–7. 'Gauss pushed the President to the Invitation, of course,' Berryman wrote, 'Princeton of itself wouldn't touch me, for I haven't concealed my opinion of the English department.'

A summer trip to stay with Richard and Helen Blackmur at their summer home in Harrington, Maine, proved more taxing than restful, for Blackmur was in an inhospitable mood. The Berrymans escaped by walking for hours by the sea, observing rocks that seemed folded and torn, a dead porcupine, a sea-urchin, and clams. When they returned to the house, tension persisted, and they presently left the Blackmurs and took refuge with their friend Nela Walcott at her house in Blue Hill. After a pleasantly sociable visit, they moved again to stay with Robert Lowell and his wife, Jean Stafford, at Damariscotta Mills, Maine.

'Too many guests had accepted,' Robert Lowell remembered. 'We were inept and uncouth at getting the most out of the country; we didn't own or drive a car. This gloomed and needled the guests. John was ease and light. We gossiped on the rocks of the millpond, baked things in shells on the sand, and drank, as was the appetite of our age, much less than now.' Their talks were literary, catholic, allusive, covering Browning, Arnold, Hopkins, Tennyson, Swift, Dunbar, Henryson, Alun Lewis, Chatterton, Chaucer, Gray, and the poets in Newman's *Apologia*. 'John could quote with vibrance to all lengths, even prose, even late Shakespeare, to show me what could be done with disrupted and mended syntax. This was the start of his real style.' Jean Stafford spoke about Yaddo, the writers' colony, and about Carson McCullers. Lowell described his five months in prison as a conscientious objector, and the texts – *The Cloud of Unknowing* and Sheed-Ward's *Catholic Evidence* (a book Berryman found very exciting) – used at his evening classes. Berryman wrote of Lowell at the time, 'I haven't found anyone so pleasant since Delmore in 1939,' and Lowell fully reciprocated his affection, writing on 19 August, 'As for your heart, we intend to hold on to it through the formless future.'

In September 1946 Berryman took up his new teaching post, occupying two rooms with Blackmur on the third floor of Pyne Hall, a half-timber building. A coffee-shop called the Balt was usefully located just a few doors along Nassau Street, the main thoroughfare of Princeton. One of Berryman's students, the novelist Frederick Buechner, remembers him vividly.

> He was slender, pale, dark-haired and rather brittle-looking. He had a chiseled, ascetic face and carried his head slightly to one side. When he walked, he gave the impression of coming at you sideways. He spoke very intently and quite rapidly, picking his way with unusual care between words and pausing from time to time to find the particular one he wanted. His voice I can still hear. It was on the high side, faintly nasal, and had something of the quality of string on a tightly tied package when you pluck it. In both the manner and the matter of what he said, he struck me always as profoundly considerate and courteous. He was of course very intellectual, very witty, but at the same time a very attentive and responsive listener. In general he seemed above all things donnish. . . . When the weather was cool, he wore an enormously long striped scarf wound around his neck and often read a book as he walked, apparently oblivious of everything else. I remember somebody saying nobody ever *looked* so much a poet.

Berryman gave a distinct impression of frailty, to such an extent that a number of students even suspected that he had homosexual tendencies, perhaps in inverse proportion to the urgency of his later involvements with women. Sidney Monas (later Professor of Slavic Languages at the University of Texas), who had just then started teaching as Blackmur's assistant, observes that Berryman's 'involvement with men was often of a very high intensity.'

First encounters with Berryman proved to be memorable; Monas's was no exception. He was an awkward, enormously impressionable young man, as intensely interested in politics as in literature. On meeting Berryman at one of the Kahlers' gatherings, he betrayed his slightly Stalinist tendencies.

John demolished me in one of those fierce assaults of his that nobody could withstand, even if they were better informed and much closer to 'truth' than I was in those days. I was mortally offended by him; crushed. I tried to avoid him. I told Blackmur I wanted nothing to do with this man Berryman, and did not welcome his presence in the Creative Writing program. Then one night, quite late, and altogether unexpectedly, John came through a drizzling rain to my dorm-room, knocked at the door and asked if he could come in. I was startled. He came in and said he had read a poem of mine in the Nassau Lit, and that he had liked it. So we started to talk about poetry, not politics. He went through my bookshelves, took down some volumes and started to read. Then he asked me to read. Then we talked some more about poetry. And then it was dawn, and he left, and I was quite won over.

All of his new friends soon discovered how much Berryman liked to talk. Often enough – if not apparently abstracted, abrupt, rude, or aggressive – he would stand and talk for hours in the street. 'Several times he told me, the day after such a talk,' Monas recalls,

'Marvelous conversation we had. Fantastic.' Although it hadn't been a conversation at all – I had merely interjected an occasional question or a very brief observation. But of course he had certainly *engaged* me, and my attention was somehow necessary to him.

It was not until 1947 that Berryman started to drink heavily; when he returned to teaching in 1946, however, it was not so much lack of control as nervous intensity that he displayed. His students were confronted with no less than an anthology of foibles. The more percipient among them construed his quirks and oddities as humane; most of them found him sympathetic and encouraging towards their work.

Berryman was far too sensitive to bear himself in a state of oblivious eccentricity. Prone to bouts of self-pity and paranoia, he anticipated opposition by being dominant and hieratic. He was well aware that he might at any moment succumb to appearing inferior, foolish and outwitted. But understanding and intelligence alone would not quiet his sense of being temperamentally infirm.

Over the years he had smarted excessively at the indifference accorded his talents. He nurtured a conviction of his own special-ness, which he sometimes held to be genius, but, more often than not, the world failed to recognise his uniqueness, with the consequ-

ence that he stigmatised himself – with a certain uncanny gratification – as both abused and psychotic. A portion of his failure and
distress, however, was quite obviously self-appointed; when he
directed some of his poems to T. S. Eliot's attention, for example,
he wrote a letter, dated 1 December 1946 (possibly, in the event,
unposted), which was couched in terms almost calculated to be
self-defeating:

> I can't suggest this precisely with enthusiasm, but if Faber were
> willing to take on my verse I should be glad. Not wanting to
> trouble you with reading a whole book, I send ten poems, the
> earliest first, running from 1939 to 1944; if none of them
> interests you their companions unsent probably wouldn't
> either. I am completely out of sympathy myself with the style
> of all but the last two, so I shouldn't blame you. They have
> readers however and are perhaps worth publishing.

Such a letter, laconic to the point of indifference, anticipated a
dismissive response; in that sense, Berryman's failure was partly
self-made, fuelling his sense of grievance. He lived the paradox
that, while self-pity was nourished by public indifference, his
defiance of public opinion was fed by self-pity, a condition of mind
which went through chronic phases.

Berryman sensed that many of his students held him in much less
esteem than they did Blackmur, to whom they felt personally
devoted. They were also better used to Allen Tate's more elegant
and courtly southern manners. After a while, in consequence,
Berryman seemed rather to resent Blackmur, or at least to modify
his previously unconditional affection and respect. According to
William Arrowsmith, the tension between them was probably
exacerbated by the students' obvious regard for Blackmur. (But, far
from being in any way contemptuous of Berryman, the students
were always respectful of his bright, aggressive manner and of his
learning.) Gerald Bentley, who was Berryman's near-neighbour
for some years, recalls:

> John constantly attacked Blackmur in social groups when we
> were together, but I think there was genuine respect and
> affection between them . . . Blackmur was very tolerant of
> personal abuse and looked at John's ideas and understood his
> acute sensitivity and was bothered little by his bad manners.

Berryman was in fact absolutely loyal to his friends; the one
unpardonable sin that they could commit was to lower their
professional standards.

As time went on, Berryman drew closer to his students, who included the poets W. S. Merwin and Bruce Berlind, and devised a set of nicknames for them: Sidney Monas he styled 'Peter Willing', Bruce Berlind, a man of pallid complexion who wrote lyrical poetry, 'Leopardi Pale', and William Arrowsmith, 'Wiley Rock'. On arriving at Berryman's apartment, they would usually hear the strains of Mozart's *Don Giovanni* playing on the phonograph as they waited interminably for someone to answer the door. It was evident to many of them that Berryman – particularly in 1947 and later years – thought of himself as an American Don Juan. He took the ending of *Don Giovanni* very seriously, and would play it over and over again. The composer Edward Cone recalls one day when Berryman reconstructed 'what would happen to all of us on Judgement Day, and how we would all be hurled into Hell as non-believers. "So it was true all along, and we never believed it!" we'll all be crying, as we go hurtling into the abyss.'

Berryman's students learned equally vivid lessons from his patience and criticism, even from his scorn. He had an astounding memory for poetry, which he could command at great length. He was always worrying references, William Arrowsmith remembers, and grew particularly vexed, for example, at finding no trace of nightingales in Aeschylus' *Agamemnon*, from where he knew that T. S. Eliot must have derived his reference to them in 'Sweeney Among the Nightingales'. (It was only later that Eliot confessed that he was referring to the nightingale chorus in Sophocles' *Oedipus at Colonnus*, with which he had confused Aeschylus' *Agamemnon*.) On another occasion, he asserted to Cone (a bird-watcher) that Frost's 'Oven-Bird' must be some kind of woodpecker. Cone explained the fact that an oven-bird was a kind of warbler that sings late in summer, after most other birds have stopped, but Berryman remained convinced that he was right.

In his apartment, Berryman had accumulated an extensive library, including complete sets of Shakespeare, endless editions of *King Lear*, as well as Marlowe, Chapman, Massinger, Beaumont and Fletcher, Jonson, and much other Elizabethan and Jacobean drama. Students learned that his grand passion was to produce the greatest textual edition of *King Lear*, and the finest commentary. He would boast openly that he knew more about English Renaissance drama than anybody else at Princeton, and repeatedly mentioned his meeting with Thomas Marc Parrott, the retired authority on Shakespeare, at which Parrott had said, 'Berryman, you and I are the only people at Princeton who know how to read. You always have the book I'm looking for.' It became evident to William Arrowsmith that Berryman found his own poetry considerably less interesting at the time than the promise of his brilliant future as a scholar. Few students knew of his extensive correspondence with W. W. Greg, who had a very high regard for his views on textual criticism. In July 1946, for example, Greg had written a letter to the editor of the *Review of English Studies* indicating that 'A recent exchange of views with Mr. John Berryman, of Princeton, N.J., who is at work on a critical edition of *King Lear*, has convinced me that at least some of the ideas on the staging of the play that I put forth in *R.E.S.* in July, 1940, (XVI. 300–03) need modifying.'

Berryman told Frederick Buechner that

> he was preparing to write a book in which, through some kind
> of new analysis of *images*, he planned to solve once and for all
> not only the authorship of the doubtful plays but also, Heaven
> only knows how, the identity of Mr. W.H., the Dark Lady and
> so on. He also told me an anecdote that he said he'd heard from
> someone who had actually been present at an exhumation of
> Shakespeare's grave. The grave was opened, the coffin found,
> and on the coffin there was a brass plate bearing the name of
> Michael Drayton, which was so unsettling to everybody's
> theory that the grave was immediately filled in again and no
> more was said about it.

At night Berryman, often troubled by insomnia, would accomplish serious and steady work on Shakespeare in his small study in the basement of the old Princeton Library (long since demolished). 'The library was locked,' Sidney Monas recalls, 'but he used to let himself into the basement window through a grate, and climb out the same way. . . . Sometimes he would come from there to my room on campus, and we would talk. Sometimes I would come by the library, at one or two a.m., talk "down" to him, and if he were in the mood, we'd go for a walk together.'

From October 1946 through the winter months of 1947, Berryman confined the expense of his nervous energies to teaching and its social extensions. All of his students found him stimulating, and very demanding. In addition to extended hours of intellectual conversation, he would play tennis with them, and parties would be organised to drive to the Jersey shore for outings on the beach. 'John needed excitement,' Monas remembers. 'We went several times to carnivals in Trenton. Eileen would worry while John would ride the loop-the-loops and the most violent "rides". It would excite him. He obviously would remain excited for some time. His eyes would dilate and his wit would speed up and he would talk even more.' Even when Berryman played chess from time to time with

Gerald Bentley, it stimulated both of them so much that neither was able to sleep afterwards.

Those students and other friends closest to him discerned the psychological pressure and pain under which he laboured, a restlessness of the spirit coupled with a deep despair of himself. 'Some of us at Princeton,' Bruce Berlind recalls, 'half-seriously referred to him as Prometheus.' His success as a teacher was conspicuous, his personal magnetism tremendous – the type of charisma which, as Bruce Berlind points out, moved an entire group:

> Friendship with John inevitably meant discipleship. It's not merely that he was older by ten or a dozen years, or that he was brilliant and a marvelous talker, or that he was publishing his poems in the 'best' places. It wasn't even that we especially admired the poetry he was publishing then – those gnarled, impenetrable, postured, pieces that are the latest in *The Dispossessed*. In part it was his monumental arrogance, which continuously asserted his superiority even when there was no question of competition. In part it was his insufferable childishness – he cd sulk, he cd rant, he cd make all manner of extravagant emotional demands, with the result that one found oneself feeling curiously protective. And it was all terribly infectious – or so I found. (There was a period when I talked like John, when I walked like him, when I imitated his style.) The point is, I suppose, that he struck some of us . . . in something of the same way that Byron must have struck his contemporaries: as the walking archetype of the brilliant, erratic, guilt-laden poet. Beneath all the posturing, he was somehow the real thing.

His achievement and promise as a writer were beginning to be more widely recognised. In December Jacques Chambrun, Inc. (W. Somerset Maugham's literary agent) offered to handle his work in the magazine field; the next year, Oxford University Press requested a verse manuscript from him (yet rejected his submission after two months); at Robert Lowell's suggestion, Paul Engle sounded out Berryman for a post at the University of Iowa; and from England, Cyril Connolly asked to reprint 'The Imaginary Jew' in *Horizon*. But Berryman was better used to rejection than to reward for merit. What he took to be public contempt for his gifts tallied better with his habit of self-chastisement.

In the spring of 1947 he found another form of outlet for his personal frustrations.

9

Art and adultery,
1947

BERRYMAN'S SONNETS

The year 1947 was one of painful self-encounter for Berryman.
During February and March he fell in love with Lise, a twenty-
seven-year-old friend who kept house with her husband and young
child not far from the Berrymans themselves in Princeton, New
Jersey. The affair was soon consummated, and there followed a
summer of fleeting ecstasy and relentless remorse. Since he found
his adultery all-consuming and destructive, the type of self-
assessment that Berryman began in the months of 1947 did not
resolve his self-doubts and punitive habits of mind. He felt appalled
that his psychic exploration led him into a labyrinth from which no
exit seemed charted. By way of compensation he absorbed himself
in the problem of consciousness and creativity, the first fruits of his
search taking the form of a sequence of sonnets and of an exhaustive
journal which ran to hundreds of pages by the end of 1947 alone.

    The journal is a serious and rewarding *journal intime*. Although
sometimes repetitious and extravagant in expression, it functions as
a serial autobiography of developing coherence and depth. For
Berryman, life yielded to an aesthetic structure under the pressure
of situations and his developing version of those situations. From
1947 onwards, his journals partake more of the purposes of *Selbst-
besinnung*, the search for inner reality. The scope and effect of
Berryman's diary may be compared to that of Anaïs Nin, who was
obliged (as Robert A. Fothergill has observed) 'to recompose
experience into dreams of her own dreaming, a mythopoeic function. From its cost in psychic energy and its failure to do more than
avert the realization of her anxieties, she herself recognizes the diary
as a neurotic solution to the problem of living' (*Private Chronicles: A*

Study of Diaries, Oxford University Press, 1974). Berryman's diary is similarly a neurotic manifestation, to which, as early as 1947, the poems he was writing acted as the mythopoeic counterpart.

What must be borne in mind in reading Berryman's private words – not only from 1947 and the later years of his marriage with Eileen, but also from the earlier periods – is his deep and terrible need to stress mostly torment and crisis, the dark parts of his consciousness. Circumstances combined with predilection to convince him that he was morally ugly, and selfish and grossly hurtful as well as hurt, when in fact the day-to-day affairs of his life with Eileen flowed with a great deal of gaiety, a sharing of jokes, parties, outings, and good friends. To the everyday pleasantness of his life Berryman gives incredibly short shrift in his journals. Always too ready to believe himself sinful, numerous pages of the journal are dedicated to anatomising his own mind, to scorning his temperament and the probable effects of his bad behaviour. What he does not on the whole record are the innumerable joys of life, periods of genuine care and intimacy with his wife, and the truth that his close friends loved his vivacious and stimulating company. Not the least, he makes hardly a mention of the facts that he shared all his writings with Eileen (apart from the sonnets written during 1947), that she always encouraged his work and sustained his morale with her own happy disposition, and that she found every reason – even until 1953 – to trust to their love and togetherness, in the manifold evidence of his kindness and overt, if complex, ways of caring for her.

Berryman's sonnets sprang from a fevered experience, and were often written without pause for reflection or analysis. They dealt with the experience even as it occurred and gave aesthetic shape – a gradually emerging thematic structure – to a series of events in themselves apparently undirected. While the journal describes and discovers suffering, the poems actualise a tormenting experience as myth, as art.

For a month and more after meeting Lise he guarded his illicit hopes, but busied himself with unfulfilled plans for a new literary magazine. By mid-April, while resentful of the distractions of teaching, he turned back to writing, and wrote a first draft of a story, 'Vain Surmise' – later published as 'Wash Far Away' (*The Freedom of the Poet*) – partly to include a 'Horrid forecast if I should stay teaching'. Therefore, he concluded in notes for the story, 'NO MORE' [teaching]. By the end of the month he completed 'The Long Home', a poem he had earlier despaired of finishing, and at the same time wrote his first sonnet of the year, confessing that his extra-marital interest had been welling: 'I wished, all the mild days of middle March / This special year, your blond good-nature might / (Lady) admit . . . / Me to your story.' Earlier, the Berrymans had accompanied Lise and her husband, together with William and Jean Arrowsmith, to the seaside for a day; at another time he encountered Lise at a Mozart concert. All these occasions are linked in Sonnet 16 (written on 12 June) which also recalls one day when Berryman cycled out to visit Lise's home. He was wholly charmed by the house, its sycamore tree, dogwood, honeysuckle, and an evening of playing Schubert's *Songs*, especially *Der Wegweiser*, on the gramophone. Another day, Lise stopped him on Nassau Street. They talked, drank some Martinis, and went back to Lise's house for dinner. Berryman bedded down on the couch, and Lise drove him home to 120 Prospect Apartments only the next day.

'Eileen talked violently about my drinking now and during the past year,' he recorded in his diary. 'I said I'd no intention of becoming a drunkard; which is true.'

While he tried to keep an air of insouciance in his bearing, his secret thoughts were boiling. Between 5 May and 17 May, he wrote an impassioned letter running to many pages, groping for an understanding of Lise and of his own feelings. It is evident from this letter that he was suffering a sudden *bouleversement* of feelings, for he scarcely knew Lise herself and was confused to find his passion outrunning an affair that had barely begun. His tone, as these extracts illustrate, was panicky and melodramatic:

Is it possible – *possible* – that we first kissed just ten days ago, on Saturday afternoon late? . . . I feel as if weeks had passed, and every minute still I wait for you. It's like a prolonged delirium, darling. . . . O my God, how little we know each other. I know you love milk, and Scotch as I do (and you're more unbridled, and this may be important), and read detective novels, not obsessively – and I am damned if I know much more about you. How much do you value money? What do you (Lise I love you!) think of as important? Who were you unfaithful with, when? Tell me darling, *all* you remember of yourself, O please – I feel suddenly, but irrevocably, as if I'd invited a half-stranger to pretend to cut my head off. You're a hedonist with a conscience about falling on people (except on *me*), and that's all I know. And of me what do you know? . . . Do you puzzle me ever, as I do you?

I've written a new poem for you, darling – I hope you may hear it – and I hope I may keep my senses a little, which you drive off like a wind – but I doubt it, and Lise I really don't care, if you will kiss me and say some time to me 'Darling' as if I

wholly mattered to you . . . O Lise, do I?
   . . . I really *don't know, can't,* whether you love me, or what at
all you feel for me besides liking and desire . . . *some,* a certain
liking, some desire. When we've been alone – mostly just in the
car at first . . . I felt you completely warm and absorbed in my
love for you – and then, all the time else, distant a million miles,
uncaring that I suffer, not wanting or needing me.

He desperately needed to win her for himself alone; intensity of
desire undercut his well-being, leaving him very vulnerable and
frightened. The letter contains a mixture of seductiveness and
self-pity. He could not help but betray the priority of passion over
the more moderate inducement of reaching mutual understanding:
he felt he would 'go mad', he declared to her, unless he could

fuck you until we're happy . . . and then begin to speak slowly
of what we are. And speech would be hard in the beginning,
because still I'd want to interrupt myself. . . . But finally we
would talk – though past our making love that seems so far
away and gentle that *driven* as I am I hardly can imagine it – and
I would learn you. This is what I want most, and next to it I
want you to learn me. Think whether it's not hard that I can't
give you my poems and stories – all this that I never care
whether anyone reads or not – to read and know *something* of
me.

On Saturday, 17 May, after drinking with Lise the evening
before, Berryman wrote, 'O we move, Lise, down levels of understanding into each other.' The sentence conjoined his disingenuous
desire for more intense sexual activity and the secondary wish to
gain deeper understanding of each other. 'It is all inevitable, but
nothing in it is easy, loving another separate all-distinct human
being until the separateness and the distinctions dissolve, and we
can be together. But I love you meanwhile as deeply as I can, or as
hard Lise as I must, and I kiss your mouth with my love.'
   One day Robert Giroux called Berryman from New York to ask
him to meet T. S. Eliot (whom Berryman now esteemed more
highly than in 1936). Berryman caught the train nervously, but
spoke freely with Eliot about literary matters, about *Little Gidding*
and *East Coker,* about the lectures that Eliot was soon to deliver in
Princeton, and about Eliot's once seeing Sarah Bernhardt. They
also spoke about Robert Lowell, who had just won a Pulitzer Prize
for *Lord Weary's Castle.* 'I like his stuff,' Eliot said, 'it's got the real
punch.'

Berryman summarised his impressions of Eliot in his diary: '"Handsome", deliberate, gracious, *honest*. Attentive, but not really to persons.'

> The poet hunched so, whom the worlds admire,
> Rising as I came in; greeted me mildly,
> Folded again, and our discourse was easy,
> While he hid in his skin taut as a wire,
> Considerate as grace . . .   [Sonnet 5].

Despite being rapt in the honour of Eliot's company, Berryman could not suppress thoughts of Lise – 'Flooding blurred Eliot's words sometimes' – and concluded that day's letter to her,

> Saturday evening: 9.30. I am on the train returning to Princeton, where you are. I have been drinking tea with Eliot and then drinking Scotch with Lowell and now reading Keyes, at the insignificant line
>
>   They cannot break our trees or waste our dreams
>
> I had suddenly a full image of you, darling, Lise, in relation to me: and knew that nothing can prevent or destroy our love. O my dear.

Berryman was irritated at the 'obsessive' lionisation that greeted Eliot when he came to Princeton but impressed with his lectures, they gave him 'confidence again in the possibility of ease and judgment'. Eliot's second lecture he considered 'perhaps the best discussion of poetic diction I ever heard *or* read.'

On 23 May, Berryman completed the year's teaching; he felt himself a writer again. Two days later, after dinner, Lise arrived at their apartment from a cocktail party and talked – to Berryman's ears, 'magnificently' – for an hour and a half. Sonnet 19 records the evening,

> You sailed in sky-high, with your speech askew
> But marvellous, and talked like mad for hours,
> Slamming and blessing; you transported us,
> I'd never heard you talk so, and I knew . . .
> Humbler and more proud . . . you . . .
>   . . . suddenly, late then, as
> Your best 'burnt offering' took me back with you.

It was on this day that Berryman could no longer contain his clandestine thoughts, and began to set them down in his diary:

> I can't any longer keep out of this journal, which I hope no one ever sees, the fact that I have been in love with her for a month, after resisting my emotion for weeks before that. I love Eileen still in some way, am fond of her, want greatly her happiness, but I am hopelessly in love with Lise and do not know if I shall ever cease to be. I went out with her afterwards home, as a 'burnt offering' to her husband who was angry at her wild lateness . . . we stopped in the lane on the way, and I got back all the sense of her after this horrible week . . . rum and music there, and then she drove me in.

Berryman remembered that her husband had sometime told him, 'Remorse does not suit you at all',

> Rightly; but what he ragged, and might forgive,
> I shook for, lawless, empty, without rights   [Sonnet 19].

That evening, in fact, Berryman and Lise had slept together.

He and Lise established a number of trysting-places, sometimes at his office, 15 Upper Pyne on Nassau Street, at other times in his library study below ground, or else at a country grove not far distant, and at their respective homes when spouses were out. Although Berryman was now neglecting his work almost entirely – he had a long book review to write, and an outstanding contract for a book-length study of Stephen Crane – the affair with Lise was an engrossing consolation. He felt impressed with Lise's steadiness of demeanour, and with her honesty of approach, and yet was he in love with this 'bold, loyal, and strange girl'? He could not give a straight answer, being too aware of their essential unlikeness of character and their continuing state of unknowing about one another. Circumstances permitted them only brief encounters alone, meetings of desire and breathless avowals.

Between times together, Berryman brooded on their status. What emerges from the diary and sonnets is that Berryman early assumed the aspect of spectator of his own drama, and that the practice of writing – although he himself was little aware of it yet – urged a heightening of his inclinations. Written protestations to the diary, and the contorted surrogates of the sonnets, served appetite rather than satisfaction. Even as early as the first days of June, Berryman reviewed his feelings, spoke in terms of 'delirium', of having been 'obsessed', and found his own unsent letter (quoted above) 'absolutely crazy'.

Occasionally Robert Lowell visited Princeton: one memorable day included lunch at Lahière's, an afternoon of play outdoors at Lise's house – where Berryman climbed Lise's sycamore tree and Lowell raced about on the ground 'like a caveman throwing up beercans and shoes', as Berryman noted – and dinner and drinks at the Berrymans'. It was probably the same or a similar occasion that William Arrowsmith recalls:

> Lowell and Berryman, both barefoot, were climbing up the big sycamore tree which shaded the small, stone Revolutionary house. Lowell was perched at the very top of the tree, on the uppermost branches. Just beneath him, trying to get higher, higher than Lowell, was Berryman . . . in retrospect, it seemed a nice image of the intense rivalry between these two poets.

Berryman confided his affair to Lowell, who advised him to 'Lie' and 'Wait six months.' For his part Berryman felt really tormented, and desired a safe hiding-place of which the sycamore tree became symbolic: 'O my God', he wrote, 'I'd like to climb back into the sycamore tree, brace myself at the top and stay until I fell out.'

On 5 June, Lise went with her family for a month's holiday, leaving Berryman 'One note, a daisy, and a photograph' (Sonnet 49) – she was pictured with her eyes lowered, hair bound, lips closed – and the memory of her cycling away in white sweater and blue jeans,

> Between the honeysuckle and the pines, among
> Poison ivy and small flowerless shrubs,
> Across the red-brown needle-bed [Sonnet 11].

and waving at the edge of the wood. The next day he went to Burke's bar (where she had never been), toasted her with beer at six o'clock, just as they had agreed beforehand, and wrote Sonnet 13 even while he drank:

> I lift – lift you five States away your glass,
> Wide of this bar you never graced . . .

During Lise's absence, Berryman played some tennis with Eileen, or with Bruce Berlind and Sidney Monas, and visited New York a number of times (once to re-encounter Delmore Schwartz 'in a hell of a state' after quitting his job at Harvard; occasionally to see his mother). One day, at dinner with Erich Kahler, he met for the first time the painter and photographer Ben Shahn, who was eventually to illustrate the book of *Homage to Mistress Bradstreet*, and enjoyed chatting with him about Cartier-Bresson, Walker Evans, and Stieglitz.

In spite of maintaining an appearance of social equilibrium, Berryman suffered appallingly from his nerves; every time he saw a station wagon, or a head of blonde hair, he thought them Lise's. Driven to write more and more sonnets, he could not speak of them for fear of disclosure. If Eileen were to discover his affair, he considered, 'It would kill her. My God, what am I? What can I do? I *cannot* destroy her by telling her, so I *must* deceive her – a whole life of deception except when I say I love her, as I do – and yet even to say this truth hurts me because it seems a disloyalty to Lise, with whom *I am in love*. All upside down, mad, guilty, and frightening.' In the forefront of his mind was the necessity to 'spare' Eileen's feelings, and to that end he felt obliged to withdraw more and more from her – 'not', as he put it, 'from lack of affection but to avoid the necessity of deception.' He thought himself insane, perhaps even 'hallucinated, self-indulgent, obsessed only?' He could not suppress the knowledge that he and Lise were still spiritually strangers to each other, that she had some 'wild false image' of him, and that the reality of their love was still in doubt. Although his desires seemed self-serving, he belaboured the diary with self-reproaches about the insecurity and privation that Eileen and Lise's husband must have been feeling. Berryman committed to the diary so many thoughts about the dubiousness of his 'love' for Lise that he himself must early have determined the way the scales would tip. He believed that, for the most part, his entries about Eileen were written from compassion, but the diary invariably runs to deeper levels of care. When he speaks of being 'in love' with Lise, for example, he is rarely able to avoid defining the term against his 'love' for Eileen. 'For weeks, for months,' he wrote on 4 July, 'my will has been at the service of my passion and my imagination.'

One Saturday night towards the end of June, he even spoke with Eileen about Lise and her husband. 'She has a personality the size of Princeton,' he heard himself declare, surprised and appalled at his own situation, and wrote afterwards, *à propos* of Lise, '*Not to tell* is the same, exactly, as to give a direct lie to an honour-question – i.e. we have no honour, and *if* we came wholly together – married – . . . we could not trust each other. But we *could* – do – will.' In a first draft of Sonnet 18, he wondered at Lise's 'strange life of mysterious calm / And reckless agitation.' Sonnet 39, which dates from 30 June, he wrote as an exercise in what he called 'foreseeing the end of this: indifference?' His very capacity for such dispassionate fore-sight is surprising. A day or so later, Eileen asked him, 'Broom, when Lise and her husband return, are we still going to be good friends? . . . I'll poison them off if we're not.' Berryman noted his sense of the remark: 'tone plaintive, half-humorous, and *mysterious*: can she have meant only the *drinking*? I didn't dare ask what she meant, yet as I simply reassured her (I wish I *could*), without asking, it was for a moment as if she knew all about Lise and was only, so mildly, asking me to preserve our marriage. My God!'

He was able to look coolly at his affair – in which his behaviour was otherwise obsessive to the point of hysteria – as fuelling artistic productivity. It is true that he often recorded writing sonnets 'helplessly', that many were 'unexpected', that he 'can't stop' writing them, that they 'go on', and that he was surprised to 'find I have eleven sonnets planned', but the inverse sense of his diary-entries about them – as deliberated (almost, indeed, as factitious) – weighs heavily in the balance. As early as 27 May, he began to see them as a sequence, running in tandem with what he otherwise felt to be the ultimate passion and squalid deception of the real affair. After a month of writing, with ten sonnets to hand, he described them significantly as 'culminating morally at the end of iii and poetically at the end of x'. What the evaluation meant was that he could work off some of his guilt by transmuting it into an artistic structure. The lowest point in his personal life could represent a point of ascendancy of illicit love which clearly (by definition) anticipated a nadir in the closing movements of the sonnet-cycle. Almost every day for weeks, he appeared to detach himself from desire in order to consider literary form and style – 'Isn't my ideal of style at present: what will be lucid and elegant, but also surprising, frightening, and various?' There emerges a discreet gap between the writer who appreciates emotion as informative and qualitative – 'surprising, frightening, and various' – and the man who suffers. 'I perfectly face the possibility that I may have to destroy these sonnets after I have stopped writing them,' he related, uncannily assuming objectivity or some quality of emotional distance.

Another feature which illustrates the moral curiousness of his position was that he constantly surveyed famous precursors of his role as adulterer or sonneteer. He saw his own adultery as con-tinuous with an immortal series. In Sonnet 75, he compared himself to Petrarch, in 29 to Balzac, in 21 to David in relation with Bathsheba; Sonnet 16 was suggested by Sidney's second sonnet to Stella. Sonnet 38 alludes to the frescoes executed by Pinturicchio relating the life of the poet Aeneas Sylvius Piccolimini, who was elected to the papacy as Pius II in 1458: 'A vanished poet crowned by the Duke for song.' At worst, then, Berryman's sonnets seem enormously self-engrossed. They reveal just how little Berryman could respond – from want of contact and knowledge, not desire – to Lise herself. More and more he drew on his own imaginative invention and on literary analogues. Much of the obscurity and inscrutability of the sonnets may be attributed, not only to the necessity of subterfuge and deliberate obscurantism, but to the fact that their content and thematic linkage were self-generated, the efflux of a personality working often in a vacuum. Absorption in himself was a necessary hazard of Berryman's isolation from the subject of his attentions; he was obliged to fashion her out of his fantasy.

In another aspect, it was salutary that Berryman should seek detachment from his passion. To formulate and structure sonnets, individually and sequentially, was to compose his feelings. On a moral level, a double standard was operative, since what became copy for the journalist and sonneteer was wormwood for his self-respect. Many sonnets, as he knew, were authentic in impulse but rendered insincere by the devices of artistry. He was also entirely conscious of times when the sonnets tended to become self-perpetuating and to generate issues of their own.

The sonnets were also serving, from an early stage, like Swift's *Journal to Stella* and Sterne's *Journal to Eliza*, as a way of imparting his feelings to Lise. In that sense, they were a form of *homage*, poems *about* as well as just *to* his love. When, on 23 June, he wrote a sonnet 'long ago planned' (Sonnet 30) about an exhilarating day they had all spent in Pennsylvania on 11 May, he recorded: 'tone light, imagery and structure *dead serious* – I must show Lise at least how *this* sonnet works or wishes to work. Lord how many are there now, 28 or 30? . . . if only I could write only wished ones, not distracted by new subjects.' The wish to write only 'planned' sonnets runs throughout the diary of this period, and signifies that he would sooner celebrate actual occasions by means of imaginative re-creation than project and invent a fictitious course of future feelings. He was wary of the expressive mandates of momentary impulses, since, it seemed to him, the instant's excitement laid traps for critical judgment. When the more immediate sonnets impinged, he lamented, '*I have no faith that they are good.*' Sonnet 71, written early in the morning of 17 July as Berryman waited for Lise's arrival in their grove, was a hymn in anticipation of love-making, imaged as a service close to blasphemy (an orgasmic sacrifice, the phrase 'simultaneous dying' prompted by the tenor of Wallace Stevens's poem 'Sunday Morning'); when Lise failed to arrive, he felt that 'all disappeared – my delight in the sonnet, anxiety to show it her, all confidence, all my desire even – and I became dull and strange as I still am.' Similarly, on 2 August, he recorded that 'the *trust* she gave me, of her coming this morning, so far assembled me that in spite of all I wrote the ninetieth sonnet, precisely to our situation, and one of the best.' Such remarks reinforce the view that many of the sonnets were written in direct response to Lise as an individual rather than an archetype. The emotion informing those sonnets was rarely spurious or solipsistic.

Aware that all too many of the sonnets depended on private reference and personal statement, however, he aimed to rewrite more and more as impersonal and representative, general rather than local, to speak to like feelings and circumstances in a potentially wider audience. It is significant that on at least two occasions he referred to the sequence of sonnets – or 'cycle', as he preferred to call it – in terms of a 'book', which answers to Robert Fothergill's observation that 'the commitment of the major diarists is to the *book* that their living nourishes.' But the notion of a 'book' of sonnets presented itself to Berryman more forcibly in proportion as the affair itself broke down, as the positive and compensatory outcome of an increasingly deficient relationship.

On 26 July, anxious about the obtrusiveness of so much private and local subject-matter, he rationalised his position:

> Sidney's [Sidney Monas] strong though tentatively put objection to the Local in the sonnets is very interesting. I told him that most have had to be hurriedly sketched, they've come so rapidly, and also that I intend more and more to generalize. These things are true. But the truth is also that it *is* the *Local* in them that is new, that is characteristic of them, and will I suppose be memorable if ever they are made public. Why did I attempt that exhausted and contemptible art-form the Sonnet Sequence anyway? (Partly events seduced me, so that I was in the thick of it, with a dozen sonnets, before (I think) I much reflected. But partly I had several things in mind. I wanted *one form* . . . in order to record (form, master) what happened. Well, but not an invented form – I wanted a *familiar* form in which to *put* the *new*. Clearly a sonnet sequence. And this gave me also a wonderful to me sense of continuity with lovers dead.

He felt that earlier sonnet sequences failed to create 'the beloved as *individual* – I would – Lise what she is. I must. And every poem would be directly *to her* – not a convention for other matters. At the same time I wanted to deal flatly and *locally* with Modern Life.'

In spite of the plausibility of the rationale, it is not difficult to recognise that Berryman still felt extremely ambivalent about both his sonnets and his audience. At the end of July, for example, he moaned about his 'desperate anxiety' to finish the book, 'though I've no hope now of Her seeing it and very little of living on to revise and re-order it as it should . . . I may burn it when I finish – why let anyone else see it if she won't.' The self-pitying assumption of an audience of one must be weighed against his 'fundamental' feeling of being pleased that 'the revision of and exteriorization-in-copying of the sonnets have worked to rid me at last of the sense of guilt about my work; in two and a half months I have made ninety sonnets – I never worked so hard in my life – to feel guilty for neglecting the *Crane* is fantastic.'

What must be inferred is that Berryman felt recompensed to the point of self-gratification by (to appropriate Anaïs Nin's phrase) 'the distillation, the myth, the poem' of his adultery. It was a shortsighted satisfaction, however, since the diminishing emotional returns of finished poems could not compensate for the longer-term effects of personal remorse. Any measure of acclaim to be anticipated from eventual publication would scarcely be consonant with the lasting depreciations of a private failure. Berryman's attempts during the later months of 1947 to persuade himself of the enduring worth of his sonnets were self-deceiving, advancing the simplistic and psychologically damaging thesis that the rewards of art might cancel out his deep-seated sense of defeat and remorse. The truth is both that the poems were a worthy achievement and that he was consumed with guilt; the pity is that he could not bear both truths to co-exist.

Berryman and Lise were reunited soon after her return on 8 July, when they shared feelings of confusion and foreboding. For his part, Berryman was so nervous and intense that he often trembled noticeably. His erratic behaviour showed so clearly that Eileen once reproached him, 'you behave like a madman when they're around. . . . You're making a damned fool of yourself.' A day or so later, while Eileen tried to encourage him to go away for a rest, Lise declared her passion again. Berryman was elated: 'How bold and loyal she is, and *permanent* – she will love me forever and I Her. We are part of each other now. . . . O my darling.' But the following days brought back doubts. Berryman's response fell into a pattern of which he was hardly aware, being abject and giddy in her company and maudlin when alone. His misgivings were not helped by knowing that he was unable to make any progress with work other than the 'draining fantastic poems', as he called them.

Late in July, Berryman paid a short visit to Sidney Monas's family farm in Pennsylvania, where he drank and ate well and walked the dogs, but his worries, hopes and fears broke out in conversation with Monas (see Sonnet 78, where 'William' is a pseudonym for Sidney). He suffered a nightmare which was poeticised as Sonnet 79. In what he later thought was a bout of indiscretion, he confided to Monas what he knew of his father's death and of his own earlier phase of 'epileptic' illness.

When he next met Lise, she said that her husband would 'never ask me for a promise – but as an honourable woman I must make it, promise not to see you again. Now I won't do this.' She decided, in fact, not to leave her husband and not to stop seeing Berryman. Her statement just exacerbated his sense of agonising insecurity. Page after page of his diary reports wish-fulfilment and self-recrimination sometimes approaching hysteria. He tried to persuade himself and Lise that there was 'a lot of horseshit in the conjugal demonstration', but he became increasingly aware of Eileen's intolerable position:

> I have been so hypnotized by Lise for months that it's as if I were coming to life again out of some fantastic dream. I am still of course hypnotized, but suddenly because of the confidence she gave me yesterday I can see other things also, and I see Eileen. Yesterday she was happier with me than for a long time. But today all my racked resentment at the deception, all my guilt-sense, and all my (I must confess it) *boredom*, returned sharply . . . incommunication and dead acedia . . . unable more to continue this pretence-of-relation-we-don't-have-and-can't-have-again and this kindness more cruel than torture since it deceives her that I *will* come nearer to her again.

The same feelings are the burden of Sonnet 83:

> When neither my fondness nor my pity can
> O no more bend me to [Eileen] with love

'O my dear I am so utterly sorry. Eileen, forgive me,' he noted privately.

The end of July, when these sentiments were written down, actually marked a distinct change in Berryman's approach to his affair. For some time he had seen a good deal of Lise in company, but little in private. From then on he began to turn his agony of resentment as much against Lise as against Eileen. Reading over some of his journal, in fact, he looked upon himself as insane – '*Small wonder*'. He could already admit that infrequent moments of love had brought out the best of his feelings, but also that Lise had left him feeling contemptible, 'exhausted, senseless, hopeless'. He accused Lise of neglecting him, considered her indifferent to the anxiety-states she aroused, and implicitly foresaw the end of their affair.

Putting things into perspective, he would eventually see the long dream of ecstasy poised against the brief day of error, but full wakefulness took a long time to come. The very next day, for example, he recorded in his diary this exchange with Eileen:

> Doing the dishes, *agony*. 'What I don't understand is why we keep up one establishment' and I said not strongly but in despair 'Let's don't' – later 'Its I who have been changed by you – you have your personality intact' – 'You're bored, so you accuse me of being' – 'If you can hold out till the Fall, I'll move out then' – 'We needn't discuss it, but it should relieve part of your burden to know it.' To the lake alone and terrified, trembling.

From then on, Berryman valued his wife's merits more highly. Although he still imagined that he wanted to separate from her, and was forced to lie when she asked about their estrangement (even as to whether he had been unfaithful), he reposed a significant measure of faith in the possibility that their marriage might last.

'Drink and mistakes and debauchery have left me dry,' he wrote on 19 July, 'only work can save me.' Within two days he had written Sonnet 110, and recorded feeling what he called 'suspension of sonnet-pressure'. Although he wanted to write number 111 – 'magical number' – for which he would 'wait, feel, recover', he felt sincerely that the weeks of writing sonnets had reached their period: '*I TRUST THIS ENDS MY OBLIGATION, MY OBSESSION, AND THE SONNETS FOR NOW.*' In the event, one or two further sonnets were written, but otherwise the cycle was substantially completed. Subject to very minor revisions and re-arrangement, the sequence remained in the order of composition. With the addition of five sonnets (107, 112, 113, 114, 115) in 1966, when he was preparing the work for press, the tale – as far as the sonnets would tell it – was finished.

Towards Lise his anger and resentment grew. Until about the end of August his alternations of mood were extreme: he would either expand with joy in her presence or become withdrawn, self-lacerating, reckoning the metaphysics of enslavement and duplicity, ideal and excess. Then distrust set in more resolutely, as well as antagonism towards her apparent heartlessness. 'She must mean to torture me to my death,' he wrote. 'As kind as a tigress, faithful as a whore, the love of an SS woman. . . . "Ring us up when you want to see us . . . any time." She knows I *can't* telephone *don't* want to see "US". Just her whip – and when she'd gone I broke and wept.'

'Mortal gloom and hopelessness! She won't make a move but to grieve me – what *is* she? And against my real, small hope, *I am back on the rack.*' The same day he wrote, in an hour, Sonnet 110, adding this comment to the manuscript: 'I have adjusted my style to her cruelty, or I begin to do. Surprisingly, I *can* write even today.' Berryman's attitude chopped and changed almost daily, as illustrated by the following diary-entries written on successive days. On 28 August, he wanted to 'slap her blind for her hypocrisy', and dubbed her 'Bitch, bitch. Empty-hearted, self-saving, untrustworthy, greedy – all she wants is *ALL for NOTHING*. . . . A blind fool I have been.' The next day he felt an upsurge of confidence in his marriage: 'If we survived these four months, nothing can separate or destroy us. I *put away* despair. . . . In fact I'm wildly happy, I *danced with joy* in the apartment alone this afternoon. . . . I feel incredible peace and confidence.'

On 1 September, he turned back to impugn Lise again for her 'callousness', for failing to see that he felt 'on the most bitter and thin edge of all things, and need help she alone could give me – if *she* could,' and for being what he called a 'cold and cocksure lover-murderer'. Disappointed in his expectations he directed more and more fierce indignation at her. In time he came to regard her as embodying two opposed personalities, and even as early as the start of September he registered – what was later to become for him a strict codification – the disparity between the woman who was warm and responsive to his love-making and the other who seemed heartless and distracted. 'You're losing me,' he noted in the diary, 'to another woman. One with no eyeballs or hair, who never lets go.' 'I ought reasonably,' he had written then, 'to kill myself tonight,' but Lise wrote him a letter which salved his feelings of (in his own words) 'antagonism and lashing and irony'. He admitted to himself that he still loved her. Yet another day, however, and his mood swung again: 'No, I can never see her. Why don't I kill myself? What is it that I wait for?'

The Berrymans spent just over a week (5–15 September) holidaying on Cape Cod, where they saw a good deal of Edmund and Elena Wilson, and of Dwight and Nancy Macdonald. Towards the end of their stay on the Cape, after periods of self-pity and of bitterness towards Eileen, Berryman recorded Eileen's remarks: '"I've been trying to be at least a friend to you . . . am I at all?" . . . "I love you" I said, truly. – *Despair.*'

After returning to Princeton, Berryman's ambivalence towards

Lise remained, but the days and then the weeks brought increasingly a sense of release and self-respect. He visited Lise in what he called
her house of 'joy and torture', and came away knowing that '*I did
not want to die*, I felt already on *my own*, I felt no love or anything but
exhaustion and escape. . . . Hatred of life is not reason enough for
suicide.'

There was no finality at all to Berryman's self-recriminating
thoughts about Lise. Within a few days he began to see a New York
psychiatrist, in order to probe tormented feelings and their neurotic
manifestations. Eileen, he noticed, began to treat him more like a
patient. His view of Lise continued to alternate between absolute
resentment and an understanding of her own vulnerable position.
He had to acknowledge that her marriage and the well-being of her
young son were seriously threatened by a continuing relationship
with him, and that indeed she could not fail to react against his
attitude of distrust and hatred of her. Berryman's own self-
protective response was to regard himself as victim – not only of
adverse circumstances but of a careless and destructive woman – to
the morbid extent of setting his present fate in the context of what
he considered the two tragic victims most influential in his own life,
his father and Bhain Campbell. He saw himself as a man deserted –
and damaged – by those he had loved most dearly. This extract
from an unpublished sonnet written on 20 September refers to the
time when he suffered Campbell's death:

> His visionary eyes,
> Hollow and ill, saw more then . . .
>
> Stricken I stood in Harvard Yard as now,
> Holding the telegram – then I walked on, slow,
> Walked on, and took my inevitable class.
> The first desertion. Now the second comes,
> Her chains fall from me, the delirium's
> Dread heart slackens to zero – I can pass.

He determined that the best refuge was to find consolation in his
writing. 'My desire *is* to write well,' he recorded on 22 September.
'I *do* also want to be happy, and I am lazy, proud, dishonest, I have
seduced, lied, cost agony, betrayed – still I do centrally want to
write well: and when I realised this last night I felt simultaneously a
small glow of self-respect or decent pride and a sense "Why then not
be humble? Why *impose*, if writing is what matters?"' The equivo-
cal story rehearsed in the sonnets was surely an ambiguous cause for
'self-respect or decent pride'. The sonnet-sequence did mark 'the

distillation of so much distress', but his art, as Berryman came to recognise, could not abrogate the responsibility for suffering and the consequent remorse. He had turned an intimate personal experience to good account as verse, but such a recourse in itself gave no sanction to a morally harmful situation. In 1966, when preparing the sequence for publication, Berryman wrote a prefatory sonnet which clearly implied a negative answer to the question posed significantly as a 'fault' in these lines:

THE ORIGINAL FAULT WAS WHETHER WICKEDNESS WAS SOLUBLE IN ART.

AFTERMATH

Towards the close of the summer of 1947, Berryman felt himself emotionally played out. For several weeks he had laboured under his grand infatuation with Lise, being inspired by her to write over a hundred anguished sonnets, often at the rate of several a day, but she had answered to his passion only on a comparatively infrequent number of occasions. For part of the time, she had been on vacation with her husband and child out of the state. All too often, however, she had been unable or even unwilling to meet Berryman for love-making. Berryman himself was working at home much of the time – supposedly on *Stephen Crane*, and on an introduction to Ezra Pound's selected poems to be published by James Laughlin at New Directions. His days burned with frustration, with the substitution of sonnet-writing for sexual satisfaction, and with long bouts of introspection.

By September his resentment of Lise, together with feelings of guilt for neglecting his literary undertakings and for adultery itself, reached the point of crisis, and almost exhausted his reserves of nervous energy. His frantic conduct had exacerbated his marriage; guilty towards Eileen, he had come to begrudge her presence and affection. Many tensions went unspoken; neither he nor Eileen acknowledged an estrangement because at heart they were still in love.

Before he could recover anything like a tolerable state of mind and a workable life-style, he knew that he needed psychiatric help. On 24 September he had a first consultation in New York, and remained in the same psychiatrist's care for some years, even after the agonised passage of his first adultery had given way to other affairs and desperate states of mind.

Firm in the belief that he was a rational human being, Berryman tended to intellectualise his feelings with an intensity that compounded the problems. He never quite believed that his self-conflicts would not yield to understanding alone. As 1947 drew to an end he did recover himself for some regular study and writing, but he also chose significantly to begin a verse play about the eighteenth-century adulteress and murderess Katharine Nairn, to whose behaviour Lise stood in his own life as the symbolic approximation. Through the last three months of 1947 he retrieved a sense of purpose and destiny in his life and work; the year ended at a high point – the lull, as it turned out, before another uncontrollable phase of adulterous involvements.

Berryman disclosed to his psychiatrist many facets of his experience and confusion, including what he envisaged of the future of his affair with Lise, his oblivion of childhood and youth, and what had been diagnosed as his 'epilepsy' first occurring in 1940. He said that Lise and he could not marry, but also that they would not surrender their feelings.

> My oblivion I said I ascribe to two causes: (1) my old belief in
> the perfect separateness of Life & Art, the poet's life being
> negligible & to-be-lost (believed dogmatically for years, though
> no more); (2) A real indifference to my own past life, partly
> because of my habit of looking back on myself as a *hopeless fool*
> at any time prior to the present moment, and partly because I had
> things to forget, notably my father, and my long waste &
> apostasy-from-intellectuality, under the fear of sissyness [at
> South Kent, his preparatory school]. The 'epilepsy' he thinks –
> as E[ileen] does – was hysteroid.

At least at the beginning of his treatment, Berryman failed to mention other neurotic symptoms that he had suffered mostly during the five years of his marriage, including his aversion to opening mail and to answering the door or telephone, and his quarrelsomeness. He also suppressed for a while what he knew to be the autobiographical elements in both of his most accomplished short stories – the 'father-substitute' (and indeed what he called a 'whole experience recovered') in 'The Lovers', and the abysmal sense of guilt in 'The Imaginary Jew'. On 25 September, he added in his Journal, 'Further to describe to S [his psychiatrist]: my intermittent emotional *numbness*; eczemal pain & horror of baldness; pleasure in pimples & blackheads; hatred of women.' The last item derived from his supposition that he felt scorn for women in proportion as he exploited and misused them. When he later wrote the poem 'Homage to Mistress Bradstreet', one line – 'Women serve my turn' – hailed, as he acknowledged, from that conviction.

As his weekly consultations progressed, Berryman began to formalise his neurotic conflicts, and to explore motives – Lise's as well as his own – more drastically than ever before. He undertook extensive reading in the subject of character-analysis, including Freud, Fechner, Reich's *Character-Analysis* and the simple *Are You Considering Psycho-analysis?*, as well as Helene Deutsch on psychological problems peculiar to women. He did not give up sex with Lise, but he was more attentive to third-party views of her. When Gertrude Buckman first met Lise, she remarked, as Berryman noted, that she found her aggressive, self-confident and vigorous: 'and persons who are vigorous are so rare'.

Berryman plotted a strategy of behaviour and work. With regard to the sequence of sonnets written during the summer, he planned that his psychiatrist might submit some of them to magazines on his behalf; to secure anonymity Berryman would take the *nom de plume* 'Alan Fury'. In addition, he applied again for a Guggenheim Fellowship, as Richard Blackmur recommended, in order to write stories. After talking to Blackmur, in fact, Berryman's sense of self-consciousness led him to detail and appraise his reactions. Above all, he felt, he had been extremely nervous, such that his scalp itched excruciatingly for hours, an itching he associated with falling hair and psychological stress. It appalled him that Eileen and Lise could find him attractive. His ill-advised conclusion was to repress his feelings.

> To be curt, formal, & *indifferent* in such intercourse as is
> necessary with all but intimates – imitate Lise's
> self-assurance. . . . With friends, *amuse myself*: don't quarrell
> [*sic*]: nothing serious, in fact, or personal. Talk less, in a softer
> voice, and restrain impatience by *thinking*, frankly, when bored.
> Bury my moods & feelings & opinions altogether in myself.

Yet nor could he bear being responsible for Eileen's misery. 'How can I work,' he asked himself, 'under these tortures of uncontrollable rejection & pain-inflicting every day? when I am forced (to hold her off) to pretend, until I *feel*, a general & absolute depression? . . . We are made wrong. Either love shd not come, or it shd stay. Man the natural bitch. This seems incredible, all. We were the *happiest* pair we knew, the one sure thing. . . . We were *happy* together.'

He began to realise that he seemed to 'need' Lise not on account of desire so much as of loneliness and fear. He sensed most acutely too that she had withdrawn her spirit from him, to the extent that she

consulted what he called 'her own cold self-absorbed heart' and her
family's interests before his. She told him categorically that she
would only have married him if things had been different – if, most
pointedly, she were not already married with a child. What was in
fact care and unselfishness *vis-à-vis* her family, Berryman took for
callousness toward himself. After encountering again and again her
putative 'indifference', he castigated her in his journal. On 15
October he wrote keenly, 'It is when [her husband's] claim and
mine come nakedly into conflict that Lise breaks up & goes numb to
me & withdraws.' (Yet, after stating that truth about her sense of
priority, he seems to have suppressed it for some time. When he
reread the journal nearly eight years later – in August 1955 – he
perceived as if for the first time, and added this marginal comment
to the entry: 'Quite right, for once.')

Berryman had begun by feeling sceptical about psychiatric treatment, particularly in view of the fact that he reserved so much
information about himself. His sense of violent self-doubt did not
seem to be emerging, a sense most striking since it amounted at
times to the feeling that he was an imposter; that feeling alternated
with his awareness of arrogance and impatience. In relation to
Eileen or Robert Lowell or Ezra Pound, for example, he felt
inadequate and shallow – in both a personal and a creative sense. As
his faith in treatment grew, his self-confidence revived. He started
working intensively on his verse-play about adultery and murder
within an unhappy marriage, Katharine Nairn's. What Berryman
regarded as his psychological 'illumination' about his relationship
with Lise impelled his energetic application, since, as he said, 'it
even suddenly revived and explained Katharine Nairn; she was like
Lise.' In his journal for 15 October he added one word: 'Euphoria'.
The next day, while making extensive notes and drafting a speech
for the play, he noted that, while Katharine Nairn and Patrick
struck him as types of Lise and her husband, he could find no
equivalent for himself in the plot.

> And I *am* missing! What excites me in this is an absolutely
> personal subject, even Lise, but *not myself*, and a perfectly
> *objective form* – as well as one fresh to me. Also the possibility of
> genuine audience . . . and work I can show to E[ileen], work no
> one expects of me. Perfect! Excelsior!
> Work, work.
> If anything can keep me from Lise, this will. I cdn't even talk
> about it to her, could I? O this may make me new.

His elation persisted for some days – even weeks – during which he brought himself to open thirty letters that had accumulated for him, including some from Ezra Pound, Dorothy Pound, and *The Sewanee Review*. Eileen, who had been ill, he found 'specially . . . charming'. Their fifth wedding anniversary passed in calm and affection.

At the end of October, however, circumstances fell out that he and Lise made love again, as he recorded the next day:

> No one was ever more affectionate & gentle & devoted & womanly than Lise last night. The first days, she said, she had a wonderful sense of freedom and liberation (just as I had); since then she's spent 90% of her time hating me, imaging herself as a rattlesnake to bite me – and her music going brilliantly; but a day or so ago all her antagonism died away – . . . last night not an impulse of hostility, only this extraordinary love. In all this we have been exactly alike. Our feeling must indeed have, as she said, *guts of steel* to survive as it has, intact, and deeper. We could never live together, we both know this, but we can't live apart either and don't mean to try again. No plans! *closer*, and yet not dependent, – with no illusion any longer of 'all or nothing'.

When Lise failed to keep their next assignation, however, he flared with resentment and accusation. 'This is not natural,' he determined, 'and it is not a love affair, and I abandon it.' For some pages of his journal his resentment of Lise rioted, but his imputations inevitably reflected more of his own sense of grievance than of her true character. He admitted that he would readily have wept for the disaster of their affair, and that he hated her. She had betrayed his rapture, injured his pride.

When rage was spent, he took the cold step of categorising her behaviour. She seemed to be two women – the one warm, receptive, loving; the other aggressive, indifferent, selfish – whom he chose to style L_1 and L_2. The bifurcation corresponded as much to his own feelings of ambivalence – to the alternations of mood for which Lise herself had reproached him – as to any duality in her personality. The significant feature of Berryman's formulisation was that it enabled him to dissociate his feelings from someone who had become an object of his study, a split personality of mostly academic interest. By oppugning Lise, he could absolve himself from self-disgust. 'TO HELL WITH LOVE. UP PLAYS!' he wrote on 7 November. 'I love L_1 and I count on L_2 to kill my love or my love to die.'

By noon on that day he was again reposing a substantial measure of faith in Eileen's understanding and happiness. What is sadly unmistakable about his sentiments, however, is the strong and delusory vein of self-gratification, and also of unfair condescension towards Lise for her part in their affair. 'I hope intensely that we will improve and improve,' he said of his relationship with Eileen,

> if I can give her confidence – in herself, in me, and in the marriage – even without physical relations she will be infinitely happier than she has been. All our talk yesterday (and how thoughtful and perceptive she is). . . . She is right, that I was never in the past interested in people as I have been recently . . . A play on the Job theme, in which a man with much, a good man, is successively stripped of everything he possesses – this notion I had last night excites me more than a poem. For all this I have to be grateful to the Lise-situation, which made me so much worse that I had to change or perish. Indeed: *I must be grateful to Lise*, who has loved me as fully as she could and who is for the most part only the unconscious agent of the elements in her that have sought my destruction. And *I must be grateful to Eileen*, who has borne altogether with more than anyone ought to have to and who found me help. And now no more of this, – but remember it.

Like all too many of his journal-observations, the passage contains elements of fantasy, self-delusion, self-centredness, and complacency. All the more sorry is its context: within three hours of writing it, he had again telephoned Lise and arranged a tryst for ten o'clock that night. Although watchful of what he had purposed to be her dual nature, he sped to betray his own sense of the reality of the situation. 'I am still in love with her,' he wrote in the small hours of the next day. 'The truth is that we were *closer* tonight, as well as more *open*, and more deeply in love, than ever we were before. *What would she be if her nature were opened more normally to warmth and sympathy and love!*'

What is made painfully clear from the pages of his journal is that he lacked the courage of his convictions; or – at best – that he lacked will-power to keep his resolutions. After a while, indeed, he himself felt disgusted by his summary statements and smugness. 'Try not to be so fucking self-important,' he chastened himself. 'Who the hell am I? It's not only unworthy & hideous, but silly.'

For a few days he recovered his enthusiasm for writing plays, and made plans to write others – about Don Quixote or Jefferson, for example – but he was evidently distraining upon his secretly renewed passion for Lise. 'Lise in my mind!' he did concede after a little; he felt that 'I mutilate my nervous system w. impossible longings.'

One further night, and another session of love-making the following day, were to be the last occasions on which Berryman gave witness to his passion for Lise.

What partly helped him to dissociate his feelings from her was his previous dissection of her behaviour. Yet more, he felt a resurgence of genuine care for Eileen, being for once authentically concerned that most of the couples in their circle were childless. Eileen herself had begun studies in psychology, and Berryman took an increasing interest in her progress.

The other crucial factor which triggered his absolute withdrawal from Lise was that he felt motivated at last to write and to *publish* what he wrote, no longer bitched by pride and fear. 'There is reason in it now, and above all I am *writing* – engaged – occupied – thoughtful – committed – as I ought to be.' Buoyed up by the resolution to write fine plays, his new literary examplars being Shaw and Lorca, he plotted what he called a 'poem-on-theatre' to be called *Thespiad* – addressed and dedicated to Beatrice, his first fiancée, who had shared his passion for drama from 1937 to 1939.

Eileen found his enthusiasm infectious, and told him laughingly, 'Poetry – then textual criticism for two years – then stories – teaching always – I'm glad I didn't marry you for peace of mind!'

On 20 November he called at the new *Partisan Review* office in New York, where he found Delmore Schwartz and William Barrett, both unshaved and looking like theatrical producers. Berryman had yet failed to produce a long-awaited review of ten books of poetry. After listening to Berryman's excuses, Schwartz first suggested that the review need not exceed 1,500 words, but at last said, 'Make it an essay: that gives you 5000–6000, or as little as 3000, and pays much better.' Berryman promised to have the job completed by the following Wednesday, and felt suffused with new capacity after having 'been so long under the love-bondage & various neurotic burdens of inhibition & guilt (E[ileen] etc.) & self-distrust from which I'm very gradually emerging.' He made little progress with the piece for four days. Then, in virtually a non-stop spell of work from 8.30 a.m. on 26 November to noon the next day, he completed the article, 'Waiting for the End, Boys', and delivered it to the *Partisan Review* office that afternoon. Delmore Schwartz anxiously tried to persuade him to write exclusively for their journal – 'John! you have a sacred obligation,' he averred, 'it's your literary duty and your financial duty to write for *us*!' – and offered to pay generously for any essay Berryman might write.

Two days later, after Thanksgiving, William Sloane Associates agreed to publish in May 1948 a volume of Berryman's poems – temporarily called *Traditional Poems* – with an advance of 250 dollars. By coincidence, Robert Giroux, Berryman's friend at Harcourt, Brace & Company, despatched this telegram on 10 December: 'I can now offer contract for your poems standard royalty terms and advance will you accept' – an offer that was too late by less than two weeks.

The release of completing the long article for *Partisan Review* energised him for more writing. In the next days he began a review of Auden's *Age of Anxiety* for *Commentary*, and pondered writing a play about a man of affectation and power such as Stefan George (for which he might consult his friend Erich Kahler, who had been Stefan George's disciple), and an article equating *The Tempest* and *The Magic Flute*, to be called 'Shakespeare and Mozart: The End', as well as another grand Shakespearean project:

> An intensely interesting & altogether new book on Shakespeare cd be made by a literary & historical critic submitting to analysis the image-findings, character-obsessions (subtracting what is taken over, *or* imposed by the company's situation), situation-recurrence, thematic continuity, etc. Besides the increased, very careful biographical findings, and such work as the feud with Chapman & Raleigh in *L.L.L.* A whole book, cautious but very bold. I might write an exploratory essay for *PR* or even say the *Atlantic* or *Harper's* . . . to see what sort of insight becomes available.

(Berryman's work in the Shakespearean vein was never completed, but he did make substantial drafts for such a book commissioned in a later year.) All told, in fact, he had to restrain himself from undertaking too many contracts, since his work on Stephen Crane was outstanding, as on the selection of and introduction to Pound's *Selected Poems*. He was also still anxious to complete his edition of *King Lear*.

On 4 December it was approximately half a year since Berryman and Lise had first made promises to one another. In all that time, Lise had come to his apartment only once or twice, his office in Upper Pyne not above three times; no more than twice to his library office, and only half a dozen times to their rural trysting-place, the Grove, Now at last, as Berryman acknowledged, the relationship was utterly finished. Yet the affair had not been altogether the 'fruitless nightmare' that Berryman called it, for, he conceded,

I owe her, besides times and days of unspeakable happiness,
(1) the sonnets, though I abhor them just now,
(2) a knowledge of women extraordinary & new,
(3) a deterioration in my nervous state such that I *had* to have
    help which now looks to draw me out of much *more* pain
    than Lise made me herself and older difficulty.

When Berryman described his days with Lise, his psychiatrist felt that he was submissive to Lise '*as you were to your mother*; . . . perhaps in *permanent rebellion*'. He also helped to account for one of Berryman's dreams – a dim dream of escape which Berryman (who regarded it as 'a charming dream in retrospect') purported to find only slightly affecting:

I've been living with *Mother* & *sisters* who dominated me:
desired to leave for *school*, breaking free, and was in the *bus*
when they came to see me off: my hat in a paper *bag* where
Mother'd put it, I *took it out*, straightened it & *put it on*; they'd
brought bags & large parcels – one vast triangular one – I took
just one bag, and kissed Mother goodbye, she hugged me &
said 'Close! Closer!' then I think I got on the bus & *went off*. An
escape dream, putting on the hat like putting on trousers, no
longer dominated, going off to school 'like a *man*'; the triangle is
mine; hat–phallus *out of* bag–vagina, I only take one '*bag*'!

Berryman later perceived for himself that the 'sisters' might stand for Eileen and her sister Marie; that 'school' could signify the analysis itself; and that the 'triangular' parcel (or situation) adverted to might be any triangular permutation of: his mother, his father, himself, Eileen, Lise, and Lise's husband. While his psychiatrist apparently reassured him that the dream concerned Lise, Berryman subsequently believed – what he considered a compelling alternative – that it was really about his mother.

What Berryman's self-searching did seem to crystallise – for the first time early in October – was a theory of the nature of his feelings towards his father. On 9 October he gave his account

of my father's lack of interest in life, .weak sexuality, & when
describing him physically as rather like the present King of
England said 'In fact he looked perhaps a little as one thinks of a
French homosexual (I was thinking of Sartre's Daniel) looking –
he shaved closely, and' – I forget what else, but why did I say
this? Is my beard-desire an answer to my fear that I have some
homosexual orientation?

He was rightly troubled by thinking of his father as neglectful of him as a child, and as cold – as, in sum, a spiritless, sexless, effete wastrel. Three days later, he drew this baleful conclusion in his journal: 'The Oedipus. I realize suddenly – I never did before – that I may have *wished* Daddy's death, and may feel permanent guilt for the satisfaction of my wish.' Such a codification accounted too simply both for his rejection of his father and for his continual sense of guilt in general. Ever afterwards, he associated his prevailing state of mental unrest with what he took to be its etiology, his father's suicide. But Berryman had been some months short of twelve years of age when his father died: what he did not realise was that he could not by himself have formed such a negative view of his father. His notion of his father's 'lack of interest in life' and 'weak sexuality' he had evidently derived from his mother.

It is clear that she imparted at least to Berryman himself – by suggestion and insinuation – her own animus. Berryman must surely have retained some sense of love for his father, and could not balance the claims both of his own residual affection and of his mother's disaffection without encountering self-conflict and distress of mind. His psychiatrist perspicaciously advised him not to see his mother for a while.

Berryman told how

> my once wondering whether Mother had killed him [his father] had the basis that he *did* kill himself because she wanted a divorce. Her loving Bob [his brother] & me, especially me, more than she loved him. . . . My horror of divorce may start there. – My not wanting to *go beyond* the dead, my father & Bhain – to whom I then added *my brother* (S talked about sibling-rivalry), *Mother* in her frustrated literary ambition . . . an amazing circle of guilt-sense to hold me. All save E[ileen].

What also emerged was his real anxiety about the change of name – from his real father's, Smith, to his stepfather's, Berryman; it seemed to him a betrayal of his natural father, for which he tried to compensate by reciting 'John Berryman' over and over again, to perhaps as many as five hundred times. His psychiatrist seems to have been especially interested in Berryman's fundamental sense of piety, which he apparently considered the result of (by Berryman's own account) 'unsatisfactory parental relations (God, & priest, as *father*). I must try to remember.' Not only did Berryman remember, but he also fixed almost an absolute understanding on that interpretation, which then unhappily served for many years to prevent him from dealing spontaneously with his current emotional disabilities. He became virtually convinced that his childhood trauma was irremediable.

As December drew on, he worked to re-establish better relations with Eileen; struck by her signs of happiness, he delighted in their renewed togetherness. But decisiveness was only the prologue to recovery; the ingenuousness of his wishful-thinking was subject to many reverses. He needed gradually to master a regimen of steadier work and rest.

He began to feel himself again a member of the literary and intellectual community. A few weeks earlier, for example, he had chatted with Dwight Macdonald and Stephen Spender. From Macdonald he sought advice about his relationship with Lise, but ended up by offering counsel. Macdonald was dejected about his work, and bored by the non-rationality of the pacifists and anarchists with whom he then made common cause.

Stephen Spender he met at a party thrown by Oscar Williams. They talked about other poets, including Laurie Lee, Henry Reed, Vernon Watkins, and Montale, and Berryman felt consoled to learn that Spender appreciated the problem of integrity for the American writer – the dilemma of whether to publish in the fashion magazines or to become academicised. He found Spender altogether courteous and pleasant, and remarked to himself, 'How beautiful, still, he is,' while scorning Gene Derwood for asking outspokenly, without irony or humour, 'Stephen, how does it feel to you to be so beautiful? Do you ever get used to it?'

He acquired a new sense of the reality of his forthcoming book of poems, and in December, excited by the project, wrote three poems for it, 'Fare Well', 'Narcissus Moving', and 'The Dispossessed', the last of which gave him a title for the whole volume.

Finally free of spite towards Lise, he wrote a coda to his affair – 'It was [Lise's] marvellous vitality I adored. This is dim for me now, but it was real, and the whole delight and ecstasy and agony are part of me forever' – and reproached himself for self-conceit and narcissism: 'In regard to the sexual matter: it would be well to keep in mind that I am *ugly*, and *hypocritical*, and spend most of my time – when I am not *daydreaming* – trying to *shit*. *Pride* shd keep me off such notions if nothing else will. I appeal to my insane Pride.' As the year ended, he derived a sense of ironic gratification from his experience of torment.

I am sitting in the Balt where I spent the summer watching for Lise, and I see snow, and feel myself well, and instead of the mad sonnets I am getting a *book* ready for the printer, and I am pleased to have her far away, and I am miraculously my own

man again. I have now at 33 been in love with a complete &
insane passion at least three times, and I hope it will not come
again. . . . I feel full of energy in general, energy & invention &
judgment. – More extraordinary for this than for the affair with
Lise even, 1947 has made me a poet again.

Throughout this account of Berryman's affair with Lise, I have
spoken of his need to exaggerate and melodramatise a changing
situation, and to schematise his hectic passion, remorse, and re-
proachfulness, as well as Lise's own necessary shifts of attention and
commitment. After reading a draft of this material, and kindly
pointing out errors of fact for me to correct, Lise herself has
provided her own reflections on the course of her relationship with
Berryman which appropriately close this chapter, since they record
both a fundamentally important viewpoint and set Berryman's
terms of reference in a just perspective. She remembers how the
affair began after she and her husband had first established a
friendship with the Berrymans,

> exchanging dinners and so on, going on jaunts in the springtime
> countryside. It was all very pleasant. I was not unaware that he
> was very attentive to me . . . I found John's candor and
> easyness, good spirits & playfulness a great delight.
>   The four of us now bound in friendship, and deceit and love.
> Still we had good times together. . . .
>   We all went together to the Jersey Shore, to Washington's
> Crossing, here & there. I was socially involved with him well
> before being emotionally involved, which caused great
> problems when it did happen, as you may well imagine. Also,
> as I found later, I had become a significant factor in his life even
> before *I* was much aware of *him*. This created a problem in the
> relationship that was never caught up with, and may help to
> explain why we never were able to get more truly well
> acquainted. He'd already provided me with an identity &
> invested me with a mystique before I'd even walked through
> the door, so to speak. And his infatuation led him to
> over-praise, over-endow and italicize everything he knew or
> imagined about who I was. Predictably, I guess, later on that
> machinery went into reverse and I became the focus for all the
> extravagances of his despairs, frustrations and rage. If you ask
> me there is very little choice between being over-praised and
> over-blamed; they both strip you of your identity and your
> exact place in things. . . .
>   The outings, the dinners together, the mild social climate

became intolerable for two of the four, and yet it's indispensable. You tremble to lose it, you shudder to endure it. Time alone has to be bought somehow no matter what the risks are, or the humiliation of deceiving people, people you care about. . . .

It doesn't seem to have been remarked anywhere that (at least in the early months) much of this time was spent fairly innocently, playing tennis, bicycling out Stony Brook road or walking around Lake Carnegie, that sort of thing. But as the relationship became more intense and the sexual aspect heated up & we both became more obsessed with each other, subtle changes began to occur. For one thing, John was feeling more & more guilty about his dealings with Eileen. . . . he was very, very fond of Eileen and hellish afraid of hurting her. . . . All this ate at him more & more. At the same time, I was buoyantly happy, basking in all the approval and praise and adulation. . . .

What wasn't at *all* clear was the black moods that sprang out of nowhere, the conveyed sense that what I'd given him before was no longer sufficient, the evidence that he was flaying & damaging himself. The more he began to live inside his own head of course the less contact I could have with him. . . .

What finally tore it was the beginning awareness that it was not *myself* John was now involved with, but some spectral ME that he was daily re-inventing; that I'd become a vehicle for his energies and problems and inventions. . . .

My guess is that while I was away the writing took over, and the resentments multiplied, and the spectral ME . . . moved into my room & threw my clothes out the window. I don't find the SS lover-murderer any easier to believe in than the incomparable blonde goddess.

It's never been clear to me why he chose me to fasten to for a while. There's something foreboding about this kind of reckless, erupting love; it comes out of wells of energy that are buried too deeply to explore. It's almost sure to spring from a source that's forgotten but not lost, and to be corrupted by that same source.

10
Work and shame,
1948-51

While he waited for *The Dispossessed* to appear, Berryman suffered tremendous anxiety about its reception. He knew that he ought to have begun work on his study of Stephen Crane, for which he had an outstanding contract, but he found himself more often consumed with self-doubt. His feelings swung between a self-approbation anticipating fame for his poetry and despair both of himself and of his work. He admitted to himself only a measure of his dire insecurity, but attempted to write ecstatic notices of his own book in the hope that friends would echo them, and planned to finish seven books by the end of 1950.

From time to time in the early months of 1948, he worked on a group of pastoral poems, in which, as he dimly realised on 2 April, his poetic talent was put to the service of a private subject, his obsessive sense of guilt for adultery:

> How is it – it's incredible – that I haven't seen, before this morning, that the general subject is *Treachery* and the guilt attendant on treachery. The specific subject is my affair of last year: obsession – 'possession' & betrayal & dominatedness (so the political analogue is omnipresent) & disengagement & (silent) forgiveness & return–escape. Man is redeemable *in time* if not in history or eternity.
>
> Adultery (political capitulation, pleasure-principle, treason) in a renegade Catholic with a friend's wife must be the particular situation. A collapsing society, worst in the best individual. Only the will-to-health can recover him to work. – *One man's story*: crime & return.

What emerges from Berryman's summary analysis is the feeling of self-congratulation, which (in other moods) he knew he had not earned. He tried to lessen his fears by promulgating his merits all the more feverishly: 'Feeling of luck', he had written on 13 January. 'All I want is *time* & I will be a great poet still. I feel, frankly, that scarcely anyone is better even now.' Much of his arrogance was in fact an effort to outface pain, as may be inferred from this diary-entry about his former mistress: 'It is 3½ months now since we said a word *to* each other (Dec. 4th), – half as long as the whole affair last year. May it keep on so. . . . Let her sweat out my fame, in continuous ice.'

It was just at this time that he suddenly wrote a first stanza for the poem that was to become after five years *Homage to Mistress Bradstreet*. Within two weeks, on 4 April, he began the second stanza of the poem, a work which struck him as a bemusing departure.

Item: I can trust myself now never to *mean*. Luxuriate therefore. Evil of Stevens, disquiet me no more. I am sober, subject-ed, formal. Riot therefore! with good conscience.

Item: after all, to please as I will, without loss else, is worthwhile.

Item: taking stock, I see Lowell as my peer. No one else. This is my real opinion. Have confidence then, be simple & easy as is natural.

In April 1948 *Poetry* took five poems from Berryman's *The Dispossessed* for pre-publication, including the title poem (even though the editor found it a 'perfect conundrum', if 'vivid in its way'). As the May publication date of the book drew near, Berryman's apprehensiveness became very strained, only to be unleashed in extravagant parades of defiance. Bruce Berlind remembers one day when Yvor Winters visited Princeton to deliver a lecture.

Bill Merwin, John and I spent much of the late afternoon together, having met at my attic-room in Bank Street, then went off to dinner and Winters' lecture. . . . John was determined to be on his good behavior with Winters. . . . Everything went well until after the lecture, when there was an informal gathering at the Nassau Tavern. Winters and Blackmur sat at a head table, and the three of us at a table some distance away. There was discussion, Winters talked – well, pontificated – and John got increasingly irritated at his remarks. Finally, John lost control, stood up, challenged Winters' knowledge of what he had been talking about, and started quoting someone – I think Corbière. I overheard Winters ask

Blackmur 'Who's that?' Blackmur: 'Berryman.' Winters: 'Is he always this way?' Blackmur: 'This is mild.' Bill, John and I left, John knowing he had 'blown it' but claiming that he didn't care, Winters was an ass anyway, etc., etc., and returned to my room. Well, it happened that the latest issue of *Kenyon Review* had arrived in the mail in our absence – the Spring 1948 issue, in which John had two poems. He opened the magazine to his contributions and immediately shouted 'That son of a bitch Ransom!' It turned out that he had instructed Ransom to print the two poems in a given order, and they had appeared in reverse order. Neither Bill nor I cd understand how this mattered terribly, and we tried to calm him. With incredible, but characteristic melodrama John announced: 'Three people are going to be mortally wounded by this.' Perhaps we shd have dropped the matter and allowed him to cool off, but his reaction was so absurdly excessive that we tried to reason with him. John got angrier and wilder with every word, shouting such things as 'You people are amateurs . . . I'm a professional. . . . In a year's time I'll be a national figure ['figger', he pronounced it].' I can't remember every detail of the exchange – Bill and I were both terribly upset – but at one point Bill used the word 'pusillanimous' in reference to John's behavior; at which point John tore off his glasses and his jacket and prepared to fight Bill. Bill was in tears, John was in a raging sweat, I was reaching a state of hysteria; but I managed to step between them, and things suddenly cooled off.

Yvor Winters's review of *The Dispossessed* eventually appeared in the Fall issue of *Hudson Review*, where, possibly influenced by that earlier encounter, he spoke of Berryman's

disinclination to understand and discipline his emotions. Most of his poems appear to deal with a single all-inclusive topic: the desperate chaos, social, religious, philosophical, and psychological, of modern life, and the corresponding chaos and desperation of John Berryman.

He concluded:

If Berryman could learn to think more and feel less, and to mitigate, in some fashion, his infinite compassion for himself and for the universe, he might bring to some kind of real fruition the talent which one can discern in his better lines; but until he does so, he will not be a poet of any real importance.

Randall Jarrell's notice (the *Nation*, 17 July 1948) managed at once to derogate the poems presently under review and to hail the poet's potential:

> Doing things in a style all its own sometimes seems the primary object of the poem, and its subject gets a rather spasmodic and fragmentary treatment. The style – conscious, dissonant, darting, allusive, always over- or under-satisfying the expectations which it is intelligently exploiting – seems to fit Mr. Berryman's knowledge and sensibility surprisingly well, and ought in the end to produce poetry better than the best of the poems he has so far written in it, which have raw or overdone lines side by side with imaginative and satisfying ones.

Berryman reacted to bad notices as in a phantasmagoria. He virtually believed that an act of astonishment had been thrown off with every poem, and accordingly took a cool reception for repudiation, disregard for disrepute. It was enormously difficult for him even to begin to doubt the quality of his poems. He would scorn his critics, suppressing the main horror (the dreadful possibility that his poems were in fact bad or weak) for utterable fears; calling outside forces – his reviewers – the enemy, answerable foes. (It was only after some months that he could bring himself to refer to Winters slyly or snidely as 'a critic sometimes so penetrating'.) On occasion he even regarded closer friends as groundlings, unworthy of his poems. 'To expose to those fat fools my unfinished poems. I am sick.' When the evidence weighed against him, however, he shifted ground, and would attempt to revalue each snub as an aspect of historical necessity – to correct or encourage his destiny.

In spite of all his protestations to the contrary, Berryman came to admit that he had expected the book to make him famous. 'Never mind that,' he announced. 'Hope the *book* does well, for the sake of the work in it, but it's on its own.' Not for long could he suppress his acute hurt, but he determined to take a positive attitude towards his defeat, especially when he came to consider Meyer Schapiro's observation about the way in which Gauguin had suffered from 'estrangement in a dream of grandiose recognitions'. 'So *I* now suffer,' Berryman felt, '& from persecution-sense, & retribution-mania. *Wait*, wait a few years . . . but I mean to *thrive* on difficulty hereafter!'

One charmingly innocuous response came from Wallace Stevens, to whom Berryman had sent a complimentary copy. The letter was disappointing only because it was clear that Stevens did not intend to read the book: 'I am a bit careful about reading other people's poetry because it is so easy to pick up things.' Berryman was amused by the note, and certainly consoled when Frederick Buechner told him that Bernard Shaw never read plays for the same reason as Stevens – the fear of influence or borrowing.

The worst manifestation of Berryman's failure was his painful sense of competitiveness towards other poets such as Randall Jarrell and Robert Lowell: 'Crane's bad luck under Kipling, mine no doubt under Lowell.' In mid-June he suffered what he called 'an atrocious nightmare in which Cal [Robert Lowell] & I were writing on poets – I on somebody, he on me – . . . and after I'd "assumed position" as it were, he treated my book with contempt.' He persuaded himself that Lowell and Jarrell were withholding from him their '"indispensable" approbation', and it was only at the end of July that he became fully aware of the extent to which the failure of his unvictorious, unhallowed verses had demoralised him: 'S said I'd lost weight, shd eat & exercise; took my gloom before Goethe – lack of sense of vision – to be a desirable coming down from my "extra-terrestrial" genius sense. I must find my life-desires in *work itself*.' There was no alternative but to resign himself to the fact that 'My poetry has not yet made a world, I realise this. *Submit*, as soon as I've a chance again, to my subjects & to my actual heart, to find it.'

Berryman's circle of friends expanded during 1948 – to include a young couple, Donald and Elizabeth Mackie, who kept a large house with a swimming pool. Richard Blackmur seemed jealous of Berryman's new friendships, and resented the Mackie 'set' – which included the art scholar George Rowley, James Worden, and Jack and Peggy Myers. These friends – and many others who enjoyed their society – formed the core of Berryman's group. Their conviviality catered to his increasingly compulsive desire for friendship and security, for social popularity (a local lionisation in place of literary acclaim on a national scale) as well as for what Berryman termed 'my apparently inescapable sexual plans'.

He took a succession of mistresses, mostly young married women, some of whom were no more than passing acquaintances. When even comparative strangers readily responded to his propositions, Berryman revelled in his role, a kind of Orpheus and his Maenads. He found success – an excellence – in sin. At least for a while, his sexuality ran so high that he occasionally felt inclined to masturbate even after love-making.

He did not refrain from disclosing the details of his ways and mind to his psychiatrist. Although it is difficult to judge the pain that Berryman must have experienced in self-searching, he seems to have been gratified by his weekly discussions and discoveries, and recorded in his journal the developing picture with such observations as: 'Again a useful hour, on the degree of intimacy which is *undesirable* – at least for me – in marriage.' Late in May he noted that 'S. was pleased with my "Stupendous" insight as to my egotism, – saving us months, he said.'

Early in April, Eileen Berryman fell off her bicycle with dreadful consequences for her back. While her sufferings – which included several specialist consultations as to the advisability of an operation – elicited Berryman's concern, he was the first to admit that his major worries centred on himself. In May, when Eileen sat for some psychology examinations which coincided with the publication of *The Dispossessed*, Berryman recorded frankly, 'I'd been jolted, when leaving after dinner, at E's saying softly she worries more about my book than her exams; a twinge, that I do not *feel* so *for* her. *Nor for anyone.*'

Eileen suffered a relapse in mid-July, and was moved to Linden Lane to be cared for by her sister Marie. Still Berryman could not quell his resentfulness and quarrelsomeness towards her, though he knew that his behaviour was invariably a form of sporting whims and making unreasonable demands for special treatment. 'What a nightmare,' he protested. 'I am lower than ever, & quite unable to feel normally.' Later – in a way quite unjust to himself, since he wanted and worked to please Eileen so constantly that it was in fact impossible for her to be angry or wounded or frightened for long, even in the worst periods, until their last year – he lamented, '*I never arrange pleasures for E. I am a monster. All for me.* (The night of August 2nd I realize this fully).' Two days later, he 'sat in agony weeping over E. *She alone knows me as I am. Unless she rejects me I am not certainly lost. Self-pity, away. I can change myself & regain her, or I can try to do it.* My foul life glares at me, and I *was* it; but also, new & rare, a grief.' That same day he recorded that his psychiatrist 'was able somehow to describe all this. *Not* "lust" he says; partly "theft" from husbands and archaic.' Berryman approved the notion that his adulteries could be interpreted as suggesting not just his need for sexual satisfaction, but an effort to assail other men's security – his insecurity being expressed in striking at forbidden women. When his mistress called the next day, he observed as a result of his insight that her 'voice sounded wonderful, but I felt absolutely calm, – and all day I'd rejoiced indeed in this sense of deliverance from the need to pursue & be absorbed in women. Get E at six. NO OPERATION – a steel brace, soon, –

and she may be able to take up the interneship [*sic*] after all.'

Eileen did eventually have to undergo a minor operation in consequence of her accident. Berryman was moved for her, and repentant for his bad behaviour, as on their sixth wedding anniversary: 'Thank God,' he greeted the day, adding, 'Not that at Mass it occurred to me to thank him. It seemed to me again all a superstition.' He was too self-intense, however, not to spend an excess of his energy in contemplating his own emotional disorders rather than Eileen's physical condition, and noted in his journal on 5 November:

> Constriction, jumping nerves, anal pain.
> 4 p.m. I must not kill myself. That's obvious. It would crucify
> Eileen. But I almost despair . . . horrified with myself for not
> having given E. [while she was having her operation] *one*
> *thought* yesterday till I got home, in utter gloom over the
> undone Crane & Pound . . . sick with longing for [his mistress]
> . . . & in despair of ever making E. happy – black, black with
> unhope of ever having *mind & soul free* for my poems again . . . I
> feel trapped! *stifled*, alone, by myself alone – will this misery,
> this vague terror, ever end?

Grieving, he felt, 'I live from day to day. Never rest, so never can work, so never can rest: on, on, no end,' but any steps he might take to right himself only scotched his sense of disgrace. By mid-November he was reflecting: 'This is my *mid*-year, my 35th, I realize tonight, 1947 was "NIGHTMARE", 1948 is "CONVALESCENCE" perhaps still.'

During the early part of 1949 Berryman made serious efforts to clarify the world for himself, but mostly he showed purpose without system. 'If, after all this, I can make the Broom happy, my life will not have been wasted,' he determined. 'I can (1) WORK (2) *DELIGHT* HER & *NEVER* cause her pain (3) "remarry" (honeymoon even) & please her.'

For months he had made up for literary unsuccess with a blaze of personality, dazzling the community of his friends. In company he drank more and more, and his social demeanour became moody, vibrant, excessive, intriguing. He could sometimes behave bizarrely by climbing onto a second-floor window-ledge or, at one party, placing his shoes in the fireplace – and walking home in his socks – where they were discovered only the next morning. He had cause to note one day, 'I have promised E to curb the latitude of my talk and *not* to interrupt.' But he was not always drunkenly assertive or looking for illusions in the wrong places; though self-intense, he was invariably sensitive to things outside himself and to his dear friends.

With prominent literary figures, Berryman (his envy mixed with docile respect) was equally watchful and receptive. In October 1948 he renewed his acquaintance with T. S. Eliot, and found him as considerate as the year before; they talked about Vivaldi and Goethe. He also met Francis Fergusson, who had been given an appointment in modern languages at Princeton – a man, he approvingly noted, 'very tentative, & attentive, cackles when amused, large & slow, iron hair combed slick.' Through his friend and neighbour Melvin Tumin, Berryman first met Saul Bellow and Leslie Fiedler in October that year. In Tumin's apartment Fiedler talked about Hamlet's play-within-the-play, while Bellow played some Purcell 'very sweetly' on Tumin's tenor recorder; Berryman took an instant liking to both of them.

He tried to continue just as discerning and considerate towards Eileen – and towards his current mistress, whom he thought increasingly timid and unassertive. Concern for both women helped only to moderate his more urgent sense of disgrace, since the strength of his resources appeared to be outnumbered at all points by betrayal and self-reproof. It seemed to him that his trousers and even his office reeked of masturbatory indulgence. It was at such times that his conscience was *à deux* with the wounds he believed to have been inflicted on him. In June 1949 he decided,

> I am *driving myself* to the verge of despair. My conscience gets worse & worse, mind & body fouled; and I cut myself off from my only source of help (E) by my bad conscience. I *am* badly isolated, but it is my own doing, & *reparable*.

At that time he thought of writing a biography of George Washington, which he might frame in terms close to his own conscience:

> Washington's (1) immense ambition (–opportunism)
> (2) doubt of capacity
> (3) bottomless resignation (as at death). . . .
> Washington's *iron –* . . . vs.
> my notion of *indolence & openness* for the poet

His deep interest in Washington's turn of mind in fact persisted until January 1970, when he drafted the poem 'Washington in Love' (*Delusions, Etc.*).

In May 1948 Berryman was appointed (on Richard Blackmur's recommendation) resident fellow in creative writing at Princeton University, with a salary of 3,750 dollars for the academic year 1948–9 – the same amount he had earned as associate in creative writing from 1946–7. In June, moreover, he received an offer from the University of Iowa to teach at a salary of 4,500 dollars. (Berryman applied fruitlessly to Donald A. Stauffer, chairman of the English department at Princeton, for an increase of the local offer, using the Iowa quotation for the purpose of bargaining.)

His dispiritedness at returning to teaching may be gauged from his response to a *Partisan Review* questionnaire on 'The State of American Writing, 1948', which he completed early in May that year. While lamenting the general state of American culture, the death or decline of useful magazines, and the upsurge of 'The meretricious in upper-middle-class popular writing (as it apes serious writing)', he drew what appeared to him a depressing lesson:

> The alternative to journalism, for most American writers, is teaching, and the dangers from it are similarly complicated. They range from pure slump to pure irritation. To write is hard and takes the whole mind and wants one's whole time; a university is the perfect place not to write. . . . Repetition of books and courses numbs . . . the writers I know outside universities read more, on the whole, more that counts, than those inside . . . it is not widely enough understood that literary criticism is an activity which bears no necessary relation whatever to good teaching. But the energy used by good teaching is very much the energy required for writing.

Berryman none the less managed his creative teaching with the intensity and verve characteristic of all his dealings. 'Berryman wanted to teach the mood, not the meaning, of literature,' Fred R. MacFadden (himself now a professor of English language and literature) recalls.

> I think he pitied the self-sacrifices of the academic professors, who gave themselves, many of them, to an early death in the service of academia. Yet out of scholarship, too, could come creative work. Berryman proudly showed us his edition of Milton, with his own annotations in the margins of 'Lycidas' [turned to good account in the apt and powerful story 'Wash Far Away', published for the first time only in 1974] . . . Berryman dealt with the creative act, not just with mere learnedness.

For the years 1948 and 1949 Berryman fitfully continued to write poems, several of them being occasional utterances in response to thoughts about death, such as this extract from 'Innocent', a lyric about a stillborn child written soon after midnight on 4 August 1948,

> The soft flesh melted from the bones
> Of the child born dead, for days & days
> In the wood's edge, Birds, nothing, came.
> Bones go. All is the same, the same, –
> Except our envy O wintry praise!

or this extract from 'Elegy, for Alun Lewis',

> Little attention we paid to each other alive
> But Death has made us friends, Your death, not mine.
> I am dying slowly; . . .
> Now envious I hear of that exploit
> And sit down to these poems of yours and grieve.

Both poems were later published by Hayden Carruth in *Poetry* (January 1950), along with a group of four sections from a work which was to have been called *The Black Book*. Knotted drafts for that full sequence, which Berryman later referred to as 'a diagnostic, an historical survey', survive among his papers; they were written in the period ending on about 1 April 1949 (a day when Berryman wept on reading about the murder of the Polish professors in *The Black Book of Poland*, a work which informs his own). The finished passages manage a dense, dissonant rendering of the Jewish holocaust, such as this extract about 'Grandfather',

> . . . blood
> Broke from his ears before they quit.
> Before they trucked him home they cleaned him up somewhat.
>
> Only the loose eyes' glaze they could not clean
> And soon he died. He howled a night and shook
> Our teeth before the end; we breathed again
> When he stopt. Abraham, what we have seen
> Write, I beg, in your Book.

or this extract 'from the Black Book (iii)' (a passage not originally published with the group in *Poetry*) about the gas chambers,

They shuffled with their haircuts in to die,
Lift them an elegy, poor you and I,
Fair & strengthless as seafoam
Under a deserted sky.

The Black Book, which Berryman termed (in July 1948) a 'suite of poems', was to have been published first by Claude Fredericks at the Banyan Press, with drawings or water-colours by Tony Clark, but the plan did not come off. In an interview with Jonathan Sisson in 1966, Berryman recalled his problems with writing the sequence:

> It was in the form of a Mass for the Dead. It was designed to have 42 sections, and was about the Nazi murderers of the Jews. But I just found I couldn't take it. The sections published . . . are unrelievedly horrible. I wasn't able at this time . . . to find any way of making palatable the monstrosity of the thing which obsessed me.

Recognition for Berryman's achievements in poetry came with two prizes: the Guarantors Prize, a sum of 100 dollars from *Poetry* for the group of five poems published in the issue of April 1948, and the Shelley Memorial Award for 1948, conferred by the Poetry Society of America in February 1949. 'I bought a bottle of Scotch & demolished it,' Berryman told his mother, 'being depressed.' Apart from such outward signs of success, Berryman's poetry brought him little cheer, at least not financially: *The Dispossessed* sold only 400 copies in the first weeks of distribution, and earned him the sum of 95 dollars – cancelled against his advance on royalties of 250 dollars.

At this time Berryman gave by far the weightiest portion of his writing effort to prose, beginning with a succinct and pertinent review of *T. S. Eliot: A Selected Critique* (a collection of essays chosen by Leonard Unger) for *Partisan Review* (July 1948), in which he judged Eliot 'inveterate and serious' as a critic. Scorning pious treatments of Eliot's work, he offered positive praise (eschewing what he called Eliot's 'perverse and valuable doctrine' of the 'impersonality' of the poet) to the distinctive suffering personality voiced in the poetry:

> One observes a certain desire in the universities to disinfect Mr. Eliot by ignoring his disorderly and animating associations. . . . Eliot's mind is grievous and profound beyond a single poet's. . . . Perhaps in the end this poetry which the commentators are so eager to prove impersonal will prove to be

personal, and will also appear then more terrible and more
pitiful even than it does now.

To James Laughlin's mounting agitation, however, Berryman
was making no substantial progress with the selection of Pound's
poems. '*First day of the new regime*', he wrote in his journal on 15
October,

> Like the summer of 1943 – stupid & ignorant, empty, not
> anything ever done, all waste & talk. *Silence now*. With
> difficulty & uncertainty, like a dead man, I reviewed my *Canto*
> selections & began the introduction: half a page. Unable to talk
> to E. or anyone. She is patient with me. My scalp blazing, my
> left foot-top row. Will I ever be able to smile again.

Finished only by late November, Berryman's introduction – which
works to demonstrate that Pound's personal life and interests are
increasingly the subject of his poetry – scored off Eliot and Blackmur for persistently attending to Pound's style and manner, and not
to his content. When Blackmur read the essay he remarked cannily,
'I wonder if you don't really have much more against Eliot & me
than you say there.'
    Though impressed with the introduction, Laughlin thought it
too profound to inveigle students and the general public. When
Berryman denied the point, calling his work 'deliberately SIMPLE-
MINDED', Laughlin skirted an argument by proposing that the
piece be used to introduce a separate issue of *Personae*. Eventually
Laughlin withdrew all his options on the essay, and Berryman
published it as an article in *Partisan Review* (April 1949).

The major work of the period from 1948 to 1949 was his book
Stephen Crane. Berryman had procrastinated for months over his
study, and only began to work intensively, to compile a bibliography, and then to write, in April 1948. He read Thomas Beer's book
on Crane that month, and excitedly consulted Beer's sister in the
hope of discovering memoranda – only to be told that Beer always
worked from memory and 'never kept anything'. Edmund Wilson,
who was currently reading all of Crane's works, told Berryman
that he thought Crane 'a great writer'. Through the rest of 1948
Berryman found it almost impossible to discipline himself with a
regular schedule of work, but he ground on with the book to a point
roughly mid-way. 'I *don't* feel today,' he declared, 'that I may die &
my book have to be published incomplete.' Still, the difficulties of
the labour seemed excruciating. 'I abhor this series,' he wrote. 'It

consists of Columbia professors and their mutual ass-licking, un-
necessary (Krutch's & Mark's) or stupid (Neff's), books, ritual
praise.' (In time, Berryman was moved to tears when he finished
reading Mark Van Doren's *Hawthorne.*)

He dogged the book for the next two weeks, drinking and
smoking excessively –

> At least I have all the help science can give. My psychiatrist after
> more than a year got me into condition to make this effort.
> Eileen puts out morning & night, for me to take, vitamins &
> anti-spasmodic. I take dexedrine morning & afternoon; martinis
> before dinner; nembutal & sherry after midnight, to sleep. . . .
> Good God.

– until, on 21 February, he had completed the first draft.

But he was not yet delivered of the manuscript: radical revision –
whether because of self-criticism or editorial strictures is not clear –
took up the next months, and reduced him to an abyss of morbid
self-doubts.

> I seem, yesterday & today, to have undergone a breakdown of
> spirit – I can't speak – it remains to see whether it will last. . . . I
> have thought of withdrawing even *Crane* from publication.
> Who cares what I write, or whether I write? I feel friendly to
> suicide. – Drank myself blind & sick last night w. Martinis, &
> passed out without dinner.

'The truth is,' he added later, 'that my book *disgusts* me. It reads
abominably & *is* abominable, almost idiotic. Where did I ever get
the idea that it was anything else?'

His lowest ebb came at mid-May, when he felt that he really
could not continue, especially when Helen Stewart, his editor at
Sloane's, wrote a blurb for the book which suggested to him that
Crane would emerge from his work as '*weak & unattractive* – so little
can readers balance things, so much do they falsify the life they
know.' The last week before delivering the manuscript, he worked
day and night in a state of alarming depression, and actually finished
and delivered the book on Friday, 29 July.

Stephen Crane is, for the most part, a sustained, elaborate biographical work, if slightly idiosyncratic in point of style, which
received some censure for appearing to use depth psychology as a
mode of literary criticism, and for using Crane's own writings as a
biographical source, a procedure which Thomas Beer had for-
borne. The most contentious chapter of the book is 'The Color of

This Soul', an intrepid final statement in which Berryman applies Freudian analysis to Crane's mentality and art, to argue the supposition that Crane suffered from an Oedipus complex: the type, he says, 'begins to desire the mother, hates the father for standing in his way.' What is evident from Berryman's rampantly inductive analysis, which occasionally strains the slim evidence of image or incident, is that Berryman felt a strong degree of identification with Crane – identifying both with his 'simultaneous desire, nervous loathing, and resentment' of the mother, and with his

> aggression against the father, first, the sense of desertion and impoverishment (with the consequent resentments) arising from his death when Crane was a boy, and second, the intellectual rebellion consciously waged by Crane against him.

One stroke of that identification can be seen in the fact that Berryman felt consoled to learn that 'Crane wd write his name, all over, again & again for hours, waiting for fame. I only *say* mine to myself.' Evidence for the fact that Berryman shared Crane's 'jealousy and hatred of the father' is rife throughout his later work, *The Dream Songs*. Here it is enough to note some of the ways in which Berryman's often anguished self-communings during 1948 and 1949 tally with his observations about Crane's psychology.

Fortified by his psychiatrist, he groped at and formulated a diagnosis of his own emotional distress which bears a striking resemblance to the psychology he imputes to Crane. In a diary-entry for 5 June 1948, Berryman remarks that 'I saw with surprise . . . an *escape*-pattern in my water (hydrophobia) imagery,' an observation which may compare with a passage in *Stephen Crane* where, in connection with 'the type of fixation to which Crane belongs', he interprets the fantasy of a rescue from water as designing a parent's death: 'Crane's fantasy had to secure father-identification by drowning the actual mother-representative' (in the story *Maggie*). Similarly, Berryman writes in *Stephen Crane*, 'Dreams of the parent's death vision as a rule the death of the parent of the same sex,' and continues, 'We can guess at masochism also in the life. . . . Now the last form of this is suicide-fantasy, as the last form of sadism is the parent's death, both parents'.' So, in the misery of his own mind, Berryman had recorded on 30 April 1948:

> Another terrible night, and my dreams of the cached murdered bodies returned – under houses, bound finally to be discovered. E. says I am naive not to recognize some *disguise*, but I can't shake off the feeling that it is my daysense of *not* having having

[*sic*] murdered that is false, – not my nightsense of having murdered.

It became part of Berryman's psychoanalytical venture to sort out the confusion in his own life of the roles in which he had cast his wife and mother. He felt it true that, for men who sustain an Oedipus complex (in Freud's own terms as quoted in *Stephen Crane*), 'the maternal characteristics remain stamped on the love-objects chosen later – so long that they all become easily recognizable mother surrogates.' Actually, for Berryman, that self-made diagnosis was both sufficient and intimidating, and goes some way to account for his alienation from his mother during the years of his marriage. The predominance of disaffection is instanced by diary-entries such as this from 1 September 1949: 'Angry, long, insufferable session with mother.' Berryman's scholarly hypothesis about Crane's mother-dominated psychology seemed to him appalling in his own person; when his psychiatrist said that he required at least a year of intensive treatment, Berryman wrote,

> Immensely depressed by this, I began to try at once to explore the incest-wife matter which he thinks is crucial, – and was spontaneous and emotional for the first time w. him in months – Mother's elaborate & continued sexuality, etc. – Eileen vs. [his mistress] whom he explained as naturally attractive to me because 'anonymous' & so incapable of mother-identification.

Writing *Stephen Crane*, and developing his theory of Crane's psychology, brought Berryman into confrontation with the most painful and urgent problems of his own soul. It was his unhappy knack to encompass his own mentality in formulae; he was able to pick out certain insights, only to eclipse them with theory. However painful the process – and there can be no doubt that it was acute – he felt compelled to compose ideas of himself, jealous of his paradigms. Once in a while, the very stringency of his self-analysis worked to an immediate end: '*the most important day of my life,*' he wrote on 15 February 1949,

> I found the Primary Scene in Crane . . . just now at noon and with my brain ready to burst with what is in it I climbed out on the terrace in the cold and sat on the edge. . . . Then I saw what my trouble is. I can labour but I can't 'come'. I am ready to burst but can't finish. First on Shakespeare at Cambridge then on Shakespeare here, – in my plays, – in my physical impotence – in my whole life. I did *not* throw myself over (to prevent my

finishing this book: 'coming' at last). I came in, & telephoned
Eileen, and now go *steadily* on to the *end*.
4.20 p.m. I feel *confident*.

Six days later, he had finished the first draft of the book.

The Berrymans spent much of August 1949 on Cape Cod, staying
first with Dwight and Nancy Macdonald, and then with the
Mackies on a large estate (complete with a salt-water pool and
precipitous rocks which Berryman loved) belonging to Donald
Mackie's grandmother at Eaglis, Manchester, Massachusetts.
Berryman himself was no doubt still suffering from the strain of
writing, and managed to engage himself in heated arguments with
Dwight Macdonald. Although they invariably repaired their
friendship, Berryman would suffer positively disabling anger for
some time after any such dispute, and withhold himself from food
and company in fits of chronic sulkiness. One row took place
during a beach party on the night of 16 August, an occasion which
Alice Kahler, who was present, finds unforgettable. Fully clothed,
Berryman marched furiously into the ocean (leaving everyone
anxious about his apparently suicidal impulse) and reappeared only
after half an hour. Berryman's quarrels with Macdonald concerned
vexed subjects such as whether psychoanalysis should enjoy the
status of a science, or the award of the Bollingen Prize in Poetry to
Ezra Pound.

Earlier in the year, the *Saturday Review of Literature* had published
two articles by Robert Hillyer (Berryman's former colleague at
Harvard) attacking the award of the prize to Pound. Hillyer's article
and supporting editorials in the magazine adumbrated a neo-fascist
conspiracy, in which not only the Fellows in American Letters of
the Library of Congress but also a larger group of unnamed writers
were implicated. Hillyer alleged serious but undocumented charges
of obscurantism, snobbery, and cultism against modern poetry and
poets. In answer, Berryman rallied a winning protest by circulating
a letter which denounced the position held by the *Saturday Review*.
When the letter was submitted on 4 November for publication by
the *Saturday Review*, the journal considered the question for a while
and to all intents and purposes declined to publish the document;
eventually Margaret Marshall issued the letter (subscribed by
eighty-four eminent writers) in the *Nation* on 17 December 1949.
Although Berryman's repudiation of Hillyer's attack (which had
taken T. S. Eliot for its main target) carried impressive weight, the
controversy was not razed: what Margaret Marshall scorned as
Hillyer's 'philistine attack on modern literature' in the name of

patriotism succeeded only in prompting the discontinuance of the Bollingen–Library of Congress Award.

Berryman held a realistic, respectful and unsentimental view of Pound, based on two separate meetings, the first of which Robert Lowell recalled as a gentle communion:

> Our trip . . . to Ezra Pound at St. Elizabeth's Hospital near Washington was . . . so soft I remember nothing except a surely misplaced image of John sitting on the floor hugging his knees, and asking with shining cheeks for Pound to sing an aria from his opera *Villon*. He saw nothing nutty about Pound, or maybe it was the opposite. Anyway his instincts were true – serene, ungrudging, buoyant. Few people, even modern poets, felt carefree and happy with Pound then.

The other visit took place on 3 November 1948, as Berryman recorded in a detailed and unromanticised account.

> He raced up the hall, 'Bring this' at a chair half-way, and while we were settling ourselves in the end (past a close-cropt melancholic brooding on the edge of a chair against the wall), suddenly shook my hand again eagerly and said 'The only liberal writer who has come out for Truman: Wyndham Lewis!' He sank down and back then, buttoning a shirt he had thrust on, arranging objects from his pockets on the windowsill beside him, and began to eat a roll, after offering me one. Later when he went away to get some British illustrated papers about the removal of Yeats's body to Ireland to show me, he brought back bananas, was very surprised when I didn't want one, and rapidly ate both. 'Too big', tapping his stomach, 'over 180 . . . 188. They send me candy and fruit.' He looks better than he did last winter, I think, though thinner everywhere except belly; less agitated in speech, but less attentive too; more coherent, a little. Certainly he remembers more. He was writing three books, he said, when he was taken, and he has just remembered recently what the third one was. (The worst thing in the cage, of which he spoke to me now for the first time, was having no work to do: he was used to thinking from two to four at night, then writing it out when he got up in the morning; and instead there was the sun on him and he was trying to read Mencius in it – the *Four Books* which as D. had told me and now he does, he grabbed up as the partigiani took him off.) Also he now speaks definitely of the sixteen cantos to come, – not of writing them, but of their being sixteen, and 'if I can finish it', and 'Of course

now I have to pull it all together . . . the piling up is done, no more need to put things in . . . but ordering. You can see where the thing is going.' I couldn't, but he had gone on meanwhile to something else.

He moves away from personal subjects very quickly and as if naturally, – when I mentioned the allusions to the Paradiso in recent cantos, he just talked about the comparative inaccessibility of the third Cantiche for modern readers.

It is striking altogether how impersonal he is. Thus, it was a long time before he recalled, or came to, what he must have chiefly wanted to take up with me: my delay over the Selected Poems, & my not writing to him. And then he was very gentle, said I was taking much too much trouble with the introduction, and a look of pain went over his face when I mentioned E's illness. 'How *are* you?' when I asked, he put the query altogether away, saying that two hundred psychiatrists asked him this all the time. . . . I seldom ask him questions, of course. But one more failure of self-assertion, following a question, is worth record also, as bearing on the development of English poetry.

He had been saying that he had gone to London to learn from Yeats how to write poetry. Yeats knowing more about it than anyone else. (Exactly as I did, a quarter-century later, but without Pound's brass; and like me had written five hundred sonnets, of which only the ten lines of 'Camaraderie' are rescued by Eliot; and Yeats's *height* – in the doorway at Woburn Buildings – astonished him as long afterwards as it did me.) He went to Yeats's Monday evenings, and on other evenings. I said that it has seemed to me more and more, in recent years, likely that the development towards *conversation* in Yeats at this time must be due to his association with Pound, and asked if he thought so. Pound said 'No'. He was going to see Ford in the afternoons, Ford full of poetry-as-talk. Yeats and Ford saw red at the thought of each other, but 'so long as Willie didn't know where it was coming from . . . I used to drill him in the evening with what I heard in the afternoon. No, papa only carried it over. Fordie gets the credit for that.'

Both gave Pound their worn-out velvet jackets, 'as they got more respectable', so he had something to wear. 'Yeats's were much better, thicker, more nap.'. . .

'To learn how it was done' he went to Yeats – this was his phrase. 'I come out of Browning, of course.' To my saying I used to think Personae the beginning of modern poetry, but now *Ripostes*: 'Yes . . . yes.'. . .

Pound now sounds as if he wanted to get out of St.
Elizabeth's, though God knows what he wants. He dislikes
being in the 'derelict' ward, likes the criminals better, 'more in
them'; misses a very tall anti-semite with whom he used to talk
before he was transferred – 'he knew all about these kikes',
glancing around and nodding as if he and I were in agreement.
As compared with last winter, he scarcely ever touched this
theme, however, and was less aggressive in other ways, more
reminiscent, less political, only commenting that 'nobody here
knows how much good they did' (the Fascists).

He urged me to stay on and on . . . insisted on getting the
Yeats photograph from his room, and quoted excitedly in very
good brogue a parody-epitaph 'Under bare Ben Bulben's bum
. . .' – and waved from the barred window – 'Ha!'

It was in response to one of his visits to Pound that Berryman
wrote 'The Cage' (*Poetry*, January 1950), part of which runs:

> . . . O years go bare, a madman lingered through
> The hall-end where we talked and felt my book
> Till he was waved away; Pound tapped his shoe
> And pointed and digressed with an impatient look
>
> 'Bankers' and 'Yids' and 'a conspiracy'
> And of himself no word, the second worst,
> And 'Who is seeryus now?' and then 'J.C.
> Thought he'd got something, yes, but Ari was first'
>
> His body bettered. And the empty cage
> Sings in the wringing winds . . .

On 27 December 1949, shortly before the publication of 'The
Cage', Berryman was appointed Alfred Hodder Fellow at Princeton for the year 1950–1, a post which presented him with a
challenging and prestigious opportunity for broadcasting his own
views and scholarship.

Early in 1950 Berryman taught briefly at the University of
Washington, Seattle, and returned to Princeton in June feeling
badly fatigued and at odds with life. Although his doctor forbade
him sedatives and alcohol, and instructed him to rest for at least two
weeks, he suffered from such crippling insomnia and rage, and
impatience for activity, that he soon returned to work and to project
ideas. The next eighteen months were to be afflicted with con-

tinuing unrest, plans and snatches of useful work but more often fitful starts ending in exasperation, and equally perfunctory affairs with young friends and acquaintances in Princeton or phases of unrequited lust; all were marked by his habit of febrile introspection. Eileen found a good measure of independence in her profession. In 1950 she gained her Master's degree from New York University with a thesis on 'Poets' Responses to the Rorschach Test', and soon after went to work for four days a week as an assistant clinical psychologist at Rutgers University. In spite of establishing her own career, however, she grew more and more anxious for the fact that her private life with Berryman had to be lived increasingly under the dispensation of his neurotic drives.

'I came back ten days ago very tired and in a very bad state of mind,' Berryman wrote on 12 June 1950, 'but live enough to be impressed by Hemingway's notion of the soul being like a lost military position – to be sold as expensively as possible – and eager to work.' The work that he began was a verse play about Mirabeau, a figure who struck him as being of Shakespearean proportions. With a burst of energetic commitment to the task, he drafted scenes 'with love & hope & desperate anxiety'. Over the years since 1936 he had attempted other plays, such as *Architect* followed by *Dictator* in New York, and in the 1940s he had troubled extensively with plays about Katharine Nairn and about the Irish rising of Easter 1916. It is clear from his description of Mirabeau that he was now labouring under a sense of wishful identification:

> Mirabeau is the Sinner *and* Hero I have wanted for years – no wonder no other man was ever so interesting to me. A subject utterly to test me. *Truth and* Imagination: or age past, a people distant & very different, a man like no one else who ever lived. At War w. his father. Loyal, intransigent, passionate, wise, the last of men so powerful who lived by scruple and desired the general good. A man of reflection & action, immensely strong, imperfect.

The resolution lasted no longer than its first burst. Berryman was capable only of similarly sporadic work for several months. Two consolations for his current lack of progress were the award of the Levinson Prize of 100 dollars from *Poetry* magazine for the group of eight poems published in the issue of January 1950, and (on 11 December) the publication of *Stephen Crane*, a work which had breasted years of seemingly insuperable difficulties in the writing and, lately, proof-reading. Although it was certainly a landmark not only in Berryman's career but also in the historical advance of

Crane scholarship, the book proved not to be an incentive for Berryman. Publication was attended by circumstances which incensed him, not the least of which was that he thought William Sloane Associates had been neglectful and officious towards him. Other factors, of which Berryman complained in a letter to Sloane himself two months later, were that the firm had apparently failed to advertise the book and had not made sufficient copies available to booksellers when times were ripe. Berryman resented the patronising way in which he felt himself to have been treated; his ill-feeling recalled the unpleasantness surrounding the publication of *The Dispossessed*, when he had refused to give autographs and had found the publication-day luncheon 'a nightmare'.

By May 1951 Berryman gave it as his opinion (prompted by the occasion of the death of Hermann Broch) that 'The world gets gloomier & gloomier and I haven't done any work for over a month except fulfil some trivial public duties.' The duties he referred to included delivering his four statutory lectures as Hodder Fellow in Princeton. Although he denigrated his achievement, the lectures on Shakespeare in fact gave him great satisfaction and represented the first public expression of his long years of textual and critical study, and they were widely acclaimed.

On 11 June 1951, almost exactly a year after his *Mirabeau* project, he resumed what he had always regarded as his 'real' work – creative writing – in the form of a new play on the subject of political treachery. His idea was to probe the mentality of a traitor, for which models included the Irish patriot James Connolly, Ezra Pound, and the recent disclosures about Burgess and Maclean. As with *Mirabeau*, Berryman's notes for the scheme show that he was in no way objective or impersonal in the venture but crucially given to project variations on his self-image:

> He is disillusioned w. Amer. capitalists *and* labor; hates U.S. in fact, though he does not fully know this, not – however – really hate as much as he says & acts. There is no Russian enthusiasm whatever involved. Wants *peace*. . . . He is taken in by the final conception of internationalism, & victimized by the exaggerated anti-patriotism to which American intellectuals were schooled in the '30's. Man my age or a little more, v. familiar with our mistakes before the War, corruption during, and weakness since. Communists as anti fascist, important to him. An intensely cultivated, able, sympathetic man: detests Amer. culture, parody-democracy & inefficiency, but is suffering also reaction to humanitarianism (dangers of world-view) tho' he hates American luxury–prosperity.

This probing of the psychology of treachery must have been incited by the fact that Berryman himself felt paradoxically so betrayed by his country, alienated and depressed by a lack of accomplishment seen as lack of recognition and support. His traitor was to be driven by a hatred of American life resulting from disillusioned idealism. As Berryman put it tersely on 13 June: 'scum to the top'. In the disillusioned idealism of his own artistic aims, Berryman would, it is clear, have appropriated the greater selflessness of his proponent. As with *Mirabeau* (a work to which he was to return periodically), however, the scheme was embarrassed too by the problems of Berryman's personal life, and was later superseded by his momentous achievements during a Guggenheim Fellowship which was to begin in mid-1952. In the more immediate future, the possibility of making progress with his play was in any case interrupted by two weeks of lecturing on Crane and Hemingway at a summer school run by the University of Vermont; there, he reported, in company with Richard Blackmur and 'an utterly charming character new to me David Daiches we formed a close corporation.' He gave additional readings and talks during this period at Rutgers and Columbia Universities, and, on the subject of 'Present Relationships Between Poetry and Prose', at the Anglo-American Poetry Conference at Bard College on 8 December 1951.

In spite of his halting work, Berryman was called to busy himself in the fevered rounds of Princeton society. He was always diverting, if often seeming manic, and it was his drunken and occasionally outrageous behaviour which set the tone of many parties. He could also moderate proceedings, however, as on the occasion when Allen Tate's young son-in-law Percy Wood threw him the provocative remark, 'I think you look like an anthropomorphized grasshopper!' Wood recalls that Berryman later took him aside and explained that the remark had hurt him as it was meant to, but added considerately that he understood how it was to feel insecure and antagonistic at such gatherings. After the completion of 'Homage to Mistress Bradstreet' in 1953, Berryman was not at all amused to hear Wood mimicking his reading of the poem. At another, earlier party, Berryman had cut a cordial, well-behaved figure in the presence of Theodore Roethke who was wildly posturing in pinstripe trousers and a pyjama cord.

Berryman slowly grew distant from Richard Blackmur during this period, possibly because Blackmur tended to be somewhat paranoid in his professional bearing and was defensive of any intellectual threat to his position. (Blackmur had also become jealous of Berryman's friendship, and had resented his 'defection' to that circle of friends which included Donald and Betty Mackie.)

Berryman was not above expressions of hostility, however; Cornelia Borgerhoff, whose husband was then director of the Gauss seminars in Princeton, admired Berryman's work but observed that, as a 'specialist in the art of the gratuitous insult', he seemed often compelled to wound others. To those he favoured Berryman extended loyal friendship and immense generosity. At that time, for instance, Robert Fitzgerald, who was then Blackmur's assistant in the Creative Writing Program, took on the additional job of presenting a weekly lecture on Shakespeare at the New School for Social Research, and Berryman unhesitatingly helped with his preparations. On another occasion, Berryman gave a lengthy oral critique of a novel written by Robert Keeley for an undergraduate thesis, even though there was no particular closeness between them. Berryman was spontaneous in his generosity and teaching, and equally eager to learn at all times.

It was during this period that he renewed his friendship with Edmund Wilson, a man of awesome repute and presence. Under the sponsorship of the Gauss seminars, Wilson delivered a series of papers which was to grow into his book *Patriotic Gore*. Berryman took the occasion to attack Wilson for his enthusiastic revival of literary interest in the *Memoirs* of General U. S. Grant, whom Berryman upbraided for his direction of many brutal and bloody Civil War battles. Wilson, who was not used to such treatment, was startled at Berryman's bitter, even vicious, attack. Howard C. Horsford, who was then a junior faculty member, recalls that Berryman made his mark at the seminars in general, 'thin, scowling, nervously intense . . . rather acidulous and combative in his questions and remarks, fairly aggressive and assertive in moving into discussions.'

He formed a new friendship with Randall Jarrell, who found Berryman's company stimulating and entertaining and wrote to his wife that he found him 'a quite touchingly modest person under the surface', but Berryman remained chiefly fond of Donald and Betty Mackie. He suffered feelings of utter disaffection from his mother, largely as a stay against her dominance and insinuating influence in his life, and seems in many ways to have taken to the Mackies for his family in 1950 and 1951. In a letter written in July 1951 during a stay at the Mackies' holiday home on the Massachusetts coast, Berryman illustrated his intimate involvement with the family in this affectionate and absorbed picture of their one-year-old daughter:

> I just had a long conversation with Diana on the terrace, she in an improvised playpen of screens, I sitting on the flags 10 feet away. First she would make a speech, then I made a speech, and

so on. I'd give a good deal to know what her speeches were about. . . . She has seven teeth, two front, v. white, & snaggle; is as fat as a butterball, & v. girlish with quantities of very fine, extremely blond hair.

It was in consequence of the obvious realignment of his feelings that Berryman's mother felt goaded to write to him on 9 June 1950:

It was because you did and do not love me that you accuse me of not loving you, John.
    Why it is true does not matter: it may be that to love your father, you must hate me, it may be any of many things . . . I do not expect you to force yourself to any show or interest or attendance. . . . As for me, I love you and hold you dear, and shall do so always. . . . is Don your brother, that you parade your affection for him before your blood brother?

Although Mrs Berryman thought of showing her letter to Berryman's psychiatrist in case it should prove harmful, and then (as she wrote in her own hand at the head of the letter) 'decided against speech, or sending', her perception and analysis of Berryman's behaviour was in this instance sound.

He spent a good proportion of his time during the period intriguing for sex. His liaisons were never as untransparent as he wished, and in fact, as Pat Warnock Eden recalls, 'his rages and tantrums and affairs were well known and gossiped about. . . . "It's all part of my biography, that's all," he said once, when he was chasing some young woman around, and obviously embarrassing and hurting Eileen.' But while he could also be gallant and entertain friendships with women, his sexual drives seemed to him unappeasable. What could not be known by the Princeton community was the equal intensity of his need to comprehend his motives, which took the form of obsessive self-analysis. He continued consulting his psychiatrist in an effort to resolve the antinomies of his behaviour.

On 4 November 1950 he recorded in his journal: 'My decision last week . . . was not to worry so but to take fucks where they turned up . . . not however to *seek* out new ones. He approved, and perhaps that is not an abominable programme *if it lets me work whereas I otherwise wouldn't.*' In the same place, however, he covered several pages assessing the possibility of having sex with a married acquaintance in her thirties. In this and other relationships of the period, his calculating, which included agonies of subtle or silly interpretation of every spoken phrase and extended even to the nuances of body-language, was both controlled and paroxysmal. In fact, the interpretation that must be put upon the excess of his writing about strategy is that his assumption of objectivity must have helped to contain the fever of his wishes. He himself recognised the 'Danger of writing, as well as thinking, myself into it', but his journal-entries otherwise took more or less passionate versions of this form:

> She did not respond very much except with her hands (lean, long, strong) and half-refused my tongue (these undergraduate details are interesting, – like my *fantastic* nervousness), but she certainly accepted fully the first long embrace, and afterwards acquiesced as it were in her having been moved *too*.

The word that Berryman uses most often about his own feelings is 'nervous', as in this extract: 'this state of nervous expectation, nervous excitement (toward the idea of her) – and – lassitude (toward everything else . . .).' He was aware that he wanted to find the woman more attractive than she actually was, fascinated himself with such features as her eyes, her oddness, her nearness and potential availability, and her apparent self-possession, and even kept a token of her in the form of a lipstick-stained cigarette stub. It was equally absorbing to him to observe her susceptibility to him personally (or even, as he guessed, to his reputation as a minor celebrity in Princeton), and to learn that she had thought him at first 'calm and conceited'. He put it keenly: 'And I persuade myself that under *me* she wd become a good mistress.'

At the same time, in November 1950, he made approaches to a younger Jewish girl, with whom he had liaisons in (among other places) his old office in the library. Despite times of mounting heat, neither relationship lasted long, but it struck him then as cause for both concern and astonishment: 'And am I about to have two new mistresses on my hands neither of whom I really want?'

For a while early in 1951 he became similarly interested in another young woman, but kept back his hopes and settled properly for friendship. Although he himself recoiled more often than not at the thought of having children, his ambivalent interest in the subject (which was to reach a peak when he came to write the childbirth section of 'Homage to Mistress Bradstreet' early in 1953) was such as to leave her with the impression that he loved and wanted them very much.* She feels that a number of phrases in that poem contain references to conversations they had together. In her copy of the poem he was later to underline the phrases 'chaste, laborious, odd'

*See note at end of chapter.

(13:1) and 'please / neglect my cries' (26:1–2). For her, the line that best describes him at the time is 'flamboyant, ill, angelic' (32:2), and she recalls that:

> He was not a pest; he did not intrude his problems on others, he was witty, courtly, sensitive, enormously erudite – he liked my serenity, he refers to that quality in me over and over again. . . .
>
> John idealized women, or at least I felt he did me; although he attacked and was ruthless to a lot of people, I was protected in an almost magic way; he was completely trustworthy in this respect, and I never once doubted it. . . .

Much more of a blunt sexuality excited Berryman's interest in a recently-married woman in October and November of 1951:

> Her breasts in the white sweater under the short suit yesterday really lookt incredible. After so goddamn much pain had, I *must* try seriously at least once: see her alone.
>
> But the difficulty of that is very great, given my nerves (wh. kept me fr. ever calling till yesterday), his unknown schedule, & the risk of going openly to their place. And will she? And even at best then we cd meet only once or twice a week? But that might be enough. But the vacation – do they go away?
>
> His schedule!!

Although, as the weeks went on, Berryman saw what he chose to regard as signs of her interest, time ran out before he could develop the relationship: he was to spend the spring semester of 1952 as Elliston Professor of Poetry (an appointment earning 4,000 dollars) at the University of Cincinnati. In the meantime, as on 21 November, he was limited to writing expressions of his agitation, in a vein betraying a contempt for the object of his desires which was characteristic of many of his adulterous passages:

> 'Empty-faced' P. said, and in fact I've never seen any real animation there but in semi-feminist bias
>
> A flirt, certainly, but v. young, new-married, and despite her body, cold.
>
> A lovely picture of a woman to pursue – and to what end? In two months I go off. But that's just the point: I don't want to love her, I want her; and if in the past month she's not yet 'sent me abt. my business', perhaps she can (w. less languishing & more address) be had, and then I'd be all right & cd be off.

Similarly, he disdained to countenance any other than sexual interest for the married woman whom he had desired the previous year: 'Note: she is *one-who-is-provided-for*. She might want to marry me. UGH.' It is difficult to study the meticulous detail of Berryman's journals without recognising both the superficiality and wiliness of his sexual energy and the pathos of the insecurity which underlay it. The wages of his continual self-inquiry was the growing sense that he was inadequate to marriage because of long-standing insecurities and of what he had come to believe were the unsupportable expectations of women. He wrote of one woman, 'And yet really, I think, I care nothing for her. I have been in this state two thousand times before. *Why*??' and came to believe his womanising 'a disease'. He purported no longer to find satisfaction in his marriage, and that he 'must divorce' Eileen: 'Managed all day to dissemble with my dislike & utter depression.' He persuaded himself then that he was too immature to support the responsibility of marriage, and to meet the demands of a partner, but it must be recognised that his willingness to believe that all women reflected for him his mother's dominance was more than a little self-serving. Although he strove consciously to reach a state of contentment and responsibility, he seems to have been little aware of the self-gratifying force which led him to succumb to disablement, and to exploit, as in sexual ventures, what was otherwise a psychological misfortune. The diagnosis that he presented to himself was that steps should be taken to solve the incapacity put upon him by his upbringing and temperament, but that (at the same time) it was probably permanent and had left him helpless. By a form of false logic, therefore, he could partly justify the unhappy selfishness of his behaviour. It was late in 1950 that he chose to concede that sex and alcohol were his 'props', and to note down this version of his psychiatrist's view:

> my distaste for 'real' intercourse (i.e. meaningful, marital) & tolerance of other = mother's dislike of girls I was *really* interested in, & indifference to sex-play. *Not* Mother herself, all these difficulties of mine, but the image. One 'shd' think of one's mother in a friendly way, not often, & not doing anything about it, he said.

As always, Berryman's life more or less served his work: that he accepted this rationalisation as the premise of his conduct went some way to dictate the theme of treachery in writing his play the following year. His notes for his hero's response to women included remarks which must have coincided with his own feelings:

> *Hatred of women* (domination by Amer. women – unthinkable in England or Russia)
> the 'girls'! well-breasted slim-legg'd shoppers . . . or *w*. falsies & deodorants & big checking accounts,
> the hags in lipstick & black locks step out. . . .

In November 1950 he had significantly recorded in his journal that one of his girlfriends 'admitted dominating men', and it is clear from the singular curiosity of the entry that he had pressed her to do so in order to confirm his theory about his mother and other women in his life.

The issue of what had been two years of maundering work and of a succession of perfunctory relationships was that Berryman rose to the challenge of change on removing to Cincinnati early in 1952.

NOTE TO CHAPTER 10
Apropos the childbirth sections of *Homage to Mistress Bradstreet* (see also Chapter 1, 'Introductory', pp. 4–5), it is pertinent to know that in later years Berryman unhappily misrepresented the fact of his experience by telling the *Paris Review*, for example, that his wife Eileen had been admitted to

> the hospital in New York for an operation, what they call a woman's operation, a kind of parody of child birth. Both she and I were feeling very bitter about this since we very much wanted a child and had not had one. So I had very, very strong emotions and solitude.

Saying that much, he was radically rewriting history by suggesting that Eileen had undergone a hysterectomy and so introducing a myth into his life story. In fact Eileen had a myomectomy to remove a benign tumor, an operation which in no way parodies childbirth but which is frequently performed to remove a fibroid in cases where a woman wishes to become pregnant because the fibroid *may* be an impediment. When Eileen was candid with the surgeon about marital relations in the months after the operation, it became evident that it was not the case that the tumor had been at fault but Berryman's own unwillingness to let her become pregnant because of his resistant or delinquent behaviour. Eileen had been reluctant to face the facts, despite all the evidence. Once the true condition of affairs became apparent, Eileen terminated treatment. Likewise, in contradiction of Berryman's statement to the *Paris Review* that both he and Eileen were feeling bitter over her operation, the truth is that neither of them was bitter, and Eileen assuredly still felt hopeful.

11
Transitions,
1952-54

The Berrymans' residence in Cincinnati was an unexpectedly fulfilling and invigorating time for both of them. Although Berryman was moved to work painfully and exhaustively on his poem 'Homage to Mistress Bradstreet' during the four months of their residence, he seemed to have no limits to his energy for teaching and social activities, as well as for producing about a hundred pages of his projected study of Shakespeare. While he fermented both his profession and his leisure, Eileen too rejoiced in the happy company of friends they made in the city. She introduced herself to the medical school and was able to sit in on courses and attend ward rounds in psychiatry.

The Berrymans took an apartment on the ground floor of 256 Greendale Avenue, an awesome, rambling house with rooms subdivided into ill-apportioned and unconvivial shapes. The ceilings reached fourteen feet, the dining-room was of such dimensions that, as Berryman said, 'you cd drill troops in it', and none of the numerous chairs offered any comfort. For the first days of their occupancy they saw no relief to the uncompromising grimness of their visit.

Cincinnati blossomed only when they met Gilbert and Elisabeth Bettman, who threw a party in their modest house, an occasion when the Berrymans first realised with wonder that a number of families kept servants and excelled in hospitality.

Berryman came to feel for their new friends what he was later to describe as 'affection, astonishment, true respect, and amusement'. The group into which they were introduced included Van Meter Ames, Professor of Philosophy, and his wife Betty; Professor George H. Ford of the Department of English; and J. Alister Cameron, Professor of Classics, and his wife Elizabeth (always known as 'Hamish' and 'Puggy'), who had themselves newly arrived in the city. Berryman joyed unreservedly in the company of Cameron and Ames, and grew perhaps especially close to Cameron, whose work on Sophocles stimulated endless hours of discussion.

Elisabeth Bettman recalls:

> At least twice a week we would have a party with the group. . . . And it seems to me that we were always dropping in on them at Greendale Avenue. We were very gay, almost feverishly so. I think John set the tempo of our social life. I think he craved this constant round of activity, although he complained 'like mad' about how it interrupted his work.

Like George Ford, who found this spirit of 'Berrymania' wholly infectious, none of their circle demurred at partying again and again until five in the morning: 'Most of us were then in our early thirties, and we felt, under John's auspices, we had reverted to our early twenties or earlier.' Elisabeth Bettman remembers too:

> We were all young and reckless of our energy. John was the spendthrift of course, and there was always the problem of his drinking, even then. . . . I used to think that he drank to ease the tension, to calm his intensity. Certainly he seemed happier and more relaxed in his cups. When he was sober, he was often very sad. One couldn't call it depression, or melancholia, but a congenital 'tristesse'. He brooded a great deal on the past. . . . He was acutely conscious of his own shortcomings – he was almost guilt obsessed. I don't think John breathed many easy moments ever. And with it all, he was so kind and so compassionate. At a superficial level he could excoriate the human race; he was 'madly' – to use one of his favorite words – impatient of mediocrity, but the truth of the matter is that he was intensely sympathetic and intuitive of the needs of others.
>
> John was a compulsive talker. He liked an attentive audience. He was disarmingly and sometimes embarrassingly candid about himself and his problems. Perhaps he sought expiation through confession. In any event he was tormented and driven and always somehow in search of release from his inner torment.

Eileen, who was an enthusiastic and expert dancer, gave added interest to the many social gatherings and revived the custom of dancing in people's houses. It seemed to their friends that she was very self-contained and exercised great patience towards Berryman's erratic life, although it was evident too that she was understandably under stress – especially during Berryman's times of being edgy and out of spirits, when, as George Ford recalls, she 'seemed to be watching him . . . like an engine-tender watching the gauge on a boiler.' Berryman himself was 'aware that their relationship was in jeopardy,' according to Elisabeth Bettman, 'and that it was his doing. But there was always that strong streak of self destructiveness that would take over, and he would proclaim himself powerless to stem the tide.'

As the Elliston Professor of Poetry, a post funded by a newspaper woman who intermittently wrote poetry, Berryman undertook a heavy amount of teaching. In addition to running a poetry workshop, he gave ten lectures on modern poets from Whitman to Auden, Lowell, and Dylan Thomas, and seven on all periods of Shakespeare's oeuvre, with a depth of scholarship which amazed audiences (invariably numbering well over a hundred) in McMicken Hall. He spent himself in the meticulousness of preparation and the tensions of performance, as Van Meter Ames, who took careful notes from Berryman's lectures, recalls: 'writing the lectures was strenuous too. I noted that one of them ruined 15 shirts. He was always hopped up.' Berryman had to change his shirt after every lecture. Much of each talk was taken up with excellent readings of individual poems followed by an explication which, despite its excellence, was often insufficient to Ames's taste, as when Berryman seemed cavalier towards Eliot's notes and allusions in his discussion of *The Waste Land*. In spite of certain shortcomings, however, Berryman's lectures were always full of strikingly personal ideas and opinions, or arresting summations. Characteristic of his remarks are, according to Ames's notes, the pronouncement that *The Waste Land* is 'the most explicit expression of the death wish in modern civilization', that 'there is no telling how good poems cannot be written. They may be written drunk, sober, etc.', or his elaboration (in the opening remarks of his introductory lecture on modern poetry) of the paradox suggested by the word 'malice':

What has happened to expressiveness, especially in the last 40 years? Today what is being expressed? The passions. Not joy, as in the poetry familiar to us, but resentment, bitterness, malice. Such are as satisfactory for poetry as the Christian emotions. *Schadenfreude* would be a better word: malicious joy. It is still joy, and this is lacking in our word malice.

In the poetry workshop, only one outstanding talent emerged, that of Janet Emig, poet and later Professor of English at Rutgers University, but the class as a whole was mesmerised by Berryman's inspirational teaching. He showed a singular interest in his students, gave readings to the graduate English Club, and would read manuscripts with endless willing. Elisabeth Bettman, who had then no affiliation with the university, recalls that 'He was a slave driver, but no one complained,' and it was as a result of his encouragement that she went on to take a degree in English.

The peculiar success of Cincinnati was that it energised and absorbed Berryman. His temperament answered to the kinds of pressure imposed on him during those intense weeks, and his literary interests, social flair, and creativity ran at full stretch. He screwed himself up to a routine which was relentlessly demanding and duly productive. Also, lionised as never before in his career, he was at last able to take the coveted role of a celebrity, and to indulge to the utmost both the courtly and the raffish sides of his personality.

Such an unremitting course could not last, and at the end of his appointment Berryman was chronically fatigued as always after concentrated periods of work. About two weeks before departure he affected a superciliousness as to:

> endless official & social activities, and am not even yet through,
> but extremely done up, and still with accumulated masses of
> junk to deal with. Undoubtedly I have been a great success,
> which is the most wearying thing that anyone can be;
> everybody loves me and goes off like fireworks when I appear,
> and I have been extremely unhappy.

In spite of pretending such disdain, however, he had accomplished a great deal, both personally and professionally. For the next year, until the middle of 1953, he was awarded a Guggenheim Fellowship for critical study of Shakespeare and for creative writing; Cincinnati had given him impetus and substantial starts in both lines. One of the lectures he had delivered there, 'Shakespeare at Thirty', was to be published in the *Hudson Review* the next summer, and he had made significant progress with the difficult work of 'Homage to Mistress Bradstreet'. He had shared the painfulness of the poem's gestation with a number of friends in Cincinnati. Although he reported that he felt 'glad to fly out of this circus' on completion of his Elliston tenure at the beginning of June, he was later to recall the city nostalgically as representing an idyllic interlude during which work and play had harmonised. For the following months in

Princeton he returned to his harrowing and seemingly inconsequential regime of solitary introspection. The crescendo of the
sorry regimen that was to come coincided with the finishing of
'Homage to Mistress Bradstreet' in the early months of 1953, after
intensive weeks of Shakespearean analysis. But the pattern and
progress of his working life – a life entirely at the mercy of his work
– exacerbated and was soon to exhaust his marriage.

In February 1953 Berryman applied for a renewal of his Gugg-
enheim Fellowship. Apart from that single contingency, his present frantic difficulties in writing his first masterpiece, 'Homage to
Mistress Bradstreet', would not allow for foresight or prudence.
Night and day became inextricable in the turbulence of his writing.
In a sense crazed by his own single-mindedness, Berryman served
Eileen ill for some weeks, and she felt deeply concerned for his
agitation at all hours.
   On completing the poem he became physically ill, drained of
energy and black at heart. 'My doctor sent me to Atlantic City . . .
for solitude,' he recorded,

> a curious idea but a good one as it turned out, I spoke to no soul
> there and did a little improve (you understand that after the
> terrible solitariness of writing, I had to give a public reading of
> the poem here – Princeton had offered me two hundred dollars
> – which brought all sorts of golden opinions and human
> pressures I was not fit for, having got out of bed to read the
> thing, then just 8 days done) – well, on Good Friday what
> should I come on, along the Boardwalk, at Steel Pier, but the
> collection on display of the medieval torture instruments from
> Nuremberg, racks, pincers, shin-breakers, head-cages, wheels,
> and – impassive, large, beautifully carved, horrible – the Iron
> Maiden – the presence of the lady in the same city made me so
> nervous I fled home.

He had balefully to think again about his many debts, but his
strongest feeling was one of unaccountable hostility. In a style
characteristic of his letters to his mother, he wrote her on 12 April:

> I saw nobody all week and *Thursday* I really began to improve: I
> was less constantly ill, less feeble, and calmer, not sullen, not
> wild. I have stopt drinking, & can eat. I am still very uncertain
> and tired, face with distaste the indispensable minimum for
> going off, and resentment can throttle me in a moment at any

fancied stupidity or imposition; but the movement downward seems to have stopped, I can even bear conversation.

Where the rage comes from I don't altogether understand, though I know a good deal about it and I think it may be an unavoidable concomitant of a certain kind of intolerable painful, exalted creation. Any artist not a saint, that is, who loves humanity as much, while torturing himself as much, as I did and was during parts of the composition of the poem, with that intensity over a protracted time, may be bound to take it out on humanity (any specimens that are unlucky enough to be by) afterward.

Apart from the melodrama of the way he expressed himself, it was equally characteristic that he should give no word of the immediate 'specimen' subjected to the almost intolerable burden of his life – Eileen, his wife. Although Berryman's fellowship was not renewed for a further term, they had arranged some time earlier to spend the summer in Europe and decided to stick to that plan. Shortly before, Viking had contracted with Berryman, with an advance on royalties of 1,000 dollars, to publish at least his book on Shakespeare; both parties now had misgivings about the commission, but there was no time to ratify the indefinite status of the work before the Berrymans sailed for Europe on a French ship out of New York on 28 April. Although Berryman invariably professed to rejoice in his own company, both he and Eileen felt a sense of relief on discovering that Louis MacNeice was a fellow passenger.

By 5 May they arrived in Paris and lodged at the Hôtel des Saints Pères, one block from St Germain des Prés, where they found themselves within walking distance of the Louvre and other forms of entertainment, including a performance of *Electra* at the Opèra. In a little while Berryman began to feel restless. While regretting an absence of hard liquor and occasionally making fractious overtures towards going home, he did manage to drink moderately of vermouth, beer, or brandy, to eat well, and to sleep with a sedative. After a few days they left with Hamish and Puggy Cameron, their close friends from Cincinnati the previous year, for a ten days' drive to Provence and the Côte d'Azure, and then on to Florence and Rome. By the end of the tour, during which they moved on every day, they were thankful to pass some time in Rome. All things considered, Berryman seemed no longer quite so obsessed with his poem, in spite of having been prompt to recite some of it to a baker in St Tropez at five o'clock one morning.

At the Pensione Svizzera they took a room away from the street, while the Camerons stayed with the poet Denis Devlin (then Irish minister to Italy) and his wife, who arranged for both couples to meet the American-born Princess Marguerite Caetani, the founder and editor of the international literary magazine *Botteghe Oscure*. Berryman went in hopes of some patronage from the lady and gave her one of his old stories, but had no success. Also in Rome they met up with other friends from Princeton, including Marian Kelleher, sister of their good friend Donald Mackie, and the art historian George Rowley. As an act which was perhaps more generous than necessary, Rowley engaged Berryman to do an editorial job on his current book. Berryman looked to finish the work within two weeks at a profit of some 200 dollars, but the task did not actually pay as well as expected and penury threatened to cut short their stay on the Continent.

The social life in Rome stepped up; they were called for parties and outings to historic sites or to the beach, for meetings with Theodore Roethke and his young wife Beatrice, and for a vivacious spree by car with the Devlins and another guest, the novelist Alberto Moravia, to the fort of Ostnia. The highlight of their days in Rome – a moment of simple and chastening theatre – took place early in June, as Berryman recounted in a letter:

> It was Corpus Christi and we'd tried to get tribune seats in St Peter's, for the procession, through the head of the Irish legation, the poet Denis Devlin, who has been uniformly kind. Well, he was told (he is anti-clerical, by the way) there wd be no tribunes & no procession except of canons. But we went to see the church anyway, which we'd seen only at night, and were among the last of thousands to enter, at eleven. There was a voice, and *applause*. I rank as a tall man in Italy and saw, half a mile off against a scarlet cloth, a small figure in white flanked by one in red & one in black. More mysterious applause. At last, men climbing up pillars, children held high to see, people w. backs turned looking in upheld mirrors, slowly the Pope came towards us borne in his chair between aisle-barriers. He waved his palms slowly towards himself, leaning slowly from side to side down the chair-arms – so Italians wave – while the part of the throng next him shouted. It was all alarmingly informal. A few feet from us he halted to ask who were a contingent of little girls in uniform. Then, a dozen feet off, at the end of the aisle before it turned out of the nave, the chair was swung to face the altar, he rose and solemnly blessed all parts of the congregation. During the few yards out, then, he blessed girls's coifs handed up to him – his outstretched arm was still visible as the chair

disappeared. Earlier, we heard at dinner, he had given his handkerchief down to a man. A very white, kind, beautiful figure. Eileen wept, and I was altogether astonished.

Although it rained much of the time in Rome (a circumstance which everyone then attributed to the recent exploding of the atomic bomb), Berryman seemed on the whole to enjoy their society and jaunts, but he had fallen into a maudlin phase by mid-June. His state of mind, and accordingly of his harmony with Eileen, deteriorated as time went on. Eileen began to experience pain in her back (possibly from too much sight-seeing) and went south on 22 June for a few days in search of sun and rest.

By the end of the first week in July she was suffering quite badly, and they moved on again to Paris. Delighting (as always against his will) in new surroundings, especially in the refreshingly sunny elegance of Paris, Berryman hurried excitedly to several exhibitions. By mid-July they left for London, to stay by invitation with Louis and Hedli MacNeice. On the Friday night of their arrival, the MacNeices threw a party during which someone playfully pulled Eileen down on the hall stairs. The sudden jerk proved catastrophic to her back, and after a tortured night on the fifth floor of the house she was admitted to hospital next morning. The specialist took a serious view of the injury since disc-degeneration affected her legs; she was immobilised for some weeks.

Berryman found himself unable to tolerate her incapacitation, not only for selfless reasons of her suffering but also for his own sake. Although he was far from feeling heartless towards her, he was more used to self-engrossment and to receiving attention than to giving it. It distressed him immeasurably to suspend his own needs in favour of the absoluteness of hers. For reasons which were deep and largely unintentional, he considered her disablement a galling burden to himself, and chafed in ways that seemed childish and hysterical at the responsibility – thrashing (as Eileen gradually came to realise) to be free again for a destiny which could well be more hapless than the bondage of his marriage. He soon started begrudging her his time and energy in visiting the hospital, a fact which Allen Tate (who was in London and visited Eileen a few times) remarked to his family. Eileen persuaded Berryman to use his time as he wished. While she hoped that he would press for work at the BBC, where he had been asked to record some programmes, he actually spent his time in visiting Cambridge again after fifteen years. In London he took MacNeice to a performance of *2 Henry VI* at the Old Vic, and also called on his former fiancée, Beatrice, who had remained unmarried since leaving him in New York in 1939.

Beatrice herself took the opportunity of paying a sick-call on Eileen in hospital.

On top of his resentment and personal neglect of Eileen, it was exasperating to witness Berryman's failure to make any financial provisions for her hospitalisation or even against their return to New York. His improvidence resulted more from procrastination than from indifference to self-promotion. The one professional advance to which he looked in the near future was the publication of 'Homage to Mistress Bradstreet', which Catharine Carver was seeing scrupulously through the press at *Partisan Review* (where it appeared in September–October 1953). In the meantime he seemed content to accept personal loans from Allen Tate and from his mother.

The approach of indigence, Berryman's habit of abandoning himself to his lot rather than searching out fresh means, and his worsening problem with alcohol, distrained upon Eileen's peace of mind. Berryman cultivated so much tension about him, and seemed so careless of matters other than the implacable needs of his writing, that Eileen was forced to put their marriage seriously in question. Piteously convinced that acute anxiety and unhappiness fed his creativity, Berryman obliged those about him to subserve the dictates of his work and his resentment of interruptions or distractions. His bearing as a poet had come to style his whole life, from teaching to social gatherings and even to the private times of his marriage. Displays of temperament had turned into a stock-in-trade. His ambivalence was such that he felt oppressed by poetic inspiration, yet needed to intensify rather than to assuage the oppression before he could manage any brief spells of quiescence. This conduct of his working life, which he believed paradoxically to calm his spirit, was accompanied by phases of paranoia or general hostility. He did not make it possible for anyone to suffer *with* him; on the contrary, self-affairs prevented him from recognising the appalling degree to which Eileen suffered from his ways.

It was as a result of the accumulation of such pressures and deliberations that Eileen decided against all her hopes to separate from Berryman on their return to the USA later in the month. She remained in Princeton, while Berryman fell back for a while into the sphere of his mother's dubious influence at 360 West 23rd Street, New York City. Realising at last that he should make proper efforts to earn his living, Berryman wrote informally to Harry Levin at Harvard with a request for employment; by October he agreed to undertake Shakespeare and creative writing courses the following summer. On the recommendation of Robert Lowell, Paul Engle at

Iowa appointed Berryman to teach creative writing in the spring semester.

By the beginning of November 1953 Berryman moved out of his mother's apartment into the Chelsea Hotel, West 23rd Street. There he reacquainted himself with Dylan Thomas, who was shortly to suffer his fatal collapse in the hotel on Wednesday 4 November. During the four days of Thomas's coma, Berryman was obliged to relinquish his vigil with the numerous 'mourners' at the hospital in order to fulfil a long-standing lecture engagement at Bard College, Annandale-on-Hudson. On the Saturday he delivered what was generally held to be a remarkable talk, running to more than one-and-a-half hours, on *The Tempest*. Andrews Wanning, a long-standing friend, recalls the lecture vividly. Berryman regarded *The Tempest* as a didactic play, to be viewed more as a moral document than as affiliated to the conventions of the Jacobean masque. That evening Wanning held a party at his rambling old house about ten miles from the campus, numbering Keith Botsford, Ralph Ellison, and Saul Bellow (currently on the faculty at Bard College) among his guests. Clusters of people waited by the telephone for news of Thomas, reminiscing and eulogising in a fashion that suggested a wake was in progress. Berryman was notably dramatic and drunken, and announced that 'Poetry is dead with Dylan Thomas!'

Pearl Kazin, who was also present at the Bard Conference, recalls that:

> Berryman was upset, but also melodramatizing his concern for Thomas. In the course of a country walk that weekend, he kept saying, as he took long gulps of air: 'I'm breathing for Dylan, if I breathe for him perhaps he will remain alive.' We drove back to New York on Sunday evening, with Ralph Ellison, and though it was almost midnight when we reached the city, Berryman insisted that he and I go to St Vincent's Hospital to see Dylan. The crowds of literary vultures had left by then, and a nun let us into the room to look at D.T., lying under an oxygen tent. . . . John just stood beside the bed for about 10 minutes, very quiet and very miserable . . . . (I think that he and Dylan liked to drink together, but they were not what I would call friends.)

It is certainly true that Berryman exaggerated his intimacy with Thomas, with whom he was in fact comparatively little acquainted, but it was less from self-seeking shallowness than from a strong sense of identification. 'Dylan was one of my oldest friends,' he wrote a few days after Thomas died (they had first met sixteen years earlier), 'but the general loss I feel far worse still.' In the same place, with what might be construed as a self-regarding posture, he added: 'my brains are broken by Dylan's illness and death, which is certainly the worst thing that ever happened.'

He called at the hospital on Monday lunchtime, when Thomas happened to be unattended for a moment, and found him dead. Careering off to tell the news, Berryman met John Malcolm Brinnin (who had been in attendance all the weekend and had just slipped out for a moment) and demanded, accusingly, 'Where were you?' Some years later he wrote a memorial poem for Thomas, in which the eighth line quoted here originally read 'I stopped out-raged a nurse . . .'

> Oh, I *was* highlone in the corridor
>   fifteen feet from his bed
>
> where no other hovered, nurse or staff or friend,
> and only the terrible breathing ever took place,
> but trembling nearer after some small time
>   I came on the tent collapsed
>
> and silence – O unable to say when.
> I stopped panicked a nurse, she a doctor
> in twenty seconds, he pulled the plasticine,
>   bent over, and shook his head at me.
>
> Tubes all over, useless versus coma,
> on the third day his principal physician
> told me to pray he'd die, brain damage such.
>   His bare stub feet stuck out
>   ['In Memoriam (1914–1953)', *Delusions, Etc.*].

It seems reasonable to take Berryman's aggression towards Brinnin as a manifestation of his shock. For a while after the death, he numbered himself among the faction which questioned the propriety of the treatment Thomas had been given. A memorial service was held on the Friday, after which Berryman spent some time commiserating with Caitlin Thomas.

Towards the end of the year Berryman met a young, immensely attractive Jewish girl, Anita Maximilian Phillips, who had recently separated from her husband. They were introduced by Berryman's friend Saul Bellow, who was then living apart from his first wife and going out with Alexandra (commonly known as 'Sondra') Tschacbasov, later to become his wife. Anita and Sondra figured among a group of bright, confident contemporaries at Bennington College, Vermont. Saul Bellow had known Berryman well at least from the period of Bellow's tenure of the Princeton Creative Writing Fellowship during the preceding academic year. Being invariably more disciplined and regulated in his conduct than Berryman, Bellow tended not to share his bizarre behaviour, yet enjoyed the *enfant terrible*. They relished each other's company for intellectual stimulus and game. On one occasion Bellow remarked that he wanted to be a poet. Berryman, who avidly admired his craftsmanship, responded brightly, 'You are!' Bellow replied, 'Oh, I mean short lines!' Sondra Bellow remembers the time in Princeton when Bellow first sold a portion of his novel *The Adventures of Augie March* for periodical publication in the *New Yorker* and threw a celebration party which John and Eileen Berryman attended: Berryman became intoxicated and proceeded to hold up Sondra's foot and recite poetry to it.

Sondra stayed with Anita at her New York home, 25 Fifth Avenue, for some weeks, and it was during that period that she and Bellow felt bound to introduce her to every bachelor in New York, a category which loosely included Berryman. Anita, who was twenty years of age, was working on an undergraduate thesis and attempting to write a first novel at the time. It was partly because of her own literary aspirations that she embraced the literary coterie commanded by Berryman and Bellow, though she recalls that Berryman's attitude towards her ambitions took the perhaps teasingly patronising form, 'Isn't she clever – she writes books too!'

On the breakdown of her marriage, she went through a phase of searching for her own identity and direction in life, and was trying to define herself against the indulgence and sophistication of her background when she met Berryman (her father, a wealthy furrier who had emigrated from Warsaw, liked to tell the story of how he had won 18,000 dollars in one weekend's gambling at the Georges Cinque Hotel in Paris). Berryman did not actually disclose that he was separated from Eileen, but Anita observed that he always spoke of her with both guilt and reverence. She recognised the deep affection that enveloped Eileen in Berryman's mind, and was made to feel very apprehensive of meeting her in his company.

She felt attracted to Berryman for his energy, excitement, and flirtatiousness. She found him intellectually adept and vigorous, nervously live – a person who, as Sondra put it to her, went without a skin. He generated a special, electrical environment with each person he met. He could also behave mysteriously with Anita, however, and would sometimes rush off somewhere, for example, and return to tell the tale of his antics in unsolicited detail. He and Bellow shared a passion for literature and would match each other with ideas and repartee. Anita felt that he wanted to exercise a talent for friendship, and (in relation to that circle of friends) fiercely to borrow the passion of the Jews and to make a real connection with them. On the other hand, he could be staggeringly childish in his behaviour, as when he once borrowed a red sash from Anita's robe and wound it around his head like a mitre in order to burlesque the Pope. She was stunned by the naivety of the show.

For Berryman, Anita represented youth and vitality; he treated her as a life-force which he felt lapsing in himself. She sensed that he was desperate at heart, and found him not only hungry for sex but deeply anxious about it. Her own forthcoming attitude flattered the needs of his narcissism, and she recalls him as 'a very attentive lover' during the span of a relationship which was in no way painful for her. In fact she sometimes felt mean or cutting towards him, a response provoked by his own air of helplessness. Because of his poverty (which appeared to concern him remarkably little), he often ate at her house and they would go for walks instead of paying for entertainment. On one occasion, as they passed a tramp in the Bowery, she remarked that he could end up like that. 'You're being generous,' he replied sardonically.

As Eileen had come to recognise before her, Anita in due course saw that Berryman was not a person with whom she could spend her life. 'I sensed that he was crazy,' she remembers. Given to brilliant or bizarre or – lately – grating scenes, he seemed in many ways unreal as a person, performing a role not by nature but by assumption, with quick wits and a conjuring tongue. Anita saw his paranoid and self-destructive tendencies, and realised that he was not fully in control of himself. As the weeks progressed into 1954, and Berryman left to teach at Iowa, she decided that she could not face what she calls 'the unreality of his expectations', and let their relationship pass away. The ending left no ill feelings between them – 'he never behaved towards me in anything but a perfectly delightful way,' she recalls, and felt regretful only of the possibility that she might have treated him badly.

In Iowa Berryman took lodgings at 606 South Johnson Street with Mr and Mrs Bristol, he a professor of business administration; she, though already elderly, at work on a dissertation. On the first night he over-estimated his knowledge of the dark hallway, tumbled down a flight of stairs and through a half-glass door, and landed bloodily in the shower. With just a week to go before his classes assembled, he was obliged to spend much of the time in bed with a broken left wrist and swollen ankles. (His landlady had broken her left wrist on the same stairs the year before.) He hurt for some weeks. Colonitis, which had come on in New York, gave him diarrhoea for two-and-a-half months, and he suffered too from a shortness of breath both morning and night which must have been evidence of anxiety. In addition, his loss of dexterity left him, he felt, unable – if not without the will – to cook. Unhappy, lonely (a condition which included a feeling of sexual deprivation), and sleeping only fitfully, six weeks in Iowa reduced him to a run-down state.

Early in his days at Iowa he took up Hebrew under Frederick Peretz Bargebuhr, a man he considered a 'brilliant scholar' who had been an architect and had come late to teaching from Germany via Palestine. Bargebuhr's field was religion on non-theological grounds with a linguistic orientation and a major in Islamology. While Berryman glowed in the light of his professor's learning, Bargebuhr could not engage in a full meeting of minds. He felt more preoccupied with his own inadequacy as a professor of religion, being the only layman among mid-western theologians – 'stuck in the values of the German Youth Movement plus Zionism' – and his conception of a poet being Stefan George. He found living in 'provincial and thoroughly unartistic Iowa, hard-core mid-western' a detrimental experience which Berryman must have shared. In his first enthusiasm for Hebrew, Berryman studied hard and outstripped the other student in the class who shared Barge-buhr's regularity of approach. Bargebuhr recalls that, 'being so pitiably stuck to my system,' he felt 'unable . . . to accept his gallop as covering the ground,' and that Berryman's 'tourist approach' to learning a language upset his principles. As an offshoot of his studies, Berryman even drafted a hundred lines of a poem ('Part is in Hebrew,' he announced grandly), what he called 'a hard-demanding unwelcome' work provisionally entitled 'Letter from a Singing Man to Saul & Peretz' (later to be called 'Testament from In Here'). He spent the best part of a week sleepless in order to hasten his output, with the result that he collapsed twice during that period. Feeling his creation unaccountable, 'what will happen to it if I ever feel strong enough to settle to composition I don't know,' he related. 'It begins in Iowa & winds up in the Pleiades, and one thing I specially dislike abt it is that it is personal. I hope it will be short.' He was sufficiently presumptuous of his abilities as to offer 'corrections' to Bargebuhr's translations of eleventh-century Hebrew poetry. Although Bargebuhr's versions were still rudimentary, he knew that Berryman could not consult the original text and had strayed from the meaning; the opportunity for any creative alliance was foreclosed. On top of his capricious routine, Berryman's sense of continuing financial dishonour and shame of life lowered his spirits so badly that he suffered a spell of what he called 'waking nightmares', as he told Anita Maximilian in frantic telephone calls.

Teaching at Iowa provided an invigorating consolation for his personal ills. Gifted to a degree, all of his students soon went into print, some to earn international reputations with their poetry: W. D. Snodgrass, Donald Justice, Philip Levine, William Dickey, Jane Cooper, Henri Coulette, Melvin La Follette, Paul Petrie, Shirley Eliason, Frederick Bock, Robert Dana, and Donald Petersen. Thirty people first enrolled for the poetry workshop. According to Henri Coulette, Berryman clearly considered it too large a number. In a seeming but perhaps unconscious effort to whittle down the class, Berryman indulged what Coulette calls the 'scare tactic' of catechising for an hour at length a doctor's wife who had written a poem which criticised her husband's profession. At the next session, only thirteen students remained, and Berryman went on from week to week to thrill all of them with a sense of the importance and nobility of writing. Beautifully dressed (always wearing a hat when outdoors), he conveyed in his personal bearing an air of eastern class and elegance, but his hands trembled from nervousness or drinking as he instilled his students with the excitement of their calling.

Philip Levine remembers vividly that

> the workshop and the night class in poetry were the best classes I've ever been a part of – John was a great teacher & he gave so fucking much of himself & there was so much in him that it was amazing. Amazing . . . We loved him; it was the middle of the shittiest part of American life, the Rosenbergs had just been murdered, Joe McCarthy was king, and John could make the study of poetry, our god damned mediocre poetry, the center of the world.

At the start of his series of poetry workshops Berryman gave two assignments, the first and most exacting being to write a sonnet, for which he included among models E. A. Robinson's 'Many Are Called' and 'The Sirens', a poem by the Australian John Manifold. Out of the assignment emerged Donald Justice's 'Sonnet' in *Summer Anniversaries*, which Berryman praised extravagantly for its technique and cunning. Another student recalls meeting Berryman for a beer that week:

He immediately began to read Don Justice's sonnet and he marveled at the opening and the explosive pause in the second line. He was deliriously excited and to this day I can hear him recite it: 'The wall surrounding them they never saw/ The angels often.'

Instantly he wrote down the first two lines of what he considered to be his own best sonnet (which turned out to be number twenty-five in the volume later published as *Berryman's Sonnets*). Henri Coulette wrote a sonnet about St Francis which, he recalls, Berryman praised for evincing such ambition and risk of subject-matter. For the second assignment – an elegy in rhyming stanzas – W. D. Snodgrass produced a poem that was to become 'A Flat One' after many changes.

Berryman was always spontaneous with applause or dislike for the exercises his students turned in, and might on occasion exult or weep openly. At his evening seminar he explicated Whitman's 'Song of Myself' at illuminating length, Paul Petrie vividly remembers, and managed to start a miniature Whitman revival at a time when the 'barbaric yawp' was regarded as mouthy, formless, and a poor risk in terms of New Critical analysis. 'It was a brilliant performance,' Jane Cooper writes.

> I also remember his speaking with great delicacy and warmth of Roethke – in particular of the poems of *The Lost Son* and *Praise to the End!* 'Why, Ted Roethke,' he would say, 'Ted Roethke is the only man who . . . *thinks* like a flower!'

> And there was even more to learn from him outside of class [another student recalls] as he talked almost exclusively about writing and writers & always in his tense, nervous, paranoid bombastic manner. Thinking back I don't believe I've ever known a more gentle yet violent individual. In private, he was marvelously compassionate about his students and their work even though in class he was often devastatingly sarcastic, nasty and generally tough. But all of this was tempered by his brilliant wit and candid openness.

Paul Petrie feels that Berryman, who was 'adroit as a moderator, excellent as a surgeon', took him often for a victim, although the part was invariably salutary.

Out of class Berryman patronised local taverns with his students, particularly Kenney's, a bar run by a tall, freckled, red-haired Irishman named John Kenney and his handsome, dark-haired wife,

Irene. It was at Kenney's that Henri Coulette witnessed what he considered to be Berryman's ineptitude at chess (since he exposed his bishops to attack from an early stage). Berryman's social candour and persistence were disarming, but could often become comic or alarming. At this time W. D. Snodgrass was working and living in a hospital and also teaching a course of his own to pay off the expenses of a divorce. He managed to attend Berryman's classes only irregularly, and while being certainly impressed by his teacher's brilliance in literary analyses he was otherwise stunned by his social conduct. 'My impression is that as soon as he liked you he began making your life difficult by tampering in your love life and sometimes by trying to tamper with your wife (much of this seemed to have a heavy homosexual bent and some of it seemed deliberate misbehavior to get slapped down).' (On the subject of sublimated homoeroticism, Berryman was later to write to a friend: 'writers are likely to have more masked–homosexual–component around than other people, and heading for friends' wives or girls is really a way of getting closer to friends.') Snodgrass found any sort of conversation with Berryman 'incredibly valuable', yet 'he did turn those sessions so painful that you finally fled howling. I remember nights in Iowa City when he would monologue till 4 in the morning, allowing no one else to speak, singing the most beautiful songs to their permanent detriment, etc., etc. It couldn't be borne.'

Berryman's personal torment was sensed by many but seen by few. At the time when he suffered hallucinations – 'w. complications' – he told Anita Maximilian on 25 March, 'I got in a friend to keep me fr. cutting my throat (of course I did not tell him this) & he stayed w. me 30 hrs or so.' It could have been another occasion, 'early morning, perhaps three or four a.m.,' when Donald Justice

had a call from John asking me to come over to his apartment because he was going to kill himself. I got a cab and went right over. (I knew my way around there because . . . my wife and I had formerly rented the same quarters.) When I looked from the hall through his living room door, I saw him sitting on the floor (in bathrobe, I believe) regarding an open case of old-fashioned razors. The sight was too much for me. I felt faint and had to lie down on the sofa. He became immediately all concern and consideration, hurrying down the hall to the bathroom to fetch damp cloths with which to chafe my wrists and so on. Soon I was feeling more myself. To my great relief, so was he. We talked a long time. He had evidently been spending most of the night telephoning friends in the east, perhaps including his estranged wife, but I observed none of this myself. Toward dawn we went into town (perhaps ¾ of a mile or less distant), had breakfast, and then up to my apartment, where he fell asleep in the living room easy chair and slept till afternoon. Nothing else was mentioned about suicide, in my presence at least, as long as I knew him.

Berryman impelled all about him to experience infatuation, disgust, anger, laughter, and bewilderment, an experience which one student recapitulates:

> What I think about most whenever I think of John was his *total* commitment to writing and his total desperation about himself, his relationships to others, and his compulsive daily self-assessment. And such awesome burdens of guilt about all aspects of his life! . . . He taught me, not only through his words but certainly his behavior too, that creative awareness affords no compromises, no mercy; if authentic, perilous.

In June, at the end of the Iowa semester, Berryman returned to stay at the Chelsea Hotel in New York prior to a summer school at Harvard, where he was to teach both a Shakespeare and a fiction course. For some of the time he was sick with gastritis and pleurisy; for most of the time he repined. He must have behaved offhandedly towards Anita Maximilian during this period, for he wrote her on 6 June:

> I felt so crusht with pain & blackness, and so surprisingly, after long isolation, & in great fatigue & some illness, that I think I attended only to my own feelings, and didn't realize until I got up last night that it must have been incredibly hard for you too – and if I had been in state to take this in I wd have acted better.

At Harvard, where (he related) his 'programme requires me to imitate a jet plane', he found his courses so stimulating as to leave little time for fretting over his dilemma in New York, an affliction which he had rehearsed at the time: 'Except when resting, or dreaming & preparing, I detest myself without occupation, and I haven't had any for a long time: therefore I drank, against self-dislike & boredom – of course I do well the jobs set me, but they give me no peace.' His students included at least one writer of enormous talent, Edward Hoagland, to whom he wrote again after fourteen years: 'I'm glad you got something out of me in Cambridge. I was engaged in a big Survival-operation and not much of anywhere. You lifted my spirits considerably yourself, not merely by being so gifted but by being devoted to it.' It was also in Cambridge that, through another student, Joan Griscom, Berryman first met a sensitive and sincere young woman named Sally Appleton, a recent convert to Catholicism who presently went to work for the scholar Father William F. Lynch, and who was herself to mature (partly through Berryman's encouragement) into an accomplished poet. In the following months he came to feel a tremendous affection for her, which she could not reciprocate. Her rectitude, and her position as a Catholic, spoke strongly to him, and her inaccessibility as an ideal in his life figured prominently during a period of radical self-assessment that he endured later in 1954. The crisis was precipitated by an incident that took place soon after his return to teaching at Iowa in September.

He was edgy and aggressive as the new session began, under the personal administration of the dynamic chairman Paul Engle (who had been absent in the earlier part of the year), a man towards whom Berryman was not sympathetic. It was at Engle's house that he met the young Irish poet John Montague, who had just arrived as a junior lecturer in charge of a course called 'Understanding Poetry' based on the Brooks and Warren textbook.

> He was ostentatiously shunning poetry [Montague recalls], teaching a course on the short story, and sharing the Fiction Workshop . . . In any case, he ignored me all evening except to point out that I should not speak about American football if I knew nothing about it . . . and that I had no right to enquire about *his* friend's health (this, in answer to a tentative question about Lowell, who was rumoured to be sick). Our host was partly to blame himself, I gathered, both for raising such topics and inviting a naive outsider like myself along. Not a promising beginning . . .
>
> I saw another side of him a few days later, when having set us a class theme on Isaac Babel, he chose my essay to read out as an example of good writing. It was done in such a polite and elaborate way that it sounded like a public version of a private apology. Things became even more complicated when, at the first Fiction Workshop meeting he came under very heavy fire indeed, for a story he had read by one of his East Coast students, which was taken as an insult to women by the lady novelist with whom he was sharing the platform. In the anti-Berryman barrage that followed I found myself coming in on Berryman's side . . . It was a nervous, fractious discussion, linked more with the personalities involved than literature, but

Berryman was clearly uncomfortable. When it was over he whisked over to thank me for my few words . . . I had gained his confidence, but perhaps lost the support of a whole department.

Montague observed a Berryman who was 'nervous, taut, arrogant, uneasy', eating alone in the local hotel, or carrying a copy of *The Caine Mutiny* into the cinema. Gertrude Buckman, the first wife of his dear friend Delmore Schwartz, happened also to be in Iowa at the time and audited Berryman's class on Babel, 'about which he was *brilliant* . . . *I* was tremendously excited and stimulated, though the class didn't seem to realise what a special treasure they had.' She herself had a teaching fellowship, part of her task being to make a preliminary selection of stories from which Paul Engle would draw that year's O. Henry collection. As it had become his habit with others, so Gertrude Buckman recalls that 'John had already taken to calling me in the middle of the night, in a drunken, revved-up state, assuring me of his genius, and reading his latest verses. I felt rather bleak about the prospect of a year of this.' Further solecisms were forestalled by the events of Wednesday, 29 September.

After what Berryman himself recalled as a 'bitter quarrel . . . with some scientist at Kenney's' during that 'fatal' evening, he returned to his house and had an altercation with the landlord, apparently after rousing him on account of mislaying his key. He was put in jail for the night, deprived of his glasses (a standard practice to prevent suicide attempts), and – at least according to his own version of the proceedings – subjected to further humiliations. The chief offence he recalled was that the police had jeered and scoffed at him and exposed themselves. '"There's a mike in the cell" those Iowa cops said, *when* I called them "You *homosexual criminals*",' he recorded later. Several persons rallied to Berryman's aid, and he telephoned others, sounding 'totally unhinged and desperate' to at least one of them. John Montague discovered him 'in a very grim mood'. The poet Emma Swan was 'discreet and helpful' throughout, and was later to drive him to the airport after the incident had reached its climax. Gertrude Buckman, who also helped to recover Berryman, found him 'shaking with fury – and helplessness, in a sweat, in a *terrible* condition – hung-over, probably unfed, most certainly unbathed and unslept.'

Iowa would not tolerate the outrage, and Berryman was dismissed from his post after appearing before the Deans on Friday, 1 October. In desperation Berryman called his old mainstay Allen Tate in Minneapolis, and it was at Tate's instigation that Ralph

Ross, professor of humanities, a man who was to become Berryman's redoubtable friend and ally, invited him to constellate with them at the University of Minnesota. 'We were pretty shaken ourselves by all this drama, and by John's knife edge tension,' recalls Gertrude Buckman, who waited with Emma Swan for Berryman's plane to depart. 'One felt he would shake himself to pieces in a moment, though he talked a defiant, proud line.' After his arrival in Minneapolis, Berryman had to pass some months before he could take up teaching, and it was during that time that he spent hours each day plotting the course his life had run so far, analysing his dreams in order to take stock of his current psychological and professional dereliction. Through all the upheavals of the following years, his ever-expanding reputation as both a poet and a professor, the exhilaration and pain of two further marriages, and the harrowing passage of his alcoholism, Berryman made Minneapolis his home until death.

12

Minneapolis and second marriage, 1954-57

Early in October Berryman moved into what he called 'the best working apartment I've had in years' at 2509 Humboldt Avenue South, three blocks from the Tates' and within a stone's throw of the Lake of the Isles. He took exercise by walking round the lake every day, a distance of about three miles; when winter gripped he walked across the ice. For the first weeks he was anxious as to whether the university could provide him with employment, but meanwhile he wrote off many letters to distant friends, mostly women, reassuring them that he had found new life in Minneapolis: 'I quit drinking by the way several weeks ago,' he told Anita Phillips on 15 December, for example, 'and am v. busy & high-spirited.'

The woman most in his mind was Sally Appleton, whom he had met in the East. Over Christmas they exchanged letters, hers addressed mostly to the problems and purpose of writing poetry, with reference to Yeats and Rilke, his increasingly to a sense of infatuation, especially as she was unattainable, a devout Catholic. It seems that her youthfulness gave him stimulus as well as, paradoxically, a spiritual perspective on his affairs. 'I realize,' he wrote on 24 November, 'that I am in a state of mortal sin & have been thro' my entire adult life.' He wrote her a sonnet ending, 'where Sally sits and sings whether to go? / The nuns catch fire. Her beauty is in bloom.' She sent him one poem called 'To Adamine', and he later considered using that title as the dedication for his volume *Homage to Mistress Bradstreet* (published in 1956). During 1955 Berryman tried to take counsel from Father William F. Lynch, who had been Sally's mentor, but a number of letters he despatched were returned in August only because Father Lynch had been too ill to respond. In letters which he drafted to Sally herself but refrained from sending,

Berryman spoke of how he had been 'for days wild w grief and disappointment at not hearing fr you', and for a while he bombarded her with phone calls.

> I get so excited when I am about to hear your voice. I feel, when you talk to me, as if I were burning up or dying. . . .
>   Stupid phone calls. Do I have to be ashamed of them? If I do, I will. I'll try not to call again for a while. They're unreal, anyway: a pretence at what can't now be: meeting. What we write is real. How strange it will be, won't it, when we do: meeting. I was going to say 'I can't imagine it' but I just, w great difficulty, can. I will probably fall in a dead faint. How extraordinary to have a drink or a meal with you. And yet we certainly will. You *are* going to be my friend, Sally, aren't you, until we die?
>   Life wdn't interest me much if you weren't.

Since her side of the correspondence was entirely disinterested, and since Berryman himself had to concede sadly that any annulment of his marriage seemed unlikely, she had to withdraw from the relation. He constrained himself to draft letters mixed of love, loss, and selfless blessings for her future. In one letter he implicitly censured himself by criticising poets such as Rilke for displaying an unearthliness based on 'an elaborate and painfully self-satisfied *fear of life*':

> it is necessary to get down into the arena and kick around. . . . I like him when he was writing out of his active grief & awe, not these lay-sermons he sprayed around Europe instead of sleeping with people like a wicked but actual man. Love affairs on paper; ugh.

Even as early as October 1954 he came to a realisation of the reasons for his own dependence on letters:

> All these letters I've written have had for purpose: self-reassurance, after Iowa's treatment, that I do have friends, am liked & respected. But it's been a good idea, *towards* friendly and business contact, regularity; and even the considerable amount of writing they represent is a start, in view of my having got written so little else. – But now less.

Being without a job in Minneapolis, and without a permanent sexual relationship, he took the occasion to ponder the state of his life and the roots of his behaviour. As often before, his sense of guilt gave him a start; in one month, for example, not only had he tried to generate three love-interests by letter, but he had also made person-al approaches to four other women. 'It is laughable or "desperate",,' he wrote. 'What's wrong that I aim so at all these *very young women*? . . . Am I doting?' Late in November he added, 'I am thoroughly ashamed of the nerve-wracking & evil complex I have got myself into. . . . Spare them! & myself! WORK.' He worried about the chronic dependency represented by the rush of his womanising, about his growing addiction to alcohol, and about penury. He tried now, as often in later years, to resolve his upsets by codifying them, but each scheme was provisional upon his re-sponding openly to fresh circumstances. His writings about himself seem to have been postulated on the belief that some fine day a specific insight might comprehend the entire pattern of his conduct. Behind many of his seemingly self-detached analyses there is a certain wishfulness: some dreams, for example, he construed as bringing drinking and sex into illuminating association:

> my woman-killing nightmares were homosexually oriented
> . . . liquor must be important, because . . . I find it so closely
> related to my adult wd-be homosexual experiences (*all* of
> them); and because, to my amazement, I experience today &
> yesterday almost no *craving* for alcohol – much as I'd been
> drinking – and this last fact suggests that it *must* be
> psychological, i.e. neurotic. I have never really believed that till
> tonight; I've always thought my will just weak.
>
> So on these two scores alone – not to add that it looks as if my
> promiscuity might disappear, as well, with the (possibly even
> imminent) clearing up of the homosexual business – I wonder if
> today is not one of the most important of my life.

In a note added later, he oddly discounted as 'irrelevant' the fact that one of his girlfriends had come 'to bed again in aft'. As for his excessive drinking, he made an interim resolution which was miserably unreal: '*Binge* perhaps once a week to take tension off.'

Since Berryman had the knack of remembering his dreams in close detail, he began to transcribe them and then to analyse his associations. On the night of 16 November the words 'St Pancras brascr' figured in one dream, together with many particulars so private and abstruse that he felt befuddled for some time. His method of analysing dreams was to exhaust every phrase and word of the transcription in terms of associations often relying on the scarcely limited possibilities of punning. The word 'pancras', for

example, gave him 'pancreas'; 'braser', 'brassiere', 'bracer', and
'brazier': 'a brazier warms you', he wrote, just as Allen Tate had
warmed him with friendship. During the next ten months Berryman analysed in obsessive detail far more than a hundred of his
dreams. On one sheet, dated 22 December, he typed short titles for
twenty-five dreams, a figure which then mounted to thirty-eight
by the end of the year. '38 in two months,' he noted with astonishment, 'wd be *228 a year!* intolerable.' In time he even considered
publishing a volume of his dream-analysis, taking for title the
occult phrase 'St Pancras Braser'. Working often hours each day at
such analyses gave him some relief from psychological pressures;
the depth of his anxiety is none the less manifested in his eagerness
to draw moral lessons as much as insight or explanation from his
numerous dreams. In particular, he decided then: 'And I now see
the psychological *purpose* of the Iowa debacle: to test Allen & get me
here.' (It does indeed seem probable that he had induced a public
crisis at Iowa in order to expose his unhappiness, but it would be
perhaps too far-fetched to believe that he subconsciously en-
gineered that crisis in order to test Allen Tate's loyalty.)

It was at this time that Berryman wrote to his mother for
information about his father and the circumstances of his suicide;
she responded with a long letter which depicted Smith as a man
confused, distressed, disloyal, and irresponsible, not meaning to be
cruel (as by any gesture for which his suicide might have stood), but
assuredly immature. In view of the current radicalism of Berryman's self-analysis, it is not surprising that he added a marginal note
to his mother's typed letter of 7 December: 'suicide is all *self-pity* &
aggression – you deprive the world of yrself – you give it lumps;
murder *w.* it??' He was still too ready to credit the theory that he
himself had been psychologically crippled by his father's default,
and to give his mother proportionately more of his own guilty
adulation for her heroic endurance. One dream-analysis includes
this sentence: 'So dream is my bloody father looking down at me,
whom he's just fucked by killing himself, making me into shit: and
taunting me before he flushes me away.'

In spite of the quick deductions and admonishments that Berryman tended to draw from his dream-analyses, the activity of
studying them at least externalised certain problems and worked to
sublimate his nervous energies; that consolation seemed sufficient:
'In this light I can't be discouraged about the 2½ months I've spent,
w. so little written, in Minneapolis,' he wrote on 14 December. In
addition, he felt lucky to have survived several weeks of 'acute
financial tension . . . without histrionics or despair.'

In the spring of 1955, Berryman started teaching courses in humanities at the University of Minnesota. The Humanities Program was an old one, far the largest of the three (the others being Social Science and Natural Science) making up the Department of Interdisciplinary Studies. It was run by Ralph Ross, an accomplished and charismatic philosopher and administrator who had formerly headed the Humanities Program (a part of Adult Education) at New York University. With his dean's approval, he had there appointed everyone in the program, drawing to New York many distinguished figures: Allen Tate, Saul Bellow, Isaac Rosenfeld, Ralph Bates (the English novelist), Adrienne Koch (the famous Jefferson scholar), her sister Vivienne (who wrote books on W. B. Yeats and on William Carlos Williams), and George Amberg. When Ross arrived at Minnesota, it was understood for some years that he might appoint individuals directly to the Humanities Program, and he promptly brought Rosenfeld and Amberg. 'Tate and I had agreed at a lunch in New York that we would both go to Minnesota at the same time, for he had been offered Robert Penn Warren's job in English. Later, Berryman visited Tate, and I got him a job. Then Saul Bellow, who would only come if I also brought his dearest friend, Jack Ludwig. I did that, too.'

Berryman immediately found an affinity with colleagues of expertise and friendly charm such as George Amberg, to whom he addressed Dream Song 63:

> He then salutes for sixty years of it
> just now a one of valor and insights,
> a theatrical man,
> O scholar & Legionnaire who as quickly might
> have killed as cast you.

Amberg derived from Cologne and was originally Hans Georg Aschaffenberg. He directed a repertory theatre, became a ballet expert (*Ballet In America*; *Art in Modern Ballet*), and was highly trained in stage design and music. With the rise of Hitler, he left for France and finally entered the French Legion in order to fight Nazis. In the days of Vichy, all non-Frenchmen in the Legion were interned, but with the aid of Spanish anarchists in the same fix, Amberg escaped and was spirited through Europe by an anarchist underground. He arrived in New York and eventually became Curator of Theatre Arts at the Museum of Modern Art. It was then that he met Ralph Ross, who persuaded him to resign and to accept an appointment in the program at New York University: a lifelong friendship began.

From the first Berryman was equally charmed by Morgan Blum, a small, heavy-set, powerful man, talented to a high degree in literary criticism, generous with entertainment, but capable too of furious hostility expressed in a terrible temper. Berryman shared one special epiphany with Blum,

> when he was at his happiest & best . . . in the summer of 1955, when on the way to the Apple River for a picnic at the falls I suddenly invented the title of the long poem already underway that has been ruining my life ever since. *'The Dream Songs!'* I said and he was delighted, and followed the murderous course of the work. [That trip took place on Friday, 5 August.]

Berryman found himself teaching courses in St Paul, Luther, Cervantes, Dante, and New Testament scholarship, and one course, 'Humanities 54', taken over directly from Isaac Rosenfeld who had called it 'Humanities in the Modern World'. He became so taken up with the course that he later outlined a textbook on it.

> I understood that it began, roughly, in 1914, a date that suited me very well. . . . It was also, such is the compartmentalization of knowledge even in a department then called General Studies, designed to omit all American material, since there exist other courses in what is called American Studies; this restriction finally bored me. . . . But it was clear from the outset that the course would deal primarily with the context of American thought and the American experience . . . the European context, that is.

As Berryman developed it, the course included Lenin's *State and Revolution*, Koestler's *Darkness at Noon*, Orwell's *1984*, Edmund Wilson's *To the Finland Station* ('as required background for Lenin's tract'), Freud's *A General Introduction to Psychoanalysis* ('for just three subjects, slips, the theory and practice of dream interpretation, and the mechanics of the development of mental illness'), and several other literary works: Eliot's 'The Love Song of J. Alfred Prufrock' and *The Waste Land*, Joyce's *Ulysses*, and Kafka's *The Trial*.

Arlene Rossen Cardozo, who took the course in the spring of 1956, vividly remembered Berryman's teaching:

> 50 students were allowed to register. Over 50 more packed the rear of the room that quarter, standing or bringing in folding chairs, hoping for a place should anyone drop out. Nobody did.
> Berryman was revered by some students for his deep

sensitivity, but was feared by others for his fiery tongue. The student for whom thought was an unknown abstraction quivered when Berryman pointed his finger, called her name and fired a question. He would continue his interrogation while she searched in vain for an answer, would finally become impatient and bellow, 'Don't tell me what you hope I want to hear! Tell me what you THINK!'

If exposure to Berryman's piercing queries, stream-of-thought lectures and searching analyses were [sic] devastating to some, the experience expanded the world for others. He appeared arrogant before those who searched for answers rather than questions, but he was humble before those who chose to question ['John Berryman: Unforgettable Teacher', *Chicago Sun-Times Showcase*, 21 May 1972].

By mid-year Berryman counted his new departure in teaching a success: 'I'm not sure I ever learnt more in six months, and it got me back into the habit of hard regular work. . . . If you want to study something, there is nothing like lecturing on it 8 or 9 times a week.' In the fall he was to return with a further course, 'Humanities 61' (on Greek thought and literature), but in the meantime he continued with what he called his 'raging stage of deep analysis' which he had been obliged to suspend since January. Reflecting on his position as early as 21 May, however, he had to acknowledge that the English Department took no account of his presence and that he was even '*v. anxious abt. Minn. job*' – his appointment in Humanities – '& *silence from Ross*, who was not at the Tates' last nt (20th). Betrayed again?'

I noticed again, & extremely, last nt. that I am not *considered* (here) now, as I have been used to being.

1) my early reputation, such as it was, means little & is fading.
2) I have no position, or influence.
3) No work is *visible*.
Possibly 2 or 3 books wd make a hell of a difference.

I. I have to recognize that I really am ambitious.
II. Also I *must* arrange for enough money to be debtless & live better.
III. And I have got to write as very good as I can.

He went on to reckon that he had wasted seventeen of his years since the age of 7, from which he drew a portentous lesson:

Yet possibly I may have another 17 years – another whole
lifetime (= 1938–1955) – bringing me to the age of 57, – to
which age, if I live & have health, I ought to be able to work all
right. Temperance, order, Self-Analysis, livelihood, & perhaps
E[ileen], are the basis.

A needed lift came to hand: his old ally Robert Giroux had
recently moved from Harcourt Brace to Farrar, Straus & Company
in New York, and wrote to express his interest in publishing
Berryman. It was the beginning of a long and fruitful editorial
relationship. On 25 June he signed contracts, with an advance of
2,000 dollars, for a Shakespeare biography and for *Homage to
Mistress Bradstreet* (which had so far seen print only in *Partisan
Review*). In the meantime, Berryman steeled himself in the hot days
of June and July to re-read 'some of the most tiresome plays ever
written', *Alphonsus, Alcazar, John of Bordeaux, James IV, Jack Straw*,
and *George a Greene*: 'I'm looking again at the whole early drama in
relation to *King John*, which seems at last to be solidly located in
1590–1, which wrecks and illuminates everything.' Although he
also ruminated about such aspects of Shakespeare as what he called
his 'strange & unattractive moral smoothness', Berryman's interest
presently reverted to the more consumingly personal task of
dream-analysis, which took up most of the year. By 19 August, for
example, the manuscript of his self-analysis had reached 650 pages.
He found occasions for absorbing his benighted sense of himself
only too pressing, as in this note:

> 10/11 June '55: 3 a.m.
>   I really feel full of despair
> & have been thinking tonight of suicide for the first time
> in many months

Among causes for his self-commiseration he included the following
remarks:

> Ross cares so little that he can
> – break my salary fr. '1800–2000 to 1600
> – promise next yr +
> without, but for my calling him
> saying anything . . .
> Giroux cares so little that he
> – apologizes by wire, &
> – without answering my letter
> – takes $500 off the advance

While he knew that he owed Ross and Giroux nothing but thanks for resuscitating his dignity as a teacher and a writer, he lacked gratitude for their failure to reinstate his self-possession. Their inability to give him wholesale job and financial security indicated to him more fundamentally that he had yet to struggle for recognition of his writing and teaching. A year later still, on 2 July 1956, he wrote a memorandum headed '*Paranoia here*', and included the comment that there were 'no other *artists* & I don't *exist* as an author' at the university. During that span he undertook only a limited amount of reviewing, but his achievements included an article entitled 'The Case of Ring Lardner' (*Commentary*, XXII, November 1956), a sharp and wily appraisal of Lardner and his art in which he may have seen something of his own case:

> Purposefulness, I think, is just what one does not see; except for the desire to escape (from familial protection and suffocation, intolerable frustration, boredom), which took the forms of alcohol and silence. He was a boozer from way back; began as a kid, and improved. . . . Apparently . . . he held liquor well. That was unfortunate. . . . Monumental remorse, often referred to, darkens the last years – for talent drunk up, self-punishment, self-loathing. . . . And he had no recourse whatever: no satisfaction in his achievement; no discernible belief or even religious sense, an overmastering hatred of humanity in general, and all its works; no freedom. . . .
>
> Unfortunately everything good in the end is highbrow. All the artists who have ever survived were intellectuals. . . . When Shakespeare mocked Chapman and Raleigh and their school of intellectual art, he did it with a higher brow than theirs. . . .
>
> The differences between entertainment and art have less to do with the audience and the writer's immediate intention than with his whole fundamental attitude toward doing what he does at all. Inverting the common notion, art for the artist we might oddly regard as a means.

Berryman believed that art could both create and report life, and that it functioned for the artist as self-discipline. His own efforts to bring life and thought into dramatic focus took the form of a start on his sequence of poems called *The Dream Songs*. A view of his awakened recognition that writing could effect a ministration for the artist himself, and of the degree to which his new persona 'Henry' should draw immediately and radically on his own emotions, thoughts, and life-history, is given by some notes he drafted not long since for a letter to Sally Appleton:

Perh. the essential thing abt poetry is that it is both rebellious (malice, fury, contempt, ungoverned grief & pain, ruleless desire, arrogance, *un*successfully forbidden knowledge) and the servant of order. . . .

I cdn't say I've ever tho't of it as stuff exactly for the heart, nor for the brain, nor for the nervous system. No, surely it must be for the whole business? I don't see any way out of it – vague, over-claiming, & crude, as it seems. Yes! The whole business; transcended, one's simplest feeling abt gd art – or mine is – is that it is *too good* for men. We don't deserve it. And yet – we call it divine – it is human.

I believe strongly by the way tho' both in inspir'n & in stewardship – altho' I don't know *who* inspires us or *whose* stewards we are.

After moving early in October, to 1929 Third Street South, Berryman made his first trip away from Minneapolis since his arrival in 1954 – a Christmas visit to New York, where he saw something of his mother and of Eileen. In the winter he worked for a spell, while teaching, on another book to have been called *Shakespeare's Friend,* an investigation of the possible collaborative relationship between Shakespeare and William Haughton. By Easter, however, Ralph Ross introduced him to an altogether different task. Antal Dorati, a charming and generous man who was then conductor of the Minneapolis Symphony Orchestra, asked Ross to find a poet who could translate Paul Claudel's 'Le Chemin de la croix' for the conductor's own composition. Ross talked to both Tate and Berryman about it, and Berryman was the more enthusiastic. 'It actually was a very close collaboration,' Dorati remembers, 'because I had already composed the piece to the French text, so the English version had to comply to a neat extent with what already existed.' He and Berryman conferred perhaps a dozen times over the following months, and the composition was performed for the first time in the spring of 1957.

I remember Berryman as a very introverted, rather shy person, trying to hide his timidity behind a certain 'roughness', which was not convincing at all. He was withdrawn, kept to himself. As long as we had the specific common interest of his translation, the contact was easy. When that theme was exhausted, conversation lagged.

Homage to Mistress Bradstreet (with nine illustrations by Ben

Shahn) appeared on 1 October 1956, to what seemed a sparse but
intense critical acclaim; by 7 December Berryman had seen only
four reviews. The keenest satisfaction came on 26 November,
however, when *Partisan Review* gave him a Rockefeller fellowship
in poetry for 1957, with an award of 4,000 dollars. 'Whee!
Bliss! . . . and the time! the freedom! Kiss me, brother,' he exclaimed to Saul Bellow, wondering if he had influenced the decision. 'I am going to write so good the trolls of language will scream
& come over to my side.' That award was followed by another 500
dollars – the Harriet Monroe poetry prize – in the spring. For a
further 500 dollars, he spent two days at a writers' workshop in
Chicago, where he sprained his ankle after slipping on a loose rug;
after two days in hospital, he limped for a month.

In May he learnt that both the Pulitzer Prize and the National
Book Award for poetry had been awarded to Richard Wilbur,
balking what must have been Berryman's own hopes for that
accolade. Nevertheless, he sent a telegram reading – as nearly as
Wilbur can recall – 'Congratulations on double sweep. Your
powerful verse will live.' Wilbur was somewhat perplexed by the
attribution of 'powerful' (since his verse was most commonly
praised at the time for its 'elegance'), but wrote him a note of
thanks. An exchange of letters took place, in the course of which
Berryman seemed to renege jealously on his plaudits, although he
concluded the matter with a generous note on 30 June: 'Wire
certainly mal-transmitted or almost certainly, but I don't now
remember what I said. Conceptual & metrical vigour all yr work
I've seen clearly has; no such irony wd do at all. Best of luck, & hope
for a meeting some time.'

Since an early stage in his career at Minnesota, Berryman's most
constant girlfriend had been an intelligent, witty, quiet Jewess
named Elizabeth Ann Levine (commonly known by her second
name), whom he engaged to marry during 1956. Sondra Bellow,
who for a time became Ann's closest friend, remembers her as being
both very peaceful and understanding. At some time during her
childhood her parents had separated, and she was brought up by her
mother. After two years at Carnegie Technical College (1949–51),
Ann eventually took a degree in literature from Bennington College, Vermont. In the summer of 1952 she attended the Harvard
Summer School, and then visited Europe at the same time the
following year. From 1953 to 1954 (and again for a spell in the
summer of 1955), she held the job of publisher's assistant with
Horizon Press, New York City. During the period of her develop-

ing relationship with Berryman, from 1954 to 1956, she lived at 604 16th Avenue South, Minneapolis, and studied for the Master's degree in English of the University of Minnesota, which she was awarded in August 1956.

Berryman scrupled for some time to attach himself to Ann, who was in her early twenties, and consequently prevaricated over putting into action the legal machinery for a divorce from Eileen. He suffered what he called 'a week of *agony*'. His lawyer informed him that three witnesses were needed to testify to his 'desertion' by Eileen, a requirement that flabbergasted and angered Berryman since the separation in 1953 had been entirely private. His mother visited Minneapolis, but left a day earlier than planned after bickering with him. Some sense of his histrionic turmoil can be gauged from a journal-entry that he typed at the time.

I am choking with nervousness over the terrible news yesterday that my divorce is postponed for *another* month, over the probability that my two superiors in the University are at last disgusted with me . . . over the ferocious quarrel with my mother that drove her back to New York the other night . . . and I am writing nothing. . . . My Department is on its way to extinction, even if with drunken phone-calls I haven't lost my job on my own. . . . Cheery, eh, and yet I feel less desperate since R. called tonight with something like friendliness in his voice to say – alas – my lawyer was right but had only misled me, not lied to me; so that the phantom-and-rage-world of yesterday a little recedes, and I did not have to call tonight to see about a second lawyer to check on the first. And setting down anything of this nightmare, as now here, mysteriously is a splinter of ease. And the last few days have been so immediately & horribly unpleasant that I've not been able to think about my wife – as, since she finally did what was necessary for the divorce, I have had to do constantly and with affection and bottomless grief. She seems – miserable to say – a little more distant. But nothing seems close. Sunday night I tried several times to hang myself – I threw my neck-tie away today. That must have been wrong; but why? For duty, obviously; but to these tiny surceases too? Watch and pray.

The divorce came through, and Berryman married Ann in Sioux Falls, South Dakota – 'MYSTERIOUS UNION EFFECTED', he telegrammed his good friends Boyd and Maris Thomes. (Dr A.

Boyd Thomes, a man of remarkable energy, learning, and enthusiasm, had become Berryman's doctor in 1955, and was to continue
to be indomitably supportive until Berryman's death.) They spent a
few days on honeymoon among the high peaks, ridges and buttes,
of the Badlands.

Saul Bellow had brought his wife Sondra and their son Adam to
Minneapolis in March 1956. He taught the spring quarter in Humanities, and was in Minneapolis on and off for the next three years,
and he and his wife were therefore able to form a close friendship
with the Berrymans. Sondra Bellow felt that on the whole Berryman made a theatre of his emotions, encircling his friends – both
men and women – with his charm and enthusiasm. Sometimes, she
remarked, he scared her when his face closed like a mask, and he
would disappear in some deep part of himself, only to return
effervescent again after a few days. He would remove himself in a
brooding self-absorption which seemed to assist his poetry. He also
often insisted on talking a baby-talk to both women – calling them,
for instance, 'Sister Ann' and 'Sister Sondra' – and would have liked
them to respond in the same rather silly style.

Ann bore a son, Paul, in 1957, and the family moved into a new
apartment at 2900 James Avenue South. Berryman found it difficult
to cope with the reality of the child, and to tolerate the necessary
changes to the continuous self-centredness of his life, though
Sondra also saw that his delight in his beautiful baby was unpreten-
dingly manifest. Berryman told his mother,

> The baby's name is King Pouperding the Great (alias Mr
> Fart-cracker, alias x & y & z), known familiarly as 'Mister Poo'
> (to be spoken very rapidly). . . .
>   Paul is obstinate, fiercely demanding (& slow to forgive), has
> strong taste-preferences (today he cast his cold eye on his first
> vegetable, a yellow veg; bananas he likes good), and still spends
> most of his waking time at visions, off somewhere, which he
> watches absorbedly. However, he has begun smiling – and his
> smiles make all of humanity's other operations look insincere –
> they wreathe out from behind his face through his face.
> Tickling his chin is one way to produce them, but only if he is in
> the mood; he still passes much time in mystery, abstraction,
> brooding. We do not know what he is thinking about, and
> neither do the psychologists. I think he is going to be
> slow-developing and am very glad about this, and meanwhile
> he is rather beautiful. A bad thing on his cheek has gone away,
> he is getting a pot, his second chin is wicked to contemplate, his

skin is ravishing all over, and he smells good. He has taken to
smiling sometimes *while* you change him; I cannot say more.

He told other friends too that Paul had 'a piercing vocal capacity
that comes from I can't imagine where'.

In the late spring of 1957 Ann and Sondra spent a lot of time
outdoors, while Berryman and Bellow worked or slept indoors,
both intent on their literary affairs which would be suspended now
and then for drinking parties, evenings of sparkling talk and
impromptu recitations, and for their teaching and administrative
tasks.

Berryman learned the good news that he had been given a joint
appointment with tenure in Humanities and English, and was
promoted during 1957 to the rank of Associate Professor of Interdisciplinary Studies, with a salary of 8,000 dollars commencing
early in 1958. In the meantime he gained leave of absence for the
summer in order to give a lecture tour of India under the auspices of
the United States Information Service. After two-and-a-half
months travelling, he planned to return via Italy, where he would
be joined by Ann and Paul. It was hardly a sign of unconditional
marital contentment that, after less than a year's marriage, he
looked forward eagerly and apparently unreservedly to a long
separation from Ann:

> what a dazed & fatigue-sodden Spring this was altogether. I've
> not been myself at all for a long time. I believe an entire &
> protracted change like that coming will restore me. I long to see
> a temple, I wish to smell ancient blood, I desire to transmigrate.

Berryman broke his journey to India with brief visits to Tokyo and
to Kyoto, where he hurried excitedly to see the Ryoan-ji Temple
and Garden. Founded in 1450, the temple consists of a vast, serene
compound extending towards the western foot of Mount Kinugasa
and commanding a magnificent view of Mount Otokoyama
beyond Yodo River in the distance to the north. The quintessence
of Zen, the garden provides the focal point of the temple – 'the most
perfect & satisfying garden even in Japan', Berryman called it. 'The
Ryoan-ji garden – sand, fifteen stones – is a work devoted wholly to
thought (tumbling Zen thought, it's true), and purely symbolic.'
He described himself as being 'dazed' with happiness and attention,
claiming 'I have never been so happy in my life as here in Kyoto',
and wholeheartedly responded to the sublime philosophy embodied in the garden.

By a series of coincidences he met Shirei Shigemori, one of the

greatest living authorities on Japanese gardens and on the renowned
tea ceremony, and participated in the tea ceremony at Shigemori's
own house, along with a Zen priest and an interpreter. Impressed
by Shigemori's eminence, Berryman sat enthralled, tried to orien-
tate his mind, and watched with a mixture of respect and irony:

> it is strange beyond expectation to hear 'ha ha' said clearly
> without any humorous intention at all, where we would say
> 'yes . . . yes . . .', but this is what the Japanese do. . . . The Zen
> priest, Suita, listening to Shigemori's elaborate discourses
> archeological & aesthetic, kept saying clearly 'haw haw . . .
> haw haw' – one of the gravest men I ever saw, who seldom
> smiled even when the others were laughing and only laughed
> once in three hours, at something he had related himself. Then
> Shigemori himself began saying 'hey hey . . . hey hey' as Suita
> talked. – A wise man will say nothing about a country until he
> really knows it.

The lecture tour of India coincided with the tenth anniversary of
Indian independence from Great Britain. In Calcutta, the first stop,
Berryman read a poem called 'Of the People and their Parks' by his
late friend Bhain Campbell, and was struck by the appropriateness
of reading a poem by a Marxist to an audience whose politics tended
towards radical socialism. Carefully studying the Indian newspapers, he felt disturbed by the country's political and economic
plights, but his own capacity was limited to educational and cultural
spheres. He would give twenty-six lectures and symposia throughout India, with the purpose of aiding the establishment of set papers
in American literature at Indian universities, and with the secondary
task of generally fostering interest in American letters. Howard
Munford, Professor of American Literature at Middlebury College, Vermont, shared the platform with Berryman. Between
them, Munford and Berryman devised a series of complementary
talks, Munford concentrating on modern American prose and the
development of a distinctive national culture, and Berryman on
modern American poetry and contemporary criticism. 'I also had
purposes of my own,' Berryman recorded, 'assisting young writers
if I found any, and the illustration of some standard of vivacity and
seriousness in approaching literature.' At the end of the tour,
however, he categorically lamented,

> I met no young writers of interest . . . but I did get an
> impression that many listeners were surprised and 'stimulated'
> by ways of critical working hitherto entirely foreign to them. I

don't think it too much to believe that the tour will have had
some effect against the deadly and incompetent rote-teaching
prevailing in India.

(In 1957, the Indian educational system sustained 920 institutions of
higher learning, including 33 universities, into all of which the
British had introduced rote learning and cramming.)

Briefing took place in Delhi, and after a meeting with the
American ambassador, Ellsworth Bunker, the two professors flew
to Bombay on 20 July, where they began the first symposium, a
five-day programme at Poona University. When only twenty
people attended – professors and postgraduate students – Berryman
commented dispiritedly, 'the thing did not seem worth doing.'
(Readers of *The Times of India* were treated to an article which told
them that Berryman 'began life' as an instructor in Wayne State
University, Detroit, and reported him as saying, 'Lowell's work is
learned, heavy, full of illusions [*sic*], with a strong Miltonian
flavour. Roethke . . . is interested in the individual soul and dwells
on children and flowers. Neither of them owes anything to T. S.
Eliot.')

Back in Calcutta, Berryman stayed at the Grand Hotel until 3
August. (At the beginning of the tour Berryman and Munford had
been told that *per diem* payments would be 17 dollars, but the figure
had proved to be mistakenly optimistic, as his bill adequately
demonstrated after just three days.)

Calcutta teemed with vibrant and depressing life. As he walked
the streets, Berryman looked in vain for fire-walking, and learned
that the rope-trick did not exist; instead, he was confronted with
seamier aspects of local life, including a street that seemed to sell
only 'rubber goods' and toys. At the side of a square a woman bared
her breasts, while pimps offered 'nice Indian student', 'nice boy
massage', 'white girl, all white', 'nice French girl', 'come see . . . no
pay if no like'. An Indian newspaper, the *Statesman*, that day
reported the incidence of nudity in Chowringhee Road – by the
Grand Hotel, in fact, as Berryman confirmed in a letter home:

outside you will be offered Anglo-Indians, young Chinese girls,
& – supreme enticement – 'a schoolteacher' (Howard Munford
. . . says he was offered a BOAC hostess, but I doubt this);
neglect this or these inflammatory items. . . . On the whole I
should adopt an impenetrable chastity & put all this
man-womannonsense behind you, in favour of 3 pair of shoes
and inexhaustible cultural determination. Beer is 5 rupees (real
money this is), but Indian rum is pretty good; mostly however

you will be living on iced coffee. I recommend (monsoon this
is) rising very early, doing as little all day as possible except
fighting off the ministrations of your bearer and his friends, and
retiring with the brain-fever bird.

His cultural curiosity was actually unquenchable, and he involved his companion in hectic schemes.

Once, on a blistering day when the better part of wisdom
would have been to stay quietly in our hotel and rest up for the
evening's activities, [Berryman] couldn't rest until we had hired
a car and gone to the temple city of Bhubaneswar. Again, we
made a strenuous trip to Juggernaut. Somewhere . . . we were
told of an ancient temple with some famous erotic carvings. It
was inaccessible by road at the time because of the monsoon
rains. Nothing to do but to charter a private plane and have
someone fly us.

Kanarak, the temple in question, is a thirteenth-century structure
located by the sea twenty miles northeast of Puri, and boasts a
ruined compound famous for its erotic carvings. Excited at the
prospect, Berryman speculated that the obscene images were the
product of Tantric Buddhism, fashioned to test the chastity of
lamas, where live women would later serve the same function.
    Berryman tried in general to comprehend the religious attitudes
he encountered, but felt compelled to saddle the Hindu and Moslem
religions together as 'evasive'. Indians, he felt, wished to evade
reality, to escape 'I AM', to 'shy away from the terrible, consola-
tory truth that "After the first death there is no other".'
    His encounters with Indians continually exacerbated his sense of
himself as a foreigner. He failed to establish a close relationship with
any individual Indian, and his feeling of alienation lasted throughout the tour.

Indians do not like us; and why should they? In the first place, as
journalists in particular admitted to me, they fear us as a Great
Power, having themselves been repeatedly subject to such. In
the second place, it is a fact that I have never in India heard a
single American – or, for that matter, any Westerner – express
any admiration or liking for the Indian character or personality;
and they are bound to feel this. Instead one hears nothing but
objections to them and disdain for them, except for the cool
sympathy of a few individuals. I simply record this fact of my
experience, and wonder whether, in view of it, not *less* candour

but *more*, between individuals of the races, would not be better.
I began myself with an exaggerated view of not wounding their
sensibilities, but I found that we got on better when I was
blunter; indeed they thanked me, saying that the worst thing
about Americans was that we never told them the truth, and
they stopped applying to me their automatic arrogance and
moral pretensions and their equally automatic self-pity.
Conversation became possible. There are two points here: 1)
they *know* how we feel, so the air is cleared by some expression
of it; 2) we really don't so fully feel that way, once we come to
express it to an Indian – that is, we have many things against
them but also, with experience, many things for them, or for
individuals, who are all that matter – and with expression *our
own feelings become truer*. I see no reason myself why nations
should love each other, and history tells us that this idea is for
the birds, and official pronouncements.

In Cuttack, Howard Munford began the symposium at Raven-
shaw College with a lecture on 'The Nineteenth Century Literary
Background', a talk which was actually more specific than general
and set the pattern of all their symposia, since both speakers
concentrated on the explication of particular works or authors and
avoided a broad historical approach. Both Munford and Berryman
felt their approach to the subject brought a gratifying response, for
at least two dozen teachers, scholars, and other students afterwards
told Berryman that his talk had altered their concepts and approach
to literary works.

As the tour progressed, however, Berryman became increasingly
tetchy, often because he wanted more alcohol, but also because he
considered that the itinerary had been badly planned, which he
found just as aggravating and officious as hotel servants, pimps,
and beggars: 'interminable, impractical, vague, positive, self-
contradictory, domineering'. Howard Munford recalls,

We were tightly scheduled, pushed here and there to lecture,
discuss, have tea, be entertained at dinner, until we did, indeed,
feel like 'servants' of the U.S.I.S., especially John. . . .
   The audiences were often hostile and would ask leading or
antagonistic questions. Sometimes, after John had been
lecturing on Whitman, or Pound, or T.S. Eliot, he would meet
such responses as, 'English poetry has lines of great beauty.
Why does not American poetry have beautiful lines?' – 'Our
feeling is that there is nothing spiritual in modern American
writing. Is this true?' These were actual questions. . . .

This was the summer of Little Rock, as I recall. At any rate, the American racial situation was very much in the news. Although we did not get many questions on this from the floor, everywhere else, at social gatherings or in private conversations, we were called upon to explain or justify 'race bigotry,' and this by the most color-conscious people in the world. . . . John bit his tongue and was polite on this score.

Outside the lecture halls, especially in Calcutta, scenes of squalor and disease confronted them everywhere, and Berryman suffered an anguish of compassion.

We had been warned not to give money to beggars, many of them were fakers and there was a danger of being robbed. On more than one occasion, though, on seeing an especially pitiable case, Berryman would exclaim, 'Howard, we have to keep our humanity,' as he gave some money. Once, in Calcutta, we were practically mobbed by begging women with children in their arms, and John literally emptied his pockets. One day we passed a beautiful girl of about eighteen or nineteen, with fine features, a leper with one foot entirely gone, hobbling around on the stump of her leg. John was haunted by this for days.

That encounter took place as they returned late one afternoon from the Kalighat in Calcutta. Calm and dignified, the girl sat and crossed her white, unbandaged stump over the other leg. At dinner in the Grand Hotel that evening, Berryman brooded about the girl, and reflected on the awful incongruity between life in the hotel – an orchestra, crooners, an oblivious dancing couple – and the piteous figure he saw again during an after-dinner stroll. The small woman sat under a streetlight, alone among the sleepers north of the maidan. By a bridge, a small angry holy man clutched a fistful of mud against the western tourist.

In Cuttack, where they were lodged by English missionaries, Mr and Mrs K. F. Weller, Berryman visited the Leprosarium, in which 490 lepers received food and 12 rupees a month, and had absolutely nothing to do. Profoundly moved by the beauty of the salaams which greeted him, and shaken by what he saw – a beautiful girl, several boys, a high-caste girl who suffered from tuberculosis and wept, a man suffering agony in the hospital, a health officer who had contracted the disease, and another man who sat mindless on the verandah – Berryman memorialised his visit in this verse fragment:

'Young Lady's Song at Cuttack'

My heavy hair
    I am beautiful
        I am not blind
It had my left foot wholly, & besides
throws out a semi-foot off to the side,
& the visitors look.
            All the others smile,
I am about to.

Much as he disliked Calcutta, Berryman regarded it as a kind of 'home' by virtue of its being familiar. More importantly he looked forward to a reunion with his family, and knew that the Grand Hotel was at least a place where mail from home might actually reach him. He even caught himself thinking 'with *longing*' of Minneapolis and his lecture-stint there. On the other hand, given his honest and open appraisal of the teaching – and of the social conditions he experienced, all of which aroused his compassion – he still felt firm in his conviction that it was right for him to have undertaken the tour.

Howard Munford had fallen sick on returning to Calcutta, and still had a fever the next day. They were due to depart for Patna on the Sunday morning, but Berryman insisted that the flight should be postponed. He learned that Indian Airlines charged extra percentage if reservations were changed later than 48 hours before the flight, a fact which served only to aggravate his prejudice, as did what he called the 'greedy and childish' contract drawn up for a radio interview the previous Thursday, which paid him only a token sum of 25 rupees. A few days later, his wallet was stolen as he slept in the Grand Hotel. 'The stolen wallet incident,' Howard Munford recalls, 'resulted from a bit of carelessness on his part and yet was practically inflated by John into an international incident.' The Florentine leather wallet, a gift from Ann, had contained about 100 rupees and 12 dollars, as well as various documents, cards, and photographs, all of which were never retrieved.

In Patna, the first day of the symposium went well, but it became marred the next day when the chairman, a man whom Berryman later dubbed a 'bastard', arrived 30 minutes late and apologised only to the audience, not to the speakers, and went on to evince a condescending attitude. It may well have been this occasion that Howard Munford vividly recalls,

Berryman, one evening, had given what I had considered to be a brilliant discussion of some recent achievements of American poetry and then a stunning line-by-line analysis of an Eliot poem. The Chairman of the evening, an elderly and distinguished Professor of English, rose to his feet to give the official summing up and vote of thanks and proceeded to say: 'America has never produced any important poetry. American poetry has no words of power, no words of passion, no words of beauty, and no words of real poetry.' I looked across at John. His face was a fiery red and his temples throbbing, but, as he later said, 'I'm a real pro, Howard, and I never lose my temper before an audience,' and he never did.

On 13 August Berryman noted, 'I came here to see: *monuments*, my friend, that you did not build – or sculpt, or dig.' As soon as the Patna symposium ended, he and Munford took a break in Benares, to witness the mysterious spectacle by the banks of the Ganges, where (as Lord Randolph Churchill had told his wife in 1885) 'a man could go straight up to heaven without stopping.' Howard Munford recalls,

In Benares . . . we had an affable and intelligent guide. John was enthralled with the thousands of pilgrims, the holy men, the turmoil of the streets, the colorful bazaars, the beggars and the lepers. The first morning we hired two boatmen to row us down the Ganges by the burning ghats and the bathing places. A gigantic copper-red sun rose as we floated by the pilgrims washing away their sins in the holy river, men greeting the sun with a deep salaam, holy men in contorted postures of worship, smoke drifting from the ghats. John . . . said later that the whole Indian venture was worth that experience in Benares.

On their return to Calcutta, Berryman and Munford took bachelor rooms at 20 Harrington Mansions, where Berryman became restless and frustrated. He was pleased to embark on a five-day symposium in Calcutta (held under the co-sponsorship of Jadabpur University), but presently fell sick. He stayed in bed for one session, but persevered with the remaining lectures, including a reading of his own poetry at the end of the week. That Sunday a man named George Isaac took him to see the infamous Sealdah Station, which accommodated between 4,000 and 5,000 of the desperately poor; Berryman felt stunned by the scene.

He passed the whole of the next week in a poor state of health, sweating and coughing. Returning through Bombay *en route* for

Ahmadabad, he saw a doctor but chose to ignore his advice and to continue with his engagements. But ill-health and exhaustion were gaining on him, as Howard Munford explains.

> John would never take things easy or relax. After a lecture he would be bathed in perspiration as if he had just stepped out of a shower. Frequently, after returning from a symposium, I would take a shower and fall into bed exhausted. John would stay up into the small hours reading or writing and, on occasion, drinking. He finally drove himself into the ground. At luncheon in Ahmadabad he suddenly rose from the table, spoke my name in a strained voice, left the room, and collapsed on the stairs outside. We carried him to his room in a neighboring house. An hour or so before the evening's symposium was due to begin, he insisted on trying to get up. I urged him to stay in bed, saying that I could easily carry on alone. 'No one is going to tell me what to do. You start your lecture, and by the time you are finished I'll be there.' Sure enough, as I was concluding, I looked up and there he was pale and drawn.

Berryman rose from his sick-bed, resumed the platform at Ahmadabad, and – as Munford remembers –

> proceeded to give a lecture different from anything he had done previously, a stunning discourse on the springs and nature of poetry. For weeks, he said, the Indians had been telling us that America had never produced any poetry, that the Indians were the most poetic people in the world, but that what he had seen of Indian poetry led him to believe that what passed for poetry with them was a loose kind of spiritual sentimentality. 'Now,' he said, 'I'm going to tell you something about what poetry really is.' He quoted from Rilke and Lorca and then gave some English paraphrases. One of these was from 'The Song of the Blind Man' and his paraphrase went something like this: 'My eyes were two sacred fonts in which the Devil has stirred his finger.' His point was that much of the greatest poetry sprang from the pain and anguish of human experience – which he went on to illustrate from a wide range of Western poetry. The audience was enthralled and would have held John in excited conversation indefinitely had his weakness not forced him to stagger out of the room and back to bed.

He was in fact too ill to attend the final two-day symposium at Nagpur – he had lost ten pounds in weight in the last two weeks – but went through debriefing, bought some souvenirs, and returned to New Delhi by 9 September. He then flew to Agra to absorb himself in the mystery of the Taj Mahal, and later wrote an impressive article about the experience which celebrates the monument as a cultural and religious enigma. 'Thursday Out' (included in *The Freedom of the Poet*) is a marvel of cultural evocation, and stands comparison with Henry Adams's writing about Chartres.

Happy to fly out of New Delhi bound for Rome, Berryman felt that despite his sickness and exhaustion the tour had fulfilled its purpose.

> I do think that they will be bound eventually to approach our literary tradition directly, not through the British (who increasingly anyway confess that their understanding of it is inaccurate and meagre); and to this end I think Dr Munford's and my tour may really have contributed . . . on the whole our audiences approached our subjects without knowledge but with prejudice, and prejudice often died and knowledge supervened.

He had in truth found the tour for the most part arduous and disappointing, but he chose to conclude his report with a mixture of magnanimity and irony by conceding that the trip was probably 'useful to my education and so, indirectly, to our culture. . . . We did not get to know much of India, working hard, but something; and the Department's job is certainly dual, the education of our people as well as of others.'

After a reunion with Ann and Paul, Berryman and the family spent the last weeks of 1957 in Italy and returned home for the New Year.

13
Breaking-points, 1958-59

During the first weeks of 1958 Berryman was smitten down by what seemed to be a series of infections, yet (bolstered by a fee of 500 dollars) he travelled to give a reading of his own works, under the auspices of the Gertrude Clarke Whittall Poetry and Literature Fund, at the Library of Congress in Washington on 24 February. Three weeks later he gave another reading in Chicago for 300 dollars. By Easter week Dr Thomes diagnosed exhaustion and admitted him to the hospital, where Berryman rehearsed events to his mother.

> I only had two weeks between quarters, and the first week was Chicago, and the second week I wrote 5 new poems besides doing other things, and I began on Sunday to feel as if I were going to die shortly. I started my courses on Monday, and on Tuesday got me a private room in the Abbott, where I am writing this. I am still very badly under weight but feel considerably better and am going out tomorrow. Nothing to worry about. For some time to come I will be under a heavy drug for part of the day (the teaching part, afternoon, after my own work is done) and he thinks I will get in shape fast. I've been suffering alternately from unmanageable irritability and a circulatory disturbance leading to partial syncope.

While in hospital, he wrote a Dream Song, 'Room 333', part of which runs:

> Comfortable in my horseblanket
> I prop on the costly bed & dream of my wife,
> my first wife,
> and my second wife & my son.

> Insulting, they put guardrails up,
> as if it were a crib!

and inscribed a clean manuscript copy to Boyd and Maris Thomes with this note: 'You understand: this is (not me, but) Henry, the – hero? – of my next poem, begun in 1955 & *nowhere*. Don't show.' Although he soon recovered energy for work, a professional disaster had struck which was to demoralise him and his chairman, Ralph Ross, for several years.

On 10 March Dean E. W. MacDiarmid chaired a special faculty meeting which voted to disestablish the Department of Interdisciplinary Studies, with the resolve that interdisciplinary courses should become the responsibility of departments other than a department of interdisciplinary studies as such. The effect of the vote was irrevocably to weaken the status of the Humanities Program within a mélange of departments. Berryman himself was so incensed by the proposal that, by 24 May, he began to draft a book which would present a rationale for the material of one of his own courses with the title of 'Humanities 54'.

The criticisms levelled against Humanities by more conventionally homogeneous departments were iterated so fiercely over the following months that even as late as 25 April 1961 Berryman felt compelled to spell out his position in a long letter to the editor of the *Minnesota Daily*.

When the department was disestablished the three programmes had no departmental home; the chairman of each reported separately to an associate dean, Jay Buchta, or directly to Dean MacDiarmid. Berryman felt singularly vulnerable in the midst of this realignment because his own status had always been so precarious; as late as the end of May 1956 – well over a year after he had first started teaching courses – he had never even met Dean MacDiarmid. Ralph Ross had a happy relation with both Buchta and MacDiarmid, but not with the extreme specialists on the faculty. Social Science and Natural Science as interdisciplinary programmes withered. Humanities continued to flourish as an interdisciplinary programme, but was under constant attack by several other departments and by individuals at faculty meetings. 'This was the painful part for John (and for me),' Ross recalls, 'who suffered and saw invincible ignorance everywhere.'

In 1958 Berryman felt so personally discredited by the faculty decision that he even initiated steps to apply for a chair of English at the University of Khartoum. 'I wish this place would calm down,' he wrote to his colleague Russell Cooper. 'It is all very undignified, insolent, and even wicked.' In Saul Bellow's absence for the year,

Berryman shared an office with Ross, where they would plan strategy and commiserate with each other.

In the summer his work began 'racing', with his attention divided almost equally between writing Dream Songs and investigating Shakespearean cruces, so much so that by mid-June he absorbedly reported that he had settled the date of *Two Gentlemen of Verona* – 'It is late 1592 – early 1593 and I can prove it.' The next month he finished chapter 4 of *Shakespeare Handbook*, a work (commissioned by T. Y. Crowell) additional to his biography of Shakespeare which was then half-completed in a manuscript draft of about 250 pages. During the summer he wrote about fifty pages – or one-sixth – of *Shakespeare Handbook*. 'Unfortunately,' he added winsomely, 'I, II & III are still to write.' In addition to hinting at his own achievements, he was lavish with praise for his friends' writings; from about this time he began unselfconsciously to apply words like 'delicious' and 'gorgeous' to Ted Hoagland's stories, for example, or to Bellow's novel *Henderson the Rain King*, which he read in manuscript. His fresh engagement with English literature was probably postulated at the time on the assumption (as he told his mother) that, after the disestablishment of Interdisciplinary Studies, 'I'll go gradually over into the English Dept., where what life will be like I don't know.'

Unfortunately, the case was otherwise; in the two years since the English Department had unanimously elected him to membership he had been subjected to what he regarded as a hurtful neglect. (Only in the summer of 1955, *before* joining the department the following year, had he given a course on Stephen Crane and Howells for a colleague named Bernard Bowron, who admired him as a witty and trenchant conversationalist and an expert teacher.) While the department chairman, Theodore Hornberger, gave him no courses to run, he did require Berryman to 'visit' student teachers (that is, to attend freshman classes and to write reports on their conduct and promise); other than that, Berryman alleged, he extended him invitations to meetings (often late or at times which clashed with his teaching in Humanities), and asked him to submit details of his publications (which were then omitted from bulletins).

Allen Tate, whom Berryman recognised as his most stalwart sponsor in the English Department, was to spend the next academic year in Oxford, and exerted himself before his departure in an effort to convince his colleagues that Berryman could most ably deputise while he was away, but Hornberger stood out against the preferment. By 17 June Berryman learned from Ralph Ross that several

members of the English Department felt 'humiliated' by the pro-
tractedly insulting relation in which it stood to Berryman. His
advocates included Murray Krieger and the lively Leo Marx, who
recalls that 'there were lots of times when [Berryman] seemed
dispirited. I do recall that he shared the sense of being kept at arm's
length by the English Department.' Another member of the department, J. C. Levenson, cared for Berryman's poetry and particularly admired his scholarship on Stephen Crane. 'When he was
pretty much his own self – manic but not *too* manic,' Levenson
recalls,

> he was one of the great people to be with, witty, intense,
> brilliant, humorous, and deadly serious. An hour of
> conversation with him was like an hour of demanding exertion.
> When you think how much energy was consumed by his
> drinking, his compulsive skirt-lifting, and just plain suffering,
> and yet he was able to conduct his academic and literary life,
> you can begin to guess how energetic he was when functioning
> well.

He remembers one evening after Berryman's return from India and
Japan, 'how intensely he instructed his friends in, and proselytised
for, the aesthetics of Japanese gardening. I felt that night that he had
opened for me an art as rich and vast as music itself.'

Berryman felt the English Department's insult more intensely
because he knew that, during the period in which he had been a
member, it was 'denuded' (as he put it) in his areas of expertise:
Shakespeare, Allen Tate's courses, modern literature, and American literature. Russell Cooper took the view that Berryman's
relations with the department were strained not so much 'because of
affronts on his part but possibly because several had an unconscious
jealousy that he seemed to know more about the English field than
they.'

Berryman's exasperation reached such heights that, on 22 October 1958, he wrote a long letter of complaint to Dean MacDiarmid
and to Professor Samuel Holt Monk (the great eighteenth-century
scholar most famous for his book *The Sublime*), a man of immense
southern charm and a subtle, supple mind. Like Allen Tate and
some other members of the English Department, Monk deplored
Berryman's bad behaviour, but he exercised a just judgment which
Berryman respected. Berryman set out his qualifications as a reput-
able scholar in American literature (most notably for *Stephen Crane*)
and in Shakespeare (including mention of his Rockefeller and
Guggenheim fellowships and work-in-progress), and his interna-

tional standing as a poet (most recently, T. S. Eliot had taken up an option on a volume of his work for Faber & Faber).

His agitation did not avail, and he had to admit in a letter (1 November) that 'any energy I've had to spare over my courses has gone off in resentment of [the English Department's] policy of pretending I don't exist, except for chores of course.' Ralph Ross had left for a sabbatical year, and Berryman now shared his office with Saul Bellow. In Ross's absence, Berryman privately directed some of his reproaches against him too: presumably, it may be inferred, because he felt that Ross, his champion, had not been able to secure and guarantee his standing in the English Department (Berryman's expectations of Ross in that respect were impossible). More significantly perhaps, Ross had recently planned to compile a volume of commentaries and questions on a wide range of literary texts, and asked Tate and Berryman to share the task with him. As part of his contribution to *The Arts of Reading*, which was eventually published in 1960 (New York: Thomas Y. Crowell Company), Berryman included discussions of stories by Babel, Hemingway, and Stephen Crane, of Eliot's 'The Love Song of J. Alfred Prufrock' (on which he gave a freshman English lecture that December) and of *Macbeth*. Judging from the scrawl of his notes about Ross, it would appear that he felt Ross had been slow in making arrangements for the collaboration, and especially in setting out the financial terms. Before Ross's departure on sabbatical leave, they must have had some sort of quarrel, for Berryman wrote: 'We'll never be friends again at all unless: we have it out, & he *forgives himself*, & understands that *I forgive him*, & we get all clear.' All his troubles had cost him 'peace of mind, in my 1 *vacation*', he professed. His complaints about Ross were quite unjust, but his sense of amalgamated grievances speaks surely for the depth of his emotional and professional insecurity.

In the following months Berryman bickered about the unequal shares of work done by each collaborator on *The Arts of Reading*: since he knew, in particular, that his own contribution was greater than Tate's, he resented him for not promptly imbursing him a proper amount of an adjusted advance on royalties. Tate's delay in doing so Berryman regarded as tantamount to fraudulent, and for a while he thought him dishonourable.

Among certain unpublished Dream Songs written during this period is one that is clearly addressed to his prevailingly bitter and mocking mood of 1958:

'O Say Can You See By The Dawn's Surly Light'

On busses, the nude thighs of gravid women
please all my decent countrymen.
The frontier, an Italian bust.
If it can be counted with two breasts, they'll buy.
James Madison was much like this, and Lee,
and throughout the whole Korean test

not one American made good escape –
a thing *brandnew* for us, full of hope.
Moreover our refrigerator boys
would not what they did not like eat, so *died*;
that showed spirit. Questioned, they spread wide
their gentle empty nervous lives

and provided our enemy with friends, one in three;
showing goodnatured treason. Soberly,
of their contempt for dad, they sang.
Without a precedent, with millioned cars
and a hatred for the mind, behind the stars,
the country's on the upswing.

The months of emotional and spiritual stress eventually took their
toll of Berryman's health; during a short break in New York early
in September he had to be admitted to a private room in Regent
Hospital, as he told Dr Boyd Thomes with grim irony:

I came East for a little vac, being as I fancied a little tired, and to
do some general thinking abt my poem (not writing: structure)
before I have to put it away until next summer. I never got any
rest, dear friends, and have lost interest in my poem. After a few
sessions with a publisher, a fine man behind whom I cd see the
polisht fronds of the Lever Bldg, I judged it best to have a few
sessions with my psychiatrist, who thought I seemed a little
tired, and put me here. Now, after only two days, I am fine: I
no longer require *any* sleep, and I have lost interest not only in
my poem but in all my other work, in all human beings
including myself, in liquor, in sex, in money (never too strong
there), in game, in the future, in the present, & even in Sung
landscape & other people's poems. I am a free man. The
excruciation that I *appeared* to be suffering, however, before I
became so fine, was hard on Ann, and perhaps this period ought
not to be characterized as a really happy one. . . . I have no
plans.

As 1958 wore on, Berryman and his wife felt their relationship being rifted more and more by incompatibility. Behind Berryman's problems with his marriage lay his history of fraught family tensions. One marriage had already broken and he took a baleful view of his broken childhood. His mother tried then and always to influence or direct his life and relationships, with the implicit conviction that he should honour her above all others, even his wife. She required him to answer for her own needs and wishes (try as he might to suppress his true understanding that she insinuated them in ways that devastated his peace of mind), and for her happiness.

When Saul Bellow's father died Berryman had told Bellow with apparent impersonality:

> my father died for me all over again last week, in a terrible
> dream which when I analyzed it turned out to be about him not
> dying at once, as I was told he did (he shot himself, on an island
> in Florida where we lived, when I was twelve), but living a
> while unable to move or call out for help, but then in the dream
> he said 'saved' – as of his soul, I mean. His father's death is one
> of the few main things that happens to a man, I think, and it
> matters greatly to the life when it happens. I can't help feeling
> that you are lucky to have had yr father for so long, and then
> just to have seen him again as A says you did. The trouble with
> a father's dying very early (not to speak of his killing himself) is
> not so much just his loss as the disproportionate & crippling role
> the mother then assumes for one.

His own mother constantly played upon his feelings, especially his sense of guilt, and manipulated him into a state of morbid ambivalence by blessing or browbeating him (as the occasion served) with a love to which he felt unequal. As early as December 1954, when she wrote him an account of the circumstances of his father's suicide which mixed apparent rationalisation with self-recrimination, Berryman wrote an exclamatory note on her letter: 'the most fantastically over-developt sense of responsibility I think I ever encountered: GUILT for what? – unless all this is retrojection (as of my father's suicide . . .).' On the Berrymans' return to Minneapolis in January 1958, his mother visited for a few days and chose for some reason not to mention her dread of imminently going bankrupt. Early in the morning of 10 January she slipped off on the bus back to New York, melodramatically leaving behind a proud but implicitly suppliant note in which she confessed:

the overpowering sense of responsibility with which I have
compensated for [John Allyn Smith's] refusal of responsibility
has given me what is a literally unbearable guilt for everything
that has ever gone wrong in your life or Jeff's. . . . I do accept
the duty of living. No one need fear my death at my own
hand. . . . I realized that you had never asked me to give you or
lend you money and that what I had done for you, and for Jeff,
was done at my own behest. . . . I am so ashamed, John, not to
be able to earn a living.

Berryman quite naturally reacted with self-reproaches and sorrow
for her, despatched a telegram, and presently wrote to the effect that
her inability to ask her own son for money made him feel ashamed
of himself. He took it as an indication of the paucity of her
confidence in him, and wrote piteous apostrophes on her note:

God forgive me. Her all these days in the apartment, . . . *afraid*
to ask this bastard son for a loan – & frantic – & not even telling
me: BUT taking the finish off the table, helping plan the
apartment, cooking, *talking too much*, reading my Indian &
Spanish books – *desperate* – & thinking 1) of suicide 2) of
'shaming' me by bankruptcy, & her *staying on*, agonized.
　　I don't deserve to live. And suppose I'd quarrelled w. her!!
my heart shakes – she wdn't have told me at all!! & God knows
her feelings & what wd have happened.
both her husbands lived in a dream world (prob. so did the 3rd)
. . . & I've always been ridiculous – grandiose – irresponsible =
n.g.

At other times he could be cool and even dismissive towards her,
as after the 'ferocious quarrel' which drove her out of his apartment
shortly before his marriage to Ann, or another when he was about
to leave for his tour of the East.
　　By late in 1958 he deliberately sloughed her interference, as he
told her on 13 January the next year:

I didn't write because I had an impression that you tried to break
up my marriage, which was in difficulties and in addition to my
physical and nervous exhaustion and other things, I did not
think it a good idea for me to take this any more. I am not now
reproaching or blaming you for this, only explaining. I feel as
you do, that people are v. unhappy & driven and that most of
them wish to do as well as they can and that some are highly
ambivalent.

Her first response was to reply with a letter – terse by her own standards – which combined wounded dignity and self-pity (including an allusion to Berryman's 'Homage to Mistress Bradstreet'):

> never in your life have I, to my knowledge, acted or not acted with intent to cause you pain or worry, to injure you in any way. . . . Much too young much too long, I am become an old woman, one not competent to endure stress or to be forced to believe she has caused it. . . . I have not felt myself a part of the family group for five months now.

On 23 February, however, she followed up her subdued letter with five single-spaced typewritten sheets of apologetics: melodramatic, specious, proud and pained.

> It is clear that you do not love me and have suffered greatly from your inability to do so as well as from the crushing burden of my love for you. For my long and, it may be, wilful blindness there is no or little excuse.
>
> What freedom it would have meant for you if we could both have recognized and accepted this fact long ago. What strains and pressures you would have been relieved of, and how much pain avoided for me, the pain of believing the impossible true, that someone who loved me needed or wanted to hurt me: the operative phrase, *who loved me*, I never questioned. . . . An unloved child is so cold, a child needs love so, until now it could not get through to me that a child might not love the warm, loving mother who loved him for himself, for what he was. . . .
>
> With your strong feeling for family, this inability to love your mother, open or hidden, has put intolerable strains on you. It may well account for much of the guilt with which you have felt yourself laden, a guilt of which you are utterly innocent. Once and forever, I recognize that you do not, can not, love your mother and I know that it has nothing to do with what I am or my life, or with what you are or your life. I hope that you can accept my loving my son and will find this love no burden since it asks nothing and expects nothing and is incapable of stopping. No child was ever more wanted than you, I feared so after a year and a half of marriage that I was barren – then, when you were put in my arms, it was you I loved, not the child I had wanted desperately but you, with your wrinkled forehead – my heart leaped out upon you. . . .

I can only take solemn oath that if you and your wife felt I was trying to break up your marriage, whatever caused that feeling was not any intent on my part. Awkward, wrong, hurt as I was I may have been in my words, but to try to break up any marriage, no, and how much less yours. . . . I could no more try to break up a marriage, than I could spit on the Blessed Sacrament. Even when just before you left for India I told you that I must advise your wife to take your son and leave you if there was a recurrence of that dreadful night, it tore me apart although it was to save not break your marriage, and therefore made in the hope that it would bring you to yourself. . . .

The greatest pleasure has been mine in the sure belief that you and Ann have a real, a true marriage. In these days not every woman can be or wants to be a wife, even to the husband she loves. But Ann has been, to me, the complement not the competitor, happy and proud of being a loving, devoted wife and mother. You and she and I all came from broken marriages. . . .

Hear me now, I am woefully weak woman [sic], and deceived no one more than myself.

Decision as to the future is yours, of course. It seems to me that it would be best and easiest for you if all relationships between your family and me were severed completely; I can still love you and have pride in your work without ever seeing you again, and most cheerfully in the hope that it will make for less strain and difficulty in your life. You may feel that in time to come the occasional visit may be possible without harm, that is for you to say. It may be that you think correspondence may be possible now, or later. . . . I leave the decision to you, as certainly the family is more important than the individual, and your family comes first with me as with you.

In the face of such a smothering, contradictory outpouring, Berryman could only shelter himself by pleading illness and disorientation. Still trying to penetrate that barrier and manipulate his soul, she responded by impressing upon him again her belief that he was a man not only of talent, but of genius, and consequently susceptible to deeper sufferings. Over the following months they played all possible variations of the game of cat and mouse. During his Christmas visit in 1960 he broke out again with hostile accusations, asserting that she was a liar who talked so much that he was nearly driven crazy. She wrote, 'The strain on you, the strain on me, of scenes is too much, too much. At last I am old, my son.' For the first time in three decades she showed him photographs of his

father and other childhood scenes; he felt unsettled by the pictures
and bamboozled by her blather:

> Ten hours of Mother's plangent babbling is about nine hours
> and twenty minutes more than I am able to stand. Moreover she
> had collected in the southwest, and showed me the first pictures
> of my father I have seen since I was a boy thirty-five years ago;
> and they bombed me.

Wrung between adulation and execration, Berryman was never
able to reach a state anywhere near equilibrium in dealings with his
mother. Later in the 1960s, and especially in 1971, he was to make a
concerted effort to love her and to behave consistently towards her,
but in the interim their relationship was subject to periodical
divisiveness of a harrowing order, particularly at certain increasingly common times when he felt under more than usual emotional or
financial constraint. After his marriage to his third wife, Kate, for
example, the taxation of a phase of heavy teaching coincided with
the worry of buying his first (and, as it was to prove, only) house,
which he could ill afford. It would appear that at that time there
occurred a ruction between Berryman and his mother of even more
than usual profundity, since she informed her other son, Robert
Jefferson, on 11 November 1964:

> It is a rather hard lot that the only person, thing or undertaking I
> have given up as hopeless should be my well-loved elder son
> whose genius I regard with awe and reverence and whom I
> finally recognize as a sadistic non-member of the human race,
> with occasional lapses into humanity. . . . And let this be the
> end of him as a subject of discussion between us or even
> correspondence, henceforth and forevermore.

Her bitterness was histrionic and far from final, but the vein of it
demonstrates the exaggerated and sometimes even hysterical postures that Berryman and his mother adopted towards one another;
both of them felt obliged to protest attitudes of love which must be
seen as belying any actuality of feeling. Whatever the state of play at
any precise stage, such a dispensation left Berryman always in a
preposterous ambivalence of mind, and was unhealthy and ultimately vicious to his life.

During the last months of 1958 and early in 1959, the fact that
Berryman attenuated his relationship with his mother was perhaps
as much a symptom as a cause of his professional stress and the
consternation of his marriage. In the New Year he found that what

he considered the saddening negotiations with Ross and Tate over *The Arts of Reading* made one more cross than he could bear. Many torturous months reached a climax in splitting his marriage.

In the early period of his relationship with Ann, Berryman had found a great deal of pleasure with his quick, clever, attractive young wife. Ralph Ross, who remembers Ann as being always sweet-natured, together with his wife Alicia shared many happy outings with the Berrymans. One weekend, for example, the two couples took a cabin in northern Minnesota, where Berryman curtailed his drinking and all four delighted in cooking steaks and playing ping-pong. On another occasion, during an outing by rowing boat to picnic not far from Minneapolis, the party was attacked by mosquitoes and Ann's face started to swell in a dramatically allergic reaction to their bites. Berryman was most solicitous and concerned about her as the men took exhausting turns to pull towards the home shore.

Berryman and Ann left other friends (such as the poet Donald Justice and his wife Jean, who visited them from time to time during the year 1956–7) with the fair impression of being a happy couple who had good cause to thank their fates for finding one another. There was trouble, however, for quite some time before they separated. Berryman began to complain about Ann, for example, long and untruly alleging that she would not feed him properly. 'I never understood this reiterated, preposterous complaint,' Ralph Ross remembers. During Ann's pregnancy Berryman gave the agitated impression that he resented the possibility that the child might replace himself at the centre of Ann's attention. 'Ann at first withdrew into herself when John complained about her in her presence' Ross observed, 'but came bit by bit to fight back.'

Though subdued in her manner, Ann became in time tensed to revolt against her marriage to Berryman, who could not suffer her to be her own woman. Deeply pained by his own mentality and problems, he could hardly recognise the true extent to which she must have needed to constrain her own disposition in order to live with his ways – and, of course, with his continual drunkenness. It is evident that as early as their holiday in Spain in 1957 Ann had started to withdraw into her own spirit, leaving Berryman (as he recorded at the time) 'completely in the dark!' He grieved for the afflictions he must have caused her and Paul. 'Ann doesn't seem to understand how *lucky* I am in knowing her, loving her,' he lamented, 'having her with me, & *with* the Poo of ours or how I love him very good or how my pride survives all the things that have happened.' It was clearly not in Ann's nature to engage in a long and potentially embittering resistance to his complex expectations and self-conflicts. Eventually her sense of survival erupted and she bid to be free, taking the car and the baby.

By mid-February 1959 Berryman was admitted to hospital at Glenwood Hills in Golden Valley Road, Minneapolis, where (as soon as he was fit enough) he set himself to upbraid Ross by letter over what he considered the shoddy and unfair arrangements for their book.

He drew on – in a way that seems almost an afterthought – to a matter that anyone else might have taken as exclusively momentous at such a time: 'This is all *aside from* my mental agony, broken health, and the double wreck of my marriage. How am I supposed to feel about this? According to 3 doctors, exactly the way I do feel.' Berryman's transposition of values was a characteristic way of coping with crisis. In the face of Ann's leaving, he set himself to work harder on a poetry review for the *American Scholar*, on his contributions to *The Arts of Reading*, and on a new contract from G. P. Putnam's Sons for an edition of Thomas Nashe's *The Unfortunate Traveller* (which was eventually issued in April the next year). On leaving hospital in March he took another apartment at 1917 Fourth Street South, where despite being still exhausted he laboured at writing and teaching. In the latter part of June he spent two weeks teaching at Utah, and then returned home to teach five weeks (ending on 28 August) of modern literature and Henry James, during which he wrote, 'I suppose I will make it, though I hardly sleep or eat, and am tortured moreover by phone calls from 2 publishers in NY whose deadlines I have gone through'. Not surprisingly, after a prodigal summer, he was back in hospital by the end of the year:

Four days in & I ain't well yet! Christ! . . .
    It's not really the mind though, it's nerves nerves nerves. *Good* signs: I eat & eat, I eat everything, I starve all the time – after all, I have six months' famine to make up for. . . . And for 3 days I did absolutely nothing and didn't worry much. *Bad* signs: I only sleep in little bits, even with 3 & 4 sedatives, so I'm nearly dead all the time. And in spite of heavy Sparine, after half an hour of any kind of work, I feel as if I were having a nervous breakdown – today I began work at 4:30 a.m. (it's 2:15 p.m.) and I have had this feeling with intolerable continuity.
    So much for your ol' fren' Henry Jackass. I'm going over to give four lectures tomorrow but then I'm coming right back – for maybe 10 days?

A regime of debilitating work served to anaesthetise Berryman from his feelings of guilt and worthlessness. As well as absorbing himself, he could punish himself in that way: when crises occurred, he could excuse himself from making decisions and put his sorry affairs in other hands. Yet he had entered on a vicious circle, since he needed both the therapeutic occupation and the money of his teaching and writing jobs, but he coped with their pressures in a way that ensured collapse. He subscribed his last letter with abandon: 'I am divorced. God bless all married persons & everybody else too.'

In spite of leading his private life on a knife-edge, Berryman conducted his teaching with thrilling intensity. He expended a vast amount of nervous energy in the classroom, a quantity that was almost certainly disproportionate to the intellectual capacity of perhaps the majority of his students. In spite of his growing weariness in the summer months of 1959, Bette Schissel, a student, recalls, 'He soared, sparkled and fairly breathed life into the material until the hot stickiness of a Minnesota summer, stuffed in Folwell Hall or wherever, just disappeared.' He always suffered from marked tremors, sweated so much that even his suit became stained, and his demeanour varied manifestly from class to class, being sometimes self-assured, at other times visibly distressed. 'He was a disturbing man to watch in action,' Bette Schissel writes; 'it helped to concentrate on the course material better if one did not sit too close to the front as he became so involved in his subject and his histrionics in describing it that he perspired profusely, his lips trembled, as did his hands.'

'He was awesome in the classroom, super-brilliant, very exciting,' Jan Jackson Druck, another of Berryman's students, confirms. 'And he loved jabbing at us, poking our egos. . . . But in all that, I don't remember that he was ever unkind or cruel or hateful. He called us stupid and ignorant (we were) but I think he liked us and liked teaching.' It was certainly Berryman's custom to throw a barrage of questions at his students in order to highlight their ignorance and perhaps shame them into reparation.

At the end of the 1950s, a young man named Lynn Louden became Berryman's graduate teaching assistant, and remained a close personal friend even after taking on his own classes in the winter of 1962.

My first visit with John was when he invited me to lunch so that we might get acquainted and chat about the courses, my duties, etc. We met on the campus, walked to a nearby restaurant, and had a most pleasant talk. Everything was quite ordinary until the check came. John insisted on buying my lunch, but soon discovered that he had forgotten his wallet. As a matter of fact, he had forgotten his belt as well.

Since Berryman became so involved and expert in his teaching, he tended to relegate Louden to lesser capacities such as keeping track of class rosters and grading examinations. On those occasions when Berryman failed to meet the class, Louden was expected to fill in by lecturing to perhaps more than a hundred students – 'usually on something I knew next to nothing about'. Although Berryman genuinely sympathised with Louden's plight, his efforts to aid him never worked out very well.

> His approach was, in general, to pose rhetorical questions and then proceed to answer them by a close analysis of key passages. The larger structure and meanings of the work under discussion emerged from these parts. What always amazed me was his ability to convey to the students, not only the intellectual content, but the dramatic color of the work as well. Two instances of this come to mind immediately. In the first case, John was lecturing on the *Divine Comedy* – he had been for several meetings. The class met on the second floor of a small building, with doorways at either end of a rectangular room. John stood on one of the long sides of the room facing the students (lots of them) arranged in long rows. I sat in the last row, almost at the end. He was talking about the *Inferno*, Canto XXXIII, and attempting to dramatize the terror as well as the logic of Ugolino's sin. All of a sudden, he was reading these passages to the class in Italian – a language, I guarantee, not one of them understood. John's previous remarks and analysis, combined with the fearful pity in his reading in Italian made the meaning clear. In the midst of all this, a few students arrived at the classroom door a bit early for the next class. It was winter, and they were noisily stamping the snow from their boots and loudly exchanging remarks. At the first sounds, I could see from my position every head in the room (except John's) jerk in unison and look with contempt at this source of interruption. I also realized that more than a few were in tears.

Louden marked the examinations, while Berryman himself graded term papers; they then collated the two marks in order to arrive at the recorded grade. When it transpired that Louden was consistently tougher in his marking, Berryman reminded him that they were simply grading students in a Humanities course, not selecting candidates for the Nobel Prize.

Berryman favoured certain students in every class, some of whom would occupy the centre front row. 'John was always infatuated with a number of the coeds,' Lynn Louden recalls, 'and generally tended, in my opinion, to exaggerate their intellectual capabilities.' Among his favourite students of the time were Bette Schissel, Judy Lebedoff, and Carole Kaplan, who were flattered but confused by his attentions. 'During the last summer in which I attended the university,' Bette Schissel recalls,

> Mr Berryman often called me, usually in a deeply agitated state, seeking reassurance that he had been 'outstanding' or 'brilliant' at his morning lecture. It struck me even then as incongruous that a man of his genius should seek the approval of an undergraduate coed. . . . He apparently felt very alone and insecure. . . . He was often incoherent and rambling . . . staying on the telephone for an hour or more.

She could not manage his sad and troubled demeanour, devised a code for her friends to reach her by telephone, and tried to avoid answering Berryman's calls. Many a night, since she had a difficult schedule to complete during 1959, she sat at her desk while the phone rang and rang and rang. On the one occasion when she did accept an invitation to a movie with him, she became so nervous as to bring on extreme stomach pains and needed to be taken home half-way through the film.

Although he did have faculty friends such as Ralph Ross, Berryman depended to a large extent on his students for company, most particularly in the years from 1959 (when he split with Ann) to 1961, when he married his third and last wife, Kate. A single instance may stand for many in dramatically illustrating his intense loneliness. One afternoon before she had to pick up her parents at the airport, Judy Lebedoff spent several hours with Carole Kaplan while Berryman, quite heavily intoxicated, recited his poems to them, accompanying the reading with dramatic gestures and sounds, and finally gave them each a copy of a slim volume he had entitled *His Thought Made Pockets & The Plane Buckt*. 'When it came time for us to leave, he begged to come along, following us to the car,' Carole Kaplan remembers. 'He ended up sitting on the curb watching us as we drove away.' Like many other students, Carole Kaplan spent time drinking with him in campus bars; one time, he diagrammed one of his dreams for her; on another occasion, he spoke against divorce, evincing a personal pain which, she could see, was largely tied up with being deprived of his son. 'He was honest and never pried, though he was interested in and concerned with people's private lives.' During her last quarter she spent some weeks in hospital, where Berryman took the trouble to call and boost her morale. When she went home at last, he sent her a record album of a Bach concerto.

Most of the students I have been able to reach agree that Berryman was incisive and inventive in the classroom – 'horseradish on an empty stomach' is Jan Jackson Druck's way of putting it. Another of Berryman's students in the early 1960s was Mary Ann Wilson, daughter of the president of the university. Meredith Wilson himself, a shrewd, kindly, ambitious man, had been inaugurated as president on 1 July 1960. He found Berryman comparatively shy in his relationships with anyone high in the administration, but recalls having a number of entirely friendly and attractive encounters with him. It was through Allen Tate, however, that he gained most of his knowledge of Berryman's mind and state of being; he shared Tate's admiration for him and considered Berryman's contribution 'one of the finest assets of the University'. Tate would visit Wilson periodically when he felt that Berryman was having trouble with alcohol or with his nervous problems, and they would contrive to arrange a quarter's leave from time to time.

Mary Ann Wilson (now Mrs John Hansen) recalls:

> I enjoyed his classes very much, worked hard, and at quarter's end was given A's, both fall and winter of my Senior year. In the Renaissance course which was given Spring Quarter, I earned a B on the mid-term exam, and since tradition ruled that Seniors were exempt from Spring Quarter finals, that by rights should have been my final grade. About two weeks before the end of the quarter, and on a Saturday afternoon, I was called to the phone at home. It was Mr. Berryman, and he was crying.
>
> 'Miss Wilson,' he said quite brokenly, 'do you know I'm going to have to give you a B in this stupid course!!!' I was taken aback to say the least to be the object of such concern, and realize now that he must have been quite drunk.
>
> 'You write me a paper! You have to write a paper to get out of this stupid mess!!' (Almost always he spoke in exclamations.)
>
> 'What should I write about, and how long should it be?'
>
> 'I don't know. You choose! It doesn't matter how long it is! But you write a paper, do you understand me, Miss Wilson?!!'
>
> I really didn't, and two weeks before graduation I just didn't have the time to write a careful research paper. I felt quite uneasy, complimented, and burdened all at the same time. Later

I learned that one or two friends in the same class who had likewise received B's on their mid-quarters received the same strange call. Some days later, I turned in a two page, very subjective paper about my reaction to that much admired 'Renaissance Man' we had talked so much about in class. Mr. Berryman never after mentioned the call or acknowledged my presence in class, but when I picked up final grades for Spring Quarter, there was an A beside his course title.

There are many things I remember about him as a teacher. When he was in good form there was none better than he. Once, though, in the Spring Quarter Renaissance-Reformation class, he was very drunk, the only time it was perfectly obvious to me. We had been reading Don Quixote, a book he loved, & without realizing it he repeated almost word for word on a Wednesday the lecture he had given us the previous Monday. We the listeners felt extremely pained and uncomfortable, but everyone sat without moving or talking through the whole interminable hour. It would have been unthinkable to interrupt or stop him; there was too much dignity and bombast in him to allow for such a thing. It was very sad.

14

Third marriage,
1960-62

For a term beginning early in February 1960 Berryman became a visiting professor in the Department of Speech at the University of California at Berkeley. He took an apartment at 2525 Durant Avenue, a bright, freshly decorated place only three blocks from work and a short walk from the beer taverns on Telegraph Avenue. Some friends took him out for a Chinese meal on his arrival, but after that excursion he found himself isolated for days on end, a situation guaranteed (as he confessed) to intensify what he called his 'flowing paranoia'. Poorly with a throat infection, he wrote that it 'has been *infinitely* beyond anything I ever suffered before, I've had to give up smoking almost completely, & live on honey in milk. I get hungry but my throat does not. If it doesn't improve, I'm going to have my throat removed.' Scheduled to teach five days a week, he gagged through his first classes, was recommended to the hospital, and went to a movie after some three days but had to leave half-way through, when strangers started to pass him lozenges for his coughing. He found a certain consolation in book-buying, for the stores in Berkeley were primed with alluring bargains, but otherwise he stared enviously from the hill out towards Alcatraz Island. He put his apartment in order, and composed himself wittily to his continuing solitude: 'This could go on too long! Wow! I took no *vows*, after all: what gives? Has Henry entered on his destined role, pariah? . . . Perhaps I am a hopeless bore, whom everybody has caught on to??' Joking apart, however, the wryness of his position led him to sleep erratically and to gloom. Some weeks later, in fact, after he had partly assuaged his loneliness, he even admitted to having urinated once in his bed.

> I was so miserable; that's a pure hate-operation, I imagine, or almost pure, the sex-imitation lying well behind. But I never

read anything on the subject and am guessing. I never was troubled with it as a child, it happened a year or so ago, out of fury & loss, and thank god it has only happened three times I think, each time drunk, so the controls are down. I get through the most marvellous quantities of liquor here, by the way: wow: I dont drink as *much* as I did in Mpls, but I enjoy it much more, because I don't go to bars, I just order it in and settle down with it.

During the first weeks of term, other members of the department also fell sick. 'It's like being in Paradise, with anthrax. I have been running my classes, but just; many people haven't.' Berryman's insomnia grew worse as he brooded and raged over his isolation, and it was some while before anyone made a move to ease or explain the neglect with which he had been treated. The large Speech Department contained forty or fifty regular faculty members representing a wide variety of academic disciplines from anthropology to English. The general field was that of human communication, and it was in the category of poetic discourse that Berryman taught his courses, under the rubric of 'Oral Interpretation'. Students were required to offer a close formal analysis of a limited number of texts (the oral reading being a pedagogical device to concentrate attention on the texture of the poem, short fiction, or play in question).

Because of a coincidence of sabbatical leaves, only one member of the oral interpretation staff remained to share Berryman's serious interest in poetry. The chairman of the department was Jakobus ten Brock, a distinguished constitutional lawyer, founder and head of the National Federation for the Blind, who, although blind himself, showed immense energy in his activities but could not be expected to understand the temperamental difficulties of poets. At the time of Berryman's arrival, ten Brock went on leave and Professor Woodrow Wilson Borah, a brilliant Latin American historian, served as acting chairman. Accordingly it seems likely that Berryman was the victim of chance as much as of ineptitude at the beginning of his stay at Berkeley, since no one in authority had thought to brief him about his classes until the very day he presented himself at the university. Most staff members were proud of the independence of their courses, and many were therefore unaware of the disregard which had greeted Berryman. Everyone simply assumed that he would run his classes as he pleased, as was the way in the department.

Anthony Ostroff, who was probably the only other poet then in residence (in addition to Josephine Miles of the English department), had taken to his bed suffering from a bad dose of flu at the time of Berryman's arrival, and still felt sufficiently ill even after another week as to make himself scarce when not actually teaching. Altogether then, the circumstances justified Berryman's sense of hurt. Furthermore, when his position was at last mitigated, he was given graphically to understand that relations between the Speech Department and the Department of English were tenuous at best. He judged for himself that his own department was 'leprous with faction . . . It was just my luck to run into so fantastic a situation after my long Mpls isolation.'

In the second week of term, Berryman had a telephone installed in his apartment, and in due course Anthony Ostroff rang with an invitation to dinner. Diffident in the face of Berryman's relative eminence, he felt convinced that he was intruding on time which would otherwise have been spent in more distinguished company. But Berryman was eager and grateful for company. Bearing a bottle of wine, he arrived in a sleeveless sweater and a bow tie, 'clean-shaven, lean, intense, humorous, a trifle wary for our first minutes together,' Ostroff recalled,

> but soon . . . completely at ease and busily working to have us relax with him . . .
>
> By the time we had finished dinner, we felt that we had already become old and marvelous friends. John was simply incandescent in his conversation, witty, learned, but never in the least pompous or arrogant in his attitude to us: indeed, he was remarkably warm and loving. But he was also excessively grateful for being with us, it seemed, when he took up the theme of gratitude for the evening. Soon, however, as he began to unfold the story of his time in Berkeley, what had seemed the excess of his gratitude became understandable and touching.
>
> The fact was that we were the first faculty people with whom Berryman had spoken (except for Borah) in his first ten days on the Berkeley campus!

Anthony and Miriam Ostroff offered to ameliorate Berryman's desperate loneliness and insecurity by, in the first instance, throwing a dinner party for him, the Mark Schorers, and the Ian Watts (whom he had spoken of as being friends):

> But after first liking the idea, John bridled at it, becoming angrier and angrier. 'Fuck them! Fuck them!' he cried. 'I have been here two weeks and they haven't bothered to call me or send a note. Who in the fuck do they think they are? Fucking Berkeley faculty! Fuck them all!' And so he raved for a while,

until, regaining himself a little, he assured us he had no *need* to see any of *them*, *we* were his friends, *we* would be together, and that would be enough.

He was, by then, slightly drunk perhaps, but certainly not very much so. His rage was clearly the result of the dreadful wound of having arrived with great expectations, only to find that he hadn't arrived at all: so far as Berkeley was concerned, he didn't exist.

Late in March Professor Borah did throw a party for Berryman, at which, Josephine Miles recalls, 'He was very high & happy and remembered all the poetry in the world, which he recited from about 8 p.m. to 2 a.m., a fantasy of bardic memory!' Coincidentally he had to correct the complete set of page-proofs for his edition of Nashe's *The Unfortunate Traveller*, which required his prompt attention (since Putnam's were to publish the volume on 15 April) and restricted his plans for sightseeing. By Monday, 4 April, he had finished a third of the text and was anxiously hurrying with the rest. 'I have lost all my imagination of happiness lately,' he wrote, at least partly in consequence, 'I mean the shreds remaining.' Nevertheless, he found time later for cultivating his friendship with both the Watts and the Schorers. Berryman had first met Ian Watt at Cambridge, England, in 1936, and now took the opportunity to draw his work to the attention of Saul Bellow (in his capacity as editor of the journal *The Noble Savage*).

In response to a luncheon invitation, Berryman met the poet Thom Gunn, in company with Carolyn Kizer, and the English critic Tony Tanner. He told them of his loneliness, and they subsequently invited him to go to some movies that evening, after meeting at a restaurant called Robbie's on Telegraph Avenue. Berryman turned up late, already drunk, and just went on drinking without eating. Excitedly he brought them copies of a Dream Song (never to be published) which he had written that afternoon, beginning 'Tanner and Gunn, Tanner and Gunn . . .' They presently went across the road in high spirits to see a double bill of *I Vitelloni* and *The Wild One*. 'Berryman laughed extremely loud at odd moments,' Thom Gunn recalls, 'not always coinciding with the rest of the audience. He also talked rather loud, and irritated some of the audience. Later he fell into a loudly snoring sleep. It was a loud evening.'

Since Tony Tanner actually lived in Berkeley (Gunn in Oakland), he had the chance to see a good deal more of Berryman. On one occasion Tanner hired a car in order to drive him about for a day. They kept company for much drinking and talking, Berryman eating negligibly but occasionally indulging his liking for a sardine and onion sandwich. Tanner introduced him to his girlfriend, Marcia Albright, an extremely attractive, vivacious, intelligent woman (reading English at Berkeley) whom he was later to marry. At one dinner-party she gave, Berryman leafed through a copy of the *Complete Shorter Poems* of William Carlos Williams (which she had just given Tanner), and said that he would read out a poem that he thought particularly fine, 'El Hombre'. 'John read very well, even movingly,' Tanner recalls, and gave the impression of feeling as 'neglected and overlooked' as Williams had been at the time of writing the poem. Berryman was attracted to Marcia, and carried on seeing her after Tanner had returned to England. He telephoned her at all hours of the day and night, sometimes to beguile her with wit and learning, more often to be maudlin.

Berryman and Gunn, with another poet, Louis Simpson, were invited by the architecture department to give a reading at an annual arts festival. When they entered the hall for the arts festival reading, it was immediately apparent that the event had not been advertised; there were only fifteen in the audience. Although all the poets chose to go ahead with the reading, 'Louis and I decided to make the best of it,' Thom Gunn recalls,

> but Berryman was in a very bad mood. He had been ill, he told me, of some complaint he had picked up many years before in the Orient. I said I hoped he was better, and I must have asked him what the illness was like. 'Can you imagine,' he said, 'lying in bed unable to move a muscle, for hours on end, not even able to move enough to reach the bottle of medicine standing on the table inches away from you? That's what it's like.' If the tone sounds a bit rhetorical here, then I'm being true to my memory. Incidentally, he seemed drunk this time also, but completely in control. When his turn came to read, he first of all addressed the audience, berating them for being so few. 'Harvard of the West! Harvard of the West!' he said scornfully (of Berkeley). He then read divinely: I think it was the first time that I had heard him read, and it was only from the time of this reading that I began to understand the tone of his poetry.

The poet Henri Coulette, Berryman's former student at Iowa in 1954, arranged a poetry reading for Berryman, Gunn, and Philip Levine at his own college, Los Angeles State. On arrival at the airport Berryman insisted on having a double Martini before they reclaimed the baggage. Afterwards the three poets, together with Coulette and Christopher Isherwood, went to drink at a dark unwindowed cocktail lounge right off that central square in Los Angeles where the down-&-outs and hustlers hang around (I remember the darkness because it was so sunny outside). . . . Some time later, maybe on the same day, Christopher told me emphatically how very charming he found Berryman. And he was, that day, he was as good as he had been at that first lunch meeting, it was total charm.

Berryman stayed over for a day after the reading, and Coulette showed him around. They walked down Hollywood Boulevard, and went to call at the Pickwick Bookshop where Berryman bought his host a copy of Terry Southern's novel *Flash and Filigree* and signed it 'Hoot Gibson'. Berryman also delighted in Forest Lawn, which, Coulette recalls, he found 'truly campy'.

The Ostroffs continued to entertain Berryman at Berkeley, finding him scintillating in conversation and appealing as a person. He read them an early version of his poem 'Scholars at the Orchid Pavilion' and some of the first Dream Songs, and returned their excitement by showing an appreciative interest in Ostroff's verses. Ostroff often called at Berryman's room on his way home from work, and Berryman spoke at times of his depression at being there, despite the fact that his teaching was evidently going well.

It was worrying for the Ostroffs to suspect that 'the gaiety of his camaraderie' with them screened a depression, and they searched for ways of distracting him. One such occasion arose when Richard Eberhart visited Berkeley to give a poetry reading; Professor Thomas Parkinson invited Berryman and other luminaries including Mark Schorer and Ian Watt to attend a reception for Eberhart after the reading. The invitation was extended to Berryman through the Ostroffs, and after some initial hesitation he agreed to come – on condition that he have a date. The Ostroffs asked an intelligent young friend, a gifted pianist, to partner him, and they would all meet for dinner before the reading. The meal plans had to be cancelled when Miriam Ostroff fell sick, but then, Ostroff recalled, 'just as I was leaving to pick up John and his date, he telephoned – to announce that he would not come, and could not, under any circumstances. He was foaming with indignation at the idea of playing second fiddle to Eberhart, and that he should go to please those fools who could not be bothered to invite him to their homes.'

Ostroff was appalled and angry at the betrayal, and even more so when Berryman refused to telephone Mary, their friend, to offer his own apologies and explanations. Ostroff accompanied Mary for the evening, and fudged all questions apropos of the renegade.

Surviving his embarrassment, he left as early as possible and took
Mary for coffee at Larry Blake's restaurant on Telegraph Avenue,
where he telephoned his wife. ' "John has been here," she said in a
strange voice. "He's just left. It was very strange." '

Berryman had called on Miriam Ostroff soon after Ostroff had
left, talked a while, recited some Dream Songs – 'some fabulous
poems', she recalls – and then 'boasted of his sexual prowess and
decided to prove it.' His 'efforts at seduction', Anthony Ostroff
recalled,

> were largely verbal, and extremely persistent, though they did
> eventuate in a brief chase round the living room, at the end of
> which, rejected and remorseful, he promised to keep his
> distance if he could but stay and talk awhile. But then the talk
> became more and more fervent with a new desire, and finally
> Miriam, thinking it best, to keep him from simply going to
> pieces, or becoming violent, submitted to it – and allowed him
> to spend ten or fifteen minutes reverently caressing her feet,
> while reciting poetry to her . . . peculiar though it sounded, the
> foot massage and recitation were neither grotesque not
> offensive but sweet and even, at times, elegant.

'Somewhere in the midst of his ardor and my embarrassment,'
Miriam Ostroff remembers, 'he noticed the room was enclosed by
windows. The house was on a hill and John was discomfited by the
realization that someone might be watching this little escapade.'

Against Ostroff's imminent return, Berryman left in a cab.
Enraged that Berryman should have tried to persuade Miriam to
bed with him, Ostroff drove to Berryman's house and traduced
him for the affront. Working himself into a lather, he finally
threatened him 'with violence if he ever came near her again . . .
But I had met my match in John. He tried to stiffen a little in his
chair, and he said, like a boy in a Horatio Alger book, "I should
inform you that I was boxing champion of my class." ' Not willing
to lose his initiative, Ostroff pursued his threat with an immediate,
albeit nervous, challenge, and left when Berryman failed to respond.

Miriam Ostroff never saw Berryman again (though she heard
from him much later), and – for the remainder of Berryman's term
at Berkeley – Ostroff himself only observed him from a distance
drinking beer in a tavern, usually alone, just once with some
students. They did renew their friendship not long after, however,
when the incident had been put in a comic, even poignant, perspective, and it was at Ostroff's invitation as editor that Berryman

wrote his celebrated essay on Robert Lowell's poem 'Skunk Hour' for the symposium *The Contemporary Poet as Artist and Critic.*

Late in 1959 Berryman had entered on a relationship with one of his students at the University of Minnesota, Harriet Rosenzweig, an attractive young woman whose marriage had broken up coincidentally with Berryman's. 'What does your husband do?' he had asked at one time. 'He makes me miserable,' she cracked. She remembers that Berryman utilised all his energies to break down barriers between his subject and the students, being urgent with the conviction that they should attain the fullest possible experience and understanding of the humanities. She thrilled to his teaching, and attracted his attention to herself not only with her looks but by acquitting herself well in class. Going out together, or drinking and talking at his messy apartment, they enjoyed playing games under the pet names of 'Lord and Lady Pussy-cat'. On at least one occasion her mother had answered the telephone at home and heard only a miaowing noise. 'It must be for you,' she remarked, passing the speaker automatically to Harriet.

For just two weeks in the spring of 1960 Harriet flew out to stay with Berryman at Berkeley. She managed to lift his depression with her sense of fun and intelligent companionship, but his relief could not outlive so short a visit. Even after he returned to Minnesota some weeks later, their relationship was not destined to last; she remembers him with happy affection for having made important 'areas of life and literature available' to her.

As the spring days expanded into summer, Berryman now and then recruited spirit enough to enjoy himself when invited by friends for drinks by their swimming pools, for a pleasant dinner with the Watts, or for other hospitalities. 'My God, I feel quite well,' he rallied himself in one letter to Ralph Ross. 'Not sick in any of my five usual ways, and I ate breakfast, and I even feel briskish & responsive to the flaring day. Maybe I will go swimming in Strawberry Canyon, after writing some letters (I owe everybody) and paying some bills (ditto *a fortiori*) and doing some chores.' More commonly he slouched through the day, mourning his lost illusions about Berkeley, armed in alcohol, unfit. He felt more or less sick throughout his stay at Berkeley; hurting, unhappy, he picked his pains, coached his loneliness. 'I have gone almost steadily down hill,' he wrote to his doctor, Boyd Thomes, 'until now I can't either think or act: if I think five minutes I decide to abandon all three of my professions, and after half an hour I am semi-suicidal. I am much less griefstricken than I was last year, but otherwise hardly better, especially physically; but I am more successful at *avoiding* thought – and even at not writing although I have some hot new Songs.'

Early in July he quit Berkeley without misgivings; eager to seek rest in the hospital in Minneapolis, he summarised his reproaches:

> I love the hills here, and some aspects of SF, and some people, but on the whole the Bay area bugs me – because, I suppose, I came out in such bad shape (though it is a fact that I have heard very very hard opinions of this campus of the University of California from dozens of people here, and found it myself – with many exceptions of course – smug and cold, as well as amazingly mediocre in area after area . . .) – if only *I* hadn't come too, I wd have liked it much better.

Late in 1960 and then more intensively early in 1961, Berryman developed a special relationship with one of his Minneapolis students, J, a petite, firm-minded Catholic. Until meeting Berryman, her relations with older men had tended to be passionless (according to notes that Berryman took from chats with her), with men her own age, 'kidding & ironical'. After a very few encounters, she began to love him, both for his evident suffering and for what she called – if his notes are to be trusted – his 'beloved intensity', and soon felt confident enough to drop what he described as 'the hurried, offhand, slightly affected way of speaking she used to use.' Berryman found her very feminine without being coquettish, and was deeply moved by 'her strengths & subtleties & lovelinesses' and by her ready capacity for caring about him. Exalted and frightened by his own emotions, he felt respectful of her position and youth (although he came to resent her being a student, which allowed only for inequality between them), and stirred as much as anything by his own sense of unworthiness. 'I feel more *comfortable* with her, knowing she's Catholic; but also even more deeply *worried*. Later I must go into this,' he noted.

The relationship quickly strengthened, she wrote him 'marvellous' letters, but he continued to be ambivalent, impressed by her integrity and fineness of outlook and by the futility of his hopes for a deeper, lasting relationship, especially since he was twice divorced and considerably her senior in years: 'to take her wd be a shattering responsibility – a man *older*, *sick*, & miserable-chaotic.' On one of her letters he wrote, 'The really bad thing so far is that I have changed you but you have not changed me – I am stubborn – but it is beginning; and, strangely, it is *both* my WANT and admiration for you are at it.' As in that note, he was wrung every day between an inclination to indulge his feelings towards her and the restraint exercised by his sense of her selfhood, her independence of mind and strong will. At an early stage in the relationship he had written:

> *Wed. at 2:30.* Weren't you amazed I taught so well! – Did you *love* me! – (I was still *dazed* from our kiss, & so proud of myself to be able to operate at all!! You were so sweet & good to me – to *call*, to *meet*, to *stay* (where did you run to??) & to kiss me!! We are both in terror (of losing love) – you from my 'getting bored', me from your finding me intolerable (my passion for honesty with you – passion to be known by you – makes me tell you things *very heavy* for you).
>
> I was astonisht (on the river road) when you said we'd only met twice – isn't it incredible?? – I feel so familiar & even intimate with you, because of all the hours of talk & *thought* & concern.
>
> The last thing on earth I am likely to mislead myself in is the degree of your liking for me. I can hardly believe in it.

The record illustrates just how rapidly he had become intoxicated by her, turning to a modest expression of hopefulness in order to prevent his ideas from running wild with an almost adolescent excess. Other notes give evidence of his framing alternatives: one moment trying (obviously in vain) to be strong and self-denying; another feeling genuinely tender and wistful:

> Suddenly, in spite of all she says, I have an unbearable conviction that it must all *stop*, *now*, instantly – that no matter what happens it will bring her nothing but grief – whether we *marry* or it *ends* or anything between and I can't even fight this feeling, because it is on her behalf, *for her* – and my hope shudders.
>
> Then I try desperately to think of something – and I see the heart-breaking loving passage in the middle of her 1st page. I *am* a good ear to her. It matters to her that I care & listen & take in. What I should most like to do about your letters is sit down with you & them and use them as a *text*: *comment* on and to them, like a theologian – explaining their beauties, their mysteries, answering & out-loud loving them.

His curiously unwitting reference to using her letters for the purposes of practical criticism discloses that he was always (if inescapably) aware of being her teacher, a role that it suited him more often to wish away. In a little while he felt nonplussed by their situation: 'an affair seems, & must be, absolutely out. What then? Is it possible to *develop it down*, so to speak, into merely a (charged) friendship? Does a term have to be used at all? But we feel, as well as think, in these categories, Or do we?' While Berryman preoccupied himself with the categorical logistics of the relationship, J herself was forced by her position as a senior student to institute a 'programme' whereby he should not telephone or meet her, except at her wish, until she had graduated: the scheme was designed to moderate their relationship so that she could study and sleep without unrest. 'Her marvellous programme', Berryman noted with an amount of naive self-delusion,

1) gives us a testing period
2) gives *me* a chance & a task
3) reduces our agonizing, freeing (a little) both of us
4) lets us get used (after *both* just 48 hrs & months) to each other
5) is both brighter & braver than any of my non–ideas
   (immersion, desperate-head-for Fate, etc.)
   but does *not* reduce my thinking about her, or my hoping
   she'll *call* (so I can say to her the new 800 things)

Somewhat later she decided that, feeling oppressed and trapped by his entreaties and influence over her, she should rectify the difficult and hurtful situation. The remedy was found, not in his weakness, but in her strength: she made the resolve to leave for California. True to her decision, she flew out one Saturday; in an unpublished poem written that afternoon, Berryman shows that he did not share her certainty but ambiguously regretted her departure from his love-life:

> My love,
> do sometimes come – through the long air – back
> and I will see you home.

After Berryman married his third wife, Kate, later in 1961, they remained friends with J. Much later – in June 1968 – Berryman wrote two Dream Songs commemorating one of her visits. 'An Afternoon Visit' applauds his recollection of J's 'spirit, tumultuous/ as if a spirit could bleed'. The other poem ends wistfully:

> She destroyed his letters: that he held against her.
> O but he loved her & he loved her still.
> To sink into that abyss
> Might be a triumph. Inconceivable.

She comes to me with her past & present a blur.
Fancy now, darling, this:

Another I, another you, long since
planned together our lives, and in the future
we will do so again.
Your colour is a joy. Your hues & tints –
Ravening thro' the world – disgrace nature,
and we will do better then   [*Henry's Fate & Other Poems*, p. 26].

In June of 1961 Berryman spent eight weeks teaching at the
School of Letters, Indiana University, Bloomington, occupying a
corner room with 'gorgeous' views on the seventh floor of a tower.
He worked hard, sweltering, 'with the best students I ever had: 15
of them – 2 beards, a nun, & a Lebanese professor', and, despite
bemoaning what he called 'a horrible demanding official social life',
enjoyed himself principally in the company of his old friend Robert
Fitzgerald. During that period he was visited by another girl, Mary,
a student from Minneapolis. Mary enjoyed Berryman's personal
presence and sense of style (at least in those days he was yet dapper),
but was not impressed by his teaching, which had tended to be too
personalised. He often mentioned his acquaintance with Dylan
Thomas, Mark Van Doren, or T. S. Eliot, and those students who
did not think it was idle name-dropping took it to be untrue and
pretentious. It was evident to Mary, who did not fall in love with
him, that Berryman preferred teaching undergraduates who would
idolise him. He seemed to need the assurance of their adoration,
although he was also genuinely self-deprecating and could scarcely
credit his own appeal. One evening in Minneapolis Berryman
walked her along the River Road overlooking the Mississippi; he
reached his arm around her, but she instinctively stepped away and
slipped down the cliff. Since she was dressed in Bermuda shorts, her
legs were scraped and bloody as she scrambled back up to Berryman. She returned huffily to her apartment. Berryman told her
lightheartedly that he had got the message: 'Out to lunch!'
He phoned her often from Bloomington, reiterating the news
that Robert Lowell and Robert Fitzgerald were his two closest
friends and asking her to come and meet Fitzgerald. When she did
eventually go, Berryman was waiting at her hotel; news of Hemingway's death had just come in, and Berryman wept in the taxi
taking them to the campus – 'in the taxi too, sick –' (Dream Song
34). Although no one yet knew the manner of Hemingway's death,
Berryman told Fitzgerald, 'The poor son-of-a-bitch blew his fucking head off.' As with all sudden or suicidal deaths, Berryman

associated Hemingway's with his own father's suicide, and later
addressed Dream Song 235 to the question:

> Tears Henry shed for poor old Hemingway
> Hemingway in despair, Hemingway at the end,
> the end of Hemingway,
> tears in a diningroom in Indiana
> and that was years ago, before his marriage say,
> God to him no worse luck send.
>
> Save us from shotguns & fathers' suicides.
> It all depends on who you're the father *of*
> if you want to kill yourself –
> a bad example, murder of oneself,
> the final death, in a paroxysm, of love
> for which good mercy hides?
> . . . .
> Mercy! my father; do not pull the trigger
> or all my life I'll suffer from your anger
> killing what you began.

When Mary left Bloomington, Berryman arranged that Fitzgerald should accompany her to Indianapolis, where she was
bound. She later called Fitzgerald and asked why Berryman telephoned her so often in the early morning hours. It seemed to
Fitzgerald, as he told her, 'Can't you see, he wants to bother you, to
hurt you?' Although Berryman gave the impression at Indiana that
his personal life was unhappy Mary always found him complimentary, never being abusive or making scenes in her presence,
and on the whole perhaps 'too gentle, too caring'. In the earlier part
of the year he had participated in outdoors activities such as
swimming and picnicking; he cared very much for the company
and attention of the young, but he was also tender to his own needs,
lonely for a more singular care which Mary could not give him.

In the spring, however, shortly before moving to yet another
address, 415 Erie Street South-East, Berryman had come to meet J's
friend Kathleen (invariably known by her family as 'Kathy', by
others as 'Kate') Donahue. Cautiously at first, for fear of betraying
J, Kate began to see more and more of Berryman. Twenty-two
years old in July that year, Kate was, like J, a good Catholic
('educated for the last 16 years by nuns. Brother,' Berryman put it
with feigned exasperation); her mother had died at an early age, and
Kate automatically became the domestic mainstay of her family – an

ageing father with drinking problems of his own, two brothers, Daniel and William, and a sister, Irene. Berryman later joked to the journalist Jane Howard that he was first attracted to Kate by 'the spindly, wobbly way she walked in high heels.' As her relationship with Berryman deepened, Kate kept it from her father for fear of alarming him; in time he felt crushed by the news that his fond daughter had become involved with a middle-aged academic poet who was already twice a divorcé.

> What are we going to do? [Kate wrote to him] In regard to being deceitful to J. your burden is heavier than mine because she depends on you more. . . .
> The fact that I have made you happy means everything to me. . . .
> I will probably always be incoherent but I am determined not to remain passive. . . .
> I think of your tenderness towards me. I have never known anything like it and probably never will again. It is such a wonderful combination of firmness and freedom. I love being able to choose to love you as a free person.

When J decided to quit her relationship with Berryman, Kate's feelings could develop naturally. Berryman suffered from a great many proper scruples, as he recognised at an early stage of what had become a lightning involvement:

> Sun/Mon 3:45 a.m.

> Kate, sweet darling –
> It is strange to write you. I know I mustn't. But you'll probably never see this. – It's only *3 days*. I tell you, I can't stand it.
> I have utterly *no right* – *and* I am old & stupid – you must marry some 'good Cath – boy' – I know that, and I even want it for you, love.
> I have *not* called you.
> *I still love J. too* – as you know, in an utterly different way. *And* as you know, I never expect to see her again.
> *But* I can hardly live from day to day without you – when I think you might be here, I curse, or cry. And yet I never expect to see *you* again.
> But where are you?

As early as 3 May, he tried writing for advice from Father William

F. Lynch. His immediate incentive to writing was that a Jesuit priest
(J's confessor, and formerly one of Berryman's own students) tried
to interfere and stop the progress of his affair with Kate. In a pained
and resentful Dream Song called 'Ode' (written on 15 August 1961,
just over two weeks before his marriage to Kate), he ends a brief list
of those 'slob's associates' who had tried to impede his happiness by
mentioning

> the nosey Jesuit.
> A tribe I lose to: *I* lose my right hand,
> she lost the honour of her word, ah well   [Song 231].

At the time of writing to Father Lynch, however, he had hedged his
alarmed sense of responsibility with what can most charitably be
described as self-delusion. 'I suppose you know that I am not
seductive to my students and pay no attention to their being so to
me, as of course they occasionally are,' he wrote, before proceeding
with assumed coolness to what he called the matter of 'professional
wariness & restraint, – which I see as double: you don't take
advantage of the *formal* relation, and you don't let them take
advantage of their access. It's simple.' Recognising that in fact the
issue was far from simple, Berryman left his disingenuous letter
unfinished and did not send it.

After his return from Indiana, the relationship with Kate developed quickly and unreservedly on both hands. She gained a
certain strength from her gentle passiveness; he found irresistible a
young and tractable nature that was generous even to a fault. 'You
will like Kate very good. I do too,' he told Saul Bellow. 'She is
beautiful as well but the best thing about her is Japanese submissiveness, silence, & attention. I'm tired of raging egos, especially my
own.' Kate's willingness to give according to his needs seemed a
precondition of their marriage; he approved her selfless demeanour
and her dependency on his approval. As Kate matured in later years
with Berryman, she came to learn that her generosity of spirit, so
instinct to her nature, was in some ways an index of her own needs,
and that her susceptibility to a certain dominance would not always
serve her self-respect and independence of being.

The wedding was fixed for late August, but was postponed
because of Berryman's sickness. On Friday, 1 September, Ralph
and Alicia Ross, and Philip and Ellen Siegelman, attended the
City Hall with the couple; because of Berryman's own mismanage-
ment of his affairs, Siegelman enlisted the aid of their friend, Mayor
Arthur Naftalin, to discover them a judge, Theodore Knutson,

who was free to perform the ceremony. In Dream Song 186, Berryman recalled after three years:

> And at the ceremony
>
> after His Honor swivelled us a judge
> my best friend stood in tears, at both his age
> and undeclining mine.

Berryman's health was in such bad shape that he could hardly sign the register, and the clerk made him practice before he achieved legibility. His beginning in sickness did not bode well for the marriage, but Berryman returned with Kate to his apartment in Erie Plaza in nothing but a glad and happy heart.

> She is a very very good woman, one of the sweetest-natured and most womanly and most loyal I have ever known. I can't describe her at all. In addition she is a raving beauty, tall, black-haired, shaped like a willow, like which also she moves, and elegant beyond praising. She is also a furnace. There are two little problems. She is 22, and a Catholic. It took us six months – and has destroyed her father and her best friend, according to them. Wish us luck, because we are going to need some at last.

In his divorce settlement with Ann, Berryman had agreed to make monthly payments in support of Paul. His salary had never been considerable – in 1959, for example, when he and Ann were divorced, he had been paid 9,300 dollars, with a further 120 dollars for occasional lectures in the English department – but the harum-scarum pattern of his life seems to have disabled him from any successful budgeting. Whenever Ann asked for him to fulfil his obligations to Paul, he would plead an impecuniosity beyond his control or else try to mitigate his delinquency by asking sympathy for his illnesses.

In the early days of his marriage to Kate, he defaulted, and Ann took him to court for 600 dollars in the third week of November. After what Berryman found a nerve-wracking period in the courthouse, his lawyer managed to obtain a continuance. So real was his plight that he spent the next two weeks working frantically on a collection of essays to be submitted in a competition arranged by the Bush Foundation of St Paul, Minnesota, with a deadline of Monday, 4 December. He had to finish a manuscript of one hundred pages, and wrote with such fever that in a matter of days he completed essays including 'The Freedom of the Don', 'Conrad's Journey', and 'The Freedom of the Poet', the last of which gave him a title for the whole collection. (In a later year Robert Giroux contracted with him for a collection of essays under the same title, containing both published material and the group written in 1962, but the volume was published only after his death.) On 1 December, Kate rushed to St Paul with two-thirds of the manuscript, at a time when Berryman was only in the middle of an essay called 'The Development of Anne Frank' (an incisive study of the process of maturation unfolded by Anne Frank's *Diary*): he was left to make up a further thirty-five pages over the weekend. Despite meeting that deadline, however, he did not win the prize.

While working on that group of essays, he had expressed the hope that 'at last maybe something will accrue from this exile': Meridian Books (World Publishing Company) rewarded some of his hopefulness at the time by paying him 100 dollars to write a brief preface for the third printing of *Stephen Crane*, which was issued in February the next year. A cheering reception greeted his article on Robert Lowell's 'Skunk Hour' for Anthony Ostroff's symposium *The Contemporary Poet as Artist and Critic* (Boston: Little, Brown & Co., 1964). Allen Tate, to whom he had sent a carbon copy, told him, 'This is magnificent. I envy Cal', and Lowell himself wrote on 18 March,

> you've made an amazing guess, more or less a bull's-eye thrust into what was going on when the poem was written – all very dazzling and disturbing.
>   What you said about other poets of our generation is something I've brooded much on. What queer lives we've had even for poets! There seems something generic about it, and determined beyond anything we could do.

Although Berryman managed to redeem his obligations to Paul in 1962, he let matters slip so badly again almost exactly four years later that Ann had to bring a civil case against him; at that time her lawyer agreed to a trial period of 100 dollars a month for six months, with Berryman's lawyer having a power of attorney over finances. Berryman had suffered from alcoholic disorganisation for some time already, and tended to stretch his expenses beyond his means, but his health deteriorated so much in the 1960s that it became increasingly difficult for him to retain any method in his daily life.

In the winter he fell sick with a combination of bronchitis and influenza; his morale had been further lowered by having to 'visit' all too often for the English department. In one report on a student teacher that February, he wrote sarcastically, 'No-one knows better than I do that if anyone marked *all* that's wrong with a student paper, empires would topple meanwhile, but spectacular nonsense ought to have a moment's attention.' He found relief to a wearisome winter from knowing that, for the next year, Brown University, Providence, Rhode Island, had invited him to be a visiting professor, and (before that) he would teach a summer school at the beautifully situated Bread Loaf School of English.

Berryman delighted in learning that Kate was pregnant. In the late spring they quit their apartment and lodged with Lynn Louden and his wife, Helen, in a St Paul apartment, prior to leaving for the east coast. 'Both of the women were uncomfortably pregnant and everything was in chaos,' Louden remembers.

> One evening the newspaper was lying on the couch and John picked it up. He told us to listen and proceeded to read a brief article. It was about a rummage sale that had been (or was about to be) held in someone's garage. The sponsoring group was a local Plumber's Union Auxiliary and there was nothing unusual about the article. Locations, times, dates, organizers, kinds of objects for sale, etc. made up the content. But listening to John read it made you want to scream. All the pathos, boredom, and anonymity attached to the lives of a group of people totally unknown to us was revealed. This was a case in which he had merely to use his voice to change journalism into poetry.

Before they left Minneapolis that summer, Berryman was appointed a full professor, and related happily too that his friends 'got me out of the English Dept, and that does matter: no more double chores & insolent nagging.'

15
Triumphs and trials,
1962-66

The Berrymans left Minneapolis for the east coast early in June 1962. Kate drove the car, despite being, as Berryman reported, 'in the worst stage of preparing to bless the world with a new person: she announced tonight that it is 3 inches long & weighs one ounce: and she is sick or sackt out constantly; what travellers!' They stayed with Robert Jefferson Berryman in New York, then visited South Kent School, and saw Mark Van Doren, in Connecticut, before taking up residence at Bread Loaf on 27 June.

The Bread Loaf School of English is run by Middlebury College, Vermont, as a summer school for teachers seeking the MA. The session lasts eight weeks. The locale is a mountain plateau; further up, the Long Trail – 'a footpath in the wilderness' – winds along the summit of the Green Mountains and extends from southern Vermont to the Canadian border. To the northeast stands Bread Loaf Mountain, for which the school is named, and fields and woods lie a few minutes in every direction. Years ago the campus was a summer inn, largely frequented by academics. The original inn building remains, as well as a large barn. There are half a dozen small cottages used as dormitories and studies for students and faculty, and two fairly large houses built in a style known locally as Steamboat Gothic. One of these is called Maple (the other being Birch), on the second floor of which the Berrymans occupied a room and bathroom on the east side, while the critic Carlos Baker and his wife were just across the hall on the west side.

The poet William Meredith was also on the faculty that summer: he and Berryman both arrived with half-gallons of gin. Berryman was going to enjoy himself, even at a cost. 'The fact,' Meredith recalled, 'that he and I drank gin at noon, which had to be elaborately overlooked and was, when that was possible, may have thrown us together at first.' It was at Bread Loaf that William Meredith first heard the Dream Songs read and even sung to him at 3 a.m. or 4 a.m. or 5 a.m., while others rested quietly in their beds. Carlos Baker remembered differently. One night in particular that summer he was vainly trying to sleep in preparation for an 8.30 lecture, preceded by a 7.30 breakfast, and, as he puts it, 'having no luck because of a persistent drone from overhead that came from Bill Meredith's room on the third floor, punctuated sometimes by what might have been laughter.' When he went to investigate, he discovered Berryman declaiming poems to Meredith, and they insisted that he listen to one. Baker listened politely for a moment, explained that they were keeping him awake, and asked them to seize another occasion. It was about 2.30 a.m. 'They clapped me on the shoulder and offered me a drink. I said no and left, feeling like a stuffed shirt for having interrupted so fine a seance and also like a resentful parent who has just given his pillow-fighting children an early-morning scolding.'

Meredith and Berryman spent many hours of those days and nights together. Kate did her best to be sociable despite being pregnant, and sometimes drank with them from the gallon jug of Gallo or Italian Swiss Colony sherry with which their Martinis were made. One time, Meredith said suddenly out of the blue, 'I never understood suicide. It's one of the things that in my worst moments has never occurred to me as a possible solution. Has it to you?' – expecting Berryman, as he recalled, 'to say "No," the way healthy people do. And he said, "Yes, I think about it a great deal." And then he told me about his father's death.' On the same subject: one day in class, according to Joy Roulston, then a student, 'he said when he was younger and spending the summer at a place in Maine, he came to the insight about death that someday he would just have to walk out into the water.' The insight had lingered sixteen years already and remained a further six years before it was given permanent form in the poem 'Henry's Understanding' (*Delusions, Etc.*), which includes these lines:

> A chill at four o'clock.
> It only takes a few minutes to make a man.
> A concentration upon now & here.
> Suddenly, unlike Bach,
>
> & horribly, unlike Bach, it occurred to me
> that *one* night, instead of warm pajamas,
> I'd take off all my clothes
> & cross the damp cold lawn & down the bluff

into the terrible water & walk forever
under it out toward the island.

Always, for Berryman, night's fears were stemmed by creativity or companionship. Meredith's friendship at 4 a.m. was no disguise, but was not known then as nursing.

All that summer the shades were drawn in the Berrymans' room. The smell of gin and cigarette smoke hit a visitor in the face. The Dream Songs, with which he was busy, were invariably written by artificial light. His lectures were at 9.30 and 11.30, followed by one o'clock lunch in the dining hall. After lunch, Carlos Baker recalls,

> he disappeared into the room in Maple, and reappeared for
> dinner at six-thirty. Kate, though pale and quiet, appeared to
> enjoy her respite from housekeeping (as did all the faculty wives
> in residence) but stayed mostly with John. The sidewalk along
> the main road from Ripton to Middlebury Gap past the school
> is paved with Vermont marble, allegedly rejected gravestones
> without inscriptions, and the Berrymans would be seen moving
> along this, commonly by themselves, John with his curious
> sidelong gait and his eyes usually downcast, and Kate moving
> lightly beside him in some dark summer dress.

Talking with some students one day, Berryman said the worst thing a woman could do was to take a man's job. He also made the pronouncement that when people were in love, they should be happy. It was such quirky, sagacious, or even absolutely provocative statements that drew many students to his classes and alienated as many more. Reginald L. Cook, the director of the school, became an intercessor, encouraging students to take Berryman's courses and persuading dropouts to return. He persuaded them that Berryman had the most brilliant mind on campus. But the teaching went very well, and the drinking heightened it.

He taught two courses, one on 'Henry James and Stephen Crane' and the other called 'Deep Form in Minor and Major Poetry'. As a teacher he was anything but orthodox. When in form he was brilliant, but he took a great deal of indulgence because of his mannerisms. One day, for example, while he was taking attendance, he looked at the Catholic priest in class and bellowed at the top of his voice, 'Priests used to dress like priests!' On this or another occasion, he announced that the purpose of education was to rumple minds, and proceeded with a method of teaching which was associative rather than logical. 'He urged the students,' recalls Joy Roulston, 'to loosen their minds and associate, using dream sequences and a newspaper headline about F. D. Roosevelt to illustrate his point.' Another student's notes indicate a considerable concern with sexual matters, especially in explicating William Empson's poem 'Aubade'.

The living situation put everybody on top of everybody else, and social life was inevitably intense. Students were aware of Berryman's problem with drinking (some surmising that he drank to kill the nervous pain that he suffered from), but it did not obviously affect his teaching. Outside the classroom his displays could be memorable. At one party when a rock 'n' roll record was being played, he commented – very loudly – 'Let's go out on the porch and sing Mozart!' – and proceeded to sing an aria.

Early on in the session, the news came that William Faulkner had died on 7 July in Oxford, Mississippi. Berryman immediately conceived the notion of holding an evening 'Tribute to William Faulkner' in the Little Theatre. He himself chose to read a selection from Faulkner's long story 'The Bear'. Professor Donald Davidson (a southerner, one of the original Fugitive group, as well as a historian, critic, and poet) read part of *The Sound and the Fury* from the closing Dilsey section, and Carlos Baker read a passage from *The Wild Palms* about the Mississippi River flood in 1927. Berryman was the star of the show, though he had prepared himself with a quantity of gin. He spoke in a curious throaty voice in which some of the syllables seemed almost to come by way of the nasal passages. But he read well, Carlos Baker recalls,

> and with a full sense of the magic and mystery of Faulkner's prose, which he projected to the assembled group of perhaps two hundred students and faculty. He reached the climactic moment: 'Then I saw the bear . . .' and paused for so long that one wasn't sure he would continue. But he did, and sat down with his characteristic half-grin and a wave of his bony hand to the applauders, who were impressed.

Berryman habitually and nervously fingered the nosepiece of his glasses or used the right index finger to push it back on the bridge of his nose. His handshake could be unpleasantly limp, inner tensions evident from the dampness and sometimes even the wetness of his palm. Extended into the air, his hand would often tremble. His fingers were long and he would waggle them to emphasise points or to punctuate sentences. They were also yellow from chainsmoked cigarettes.

During this summer Berryman shook hands with Robert Frost, then a man of eighty-eight whose reputation and physical eminence were overwhelming. Frost seemed to want to dominate the Morrison family (Theodore and his wife Kay, Frost's secretary, their daughter Ann, and her then husband Chisholm Gentry), especially the women, at the Homer Noble Farm about a mile and a half away from the Bread Loaf campus. Berryman felt grateful to all of them for understanding and perhaps for mediating between Frost and himself, and praised them in a Dream Song:

> ah but it's Kay
> & Ted, & Chis & Anne,
> Henry thinks of: who eased his fearful way
> from here, in here, to there. This wants thought.
> I won't make it out.
>
> Maybe the source of noble such may come
> clearer to dazzled Henry. It may come.
> I'd say it will come with pain,
> in mystery   [Dream Song 38].

There were not many visits to Frost, as William Meredith has testified. Perhaps Berryman found Frost too awesome a figure or too affronting, or perhaps it was the air of regality about him, but certainly he was never so quiet as when visiting Frost. He became a child, without the characteristic rough edges, and kept calling Frost 'Sir'. There was also another matter: Berryman believed Frost had somehow slandered him once – or twice, as Dream Song 37 relates:

> He had fine stories and was another man
> in private; difficult, always. Courteous
> on the whole, in private.
> He apologize to Henry, off & on,
> for two blue slanders; which was good of him.
> I don't know how he made it.

A manuscript of the poem gives a variant reading: 'He apologized to Henry, repeatedly, / for a violent red slander.' In the last analysis, Berryman's memories of meeting Frost were all favourable. Long afterward he commemorated the occasion in 'Lines to Mr Frost':

> I wonder toward your marvellous tall art
> warning away maybe in that same morning
>
> you squandered afternoon of your great age
> on my good gravid wife & me, with tales

gay of your cunning & colossal fame
& awful character . . .   [*Delusions, Etc.*].

The Berrymans next moved just down the road from Bread Loaf to a cabin owned by Dulcie Scott, a good friend of William Meredith. There Kate took a photograph of Berryman with an enormous stack of Dream Songs. For good reason: the cabin provided an interlude of peace and quiet, a time for taking stock interrupted only by what Meredith called 'a brief philosophical exchange' with a rabbit (Dream Song 62) and a rather more exciting rumpus with three racoons rummaging in the garbage:

it seems, and is, clear to me we are brothers,
I wish the rabbit & the 'coons could be friends,
I'm sorry about the poker
but I'm too busy now for nipping or quills
I've given up literature & taken down pills,
and that rabbit doesn't trust me   [Dream Song 107: Sept. 7].

What Berryman found more exasperating than fauna were his efforts to weld the Dream Songs into a form. They seemed resistant to any possible shape or scheme. Late in August he set down one attempt at a conspectus; but then, starting a fresh page, 'ugh,' he wrote, 'so many schema: + minstrelsy.' His misgivings about the Songs were many. They included uneasy feelings about the fact that most of the Songs seemed very picaresque (like one of his favourite novels, Saul Bellow's *Adventures of Augie March*), that all the adventures were what he called 'bad', and that they smacked of paranoia. He then noted down what he considered the outstanding themes of the Songs, such as '*American*, then & now', including what he described as the government service done by 'Henry', the persona of the Songs (harking back to Berryman's own cultural tour of duty in India for the US State Department). Other collocations were:

Father – Mother – child
sex – love – woman
citizen – teacher – artist; scholar
Friend
Religion + illness, – Death

On 1 September, a rainy day which marked their first wedding anniversary, Berryman returned from a dinner party to work on his Dream Songs. It was clear to him that he should at least arrange what he was originally to issue as a set of seventy-five, foremost of which was to be a minstrel '1st part'. In this part, according to the ministrel tradition, he could include dances, superstition, fear, ballads, weird costumes, burlesques of opera and of personalities, which would end 'in a "walk around" of ALL'. In fact, it would seem, the formula would countenance just about every last one of what seemed a ragbag of Songs. Most of the Songs written up to this time were included in the volume eventually published as *77 Dream Songs*, but whether they function as a whole is still in question. 'But,' Berryman ended his note-page, 'keep pressure *low*; phantasmagoria, entertainment, switch.'

He did not have long to juggle with the manuscript, for pastoral clemency was short-lived. The next move was a day's drive to Providence, Rhode Island, where Berryman was to take on for the academic year Edwin Honig's classes at Brown University. (Charlotte Honig was dying of cancer, and they had to rent a house in South Woodstock, Connecticut, not in the grips of city life yet near enough to the hospital.) In Providence, the Berrymans, after much telephoning about problems coincident to the move, sublet 24 Congdon Street from the Honigs. On arrival the newcomers went out to dinner with their hosts. Kate was quiet and amenable, Berryman very courteous to Charlotte Honig, and the jokes turned upon literary figures.

The faculty party for new staff followed soon afterwards. Berryman did not cut an impressive figure. He was quick in his movements, but looked rather clerical, his eyes being masked behind his glasses. Clean-shaven, his face was longish, with a very square and stubborn jaw, a rather pursed-up mouth, and his chin was commonly elevated or else pointed down. As a novice at Brown, Berryman exhibited something at least of his stuffy side, his elegance. But he carried with him a reputation for wildness hardly suited to Brown, and one might have been forgiven for doubting his fitness as a substitute for the gentle, amiable Honig.

What could not be doubted for long was the intensity and skill of his teaching, nor that of his creative work. One morning Berryman called Daniel Hughes, then acting director of the Creative Writing Program, and asked him to come over and listen to some poems.

> I went grumbling, thinking it part of the job. But that was the turning-point for me with him because when I got there the evidence of the hard thinking and writing were everywhere; in his fierce hand on scraps of paper, in the full ash-trays, in the grey resistance of the light through a dreary New England dawn. I envied him because I write poems too but could never

concentrate as he did. I have never seen before or since such concentration; it seemed to me, it seems, life's major chord. Whatever difficulties there were after that, I felt the presences of his terrible cost and commitment, and I loved him.

The poems that Berryman was writing that fall took a dismal cast. They included Song 45, in which 'He stared at ruin. Ruin stared straight back,' and Song 70, which celebrates the fact that, when an undergraduate, he had once endured a feat of rowing, but turns with sick irony to these lines:

> Forever in the winning & losing since
> of his own crew, or rather
> in the weird regattas of this afterworld,
> cheer for the foe. He set himself to time
> the blue father.

On the manuscript of the poem, Berryman noted in parenthesis that the last line refers to 'Allyn' (John Allyn Smith), his natural father who had lost his life.

The National Poetry Festival, an event of some importance, was convened in Washington for three successive days from 22 October. Just about all the foremost poets of America participated. John and Kate Berryman flew to Washington from Providence and stayed at a hotel near the Library of Congress. They had lunch with Delmore Schwartz and his girlfriend Victoria, who had an immense enthusiasm for the Dream Songs: Schwartz complained that she was always reading him Dream Songs. Schwartz himself was suffering from the delusion that his ex-wife's detectives were following him, and accordingly behaved as if he and Victoria were not together.

Schwartz read on the afternoon of Monday, 22 October, when his voice went up in pitch so high and so hard that Richard Eberhart, who was in the audience that day, thought it a new style. Only later did he realise that it was part of the mental collapse that Schwartz was suffering.

Berryman himself opened the readings on Tuesday afternoon and included some of the Dream Songs in his recital. They were heard with enthusiasm. Later he told Richard Wilbur that he had written a great number of such poems and had in mind a vast structure into which they – and others yet to be written – would ultimately fall. Both Wilbur and Robert Lowell urged him to publish some of the best of them as soon as possible and not to wait for the pattern to be filled up.

A large party was held one night at Stuart Udall's. Kate did not go, for her ankles were swelling from her pregnancy. Later that evening Berryman and Richard Wilbur called her from a police station. Word had come during the party that Delmore Schwartz had been arrested for drunkenness and was in jail. When Berryman and Wilbur went to investigate, it turned out that Schwartz had gone berserk in his room, had torn the telephone from the wall, and had hurled an ashtray through the window. The police thought he was only drunk and kept him six hours, but he was more mad than drunk. Discharged at last, he was not at all grateful for being rescued: for one thing, his belt had been taken away from him. He abused Berryman violently and was heard with perfect patience. Berryman was equally unruffled when Schwartz stole a taxi booked by Wilbur and himself and left them with a long walk in the early hours of the morning. Schwartz, sloppily dressed but carrying his umbrella, arrived in a state of bedraggled ferment back at the hotel. Victoria, who loved him, was forbidden to enter the room. 'Go and sleep with Berryman!' he screamed at her. In any event, Berryman stayed in Wilbur's room, and Victoria with Kate. In the morning Schwartz received his money and left town. Throughout the incident, as Richard Wilbur recalls, Berryman was a solicitous and loyal friend. Dream Song 149, one of Berryman's elegies for Schwartz, records that: 'I got him out of a police-station once, in Washington, the world is *tref* / and grief too astray for tears.'

By Thursday, the Berrymans were back in Providence in time for his forty-eighth birthday party, at which he was able, at his own request, to meet S. Foster Damon, the great Blake scholar. Remembering his Princeton and Harvard days, Berryman was the soul of respect and attention in Damon's presence. But he was short enough with another poet who came to the party: 'I don't know,' he remarked, 'whether he wants to get my autograph or sock me!' (The poet wanted both.)

During Thanksgiving week, Berryman wrote fourteen Dream Songs, including 'Big Buttons, Cornets: the advance', a poem which combines the frustration of finding all the bars legally closed on Thanksgiving Day itself with that of being black and lacking legal rights; the poem is a defiantly gay doggerel in true ministrel tradition.

It was during this period that Berryman began to show signs of serious disturbance. Kate did not yet fully appreciate the extent to which emotional disturbance was caused by alcohol, and considered them separate problems. But Berryman was suffering – and drinking. There would come a time in his life when he would mistake the whiskey for the work and think it indispensable to his writing a poem. At this time, late in 1962, the consumption of alcohol was not adequately reckoned, but then the course of it did not look morbid, despite the fact that he had been drinking excessively for nearly fifteen years.

With less than a week to go before the baby was due, they decided to visit Berryman's friends, Monroe and Brenda Engel, in Cambridge. Berryman's behaviour now became very erratic, loud and upset, and he cried. He was admitted to hospital, under pressure – 'Cal's hospital – Maclean's –,' where he spent the rest of the time until Kate's confinement, hating himself and hating her. 'I'll never forgive you for this!' he bellowed at her. He experienced an enormous sense of resentment against Kate as never before or after. Kate herself stayed overnight with the Engels. It was arranged that Berryman would be discharged when the baby was due. Part of his trouble at the time might be attributed to his feelings of apprehension about the oncoming birth. His doctor in McLean Hospital was of the opinion that he would be greatly upset and feel replaced in Kate's affections, and predicted, mistakenly, that Berryman could not go through with it.

Berryman was discharged from hospital on Saturday, 1 December, and took the train to Providence. Later that night Kate was taken to hospital where, at 1.30 the next afternoon, Martha was born: '7 lb., 4 oz., very frisky, much hair all black, heredity atrocious,' as Berryman recorded. 'Kate is radiant; the labour about 10 hours, never bad. Father survives too, owing no doubt to double dosages of chlorpromazine & dilantin.'

That evening, direct from hospital, he visited Daniel and Mary Hughes with his delightful news. The Hugheses, who did not have a car, put him in a taxi after the proper congratulations. He was not drunk when he left them on a snowy, icy evening. Twenty-four hours later, Berryman's psychiatrist in Boston called Hughes at about 11 p.m. and urged him to find out what had happened to his patient. Berryman had missed an appointment that day (Monday, 3 December) and was not answering the telephone. He was discovered helpless in bed upstairs, unable or unwilling to get to the phone. Daniel Hughes recalls:

> The taxi had backed over his leg upon depositing him at his door the night before. Why he hadn't sought help is still unclear to me, but we called the fire department and got an ambulance to take him to the emergency room. I rode down with him, more voluble and upset than he was. A grim stoicism, even a confirming sense of the ironic, was his dominant mood although his leg looked mangled and festering to me.

Hughes sat with Berryman until he was rolled away. 'I feel,' Berryman called out, 'like a minor character in a bad Scott Fitzgerald novel.'

All this was taking place within a matter of hours of Berryman's having been blessed with a daughter. Is there any good reason why an injured man in pain should not seek help, unless from some sort of distress of mind? A reference to 'couvade' in one of the Dream Songs should probably be taken with a pinch of salt in this connection, although the notion was certainly on his mind. When Mary Hughes visited him in hospital, Berryman barked: 'Don't give me any tenth-grade Freud about my having to be in the hospital while my wife is there too!' At the least, it must be said, they were not in the same hospital: Kate was in Providence Lying-in, Berryman in Jane Brown. But what must be understood is that often, for Berryman, delight would be only apparent. He was a man who considered death constantly and devoutly, one for whom the weight of a new birth would instantly jog the other side of the scales. He was always apprehensive about what an eternity might lie in every next hour. He could be simultaneously sad and witty: it took only the slightest shift of mind for brilliant gaiety to gall.

Even as he lay in hospital (his daughter now four days old), Berryman wrote a first version of Dream Song 40:

> I'se scared a lonely. Never see my son,
> easy be not to see anyone,
> combers out to sea
> know they goin' somewhere but not me
> got a little poison, got a little gun
> I'se scared a lonely.
>
> I'se scared a only one thing, which is me,
> from any else I don't take nothing, see,
> for any bugger's sake,
> but this is where I *livin*, where I rake
> my leaves & cop my promise, this' where we
> cry ourselves awake.

Such a verse at such a time is expressive of great emotional dereliction. Professedly happy, he was evidently in an ambivalent state of mind. He felt joyous about his daughter, but his piteous condition was to inhabit a mixed mind: a mind in which even contentment could not readily be accommodated.

While students visited the patient and signed their names on his plaster-cast, Berryman continued thinking out his projected volume of poetry: 'I see why I hate putting the "75" together (I did 51 today – there's 52nd. – the good ones seem to me *so* good I can't bear to hide them with their inferiors.'

John and Kate Berryman both returned home from their respective hospitals on the same day, Berryman still in an enormous cast. He began to get very drunk and accused Kate of neglecting him, true to the warning given a few weeks before. Kate became so upset that she threw a tray of dishes on the floor. The Hugheses helped to pacify the situation: Berryman calmed down. The plump baby Martha enlivened the room to Berryman's affectionate cries: 'Con! Con! Look at her wanting to con us!' He was enthralled with the child.

On 26 December he wrote Song 68, a paean and lament for the stars of the Blues. With the sick Christmas spirit in mind, he recalled ironically the fact that a hospital for whites – 'sick-house's white birds' – would not admit the stricken singer Bessie Smith. He also wrote Song 285, none too confident of the New Year:

> Henry peered quite alone
> as if the worlds would answer to a code
> just around the corner, down gelid dawn,
> beckoning like a moan.

With the New Year his teaching also resumed – with characteristic fervour. His courses were largely carried over from Bread Loaf, one in 'Deep Form', another in creative writing. Ken Snyder, a graduate student, attended one of the courses. Although Snyder himself admits that he was not a 'bomber' (Berryman's term for a brilliant student who knew it: 'His word for or about me was "Horatio", i.e. steady but dull'), he yet found Berryman a 'devastating' teacher who exercised a tremendous influence over his mental or spiritual life: 'If you heard him at all he scarred you, if you didn't, he looked & sounded a belligerent drunk. It was not at all difficult in those years just before *The Dream Songs* for people to respond with a mixture of terror & something like contempt.'

That spring Berryman could be seen getting out of a cab on crutches in front of Horace Mann house, where his classes waited, and 'swinging on into his office and classroom like a clarifying spirit'. The class would hear him coming up the wooden stairs to the classroom on the third floor. His trouble with the broken leg seemed oddly serious and fuelled the constant talk among the students about his health. Nearly everyone felt protective toward him, suspicious that something terrible was happening or about to happen to him. He was the tireless subject of discussion: his illnesses, Kate, the baby. He seemed frail, his long hands shook all the time, one dangling a cigarette and gesturing with it.

On the whole his students that year were a remarkable set, although there was not a predominance of women. There were those who found their way into the *Dream Songs*: Riva Freifeld, a splendid-looking girl with an abundance of red hair, and the two outstanding writing talents of Ellen Kaplan and Valerie Trueblood, as well as others who were not poeticised. Berryman exercised a tremendous involvement with all of them, while Kate took more of a mothering role. Valerie Trueblood, who was eighteen at the time, entered into a kind of hypnotised veneration of Berryman that must have been a crush. Her response was common, and with good reason:

> He gave off a promise in his bearing toward the students, his appearance before us hung-over, or devilishly gleeful over a letter he had had, or passionate about a story he was going to read us ('I've brought you a little story, ladies and gentlemen, and it will *kill* you'), that we could exchange whatever we were doing for something far more dangerous and comical – with his help, *if* we deserved it.

Valerie Trueblood recalls further:

> He would always enter the room looking disgusted after his struggle up the stairs, and immediately a wonderful, ferocious smile would break across his face as if he hadn't expected to find *us* there, a feast of trembling students. This smile was accompanied by elaborate greetings to one or other of us, always '*Mr.*' and '*Miss,*' which were thrown out in a mocking voice as if the names were ridiculous in themselves and we might want to defend them. But then he would sit down and the smile would become a sweet-natured, pleased, expectant expression as we got ready to read the story of the day.
>   In the first class I attended he said, for the benefit of those of us he didn't know, that never in his presence might we use 'fascinate' or 'intrigue'. He said the theme of the course would be shortness. Here the note that he struck again and again sounded: he was going to teach us strictness, discipline, and the way out of the miserable tendency to inflate everything we wrote. He gave precise assignments: set a story in summer, involve notations of freedom and bondage. Imitate each other (a nice way to handle our flagrant imitations of each other); show your work to each other. Write a story that does not come to an

end or write an ending with future conditions implicit. Don't write poetry when you mean prose. Poetic prose was a 'very, very risky business.' He was astonishingly generous to our cramped efforts. He could read a perfectly awful story and fly it into another realm with his delight in the two good sentences. He made every one of us see what we *might* have written. For a man who could be, if provoked, malignantly unfriendly to fatuousness, he was as gentle as a nurse. He tried not to hurt anyone in this class, let alone demolish anyone, as it was clear he was fiendishly tempted sometimes to do. He could not help, sometimes, setting the stage for an all-out attack by the class on somebody's effort (the story would have to be pretentious, for him to let things get this far), but he would stop it, at a certain point, by asking the mildest and least outspoken ones to judge – and allowing this opinion, usually gentle and undamaging, to stand. He would say, 'I think we've all been duped! Mr. P— is correct in assuming this story is *not* an allegory! As a simple *story* it's quite well done. Deliciously clever!'

In the spring semester his course in 'The Short Story' used the Allen Tate–Caroline Gordon anthology *The House of Fiction*. He read out Tolstoy's 'Master and Man' on one occasion, and then hobbled all the way downstairs to walk around and dry his tears during a break. In his poetry seminar, the atmosphere seedy in a darkened room, he again laid out the secret workings of Empson's 'Aubade', Elizabeth Bishop's 'Roosters', and Frost's 'Provide, Provide', as well as discussing *vagina dentata* legends and medical anomalies. The fact that the students seemed unread appalled him, or he pretended it appalled him. Inexcusable ignorance actually seemed to delight him. His almost unbearable itch to quash fools went hand in hand with a curiosity and a lenient half-commiseration with them. He associated the ability to make a fool of oneself willingly with the daring of the artist; he said again and again, Valerie Trueblood remembers, 'Whenever you write any-thing you run the risk of making a *fool* of yourself' – in his violently italicised speech.

On another occasion he gave a reading from *Time* magazine, to show what 'the unlearned could unleash' on the country. He read from *Time* in a prissy voice that grew more and more savage. His scorn, like his praise, always managed to demonstrate just how much more there was to writing than anyone would credit.

His literary loves were intense and he could be arrogant in connection with them. He assigned 'Lycidas' and asked the next week how long students had spent reading it. When one girl was

fixed upon, she said proudly that she had spent three hours. He
pursued the matter with great menace and declared that *300* hours
(the amount of time he had given it when young) were inadequate.
Valerie Trueblood also remembers that 'His discussion of "Resolution and Independence", and reading of passages from it, changed
the poem forever for us.'

Students were often invited to his house. Valerie Trueblood
experienced her first Martini at one such session, while Berryman
read out Dream Songs. In class he mentioned his own work only
obliquely, with bitter but sprightly allusions now and then to what
poets 'went through'. At home the poems reigned, the master
sitting in a rocking chair and reading very merrily, occasionally
asking Kate, 'What do you think of that?' and telling the students,
'She says it's wonderful!' 'His baby Martha was up late,' Valerie
Trueblood recalls,

> and everyone admired her. He asked us all questions: were we
> friends? did we read each other's work? what did we read? He
> could ask outrageous personal questions but asked them rather
> as if it could only be a relief to everyone for him to know the
> answer, and get the matter out of the way. You were not
> expected to answer them; he was a courtly, discreet man who
> could not tolerate social trespass or bad behavior. People who
> tried to match his audacity were often cut off.

On the afternoon of 20 January, Berryman wrote Song 25, with
the last line: 'Thank you for everything.' At the foot of the page he
wrote, 'Sunday afternoon, January 19th or so, 1963 – *no more*: this is
the end,' and underlined three times the word 'end'. It was one of
the many occasions on which he tried to conclude the poem – in any
event he was still writing Dream Songs at least as late as 1969 –
straining always to release himself from the terrible incubus of his
inspiration. To Allen Tate he lamented the fact that he found
himself constantly writing Dream Songs, but explained that he was
'self-trapped'.

At 8 a.m. on 29 January, Delmore Schwartz arrived on the
doorstep of 24 Congdon Street. He had just taken a taxi all the way
from Cambridge, Massachusetts, and told it to wait. The spectacle
was memorable:

> He walked my living-room, & did not want breakfast
> or even coffee, or even even a drink.
> He paced, I'd say Sit down,
> it makes me nervous, for a moment he'd sit down,

then pace. After an hour or so *I* had a drink.
He took it back to Cambridge,

we never learnt why he came, or what he wanted.
His mission was obscure. His mission was real,
but obscure   [Dream Song 155].

Schwartz talked wildly about Nelson Rockefeller and about other unintelligible matters. He was so *high* that he refused a drink – no drink was needed. He walked up and down the room shouting, 'Literature doesn't matter! The only thing that matters is money and getting your teeth fixed!' At midnight the same day – or perhaps the next day – he called from New York, and asked Berryman to go and stay with him at the Hotel Earle, 'leaving my job' – 'All your bills will be paid, he added, tense' [Song 154].

Later that day Daniel Hughes dropped by and Berryman told him about the incident. He had been upset by Schwartz's visit and his wild talk of a few hours before, and wondered aloud, 'You know, I think he's crazy.' But Hughes had brought his own tidings: Robert Frost was dead. Berryman greeted the news with a wide-eyed question: 'Dan, it's *scary*. Who's number one? Who's number one? Cal is number one, isn't he?' Hughes was aware that Berryman wanted him to say, 'You're number one, of course,' but he did not say it. He was in fact mildly shocked by Berryman's competitiveness, which he later came to understand better and to accept.

At the beginning of April, Charlotte Honig died. A memorial service was held on 10 April, of which Berryman reported, 'We are low. . . . It troubles one to live with a dying woman's things.'

On Sunday, 19 May, Martha, in Berryman's own turn of phrase, 'got Xtianized.' Robert Fitzgerald stood as godfather. Before departing, his final endearing action was to bend down and kiss Martha's toe.

The year at Brown University drew to a close: Berryman's efforts with his students had been rewarding. For so long he had looked on teaching as a spare horse, a second choice to writing. Yet the second had responded to use and experience. Now he rode it like a charger. There was even a 'Berryman style' that developed among the students. Edwin Honig, who inherited a number of those students the following year, found that some of them 'whom I'd known before as lugs', had been sensitised by Berryman. 'They even affected Berryman's mocking Cambridge accent, which he could put on very easily. It was a sort of combination Cambridge, Oklahoma and Yankee.' Otherwise, Berryman had been basically ignored while in Providence. Only the Hugheses managed to give

him any real connection to the school. It is probably true to say that
Brown was apprehensive of him and his later success, and high
fame was only imminent at that point.

For the summer weeks the Berrymans occupied an old Gristmill in
rural Rhode Island, and were able to cool off under a private
waterfall. The place was happily primitive; at night they had to
grope outside for the toilet, with the help of a torch. Learning that
the University of Minnesota had granted him a sabbatical leave for
the next academic year, Berryman applied to a number of foundations for assistance towards writing his critical biography of
Shakespeare, on which he planned to work at the Folger Library in
Washington, D.C. John Thompson held out hopes of a travelling
fellowship (5,000 dollars) from the Farfield Foundation, but Berryman had already earned a reputation for being a poor investment as
a drunk, and the money fell to Saul Bellow. (On 3 February 1964 –
late for the purpose but none the less welcome – the Ingram Merrill
Foundation, New York, awarded him 4,000 dollars.) His enthusiasm for the project went undimmed, however, as he told Ralph
Ross on 19 September that he had already started a new draft of
Shakespeare's Friend, 'which I want out in the spring; I LOVE
scholarship.' (Earlier in the summer he began five pages of quite
another book, an autobiography – 'It starts with my father's suicide'
– but made no substantial progress with it.) Despite his apparent
buoyancy, he had to admit to a certain sluggishness of spirit:

> The consciousness of age you spoke of some weeks ago is with
> me always now. I feel as if I were rushing to death, with
> nothing done. It is an unworthy and debilitating feeling – but
> how to get rid of it? We must have a talk about this. Maybe one
> can take steps, maybe it's just another thing to be put up with.
> Dante seems to have been marvellously free from it, but in
> Shakespeare and Villon say it's like a poison. There appear to be
> no rules. Who among the philosophers have dealt with it? – here
> in the summer woods I am feeling very ignorant.

Proceeding to more immediate matters, he added: 'It is weird how
people fail to mention money. Somehow, having ignored money
all my life while at the same time agonizing over it, I now
occasionally feel that there is no point in mentioning anything BUT
money.'

He felt somewhat consoled to learn that a reviewer in *The Times
Literary Supplement* (31 May) had objected to Donald Hall's prefatory remark to his anthology *Contemporary American Poetry* (that

'Homage to Mistress Bradstreet' was a 'failure') as being 'grossly unjust to a path-breaking masterpiece'. Berryman observed ironically, 'Ha ha. When *TLS* never even reviewed it.' It was also a balm to hear from another poet, James Dickey, 'You are the best living poet in English.'

It was characteristic of Berryman's financial innocence that when Brown University suddenly deposited to his account a final cheque of 973 dollars, he was utterly surprised. 'My balance was under a hundred dollars. My God. Imagine being due a thousand dollars and not knowing it! How have I crept in darkness to 48?' He was overjoyed enough to write an *ad hoc* poem:

> Praise we then, barefoot, after *no* (dear) thought,
> days when one thousand extra buck arrives
> already earned, known about
> by any counting boob but Henry Cat
> who just is was to dive down debt again
> is in his earlier lives
>
> and numerous & penniless his wives
> & daughters which they do need dressing, man.
> Praise, while the robins
> treed in his territory worm their littles –
> four is – ha ha, such lucky-bucky days
> which come almost every decade.

but lightly dismissed it as a poor Dream Song, since it seemed 'The only gay one of the lot (batch, group, pride, gaggle, clutch, constellation, murmuration).' His gaiety even went so far as to tolerate a moment of careless joy from Kate. 'The *medical* fact being: she do a little jig & kick me in the BALLS. *ow*. Lousy muse! . . . We do our Super-Extra-Dough dance. Few get hurt-up.' For a while he could delight unequivocally in his family, 'we love each other good – and the baby is so adorable (she now wags her head back & forth to show is adult) the day's a joy.' He found Martha 'so heavenly & so various that it makes us feel like jets taking off, children have *far* more facial expressions than we have: she do:- Napoleonic triumph, the weepy-betrayed statesman, cozy-cozy, cunning, who-the-hell-are-you, shy-shy, drop dead, I'm-thinking-it-over, that-food-was-terrific. We drool & adore.'

The climate changed drastically when his mother came for a visit in the second week of July. Berryman wrote to Dr Thomes begging for sleeping pills.

Mother is herc a week . . . Like do me a favour, Boyd. Neither
for murder nor for suicide will I use them heavy sedatives. Old
baby croon: mother figure she's hers, & hopeless' exagg' –
please send me something at the Gristmill will make me sleep
22 July: Insomnia!!
Sedatives!

His emotions compact of veneration and rage, Berryman commonly suppressed his sense of opposition to his mother since it cried out
against a force as of his own being. The growth, structure, and
policy of his life had been subject to her management. The younger
Berryman had taken her will for his will; later he could cope with
her love and her will, which had to a great extent designed his life,
mostly by way of self-hatred and self-conflict. His mother arrived
in a state of high excitement about landing a job at the Catholic
University in Washington: so excited, in fact, that she talked of
nothing else for three hours. She was completely overwhelming in
the confines of the Gristmill, and Berryman was soon gibbering
with nerves and exasperation. Terrified to have her in the house, it
seemed to him that he lacked any control over how long conversations went on. One day when he rushed off to bed screaming, 'Get
her out of here! Get her out of here!', she heard his outburst and left
quite early in the morning. 'Henry in trouble whirped out lonely
whines,' he wrote in mid-July, and then (within a week) Song 66,
which includes the quoted admonition, 'that a man should always
reproach himself.' A day later, 20 July, he wrote Song 243 compar-
ing himself to a sorry Odysseus.

The time had come to put together a volume of Dream Songs.

> I am closing in on this damned poem. I swear to God & you it
> contains – repeat: contains – more bad writing than either of us
> has ever done before . . . and Kate says if I write just *one* more
> she will vanish in orbit, flourishing the baby . . .
>   Let us anyway be happy, heh-heh. Not *all* the Dream Songs
> are contemptible – tho' if you saw Alvarez's elucidatory
> comments on two of them (proofs just came from *The Observer*)
> you'd say so. I have decided that it is my fate to be the worst
> writer of our time.

Although he reported to Richard Wilbur in mid-September that
'There are 150 more "finished",' he planned on 22 August to
publish just sixty Songs. He calculated that, at least in terms of
quantity (a line-count), his output showed an advance on 'Homage

to Mistress Bradstreet'. He had as yet no other yardstick to measure the opus by. There had been a flow of appreciation from friends, Boyd and Maris Thomes, Robert Lowell, William Meredith, Richard Wilbur, and Robert Fitzgerald (who had thought 'marvelous' the verses that he had read at Indiana), but who really understood the reach of this poem? By the first week of September he had sent seventy-five Songs to his publisher, Robert Giroux ('He made me an offer sight unseen & I capitulated,' Berryman told Lowell. 'But why publish verse anyway? It's all right for you to do, but why the rest of us?'), and had chosen to dedicate the volume:

> To Kate, and to Saul
> 'Thou drewest near in the day'.

The following weeks were ordered by marking time; having stitched his poem together, Berryman languished, ill, awaiting judgment. He reported to William Meredith: 'I've been ill practically every day for weeks . . . my thought drags, is uncertain, and inventionless (though I've written some new Songs) . . . Also: waiting, waiting; still no plans, because no money . . . I gave up writing new Songs long ago but your head fills once twice thrice and you've had it: you reach for a pencil.' At the mercy of a temperament disposed to painful self-scrutiny, he could only be restored to himself by high praise. He feared that critics might misunderstand his work, his fear being underpinned by an awareness of the perhaps dubious shifts by which he had yoked the parts of the poem together. Certainly he wanted the little, each section, to be measured by the lot, the entire volume: as a poem, not poems.

On their second wedding anniversary Kate drove Berryman out to Cape Cod, where they 'got woofed into a party of 100 or so' with old friends from days at Princeton, including Edmund Wilson, Conrad Aiken, and Joan Colebrook. In October he read at Boston University, and then, with Robert Lowell, at the Guggenheim Museum under the auspices of the Academy of American Poets. (His earnings from readings in 1963 amounted to approximately 700 dollars.) But despite such occupational distractions, Berryman continued to show all the symptoms of withdrawal even through their final day at the Gristmill; he sulked in bed and was the last piece of baggage to be moved. They drove to New York City and stayed at the Chelsea Hotel, where Berryman still sustained only vague plans about being near Princeton, rescuing his library which had been in storage for years, and working again on Shakespeare. Instead of organising himself, however, he drank heavily, and spent one night in the hallway of his brother's apartment. He made

several unavailing trips to Princeton with Kate to find a place to live
and to arrange for the redemption of his books, but Kate's time was
taken up with the baby. In Princeton they visited Richard Blackmur, who seemed aloof, perhaps because of illness, and made the
parting shot, 'Why don't you go see those rich friends of yours?'
(probably referring to Berryman's old friends, the Mackies). As
time passed in New York, Saul Bellow called and asked if they
needed money; Kate said, 'Soon.' They stayed at the Chelsea Hotel
six weeks in all, a period Kate found so trying that she came close to
getting in the car and driving back to Minneapolis. Eventually
Berryman's mother called and said that an apartment was available
in Washington at 103 Second Street (two floors with a separate
entrance), opposite the Supreme Court Building. Berryman started
frequenting the local bars, and during a stay of several months in
Washington he never once visited the Folger Shakespeare Library.

Early in 1964 he flew to California for a reading tour (earning 500
dollars, his highest fee to date, for reading in the Fine Arts Festival at
Los Angeles State College). His health was such, however, that he
collapsed from exhaustion after only a few readings and was
admitted to room 132 of the Riverside Community Hospital.
Either before or just after hospitalisation, he was looked after by a
young woman, as Song 188 records. When Berryman's mother
exclaimed against his behaviour, and said how typical it was, Kate
retaliated with the words. 'But he's an alcoholic!' They had never
thought in such terms before, and she had never used the word.
When Berryman returned to Washington, other doctors diagnosed
acute bronchitis and an ear infection.

> 'Gynecomastia' the surgeon called,
> 'the man is old & bald
> and has habits. In this circumstance
> I cannot save him.' The older you get, at once
> the better death looks and
> the more fearful & intolerable   [Dream Song 185].

By April Boyd Thomes admitted Berryman to the Abbott
Hospital in Minneapolis, where he stayed until the first week of
May. While in hospital he wrote at least eleven Dream Songs,
including 'Room 231: the forth week' on Monday, 27 April, the
publication day of *77 Dream Songs*. Ellen Siegelman had brought
him roses; Isabella Gardner, Allen Tate's wife, sent a tulip plant, to
which the poem (which became Song 92) was his response.

> Something black somewhere   in the vistas of his heart.

Tulips from Tates teazed Henry in the mood
to be a tulip and desire no more
but water, but light, but air.
Yet his nerves rattled blackly, unsubdued,
& suffocation called. . . .

Berryman drew tremendous reserves of faith and energy from
the love and support of his friends. When he remet Robert Lowell in
1962, for example, it had been almost ten years since their last
encounter, but Lowell always made himself available for boosting
morale, even though, after their times together at Princeton, he saw
so little of him in person even until death. On 18 September 1959,
when Berryman telephoned Lowell in a mood of dereliction after
the breakdown of his marriage to Ann and in the face of his
professional problems, Lowell wrote the next day to steel him with
confidence.

> I have been thinking much about you all summer, and how we
> have gone through the same troubles, visiting the bottom of the
> world. I have wanted to stretch out a hand, and tell you that I
> have been there too, and how it all lightens and life swims back.
> And it's a sorrow to think of your being alone, seeing your son
> and not being with him. I've thought of your dazzling
> brilliance, so astonishing to your friends, of reading in Chicago
> two years ago and hearing the uproar of admiration you had left
> behind you . . . Then our talks in Maine, meetings in New
> York. There's been so much fellow feeling between us, and for
> so long now. I am afraid nothing of this got said last night, yet it
> was as though we had been waiting for months for your call.
>   Well what is there to say? The night is now passed, and I feel
> certain that your fire and loyalty, and all-outedness carry you
> buoyantly on . . .
>   We have been delighted with the English reviews of Mistress
> Ann [*sic*]. The new poem about Harry [*sic*] in its sixty parts
> must be a deluge of power. It will be exciting to see the parts
> you are about to publish. I wish you'd send me more of it. You
> must believe that it will reach its finished form . . .
>   I still haven't at all said what I want to, but our hearts are with
> you and we love you very dearly.

Berryman trusted to Lowell's loyalty, and keyed his work
according to his encouragement. It was Lowell who first suggested
– in what Berryman called a 'marvellously generous and free letter'
of 29 April 1962 – the saving idea that he should publish an interim

volume of Dream Songs, with a provisional aesthetic shape. Whether for good or ill remains a critical issue to this day, but the notion gave Berryman a tremendous psychological lift by providing a clear schedule and an ascertainable goal. Lowell wrote on 14 April:

> Just a note to say that I think the Henry poem is terrific. I'm guessing that the whole holds up to the short sections I read the other day, and no doubt adds immense momentum to those high spots. I think everyone who liked Ann Bradstreet will like this, and maybe much more, for it is more lyrical and a much longer sweep. Speaking in the dark about the whole, my guess is that some moderate length a hundred pages or so, ought to be immediately shuffled together and gotten off to the publishers. You are way beyond needing magazine attention, and might gain by letting the whole drop on the world like a bomb. I think so. Then maybe the short form will be the best form, and the rest will seem like shavings, the wood out of which the permanent arises. But I don't know. Some things like the Prelude have to be too long. But I think a hundred pages of quite hard and intense lyrics would carry as much as reams more. Still a first version would do no harm and would hardly seem a trickle.
>
> Glad to meet your lovely Kate. Do take care of yourselves. I think you should feel your seven years labors are over, and that now all you need do is arrange, breathe and stop battering yourself. No, don't batter yourself, life's too good for that. I could say a lot more about the joys of remeeting, those moments when all the fevers of one's own writing clear and make sense.

While Lowell's assurance, which was later reinforced by the remarks of others such as Richard Wilbur, gave him the resolve to publish a volume as soon as possible, Berryman anticipated all the adverse comments that would eventually be made about the book. It is not surprising that, among all the reviews of the book, he found Adrienne Rich's uniquely satisfying, for her perceptions seemed to validate his procedures:

> it is the identity of Henry . . . which holds the book together, makes it clearly a real book and not a collection of chance pieces loosely flung under one cover. None of the poems (except possibly the elegies) carries in isolation the weight and perspective that it does in relation to the rest; partly because the

cumulative awareness of Henry is built from poem to poem
['Mr Bones, He Lives', *Nation*, CXCVIII, 25 May 1964].

She concludes that the work is truly original because of its superiority in 'inner necessity and by the force of a unique human character'.
But her phrase 'inner necessity' tends to beg rather than to answer
questions concerning narrative unity: the direction in which a long
poem may be seen to move (according to customary expectations)
and its reasons for that movement. Many critics remarked on the
obscurity and incoherence of some of the Songs, and the more
favourable correctly found the novelty of style an appropriate
vehicle for the poet's vision, but Adrienne Rich's was the only
notice which Berryman considered 'serious & stunning' (presumably for calming his just apprehensiveness) – 'the most serious study
any large area of my work's ever had.' (Adrienne Rich later
introduced his reading at Harvard – in 1966 – and became his friend
and firm critic.)

Berryman had spelt out his proper fears that the volume might
not be unitary in a letter of 29 April 1962 responding to Lowell's
encouragement.

> The grand problems are two. [The Songs] are partly
> independent but only if – as Saul does (is) – the reader is familiar
> with Henry's tone, personality, obsessions, friend, activities;
> otherwise, in small numbers, they seem simply crazy . . .
> Second problem: the poem is hopelessly unfinished; so the 75
> *Dream Songs*, say, will be just a dry run, and may not convince
> anyone, including me, and why should it? Yet slabs of these
> things have made people laugh & cry. And I have another little
> feeling, which perhaps I would only tell you: after the
> long-drawn artistic austerity and daring – if those terms are not
> exaggerated – of the Bradstreet poem, it seems to me that I
> might be trusted a little by such readers as care. Even you, and
> you seem to do. Only, if they seem inchoate in the 75 or so,
> don't mind . . .
>   I can't help feeling that it's *irresponsible* to publish – not 16 and
> 30 cantos as Pound did – but a large number of sections which I
> still however retain completely control of. I wonder, wonder.
> But you cheer me up.

He was particularly disappointed, then, to find that when Lowell
reviewed the volume in the *New York Review of Books* (28 May), he
was not altogether supportive, commenting on the dangers of
mannerism and incoherence, and (for all that he had previously

shown an understanding of Berryman's method and intentions) failing to perceive that 'Henry' and his friend were supposed to be distinct characters in the poem. Berryman compared himself to a turtle that 'withdraws, alarmed, into carapace = Henry', started nervously listing the Songs and their characteristics, and decided, for example, that the first seven Songs were all grievous and dealt with privations. Breaking off from the vain task, he decided, 'I am satisfied as to *sequence*, but extremely worried about an illusion of *inevitability*, since Cal uses "at random", (like the usual view of [Pound's] Cantos).'

Although Lowell's criticism contributed to a 'bad week' for him, Berryman did not smart for long; his regard for Lowell could never be seriously threatened. His friendships, which he called loves, ran (as commentators have pointed out) to a kind of ardent hero-worship. They were founded on what was virtually a system of mutual indebtedness, a paradoxical combination of rivalry and disinterest in which the scales of obligation should always appear to be even. Berryman could scarcely tolerate a favour unreturned, it weighed too heavily on his sense of vulnerability, even of his inferiority. Since he dreaded criticism of his work, it was useful not to be exposed in front of the field; in poetry, his pace-setter was Lowell. After Robert Frost's death in 1963, he stated a self-regarding truth, 'I've been comfortable since 1946 with the feeling that Lowell is far my superior,' and perhaps discovered a safe and secret satisfaction in knowing that some of his readers must have thought otherwise. In 1958, Berryman had asked the poet Howard Nemerov a question that obsessed him, 'Howard, if you ever really made it big, would you want to be the only one? Out there in front all by yourself?'

Berryman sustained a similar friendship with Saul Bellow, and was happily grateful for the fact that Bellow had set him an example of ambition and style in the novel which he could emulate without competition in his own genre. When staying at the Gristmill in 1963, he told Bellow that he would 'be dreaming out an agrarian existence' were it not for what he called 'the adrenalin heaved me by your raving master-works' – *The Adventures of Augie March* and *Henderson the Rain King* – which he had studied through manuscript and proof stages. He favoured those novels to the point of raving because he had been able to assume to his poetry their qualities of vision and energy, reaching out towards the exhilarating, the eccentric, the suffering, and the absurd. From 1963 to 1964, Berryman read through *Herzog*, his first comments marking time: 'So far it looks much more *normal* than Augie and Henderson, more continuing the line of *Seize the Day*, though of course more mature

& complex.' When he finished reading the book, he could announce unreservedly, 'I don't know how you did it . . . – I suspect the 'vacation' of *Henderson* made it possible . . . Nobody has ever sat down & wallowed to this extent in his own life, *with* full art – I mean: novelists. I don't know of anything to compare it to, except you . . . Go to heaven.' There is no reason at all to doubt the genuineness of his enthusiasm.

When in 1962 Edward Hoagland wrote Berryman to give his thanks for supporting and encouraging his work at Harvard eight years before, Berryman responded with a succinct, pragmatic letter (unfortunately undelivered and returned) which composed his rationale of friendship.

Don't be so damned grateful, will you? It's oppressive. I suffer from sort of hopeless gratefulness myself – to the men and women who have done for no reason marvellous good things for me, or just *been* such that the universe seems (almost) worth living in. It's stupid. For there is usually a big working the other way – e.g. in our case. In six years I cd not explain properly the joy you gave me that summer – and not only joy, but – I don't feel witty enough to put a name to it . . . so I'll pass you on a staggering sentence of Einstein's. He's been talking about his early (12 or so?) loss of religious faith, and then says: 'Similarly motivated men of the present and of the past, as well as the insights which they had achieved, were the friends which could not be lost' – only the German is on another plane, 'waren die unverlierbaren Freunde' – the *un-lose-able* friends. You seemed to give me then, gave me, a fresh hard glad look at what I thought I knew something about, the artist's conscience. I have tried to use that standard since – but I won't say successfully. So no more gratitude; we're quits, – not that I have ever been able to do anything for you. . . . Two of the men I feel *most* grateful to, with full reason, are Saul & Cal Lowell: I try to remind myself, against prostration, that when Saul was in *real* doubt over *Augie* – the ms. was then 900 pp. or so – I cheered him, & I've helped him, by being around, a hundred times since – and so with Cal: he wrote me last week for no reason a letter *so* generous & vivid about my poem (7 years in the works, and he saw some 20 sections when he was here just before) that you would think you could never get even – so: I try to remember that I helpt him in Maine on the proofs of *Lord Weary* fifteen years ago & helpt make his American reputation with an endless review in *Partisan* & held his hand many times, between marriages (his & mine), in New York, and when he was going

out, and just did a living essay (in a symposium – with Wilbur &
somebody) on his 'Skunk Hour', for *New World Writing*. I try.
As for you, pal, succeed. No quantity of reminiscence takes the
happy burden of gratitude from *me*.

Those who came close to Berryman were rewarded with a sense
of his generosity, as Valerie Trueblood witnessed.

> He loved to discover happiness in people; that is he took a
> delighted interest in it when he found it. I remember going to a
> party after a reading he gave in 1966, and being led by him to a
> beautiful, tranquil woman standing in a corner of the room. He
> told me, 'Talk to her! She's happy! She's just married her second
> husband, the right one this time and she's happy as a lark! She's
> been telling me about it. Talk to her!' She told me about her
> happiness while he stood there nodding his head, and staring
> around the room, gradually losing his buoyancy as the evening
> wore on. Nobody was happy enough.

Similarly, the poet James Wright recalled that when he fell ill at 'a
certain distressing period of my own life . . . you can understand
how startled and awakened I felt to see John Berryman, to me a
shockingly great artist, appear at my bedside, asking me if he could
help me. As long as I live on this earth, I will never forget his
request. I answered: Will you please take care of my students while
I'm ill. And he did. I have since learned that John at that specific time
was having a hell of a time himself.'

Berryman spoiled his credit on certain occasions, however, and
provoked antipathies, sometimes because of drunkenly losing control of himself, at other times because of a competitiveness which
both scared and stimulated him. He was brash and offensive
towards Denise Levertov, for example, and often enunciated his
antagonism towards Richard Eberhart. When a reading he gave at
Buffalo in March 1966 coincided with one by Allen Ginsberg,
Berryman was rude, drunken and sulky at a party held afterwards in
Leslie Fiedler's house; 'they call this music,' he remarked as people
began to dance.

Isabella Gardner came to Minneapolis as Allen Tate's wife, but
when she deferred to her husband in conversations about poetry,
Berryman grew tense and angry, '*I'm* a poet too, you know.' She
recognised that Berryman disliked her and perhaps all 'women
poets' with the exception of Elizabeth Bishop. 'He was brutally
rude but I was always aware of his intense compassion that underlay
this *superficial* cruelty. Allen had *little patience* with him but I know

that he respected him.' The Tates found Berryman's difficult behaviour taxing to their tolerance, though they 'loved & revered his wife Kate. We called her, among ourselves, "Saint Kate" – saintly not because of rectitude but because of radiant serene warmth, humor, understanding & total love.' Although by 1966 Berryman had come to find Tate 'too weird & pompous to be close to any more', Tate had been given just as good reasons for feeling exasperated with him. On 8 January, for example, Berryman subjected him to a preposterous telephone-call in the small hours of the morning, and Tate remonstrated by letter that day. Berryman apologised, and rightly attributed his offensiveness to inebriation, but his conduct on the telephone became a by-word among all his friends and even among remote acquaintances. In what was sometimes the stuporous pattern of his life and the timelessness of his absorption in work, he failed to take stock of social propriety.

'I do know that I felt often that he shed *crocodile* tears about the deaths of his friends,' Isabella Gardner recalls. 'But I also know that he suffered almost intolerable pain, the anguish of the spirit.' Berryman showed curious and ambivalent aspects of his character in his bearing towards the dead. In one respect, he enshrined his friends as (to use Saul Bellow's expression in conversation) 'the sacred dead', who offered him no further competition and unquestionably received his jealous identification. But he could express himself with a seemingly equal emotion for those who were not his friends, especially if their deaths were violent, or suicidal like Sylvia Plath's, and triggered both an old manner of grief for his father and his theory about the dispensation of his own life. He could arrogate the dear dead to himself as emblems, and sometimes expressed a grief in excess of familiarity. There is no reason at all to doubt the reality and intensity of his mourning, however, since it was proper only to himself. Yet there is an ambivalence evident in the degree to which those deaths readily served Berryman as copy for his verses. It can perhaps be seen in the way he addressed Ralph Ross about the poet Theodore Roethke's death:

I was slugged . . . and for the final time I revise the 2nd of the Songs for him I'd been reluctantly & despairingly working at. *That is the last 'free' Dream Song.* I send it to you. I don't know what its fate will be. But I imagine it will be around a while. I sent it to Beatrice, his widow, with a letter pseudo-consoling: (1) he went thro' 3 phases, & was in at least the 2nd a daring & true & beautiful poet, (2) he cannot suffer any more. I haven't decided who to give it to yet; I'm tempted by *Kenyon* . . . I haven't decided.

Berryman's tenderness towards another poet, Louis MacNeice ('one of my best-loved friends', he told Richard Wilbur), is indicated by a simplicity of expression in this letter to Robert Lowell at the time when MacNeice died: 'Hell of a year, isn't it – Mr Frost, Ted [Roethke], & NOW Louis whom I loved. Keep well, be good. The devil roams.' That tone is certainly different from what seems an unhappy lapse into bathos in a letter (18 October 1965) to William Meredith about the death of another poet, Randall Jarrell: 'Randall's death hurt me – shock and sorrow to Mackey, please. Everybody is dying – I personally am dying of diarrhoea & nerve-ends.' On the other hand, Berryman may have chosen to avoid any show of sentimentalism by such a brisk, if unfortunate, transition. In the early part of 1966, Yale University organised a memorial for Jarrell, with about a dozen speakers; Richard Eberhart remembers emphatically: 'Berryman was pretty far gone when I saw him last at the Yale Jarrell memorial. He was pathetic. I felt sorry for him but also felt that he should not have appeared in public.' Robert Penn Warren recalls, in contrast, that 'Berryman's witty, funny, and moving remarks made a profound impression . . . he was coherent, amusing, and effective – in spite of, or because of, his favorite beverage.' Berryman ended his comments by reciting Dream Song 121:

> Grief is fatiguing. He is out of it,
> the whole humiliating Human round,
> out of this & that.
> He made a-many hearts go pit-a-pat
> who now need never mind his nostril-hair
> nor a critical error laid bare.
>
> He endured fifty years. He was Randall Jarrell
> and wrote a-many books & he wrote well.
> Peace to the bearded corpse.
> His last book was his best. His wives loved him.
> He saw in the forest something coming, grim,
> but did not change his purpose.
>
> Honest & cruel, peace now to his soul.
> He never loved his body, being full of dents.
> A wrinkled peace to this good man.

If Berryman was offensive to those who took offence, he rarely intended to be gratuitously insulting. Immensely generous by nature, he meant no harm to the weak or unwitting. The true quality of the friendship he both gave and inspired is manifest from an attractive letter that Robert Lowell wrote on 10 March 1966:

> This is really just to say that I love you, and wonder at you, and want you to take care. Your reminiscences of Randall were the height of the evening, and seemed for a moment to lift away all the glaze and constraints, that dog us, and yet it was all in order. All so like what you have done in your poetry, freedom for us too, if we had the nerve.

On 20 May Berryman was awarded the Russell Loines Award of 1,000 dollars from the National Institute of Arts and Letters. In the weeks before the formal presentation in New York he began to feel 'less erethistic & lethargic', as he told William Meredith. 'My trouble now is largely neurological – no longer much physical, and not mental or emotional,' he assured Van Meter Ames. What excited him as much as anything about the day was that Paul was able to attend the ceremonial. Separated for five years, Berryman had seen his son all too little, and fostered an image from selected memories. During a Christmas visit in 1960, for example, Paul dropped his father's electric razor in the toilet bowl: Berryman, with so few fragments to build his picture on, commemorated the incident in an unfinished lyric on Paul's fourth birthday.

A Father's Song

> When I think of all his lost things, and I do –
> balloons, & the fearless afternoon at the zoo,
> the plastic first train of the *Little* Poo,
> and how on Xmas in the toilet-bowl
> he drowned Electric Razor, how my soul
> lurched as that morning earlier he said
> without emphasis 'You have pretty feet', – instead
> (I promise nothing: the weird world is wide)
> of weeping that he's growing a great boy
> so far away, it's true with a dim eye
> I seethe for joy.

Shortly after his own birthday that year, he wrote this letter (probably unsent) for his son.

> Dear Poukie, . . .
> I miss you. I miss you every day, and I have done ever since I saw you last. I have long dreams (one last night) about you.

(Draw me a new picture, like of cliffs and sand-dunes below and where we are; your mother will explain this.) I also get to have long talks . . . with the people who know you – the Siegelmans, the Rosses (you *might* remember Peter and Stephen – Stephen, *his* mother tells me, got down on all fours lately & said 'I'm Alice' – Ellen, his mother, said 'You can't be Alice – that's a *girl's* name' – he said, wumphing across the floor, 'I'm Alice the Dog'; when he then called 'Alice! Alice!' Ellen said 'But why are you *calling* that? That's *your* name' – he said 'I'm talking to myself.') – and I also can talk about you to: just myself, and in lectures (your mother will *try* to explain this), and to a good lady who (after years) is my new wife. We look at pictures of you, so far off.

Now, you must remember what I say:

1) It is not possible for me to see you, much, if ever again. But you are to know that I love you. I will come as soon as I can. There is more to say about this.

2) You must be a *good boy* – obeying your very good mother – heading to some end *outside yourself* (far later, your mother will be able to explain this) – and with respect for your father, who has not been the most useless man in the present American world.

3) Then kick it all aside, – except for your veneration for your mother, – and do *what seems necessary* and consonant with your gifts, training, & allegiance.

4) *Strong fathers crush sons.* You are spared this, I think. (I am not able to form *any* conception of how my work will be regarded.) *Go on.*

Yours, and w. love,
John Berryman

He sustained the hope that his son would eventually feel proud of him, less – curiously – as a person, than as a poet of standing. He suggested that thought in another letter early the next year. 'Boasting is *out*. But if anybody boasts about their father, it is all right for you to think privately: "Well, my father did something that was thought interesting five thousand miles away and years later and that nobody else could do." I think your mother will tell you that that is all right.' It was characteristic of Berryman's frame of mind to presume that Paul would grow up with his own standards of value, setting perhaps as much store by creative achievements as by the man. There was sadly as much vanity as paternalism in the sentiment. 'A matter that hurts me is that I have made many hundreds of people laugh, in various cities, during the last year or so, but not you – and your father is thought to be a wit,' he wrote in a letter from Washington early in 1964. He projected the response that he wished Paul would ultimately feel: 'My father was involved once in a hopeless tragedy, and for many years my feelings about him altered & altered, until they settled again, long ago, on sympathy respect & love.'

Shy and happy to see Paul again at the ceremonial of the National Institute, Berryman discovered – then and at later meetings in the 1960s – that the image he nourished of his son was always out of step with the reality of the growing boy. The disparity made for an awkwardness between them; too much absence diminished his hopes for maturing a relationship with his son, but not his enthusiasm for rehearsing the part. He told Ann proudly that Paul 'not only looked well at the Institute but behaved brilliantly, neither forward nor shy.' Going to the ceremony itself, however, he counted a great mistake – 'it set me back weeks' – and he returned to the terrible heat of Washington for two months, 'unable to eat, scarcely to stand'. From this time, it should be said, Berryman never recovered his health and took medication, except for brief intermissions, for the rest of his life.

Since they could not afford *not* to return to Minnesota, Kate drove back with the baby, and found them an apartment at 3209 Lyndale Avenue South, while Berryman lay exhausted in the capital. At one point his mother threatened to take him out to the airport in a wheelchair, but eventually he returned of his own accord. By August his physical and nervous exhaustion again required him to enter Abbott Hospital – 'It's simply my mind tearing my body to pieces' – where he improved enough to be able to climb five flights of stairs without using the bannister and without stopping. Because of Berryman's debilitation, Lynn Louden had to take over both of his summer-session courses. Despite the financial hardship that resulted from his lack of employment over the summer, Berryman undertook to buy his first and only house by September – 33 Arthur Avenue South-East (in a select residential area about a mile from the University) – at a cost of 17,000 dollars, for which he had to borrow the entire deposit. Harassed for want of money, the Berrymans moved into their house without furniture on 1 October, and Berryman came home to a party after teaching that day. By December Dr Boyd Thomes loaned him the sum of 442 dollars to have his library removed from store in Princeton (after eleven years) and transported to his new home, where Berryman had for the first time in his life designated one room as his study.

His health remained so bad that he needed hospital treatment in
March 1965, when, as he told Saul Bellow on 9 April, he decided to
'quit drinking . . . and my nervous system is giving me every
known & unknown form of hell. I live hour to hour. Did I ever
write poetry? I feel like Herzog only worse. My lectures & seminar
take every inch of my will. . . . In the snatches of sleep I get, even
my dreams are worse than usual.' Two timely consolations arrived:
he was awarded the Pulitzer Prize in poetry for *77 Dream Songs*
(Bellow's *Herzog* took the National Book Award), and a Guggenheim Fellowship worth 9,500 dollars for the academic year
1966–7, which he opted to spend in Dublin. Students and news
reporters raced to Berryman's house after Robert Giroux telephoned him about the Pulitzer Prize on 3 May; Berryman told the
Minneapolis Star (4 May):

> 'My first reaction was that this prize was nothing. I said to him,
> "Do you remember the boobs that used to get this stuff when
> we were kids?"'
>   The poet blew smoke from his always-present cigarette
> through his nose in two even streams, paused, and then said,
> 'Now they give it to serious men. In the past, I might have
> refused it. Now I say "Yes!"'
> Berryman paused again.
> 'Hurrah!'
> 'It is delicious!'

Dorothy Lewis reported for *St Paul Dispatch* (12 May 1965):

> 'But I'm not fooling myself that this makes me better than
> many of the "greats" who haven't had Pulitzers – William
> Meredith for instance,' he added.
>   Berryman openly declares his distaste for the stupid and
> prosaic things in life. And he'll call almost anything stupid that
> stands in the way of poetry.
>   A passionate non-materialist, he is most contented minus a
> necktie and dressed in old clothes. His favorite chair (no one else
> in the house may sit in it) is a battered old overstuffed piece with
> a foot-stool where he lapses into oblivion while he works over
> his verse.
>   He admits he is a man obsessed. 'It's hard work. Hard.
> Nothing easy about it. But eventually you reach a point where
> you say, "Let it go."' . . .
>   Asked the most important elements of good poetry, he replied,

'Imagination, love, intellect – and pain. Yes, you've got to know pain.'

Allen Tate told the *Minnesota Daily* that he thought the prize 'long overdue and richly deserved'. As reviews of *77 Dream Songs* appeared in journals and newspapers over the months, the balance of critical opinion showed in Berryman's favour; in 1965 his royalties amounted to 1,130 dollars (above his advance of 500 dollars), a figure which doubled by the next year. Further income accrued from poetry readings around the country, which he continued to give in spite of ill health. At the beginning of November he fell down and broke his left arm; after returning home from ten days in hospital he fell yet again on the night of 1 January 1966, probably as a result of the side-effects of the drug Thorazine.

By the summer he felt fit enough to play only a bad game of tennis every day. In June and July he began to sort the already voluminous Dream Song manuscripts in preparation for the family's departure for Dublin, where, he had determined (since he had already written what he called 'THE LAST DREAM SONG: 161' in 1965), he would cull precisely eighty-four songs to complete the poem with a second volume. He told Valerie Trueblood on 7 July, 'it's no less than 259 Songs, of which only ten have been published and 15 are brand new, besides 35 unfinisht & scores of fragments – I feel dazed: . . . you can see that I have my work cut out.' In June he had told Jonathan Sisson in an interview for the University of Minnesota student magazine *Ivory Tower* (3 October), 'There's a large body of manuscript which is fragmentary, dealing with beginnings and ends, and some middles. I'm taking all that stuff with me. Some of those are much better than some of the finished songs. That is, often after the inspiration has failed, you keep on going out of a sense of duty, and turn up with nothing, so that some of the fragments are much better.' Concerning the problems of constructing a long poem without systematic progression, he added, 'You have no idea when you get up in the morning what, if anything, you're going to have. Some songs take weeks or even months and others are done in ten minutes. You're at the mercy of the notion of sustained inspiration. Nothing else will do.' Sisson prefaced his interview with an absorbed sketch of Berryman:

> sitting with his feet buried in his manuscripts and letters from various literary notables, primarily English. He had run out of matches, which I supplied, but not scotch, which Mrs Berryman brought us. Mr Berryman has a way of holding his cigarette at the base of his fingers, often between the right

second and third fingers, so that, with the cigarette in the right
corner of his mouth, his index finger stands before his right eye;
but his glasses never seem to get smudged. The dog Rufus and
the Berrymans' daughter withdrew, leaving several toys
comfortably scattered about.

Mr Berryman has astonished eyebrows and a prominent
tongue. His reddish face looks soft; in repose the cheeks are
somewhat pouched: his expression is lively only when he
speaks. When he turns his profile and one notices the handsome
grey and light-brown hair, Mr Berryman resembles Frederic
Dorr Steele's drawings of William Gillette as Sherlock Holmes.
It is this contrast – of the hard profile and the vulnerable face
head-on – which makes the deep impression. Mr Berryman's
voice, by turns querying and relaxed, also echoes the extreme
tension between pain and numbness that is the essence of the
Dream Songs, his magnificent, risky long poem.

Berryman was thinking of his own plight when he described how,
for Mozart, 'His whole life was at the mercy of his art. It was
incredible. I'm thinking of that and I'm also thinking about the kind
of hysterical states that modern artists go in very much for – an
extreme case would be Van Gogh's cutting off his ear – periods of
masochism and blasphemy – that kind of business, which in the
Dream Songs is temperate and held in control.'

Shortly before his departure for Dublin, Berryman felt doubly
stricken at having to take leave of Ralph Ross and Philip Siegelman,
both of whom had accepted fresh appointments in California. At
the end of June he wrote three pointed songs under the title 'Henry's
Farewell' which found their appropriate place at the end of Book VI
of *The Dream Songs*, before 'Henry' leaves to embrace the experiences and reflections that constitute the bulk of Book VII, in
Dublin.

>   One decade's war forget, in which, I may say,
>   we've scarcely won a battle to this date. . . .

>   Faction ran wild & so did many vermin
>   fresh from their woodwork and we bore their blows
>   & carried on our work alive.

>   I fear the queen is swarming, toward the west
>   taking her chosen workers, for a stunt
>   leaving behind her Henry   ['Henry's Farewell – III'].

Henry repaired to Dublin, showing his back,
to thrive on shanty-talk.
'*They'll* miss *me* too' he muttered, and 'A sorry pass,
when the best are so dispersed one has to chalk
up thousands of miles for one crack

or canny reference' shaking his head he groaned
and grinned at his green friends across his stout
but his heart was not in it, his heart was out
with the loss of friends now to be telephoned
only when drunk and at enormous cost:
he gnashed out a lonesome toast   ['Henry's Farewell – I'].

16

The sick and brilliant public man, 1966-69

After crossing from Montreal, the Berrymans spent the first week of September in the Majestic Hotel, Dublin, a place Kate found 'so public for this kind of falling-apart family' that she was happy when they moved into a modest semi-detached house at 55 Lansdowne Park, in the suburb of Ballsbridge. For the span of what she called their 'voluntary exile', Kate assumed the role of 'a good Irish Housewife – shop everyday, wash clothes by hand, & don't wear slacks,' while Berryman feverishly wrote Songs and steeped himself in alcohol. To outsiders he gave the entirely credible impression that the poet John Montague records.

> Berryman is the only writer I have ever seen for whom drink seemed to be a positive stimulus. He drank enormously and smoked heavily, but it seemed to be part of a pattern of work, a crashing of the brain barriers as he raced towards the completion of the *Dream Songs.* For he appeared to me positively happy, a man who was engaged in completing his life's work, with a wife and child he adored. He was delighted to talk about literature, which he clearly loved with an all-absorbing passion; he would cry as he recited the Paolo and Francesca episode from the Inferno or suddenly leap up to shake the hands of some one who had agreed with him about the merits of a Henry James story. He no longer cared, he was no longer concerned with appearances, as his long, hacking coughs halted conversation, or an elbow sent a glass flying ['Memoir of the American Poet in Dublin', *Hibernia*, 24 May 1974].

But Berryman was suffering severely from alcoholism and a sense of insecurity about his poem and his life; by April he had to spend a week for treatment in an open ward of Grange Gorman Hospital. Kate tried hard to 'get inside his skin', but she had come to experience such disequilibrium that she sought psychiatric help for herself.

The first problem was, as always, financial: on 9 September Berryman cabled his bank in Minneapolis to request a transfer of credit to Dublin, and when it had not acted for ten days he asked Maris Thomes to intercede. 'When I went to see Mr Stotesberry with my sword and coat of mail I was greeted by welcoming smiles and sighs of relief,' she told him: apparently Berryman's telegram had been mistranscribed and needed to be clarified. In thanks, Berryman addressed Dream Song 295, based in part on phrases from her own letter, to Maris Thomes.

> You dear you, clearing up Henry's foreign affairs,
> with your sword & armour heading for his bank,
> a cable gone astray

In connection with money matters, Berryman had to retain the services of a Dublin accountant the following April to penetrate the riddle of his laggard American income tax return.

Song 295 was one of many that he wrote in Dublin during 1966, to add to the several that he had written on board the *Carmania* while crossing the Atlantic. In Dublin every event became the occasion for a poem, since he readily succumbed to his aptitude for improvising verses rather than to confronting what seemed the monstrous task of selecting, editing, and ordering a volume of 84 Songs out of hundreds which were available. On 6 October, for example, Jean Bennett, who had been his girlfriend in 1936 ('my ex-fiancée', he called her), came for drinks with her husband, Sidney Lanier (he worked with the American Place Theatre and had brought his production of the play *Hogan's Goat* to the Dublin Theatre Festival).

> An old old mistress recently rang up,
> here in Ireland, to see how Henry was:
> how was he? delighted!
> He thought she was 3000 miles away,
> safe with her children in New York: she's coming at five:
> we'll wélcome her!

Berryman wrote those lines for Song 311 in her presence, while the party killed bottles. Jean saw that Kate was unhappy about the excessive drinking, but she observed too that alcohol made him

'more entertaining, more brilliant'. As the evening ended, Berryman asked Lanier, 'By the way, who are you? . . . My God, now he
tells me!'

'Some of my travel & Irish songs are beauties,' Berryman told
Maris Thomes, '("It's *beautiful*" said to me Kate about one, as if I
had never written anything "beautiful" before) and some take it out
on the Irish – I'll teach these bloody islanders. But we've met
excellent people too.' Although he evaded the need to organise a
volume by writing new Songs ('30 or 40 . . . since Minneapolis', he
told William Meredith on 20 September) and by haunting the local
bar, he did resume the onerous task by November.

> I have been working like bloody hell on Book VII (the last in the
> sequence) & to my horror Kate counted it out recently at 74
> Songs – revised, accepted by me, & located – besides 12 or 15
> always destined in order for the absolute end of the work. This
> version, that is, is already longer than the whole volume was to
> be; – without V & VI, both elaborate. Do you know of a warm
> cave where I can go & hide?

His sense not only of isolation but, more fundamentally, of uncertainty about his work is shown in the fact that he wrote to several
friends who had proved to be most loving and supportive of his
work for their appreciation of his achievements. 'I have done
without readers all my life,' he wrote, for example, to Valerie
Trueblood, 'but now that I am *both* famous & isolated, I *need* them.
Just locate my errors & weaknesses, that's all, exc. also obscurities.'
Berryman always admired Valerie Trueblood's looks and intelligence, and felt solicitous for her happiness. In Dublin he addressed a
number of Songs to her, and later explained, 'You ask "Why do me
honour", I reply: first place, no honour, I just think about you a
good deal – and, second place, why not? You are a beautiful & gifted
American girl: if I perceive this & want to write about you, why
not?' (even as late as March 1969, he was to write, 'I have been half
in love with you for years, but your fate was not entrusted to me'),
but it was as much his own insecurity as his admiration for her that
he betrayed by imploring her judgment. 'I am counting on the
interstices of your fresh opinion.' He relied perhaps most heavily on
William Meredith's approval, which he sought at this time. 'With
Randall [Jarrell] & Delmore [Schwartz] gone, I don't know whose
judgment I trust more than yours.'

He sent Book IV, the opus posthumous sequence which then
consisted of thirteen Songs, to Meredith for his counsel, and also to
Robert Lowell. Long since, when he had first written that group, he

had recited them to Robert Fitzgerald, 'full of mad glee sometimes, thinking he had really outdone Cal.' It was cause for particular satisfaction when Lowell cabled in October that he considered Book IV 'a tremendous and living triumph', gave it to Robert Silvers for publication in the *New York Review of Books*, and then followed with a letter on 5 November enlarging upon his view. 'The Opus posth. poems seem to me the crown of your wonderful work, witty, heart-breaking, all of a piece. Somehow one believes you on this huge matter of looking at death and your whole life. I'm sure it will be read on and on, one of the lovely things in our literature.' In the face of his own implacable, though innocuous, competitiveness towards Lowell, Berryman found that reassurance tremendously fortifying. *The Times Literary Supplement* filled a page with nine Songs from the sequence, an accolade which was only rivalled when the Chancellors of the Academy of American Poets voted him an award of 5,000 dollars.

In addition to begging the indulgence of Valerie Trueblood and William Meredith, he leaned most heavily on the love of two other women, Maris Thomes and Ellen Siegelman, as Song 304 declares.

> Maris & Valerie held his grand esteem
> except for maybe Ellen on her hill-top
> in northern California:
> Maris the vividest writer yet, a team
> not a woman, bringing bank mysteries to a stop,
> relishing garden mysteries,
>
> with the enigma of Boyd ever at her elbow
> as Ellen has the enigma of Phil, while Valerie
> has only & always her own
> in her daring & placid beauty, which bestow
> warily, my dear, warily, warily,
> lest they want that alone.
>
> I wrote to the White House yesterday, regretting
> the lateness of an invitation there,
> we couldn't accept:
> I should have consulted him on my splendid getting
> four ladies to write to Henry: who is most fair,
> ingenious & adept?

(In a letter to Maris Thomes, he told the story behind the last stanza: 'Joke: apparently, along with Johnson's other economies, putting out lights: there are no airmail stamps in the White House! We received an invitation to a reception there, which came by ordinary

mail & took *weeks* into October (p.m. Sept 2, reception 8th). I wrote
without irony, regretting & explaining that I had not boycotted the
affair, hating his conduct of the war but thinking like Bellow that he
was doing his best. Mrs. Johnson wrote me, concluding "It was a
lovely evening."")

Tussling with his manuscript, and feeling that his judgment and
faith were inadequate to the task, Berryman relied wholeheartedly
on the contact and reassurance of letters. He had earlier decided to
publish the sequence of love sonnets that he had written in 1947
(they were issued as *Berryman's Sonnets* in April 1967), for which he
had gained Lise's permission in Washington the year before. He
made necessary editorial changes with comparative ease (together
with writing a handful of new sonnets to shape the sequence), but it
augmented his confidence immeasurably to learn that William
Meredith, who is the 'old friend' of Song 297 (the first poem written
at the Majestic Hotel in Dublin), liked them. What seemed the
imponderable job of organising *His Toy, His Dream, His Rest* could
only be accomplished alone, however, and took many harassed
weeks in Dublin, far beyond that point when he told his mother on
15 December,

> I finisht my poem some 5 days ago, with a spurt of 'Henry's
> Crisis' & two others & then a terror 'Henry's guilt'. I have still
> the terrible editorial & administrative labour of making Books
> V & VI of the 300 but I can't *write* any more, at least until I am
> thro' with the second volume & open the great yellow folder I
> brought from Minneapolis, with fragments better than many of
> the finisht songs. But I feel remote & lost without my poem.

Even three months later Kate recounted with studied patience: 'We
have been burdened with Dream Songs all winter and now everyday is a day of reckoning. Me typing and John organizing and not
writing any more which is a good thing since there are over 300
contenders for *His Toy, His Dream, His Rest*.'

Work was shared with bouts of drinking. John Montague hired a
hall for Berryman to give his only organised reading in Ireland,

> and with the help of Liam Miller and Basil Payne . . . made sure
> that it would be filled. For the reading he gave us his lovely
> Yeats poem, *I have moved to Dublin to have it out with you/majestic
> Shade* . . . But, as the hall was filling up with a motley mob of
> admirers, recruited from every pub and college we could think
> of, we were told that Berryman had disappeared. . . .
> He did appear eventually, and one of the strangest poetry

readings I have ever attended took place. With great difficulty
Patrick Kavanagh had been persuaded to come, on the
condition that the name of a certain Irishman was not
pronounced in public. Kavanagh lurked in the back with his
troops, coughing as he waited, while I tried to create an
atmosphere for the reading with an introduction, in which I said
that this was the most important occasion of its kind since
Robert Frost had read in Dublin. Unfortunately, he mentioned
our first meeting at Iowa: protests from Berryman, who loped
out to greet old friends in the audience, one of them Brian
Boydell, whom he had known at Cambridge. The sight of
Boydell being warmly embraced by Berryman distracted the
audience, so that I was able to weave to the end of my
introduction without further interruption. But when Berryman
consented to come forward, he began his reading very
graciously with a vote of thanks to those responsible for the
recent recognition of Irish poetry abroad, in particular the man
whose name Mr. Kavanagh did not wish to hear.

Uproar, and exit Kavanagh. But many of his associates
remained, including one critic, who could not restrain his
admiration for Berryman's more intense works, but kept
publicly declaring his praise when a line or word struck him.
Another unexpected but very loyal supporter of Berryman,
Ronnie Drew of the Dubliners, who had been a Majestic
drinking pal of Berryman's, took umbrage to this as an
unprofessional intrusion, and kept calling on the critic to shut
up. Since the genial offender bore the same name as ourselves,
Berryman kept glancing up in a puzzled way, and once stopped
to look over at me: 'Am I doing all right, John?' He was not so
much drunk as splendidly oblivious, and soon he and the
audience were talking away as if he were reciting in some bar, as
he sometimes did. 'Do you really like that poem?' he asked,
after one woman had insisted that he re-read that terrifying
poem on his father's suicide ['Memoir of the American Poet in
Dublin'].

In May Berryman returned to New York to receive his award
from the Academy of American Poets and to give a reading
organised by Elizabeth Kray at the Guggenheim Museum. Isabella
Gardner and Elizabeth Kray both judged that he did not look well,
and while attending James Wright's wedding reception that week
they decided independently but simultaneously to inquire into
Berryman's health at the Chelsea Hotel, where he was staying. 'We
went to John's room and he was vomiting his guts & blood out,'

Isabella Gardner recalls. 'I knew a doctor *in* the hotel. He came to
John's room at *once*. He took him to the French Hospital – Betty & I
signed things to get him in. He was all but dead. A couple of days
later I went to hospital and he had a ½ pint of whiskey by his bed –
no more intravenous feeding, & *soon* he was out of there!' Berryman
had collapsed from exhaustion and malnutrition, but recovered
with enough alacrity to write Dream Song 380 – 'From the French
Hospital in New York, 901' – memorialising the occasion of 3 May.

> Punctured Henry wondered would he die
> forever, all his fine body forever lost
> and his very useful mind?

He returned to Dublin with the journalist Jane Howard, who had
been assigned to spend a week writing a story on him for *Life*
magazine. (The photographer Terence Spencer, who was to take
1,200 shots, joined her from London.) During the flight he indulged
in embarrassing matchmaking, and bullied her to scrape up an
acquaintance with likely men across the aisle.

All ladies, poets and otherwise, are an obsession of
Berryman's. 'I *should* know about women,' he says. 'I've been
married to three of them, and had dozens of affairs. I don't think
I'd like to teach at a girls' college, though. I'd go crazy there in a
week. To be in *any* room with more than four women makes
me feel a little nervous and threatened. And at a girls' school I'd
fall in love with my students, which would be troublesome for
me and bothersome for Kate.'
As might not be guessed by readers of *Berryman's Sonnets*,
which tell of one real extra-marital love affair the poet had 'a
thousand years ago,' their author is now evangelistically
opposed to adultery. 'You mustn't love a married man,' he
counsels woman. 'Not only do you get hurt, but you find
yourself capable of actions you would never have thought
possible. You behave like a spider.' Probably because he is so
content with Kate, who he says 'has no faults at all, and yet she's
still not boring,' he is impatient for the whole world to pair off
like characters in the finale of a Gilbert and Sullivan operetta.
'It's terrible to give half your life over to someone else,' he
admits, 'but it's worse not to. It's too bad that when you get
married, they don't let you say "I hope so" instead of "I will,"
but it's still important to try. You've *got* to try!'
When Berryman's marriage-broker instincts get the better of
him, anyone is fair game: friends, cab drivers, waitresses,

stewardesses, students, former students, receptionists in offices, guys who pick up litter in parks. When he comes on some stranger, he says: 'And what might your name be, sir or miss? And are you married; Ah! You're not? *Why* not? And how are your prospects? And what's wrong with that man or girl right over there across the room? Up you get! Go to it!'

Jane Howard's article ('Whiskey and Ink, Whiskey and Ink', *Life*, LXIII, 21 July 1967), accompanied by Spencer's superb photographs, served as much as any other report of the 1960s to sell Berryman in an image reminiscent of Dylan Thomas; she perfectly reflected the eccentric style he had encouraged in his conduct.

He has enough personal style, in fact, for any dozen of the rest of us. You never know whether to treat him as an august man of letters or as a prankish little boy, because he is always, simultaneously, both. His wild beard looks like steel wool and spills in a bib down his throat, freeing him from having to wear a necktie. His colleagues at Minnesota, it is said, have to wind his scarf around his throat before he proceeds into the winter cold, because he forgets things like that. He sweats a lot and swears a lot. Sometimes he plunges into silent, private gloom. Sometimes he won't eat. . . .

Then there is his voice. If there's anything he isn't, it's a mumbler. Waiters in restaurants, clerks in stores and sextons in historic churches he visits are always coming up to ask him *please* to quiet down, because when Berryman is emotionally moved (which is most of the time), HE LOSES CONTROL OF THE VOLUME OF HIS VOICE AND SHOUTS AND ROARS. . . .

Berryman started teaching because he had to eat – 'though,' as he says, 'when it came to a choice between buying a book and a sandwich, as it often did, I always chose the book.' And he started writing, 'because I had to and have to. It's what I *do*, the way beavers build dams and presidents make decisions.' . . . He lives, and he writes, with a sense of urgency. . . . 'We're supposed to do what we have to do RIGHT NOW.'

On a good day Berryman feels pretty sanguine about accomplishing the tasks he has set out for himself, and about things in general. 'This world works so well!' he says when he feels at his best. 'The older I get the more I'm impressed by how brilliantly this thing is administered. I would have cut my throat in 1947 if I hadn't thought then that I was in the grip of something infinitely beyond my own recognition.' But there are bad days when he all but weeps as he quotes Henry James: 'I too have the imagination of atrocity, and see life as ferocious and sinister.'

Sensational, temperamental, learned: Berryman liked the article for the colour she gave his reputation, and directed his friends to it in the following months. A. Alvarez also travelled to Dublin to film an interview with Berryman for the BBC.

Life had hired cars to take Berryman around – to Joyce's martello tower, and to Tara – for location pictures. 'This hiring cars business became a habit, you know, so we hired one ourselves and did some traveling,' he later told Elizabeth Nussbaum in an interview for *Minnesota Daily* (9 November 1967). For four days from 16 June the family drove to visit Achill and Sligo in the west of Ireland, before they left for a week in Paris and then a further week in Venice. Kate flew via Rome to Athens, where she finally found them a furnished apartment near the Hilton Hotel for the remainder of the summer, while Berryman took a bus to Ravenna, where he visited Dante's tomb, and then Spoleto to participate in an international poetry recital, the 'Festival of Two Worlds', with Allen Ginsberg.

In mid-July he travelled again to London, to play his part at 'Poetry International', where he suffered so badly from alcohol that he urinated in his hotel bed (after just six nights his bill for extras alone mounted to £84 on that account), and rejoined Kate in Athens for the next month. In addition to sightseeing ('the Acropolis . . . I nearly fell off of, it is dizzying,' he told Jane Howard), they toured Sounion, Marathon, Delphi, and the islands.

By chance they shared their voyage on the *Semiramis* with Professor Ernest Samuels of Northwestern University, who had won a Pulitzer Prize for his biography of Henry Adams the same year as Berryman. Although Samuels was not familiar with Berryman's poetry, he was won by his outgoing manner and enjoyed their talks. During the evenings aboard ship, however, Berryman would gather about him an admiring group of young people who sat enthralled on the deck listening while he downed one drink after another; Samuels and his wife grew concerned for his health and for Kate's 'saintly forbearance'. Though unathletic, Berryman proved himself sufficiently agile and determined on Patmos to ride up to the monastery on a donkey, while the Samuelses together with Kate and Martha took a hair-raising ride up by taxi.

They departed from Athens at the end of August, took ship from Liverpool to Montreal, and flew in to Minneapolis at last on 8 September.

Mayor Arthur Naftalin and his wife Frances threw not one but two welcome-home parties for the Berrymans, to accommodate all their guests. Beforehand Kate had struggled to trim Berryman's exile's beard with scissors. For the second week of October he was visiting poet at Trinity College, Hartford, in Connecticut, and within another week he was notified that he had won a 10,000 dollar award from the National Endowment for the Arts 'for disting-uished service to American letters'. 'You're kidding,' he responded. 'I never heard of them, but I'm glad to hear they exist, throwing money around like that. I hope it isn't a matching grant, because I couldn't match the ten thousand, could you?' Berryman's sense of grandiosity, built upon the acclaim and financial rewards that came his way from 1967 onwards, is indicated by an interview that he gave more than three years later:

> In 1968, Congress voted me a ten thousand dollar grant as part of some federal arts program and a reporter called me to ask if I expected to get it. I said, 'Expected it? I never even heard of the god-damn thing!' And this was spread all over the country and some guy on the floor of the House said, 'Why do we give money to these jerks when they've never even heard of the program?' and pretty soon the agency was wiped out.
>
> Well, this means that some of my friends, and some of the younger people who need it, won't get a very useful 10,000 bucks. So I'm very ashamed of myself. That is, I hadn't adjusted to this notion of myself as a sounding board. Anybody lifted out of obscurity has to be goddamned careful what he says and there's no excuse for me because that was three years ago and I had been in a very special position for a number of years.

By November 1967 he entered the hospital again for alcoholism and nervous exhaustion. Boyd Thomes, who treated Berryman on this and many other occasions at Abbott Hospital, recalled in an interview a situation characteristic of Berryman's sickness. 'I've come into the hospital room to visit him when he's hallucinating and have him brush me aside until he's past the good part, and then he'll talk.' During the later 1960s, he told Carol Johnsen,

> John would labor under the conviction that his time had come . . . he was a ruined man, that he was dying, that his health had left him. . . . I would tell him that he did not seem to be dying. Now this was generally true for a long time but toward the end of his career he obviously *did* seem to be dying. What he was dying from was alcoholism. And I would assume that it

wouldn't have been long before he would have been dying from pulmonary disease because of his smoking and coughing which had reached a point that was *so* alarming that it sometimes made it almost impossible for him to communicate. And I don't know that anybody ever counted how many cigarettes he smoked in a day but I suppose five packs wouldn't be an unreasonable guess. But basically John was as strong as a horse with a very splendid physique and if he didn't have the shakes so bad he might even have made a pretty good athlete.

Apart from working on Berryman's physical recuperation, Thomes had to reckon with the knowledge that his 'despair was real. And so a good deal of the action in being a friend of John's has to do with trying to manage the problem of his whereabouts, his psychological integrity, his spells of depression, his moods and attitudes. But when left alone, he would very commonly lapse into very black despairs.'

Berryman's agitation late in 1967 and in the early part of 1968 attached itself to the difficulties of finally organising *His Toy, His Dream, His Rest*, (the second volume of *Dream Songs*) for publication. He took the suggestions of his trusted friends, most prominently William Meredith, but could find no way to rectify Robert Giroux's sound judgment that 'the latter two books are longer than they should be; a number of the Dream Songs written on the voyage to Ireland and a few of the Dublin poems seem to be candidates for deletion.' In the following weeks he deleted from the manuscript four out of six Songs that Giroux specifically questioned, but he also inserted one or two Songs (such as number 193 written for Mayor Naftalin who underwent a throat operation in February 1968). The poem was ready on 9 March, but he planned 'to give the galley proofs a hard time' and looked forward then to a summer of rest, swimming and playing tennis.

'We have no friends here, it's hell. . . . of course we see Boyd & Maris, but that's about it,' he complained to Ralph Ross. 'Also I've been on the wagon much of the time, which makes social life almost impossible.' He and Kate began to visit a psychiatrist 'to rehabilitate our marriage' ('God knows, won't say'), and Kate had decided to find herself a career interest outside their increasingly tense and demanding home environment by 'taking courses leading to teaching'.

Robert Lowell heralded *His Toy, His Dream, His Rest* when it was finally published on Berryman's fifty-fourth birthday. 'What I like is your ease in getting out everything – I mean everything in your experience, thought, personality etc. mills thru the poetry. I think age helps; but most poets are dwindled by age. Like you I want to go out walking.'

Berryman read from his poems in New York on the publication day of *His Toy, His Dream, His Rest*. Two days later, in a fine interview conducted by the undergraduate journal the *Harvard Advocate* (CIII, spring 1969), he was asked about the relation between his teaching and his poetry.

> 'There's no connexion. Teaching keeps me relations with my bank going. Otherwise they would be very stuffy with me . . . being poet is a funny kind of jazz. It doesn't get you anything. . . . It's just something you *do*.'
> 'Why?'
> 'That's a tough question. I'll tell you a real answer. I'm taking your question seriously. This comes from Hamann, quoted by Kierkegaard. There are two voices, and the first voice says, "Write!" and the second voice says, "For whom?" I think that's marvellous; he doesn't question the imperative, you see that. And the first voice says, "For the dead whom thou didst love"; again the second voice doesn't question it; instead it says, "Will they read me?" And the first voice says, "Aye, for they return as posterity." Isn't that good?'

Although he told the *Advocate* that being a poet 'doesn't get you any money, or not much, and it doesn't get you any prestige, or not much,' the publication of *His Toy, His Dream, His Rest* presently brought a good amount of both money and prestige. In the first week of January 1969 he shared the Bollingen Prize in Poetry – 5,000 dollars – with Karl Shapiro (for his large volume of *Selected Poems*). (At a reading with Berryman in Minneapolis earlier in the 1960s, Shapiro recalls, they had found themselves entering a packed auditorium without available seats. 'Stand up, we're poets!' Berryman commanded the first row of the audience, and they had obeyed.) Berryman's royalties for 1969 reached nearly 13,500 dollars (more than a fourfold increase on the previous year) at least partly as a result of his winning the National Book Award, for which he delivered his acceptance speech at the ceremonial on 12 March.

> Both the writer and the reader of long poems need gall, the outrageous, the intolerable – and they need it again and again. The prospect of ignominious failure must haunt them continually. Whitman, our greatest poet, had all this. Eliot, next, perhaps even greater than Whitman, had it too. Pound

makes a marvellous if frail third here. All three dazzlingly
original, you notice, and very hostile, both Pound and Eliot, to
Whitman. It is no good looking for models. We want
anti-models.

I set up the Bradstreet poem as an attack on *The Waste Land*:
personality, and plot – no anthropology, no Tarot pack, no
Wagner. I set up *The Dream Songs* as hostile to every visible
tendency in both American and English poetry – in so far as the
English have any poetry nowadays. The aim was the same in
both poems: the reproduction or invention of the motions of a
human personality, free and determined, in one case feminine,
in the other masculine. Critics are divided as to the degree of my
success in both cases. Long may they rave! [New York: The
National Book Committee, 1969].

He also began to make considerable earnings from poetry readings throughout the country (though never in the South), with fees
commonly reaching 500 dollars and exceptionally 1,000. For three
days from 23 January, for example, he was in residence at Skidmore
College, where he watched while fifteen young ladies (one named
Cookie Palmer being, he considered, 'the best') 'sang out Henry's
Songs', and observed their young pains with perplexity.

> God knows what they're about, but I can swear
> they're not worth her attention,
> Cookie's I mean, I think I mean at all
> any of theirs, any of all their care
> with the drinking & the tension   ['Skidmore Fête'].

He gave the sixth annual Theodore Roethke Memorial Poetry
Reading at the University of Washington on 27 May, in succession
to John Crowe Ransom, Robert Lowell, Rolfe Humphries, Archi-
bald MacLeish, and Robert Penn Warren. The evening before, he
was met off his plane by William Matchett, who was so apprehensive of a night's bar-hopping with Berryman that he deposited him
with some graduate students. As Berryman arrived, Paul Hunter
recalls,

> I got the impression of a painfully shy man, blinking out
> through his beard as if through a mask. But as soon as he
> opened his mouth, and the cavernous tones and
> pronouncements began to roll, I forgot that first impression.
> The characteristic style of his speech that evening was mostly
> drumbeating – who he'd known, where he'd been. But early on

I saw that one could slip under the rolling thunder of the
pronouncements, and touch the difficult, painfully alive person
inside, who clearly had made his identity and art merge with no
inconsiderable effort. I have one other explanation for the
remarks Berryman made that night; he was the oldest person
there, and he'd been led into a den of children, so had to content
himself with playing curmudgeon or king of the mountain. . . .
We were all shaggy and smoked dope and looked the part of
bomb-toting activists, bent on forging the new world, even
though everyone present that night was deferential and
subdued. With the possible exception of myself. Because once I
sensed I had nothing to fear from him, I did begin to prod
Berryman, egging him on to thunder his loudest . . . with
questions about, for instance, pop art and culture . . . 'I can
never forgive that young upstart for stealing my friend Dylan's
name,' he roared about Bob Dylan. 'Yes, but don't you agree
he's a poet?' 'Yes, if only he'd learn to sing!'

The next morning Jean Cox, then an information specialist for
the university (handling publicity for the Roethke Readings), picked Berryman up at his hotel at about 7.45, prior to a television
interview on an early morning talk show. Knowing that Berryman
was an alcoholic, she had arranged with the show that Berryman
should appear in a taped, rather than live, slot, a precaution which
proved fortuitous when he was embarrassingly unable to attend to
the questions and simply rambled on, frequently unintelligibly.
Afterward he insisted that he needed to purchase his liquor, and Jean
Cox was compelled to drive him to two state-owned liquor stores
(which reserved a monopoly on selling liquor by the bottle) before
he would really believe that they were closed during the mornings.
Acutely sensible of the university's reputation, Jean Cox cringed as
Berryman stumbled up the steps of the platform in the ballroom of
the Student Union Building that evening, but she was gratefully
astonished at the clarity of his reading, as Paul Hunter confirms:

his first remarks drawled and snapped forth over the audience,
and people near me remarked that he must be drunk. But
strangely, the remarks were occasionally blurred, while the
poetry was not. I was struck by how musical and full the poems
were, how the eye and page could not do the poems this kind of
justice. The timing was impeccable, precise, even musical;
pauses for lines . . . could have been noted with musical rests
and counted out.

The effect of such precision and music (and tenderness, and

dirge-like elegiac intonation) was to convince me very soon on
in the reading that the drink was probably an unconscious
strategy. I'd already by that time known too many alcoholics to
simply pity or dismiss him out of hand. But this sweetness and
accuracy coming out of what appeared on first encounter to be a
self-important posturing academic out of step with the
moment, took me completely off guard. As the reading
progressed I found him picking again and again my favorite
pieces from the *Dream Songs*. By the time he had reached the last
poem – 'My house is made of wood and it's made well,/unlike
us' the overflow crowd was breathless; most eyes were wet;
most too sprang to their feet as he ended with that backhanded
expression of love – 'I wouldn't have to scold my heavy
daughter.'

At a party given afterwards by David and Patt Wagoner, Berryman
seemed subdued and satisfied. 'It had been a high moment for him,
an audience that he'd wooed and won on his own terms, and he was
justly proud. But it was a quiet pride, unaffected and open.'
     He thought that his readings were necessitous to his income, but
equally he found them grossly taxing to his nervous energy and
subject to odd contingencies.

> Too much can hardly be made of the eccentric view
> that sees liquor in quantity as a sedative
> & for poets dissociative.
> I won't linger over that. That's up to you.
> Like the 3 kinds of marijuana I was recently offered
> in Illinois, like a bird
>
> of passage, bard of passage, oh well I
> somehow refused them all & got home safe.
> Also a 'sexy' fat woman
> was offered me, whom likewise I refused, I
> with my intent to be true beyond belief,
> which is merely human   ['An eye-opener, a nightcap, so it
>   goes', *Henry's Fate & Other Poems*].

As more and more newspapers and journals urged him for interviews during his reading visits, he took readily to the vulgar role of
pundit, passing opinions not only about artistic values but also, as
to Pat Murphy of the *State Journal* (Lansing, Michigan, 11 May
1969), about public issues like the Vietnam war. 'In this war, it's
Americans killing Asians, we should have no part of it. . . . I'm

glad I don't have to make the decision as to how to get the United States out.'

Daniel Hughes witnessed his reading at Wayne State University in the late spring of 1969 and the ritual that attended it. Shortly before, Hughes had spent a weekend in Minneapolis and had naturally told Berryman about his own sufferings from multiple sclerosis, which 'unquestionably gave me a place in his mournful view'. That visit had also given him an insight into the way Berryman lived: 'too much smoking, drinking, silence, sudden availabilities and quick retreats – and Kate's difficult life with him. In the midst of this disorder Martha had blossomed into what she is called in a Song: "my almost perfect child". High manners, intense verbality, confidence and emanations of love.' At Wayne State after a night when Berryman had made an appearance at a community college in Detroit,

> We met him at his motel the next noon and drove him to his luxury hotel in Detroit. He looked sicker than he had in the fall, and, in fact, a fragility I had not seen in him before seemed to dominate him; he was warm to us, tired in his bones, a kind of walking, ill-clad nerve. We sat in his hotel room while he dozed and talked about, for example, the first edition of Lowell's *Notebook* which he thought (as I did) was an attempt to rival or catch some of the play from *Dream Songs*. We had to get him to dinner at a nearby restaurant and then to school and things seemed under control until, upon leaving, he asked us to meet him downstairs. Of course he had a bottle with him and kept us waiting while he fortified himself. He couldn't eat and shook through another drink while *we* stuffed something down. John's reading was the big poetry event of the season, a thousand dollar 'job' as he would call it, but there was some hostility to his coming too. A counter-culture poetry reading across the way, a room too small for the large crowd, and a poet more sick than drunk . . . He was heroic and frail; soaring and slumped; finally triumphant. I remember telling him in Minnesota that Song 382, 'At Henry's bier let some thing fall out well' was an act of moral grandeur and so was this reading.

The next month Berryman suffered an accident which gave him prostrating pain for many weeks, as he told Lowell after three months.

> This is the greater occipital nerve beginning in the back of the neck and going up over the skull which got crushed between

two vertebrae, apparently in a muscle spasm 3 months ago. I
was in and out of hospital for weeks and still go daily for
treatment, hot packs, deep massage and traction. It is not a
favorable situation but there seems to be no brain damage, just
pain like a jumble of rocks in the upper back of the skull.

His suffering gave him a subject for perhaps the last Dream Song
that he ever wrote, 'A Nerve Is Pinched', which concludes fatefully:

> Masada saw a bloody serious action
> against the alternatives, Roman slavery.
> All killed themselves   [*Henry's Fate & Other Poems*].

The university chose at this time to bestow on Berryman the title
of Regents' Professor of Humanities, an honour which brought an
annual gift of 5,000 dollars, for outstanding contributions to the
teaching profession, to the university, and to the public good.
Before the convocation ceremonies on 2 October, Berryman told
E. W. Ziebarth, the dean, 'that he could go through the ceremony
only if I stood by his side and told him what and what not to do. He
was just plain nervous, and although he often made scathing
remarks about academic honors, he was deeply moved by this one.'
Although Berryman had a singularly ambivalent feeling about
administration and administrators, he respected Ziebarth and was
sufficiently confident of his friendship to subject him to a number of
telephone calls at two o'clock in the morning for a 'rambling
monologue' about past relationships, for example, spiced with
comments such as 'at this hour I thought you would still be up
combing your moustache.' 'He could react with enormous humor
to an unexpected response, and in my experience at least, never
resented (or *held* resentment) if he was told to "go to bed and stop
bothering me".' He showed an unadmitted interest in what
Ziebarth would think of his work: 'when I discovered one of his
very early works in incomplete form and asked where I could find a
complete copy, he said, "it is totally unimportant, immature and
sentimental, mostly nonsense." But, within a week I had a copy
from him, with a note, "this is silly stuff, but tell me how you feel
about it".'

For twenty years Berryman had suffered acutely from drug dependency: it was only the next month, in November 1969, that he
was faced with the radical truth about his abuse of alcohol. Shy by
nature, scared of criticism, sickness had long screened his torment.
The time had come to resolve the shocking discrepancy between his

public performance as the bombastic, outspoken, lusty, liquor-sodden bard which thrilled and sometimes outraged audiences at readings (and at the entertainments that followed) and the fatal disease which buttressed that role. At least as the public entertainer, he was acclaimed or derided for a display which was to a large degree suggested by a chronic sickness that altered or exaggerated his temperament. On 10 November, after taking three Thorazine tablets and two Tuinal capsules, he fell down in the bathroom, spraining his left ankle and striking his ribs and right big toe. After X-rays at the St Croix Falls Hospital, he was taken to Hazelden, a famous alcoholic rehabilitation centre, where the admitting doctor described him as 'a well developed, poorly nourished bearded male who appears very weak but is alert and cooperative' and made the following terse diagnoses:

1 Chronic severe alcoholism with acute withdrawal, evidence of alcoholic peripheral neuritis.
2 Drug abuse.
3 Recent injury, contusion right ribs, sprain left ankle, contusion right great toe.

After a week of treatment for injuries and withdrawal from alcohol, he began to feel restless and asked permission to continue his lecture series at the university, but surrendered himself when he was told that the minimum stay on the unit was three weeks. Staff elicited the information that he had first taken a drink at the age of 17, first become intoxicated at 20, realised that he had a drinking problem in 1947, and that, since then, his longest dry period had been the four months from September to December 1968. The tally of his drug-taking revealed: sleeping pills irregularly since 1949, nerve pills irregularly since 1955, Phenobarbital since 1959, Haldol and Vivactic daily, and Tuinol several times a week, since May 1969, Serax in November 1969, Librium during several hospitalisations, Thorazine several times a week since May 1969, and Nembutal for several months during 1961. (In June 1968 he had written a Dream Song which ends unwarily,

Haldol & Serax, phenobarbital,
Vivactil, by day; by night deep Tuinal
& Thorazine,
kept Henry going, like a natural man.
I'm waiting for them to work, as sometimes they can,
honey, in the bloodstream   [*Henry's Fate & Other Poems*]).

His medical history concluded, 'Pt. states he visited psychiatrists from 1949 to 1953 for hysteria and marital unhappiness and every other week during 1969 for marriage problems and alcoholism,' but recorded most significantly of all: 'Pt. admits that he is an alcoholic.'

In counselling sessions Berryman was conducted through what Vernon Johnson (*I'll Quit Tomorrow*, New York: Harper & Row, 1973) has called the 'baffling barrier' of admitting alcoholic dependency and his depressed and powerless condition. Extracts from the counsellor's notes illustrate the course of Berryman's self-questioning and discovery.

> 28 November. patient discussed his arrogance, selfishness, self-pity, fear, guilt – says he's starting to put the emphasis on the 'Now' – is trying to stop comparing himself with other people. We discussed his fear of failing to live up to the phony image he has of himself. Patient still seems somewhat patronizing. . . .
> 1 December. Pt. admits he is an alcoholic. . . . Indication of depression, anxiety, immaturity, lack of insight, high aesthetic interests, feelings of alienation, & dependency.
> Pt. began interview admitting he had reservations about staying on. Discussed his feelings of inadequacy. Also his impaired mental ability. Admitted he is full of fear. . . .
> 2 December. . . . patient's attitude seems improved – talked quite freely about arrogance – irresponsibility – selfishness – impatience – intolerance of others not living up to his standards – his being overbearing – he also talked about his fear of being found out – that people will find out he's a 'shit', as he put it. . . .

Though allowances may be made for differences of interest and temperament, it is certain that Lars Mazzola, who knew Berryman for the last three or four years of his life and assisted him for four courses at the university, had cause to remember his intolerance:

> he struck me as an autocratic, brilliant, and difficult person . . .
> He treated me as a lackey, to whom he would occasionally condescend to be friendly . . . His reflective powers tended towards the sacrificial and egocentric – his joys almost always had a hidden sneer – he gloried in complication and drama rather than commonality, sweat, and the earth. And yet I believe he heard the whisper of an angel more than once . . .
> What talent he had to offer the world was considerably diluted

by the time I met him – he loved to think of himself as the often-propositioned male – he was obviously sick – most everyone saw it except his close friends, who saw the memory he projected to himself. . . .

After his discharge on 19 December, Berryman wrote to Ralph Ross with a confidence that was unwarranted and perilous,

> I feel marvellous, better physically mentally and spiritually than I've felt for many years. The programme is almost as much interested in your character defects, personality disorders, as it is in your drinking problem, and I corrected some of my wrong thinking about myself, helped by the lectures (3 a day), group therapy, various excellent books they give you to read, and interviews with my counsellor, a psychologist, & a priest.

The English department asked him to run an undergraduate seminar on *Hamlet* during the winter quarter, a prospect which further stirred his dangerous self-assurance. 'I'm having a delightful time. . . .'

17

Drink as disease,
1969-70

Elated by what he thought was his redemption from alcohol achieved at Hazelden, Berryman ended 1969 in hopes that the tide would run and run. 'I am extremely happy,' he reported to his friends,

> working very hard on *Hamlet* for a course on it I'm giving this winter for the English Dept. But I'm nearly done and am branching out back into comprehensive biographical & critical Shakespearian studies. A few months ought to see my biography at 500–600 pages, when I'll cut it back to some 450 and give it to my amazed & delighted publisher.

The critical biography of Shakespeare had first been drafted in 1951–2. Now, within a month of starting afresh – without looking at the draft – he spoke of being almost through Chapter 3.

Still, for all that the work was accelerating, there was a new element of hesitancy in his attitude towards it. He started to ask for reassurance and opinion, and sent the first three chapters of the biography (covering the eight plays of Shakespeare's early period, and the *Sonnets*) to William Meredith for 'suggestions'. Sir Walter Greg, who had given his imprimatur twenty-five years earlier to certain of Berryman's suggestions about the editing of *King Lear*, had died, and his passing left Berryman doubtful about his credibility as a modern Shakespearean scholar. The times were fluid, research and discovery bounding: 'Off here in the Middle West I suffer a little from the feeling that I am working in a void.'

The following weeks contain a telling sequence of events which it is important to set out, because the result was that Berryman ended up devastatingly drunk and in a hospital. It would seem that after being discharged from Hazelden on a gust of euphoria, Berryman pursued his work solidly for some weeks until he collapsed, not so much from outside causes as from his own failure of nerve. He was admitted to the Abbott Hospital on 26 February, and discharged about ten days later. His psychiatrist wrote, 'for no apparent reason, he began drinking once again and had remained intoxicated for 2–3 weeks.' Berryman was in an overstimulated condition. Inspirited by the strides the work was taking – in Shakespeare, in a long poem, in ordering old work – there occurred what he called a 'revolution' on 4 February: 'Day before yesterday I suddenly wrote a *Lyric*, my first short poem in many many [sic] years.' The poem was 'Her & It', written in one hour of the afternoon, complete with '8 changes' and originally including this boastful stanza:

> I'm hot these 20 yrs. on his collaborator
> in *The Taming of the Shrew*
> and I know many other things abt him
> nobody else understands. I'm hot.

He had some cause to brag: he had done a considerable amount of work on Shakespeare, was certain of his discoveries in that line, and now 1970 saw them rejuvenescent. Here too was a poem written in heat which celebrated the fact; it seemed to him, after a long lapse in substantial creativity, uncommonly successful: 'Intoxicated with it, I wrote another, and in the evening two more. Yesterday, two more.' The poems were flowing red-hot as never before, but the poet did not stop for self-criticism. While inspiration lasted, he seemed to regard the verses as finished and immaculate, but his self-doubts became evident when he began to ask friends for their approval of his efforts: 'I can't wait to hear what you think of them. Be candid though, and if you find any blunders or numb spots for Christ's sake point them out. These poems aim at nothing short of *perfection* of tone.' The danger signs might have been clear: outwardly overjoyed, inwardly Berryman was prey to dire doubts about the quality of what he was writing.

The friends he had applied to were all practicing writers in the forefront of critical opinion. Clearly they would judge by high standards, especially since Berryman had asked for nothing less. Equally, however, nothing less than their abject praise would have served his precarious state of mind. His ambivalence could be perceived, but not its morbidity. Richard Wilbur recalled:

> The arrival of the manuscript was prefaced by a number of
> telephone calls from Minneapolis, over a long period of time

and the damnedest hours, in which John expressed anxiety over his new poems, or contrariwise showed a great confidence in them and in the novelty of their form. . . . The manuscript, when it came, seemed inferior to the Dream Songs, yet interesting in some of its materials, and fascinating in some of its transitions and collocations. Out of a sense that he was feeling his way from one style to another, and should not be discouraged, I think that I soft-pedaled my reservations and concentrated on the good qualities of John's new work. I did say to him that some of the lines and passages needed more brilliance of the kind he could supply, and that he ought to write an additional poem or passage in which he explained that he was *not* writing a full literary autobiography [see line 4 of 'Message'].

William Meredith was equally shrewd in his judgment of Berryman's motives:

Since when does your critical judgment need support or comparison? You are one of the most considerable poets of our time, and have become so by a process of lonely, pig-headed self-editing. You could tell good from bad and true from false in your work long before I could (in your work). As a loving friend, I am *bothered* at your wanting either criticism or praise, at this point and with this urgency, from [Elizabeth Bishop and Richard Wilbur] or from Mark Van Doren or me. An insecure Berryman is a contradiction in the adjective. When you have a hot streak, you know it. If, as is possible, you're not having a hot streak with these poems (and it would be my opinion on the grounds of the ones you've sent me you're not), you suspect if you know that, and you sit on the poems doubtfully until they declare themselves.

Meredith could hardly have been more perspicacious; Mark Van Doren endorsed his sentiments: 'Your letter says *very* wisely what I've been trying to say to John on the phone – with no result except long silence and then screams.' In short, most of his friends were doubtful about the quality of the poems. They were not to know that he was disproportionately vulnerable to even a misheard whisper of criticism. Where he looked for perfect sanction, they could only give him back his human nature. Being the man he was, sick – not from vanity, but in the flesh – he turned to drink.

Within a few days, Berryman was admitted to the Abbott Hospital in a state of alcoholism. The narrative summary by Dr

Donald M. Mayberg included these remarks: 'He was unable to walk and so entered the hospital voluntarily. Physical examination was consistent with that state of alcohol withdrawal in that he was markedly tremulous and showing nystagmus and palpable liver, bruises on both shins and inability to walk or stand.'

Dr Mayberg's treatment of Berryman, whom he recalls as an 'exquisitely sensitive man', was no more than 'a holding action', its purpose being 'only to maintain him alive, functioning, and productive.' Berryman was back in the hospital again for three days from 17 March: diagnosis, the same. There, he discovered,

> It's all girls this time. The elderly, the men,
> of my former stays have given way to girls,
> fourteen to forty, raucous, racing the halls,
> cursing their paramours & angry husbands.
>
> Nights of witches: I dreamt a headless child.
> Sobbings, a scream, a slam.
> Will day glow again to these tossers, and to me?
> I am staying days   ['The Hell Poem', *Love & Fame*].

At 7 o'clock in the morning after his admission, he wrote a poem about another patient, Tyson, who had arrived in the hospital with the words, 'I have come to announce my death.' The poem, 'Death Ballad', expresses painful witness to the spectacle of Tyson and Jo, who were 'United in their feel of worthlessness/& rage,' and ends with the sympathetic consideration that one way to save oneself is to care for others, as Berryman himself was doing:

> take up, outside your blocked selves, some small thing
> that is moving
> & wants to keep on moving
> & needs therefore, Tyson, Jo, your loving
>   ['Death Ballad', *Love & Fame*].

Anything ugly or painful was a source of excessive hurt and suffering to Berryman. He was both sensitive to suffering and sensitised by it. As Dr Mayberg observed, he would weep 'copiously for the trials and tribulations of those with whom he came in contact.' In addition, he would extract suffering from others in order to augment his own suffering. It was Dr Mayberg's opinion that separations from loved objects were the key to his constant and chronic depression: one such separation is commemorated at about this time in the poem 'Heaven', which concerns a woman who, as a draft of the poem reads, 'was killed in a car incident soon after she married.' The same draft includes the lines (emended in the published version): 'She forgave me that golden day my lust for her / but what might persuade me to forgive her loss?'

He left hospital this time after three days on 20 March. Three days later he was readmitted 'with a flight of ideas, excessive creativity, hypersexuality, over enthusiasm and excessive drinking.' Dr Mayberg saw clearly Berryman's feeling that sobriety was not productive for him as a lover or as a writer. Dr Thomes gave him a general physical examination which revealed 'excessive cerumen, some shortness of breath and tachycardia'. He was accordingly treated with supportive medication and individual and group psychotherapy, and, as the phrase had it, 'made an uneventful recovery'. The discharge diagnoses were: '1. Cyclothymic personality. 2. Habitual excessive drinking. 3. Impacted cerumen, both ears.' Such brief hospitalisations would rely heavily on medication, though it was obvious that he was medicating himself so heavily with alcohol that he increased his tolerance for anything else.

The first week of April brought another period of excessive drinking, at the end of which he was back in the hospital. The patient, according to Dr Mayberg's chart, 'was lethargic, stuporous, uncoordinated and diaphoretic on admission.' He suffered from a marked tremor. There was no doubt that his alcoholism was acute and chronic. Again, three days later, he was discharged with quantities of Librium, Haldol, Thorazine, Tuinal, and multivitamins, after a course of treatment called 'supportive with withdrawal'. The vortex created by his undisciplined use of alcohol had become intolerable either to witness or to live with. Berryman and Kate kept an appointment with the psychiatrist on 24 April, when Dr Mayberg noted: 'Kate has made an ultimatum about drinking – At the end of the term he must go into Hazelden or I will leave. None of us can tolerate John's deterioration – It's too painful to sit by & watch.'

Until April 1970, Berryman had too often taken alcohol for the blood of his life, the force behind his poetic powers. Then – at last – he understood the indisputable fact that 'Alcoholism is a fatal disease. 100 percent fatal. Nobody survives alcoholism that remains unchecked.'

He did not go back to Hazelden. Instead, on 2 May, he entered the Intensive Alcohol Treatment Center at St Mary's Hospital, Minneapolis. Diseased by drink, he had exhibited over the years all the symptoms of chronic alcoholism, including projection, manipulation, blackouts, and euphoric recall. The *Patients' Handbook*, given him on arrival at the unit, declared that:

> Alcoholism and other chemical dependencies are chronic diseases affecting the total personality and all the interpersonal relations of its victims. Chemically dependent persons typically suffer progressive deterioration of physical, emotional, mental, and spiritual health. Their addiction to mood-changing chemicals produces this havoc.

John Baudhuin, an undergraduate student in English literature and himself a poet, was the orderly on duty the night Berryman entered treatment. He had checked the waiting list earlier that Saturday evening and was quite surprised to see Berryman's name; Baudhuin was the only one on the staff that night who knew of Berryman's reputation. Chris Fall, the ward secretary, certainly did not recognise the wretched figure when he arrived. 'Who's Moses?' she asked, to be told he was a Pulitzer Prize-winning poet. John Baudhuin went down to the admitting desk, and remembers feeling surprised

> that such a man of wit and genius could be so incredibly broken down and so ordinarily intoxicated. . . . I went through the usual admitting procedure. His beard at the time was untrimmed and shaggy, his eyes hollowed out, and there were large blisters on his hands from wayward cigarettes. He trembled a bit, and talked incessantly. He was still quite intoxicated. After the admitting procedure and a brief interview with Kate, I had to attend to other duties.

Berryman proceeded to chat volubly to Chris Fall, and

> quoted excerpts from everything written and perhaps from some works yet to be written. He offered some passages in Greek, then a few haiku poems in Japanese, which he then proceeded to translate for us. He stood up and sang an old blues song, and he later offered some rather garbled philosophy. Beneath the wit and charm and the alcoholic haze, I think he was incredibly lonely and acutely aware of the deteriorated state of his life.

According to Vernon Johnson's book, *I'll Quit Tomorrow*, the patient 'goes through admission and detoxification, if needed, and spends twenty-four hours under observation. He is in bed, with a medical regime for withdrawal and a routine medical checkup. Contrary to popular belief, physical withdrawal usually presents no major problems and can be handled simply with good medical management.' Dr George A. Mann, then an anaesthesiologist, now director of the program, remembers Berryman's withdrawal as being vigorous. His state of nutrition was very poor. He stayed in withdrawal for a long period of time, and was physically ill for at least three weeks after admission, with cold sweats, insomnia, tremulousness, nausea, inability to eat, and severe anxiety. John Baudhuin remembers Berryman sometimes pacing up and down most of the night, threatening suicide if he did not sleep.

He was so toxic that he would hallucinate a great deal. In this connection, one of the cogent differential diagnoses that must perhaps be made about Berryman is whether or not he was psychotic. Dr Mann thought him psychotic only when toxic. When he was not toxic, he would express most of all an overriding anxiety, a terrible sense of inadequacy for which he would overcompensate with a loud voice and bragging. This, what the jargon would call 'input', was basically a self-protective device, preserving the defences which were his very enemy. Berryman himself knew in the back of his mind the cause of this mechanism: in his copy of Trollope's *Last Chronicle of Barset,* which he had read only a few months before, he marked for particular attention a line that speaks of 'the arrogance which so generally accompanies cowardice.' Berryman was probably not then truly psychotic except when drinking. Dr Mann was left with the impression that Berryman had a great fear of insanity and of suicide. He felt he was insane or was going insane. He seemed in fact more fearful of his insanity than of alcoholism; perhaps alcoholism was even a manifestation of his insanity. Above all, life was totally threatening to him. He experienced great difficulty in coping with his day-to-day existence. The difficulty created in him an overwhelming, all-encompassing feeling of anxiety, what Dr Mann called 'an existential anxiety'.

Two days after his admission, Dr Clifford O. Erickson wrote of Berryman:

> After admission he became severely grossly tremulous, insomniac, experiencing some frightening dreams, and was obviously on the verge of delirium tremens. He was, of course, then placed on tranquilizing drugs, vitamins, and, also, anticonvulsants, and within a couple of days appeared to be beginning to settle down somewhat.

Berryman continued to experience symptoms of sickness for some time after admission, and was kept in the room next to the nursing station. As soon as the acute phase seemed past, he was assigned to his counsellor, Jim Zosel. He also began to attend the lectures that made up the mental management phase of his treatment. Their purpose was to bring him to an intellectual understanding of the primary nature of the chemical dependency syndrome. Patients would attend approximately sixty lectures on all aspects of the disease, including the effects on the brain, the operations of psychological defence systems, the dynamics of interpersonal relationships, and the emotional effects of desocialisation. Clergymen and social workers lectured on value systems and spiritual impoverishment.

Jim Zosel's group met every day for two hours in a therapy session. The goals of the group are stated in the *Patients' Handbook*: 'To discover ourselves and others as feeling persons, and to identify the defenses that prevent this discovery.'

Patients learn to confront and level with one another. They also learn to recognise repressions and other defences, which are called to their attention and named while they are actually employing them.

Jim Zosel's method as counsellor (and himself a recovering alcoholic) fell

> loosely within the format of what we now call reality therapy.
> In this approach relatively little attention is paid to *why* the
> condition has come about, though in many cases that
> information might be useful. But lack of time prohibits it. The
> approach stays zeroed in on the present existence of the
> condition. The counselor's goal is for the patient to accept the
> truth that the disorder *is* – and that he *has* it. The patient has to
> understand all the implications of the disease and how it affects
> his life *now*.

Berryman joined the group shaking, smoking, and coughing. Soon, aware of Jim's intentions and methods, he felt threatened. ('The patient's chief fear is that his presentation of himself will be destroyed. That is, he feels the counselor is out to change or correct him.') He accused Jim of being sophomoric in some of the things he said. His hostility would take the characteristic form of barking and roaring at Jim whom he thought was his antagonist. Jim would attempt to bring him to his own awareness of the discrepancy between his behaviour and his professed ideals and values. The counsellor is not concerned with any supposed root problem. He takes alcohol as primary, with the emotional problems unresolvable until the alcoholic himself comes to terms with the pathological relationship to which he is subject.

For his part, Berryman would have liked to talk about his problems, or at least to touch on them. He was very good at 'intellectualizing': 'He had himself very well figured out,' and would retail many theories about himself. Jim would tackle the problem by trying to describe to Berryman how he looked, and how he was behaving. At times there seemed to be progress, often followed by regressive behaviour, probably because he became frightened. Berryman was, as Zosel recalled, 'good at hating himself'. He cut an aggressive and decrepit figure, shattered in spirit and body, and unclean. Many other staff members became disgusted with him, some because he was always, as they would put it, 'talking the program'; others, themselves neat and clean, reacted badly to his arrogance and dirtiness. He would wear the same shirt for days, and joked with his misery.

Berryman later regretted his antagonism and defensiveness towards Jim Zosel, whose function he misunderstood because he himself was in what is called the highly locked-in state of the alcoholic. The autobiographical novel, *Recovery*, contains Berryman's rationalisation: 'I *admired* him all right – he's spectacular, blazing with invention and knowledge of life, wonderfully creative and quick – but I thought he was arrogant and cruel and I wasn't at all clear that he was *sincere*.' Eventually, while doing 'a lot of hibernating with Carrington' (Archbishop Philip Carrington's books on St Mark's Gospel and the Early Christian Calendar), Berryman came to open up more when Kate was present at conferences. He told how he had manipulated her, and confessed that he had acted miserably towards her; his sincerity was evident. The spouse of any alcoholic has 'her own highly developed and inordinate defense systems and negative emotional postures,' which she must learn to recognise while the patient is in the hospital. She too experiences feelings of rejection and resentment. If Berryman had made a rapid recovery, it would have been very threatening for Kate, demanding a reassessment of her role. The relationship between an alcoholic and his spouse is one in which both partners become immobilised and depressed. In private counselling, Berryman often spoke to Jim about his sex life, and conceded that he was excessively interested in women.

On Tuesday, 12 May, Berryman had what he called an 'exterofective' crisis – '*real life* I mean.' He had permission from Dr Erickson to take two hours out of the hospital in order to give his afternoon lecture at the university. Jim Zosel did not approve of this licence and enlisted Dr Mann's help to oppose Dr Erickson's decision. According to Berryman's own account in *Recovery*, Jim came in that morning and told him:

> 'I've just talked to Dr. [Erickson] on the phone and he's withdrawn his consent to your pass.' I was horrified. I am not sure I have ever been so shocked in my life. I said, 'You and he have no authority over me, I'll just call a cab and go.' Then the heat began. 'You're shaking like a leaf.' I said, 'I don't shake when I lecture' (and on the whole that's true). 'You can't walk.' 'I can walk well enough. There's an elevator.' 'We're afraid you may have a convulsion.' 'A convulsion,' I said grimly, 'That's science fiction, I've never had a convulsion in my life.'
> The Chief Counsellor, sitting in, after some speech of mine about my duty to the kids, said, 'I read: grandiosity and false pride.' Later he described me as a blind man who has hold of an elephant by the tail and gives a description of it; I looked at him bitterly and said, 'You're witty.' 'Judgmental as ever,' he smiled at me.

Eventually, Berryman gave in and said he would not go. Marion Mann, who was in the therapy group at the time, grew very concerned about his class. 'They were all consolation, advice, sympathy, even praise,' Berryman recalled. 'I couldn't understand it and did not give two ounces of gerbil-dung.' He felt he was irreplaceable, but Marion Mann suggested that Jim Zosel, himself an Episcopal minister, could undertake the class, 'and there was [Jim] looking hot-faced at me saying, "I'll give your lecture for you." I felt stunned . . . I said, "I could kiss you!" He said – he's a maniac – "Well, do," and so help me I leaned across Keg (who, it vaguely and irritably even in that moment came to me, was *laughing*) and [Jim] and I embraced and kissed cheeks.' Berryman felt overwhelmed with gratitude and self-reproach; he wept copiously and had to be escorted from the room.

Zosel remembers being 'scared to death' during the lecture on St John's Gospel. He presented some of Berryman's good but sketchy material, and some of his own. Berryman's notes emphasised the powerful, majestic elements in the Gospel. About seventy-five students turned up, but they were bored and restless – probably because that day coincided with a student strike against the war in Cambodia. The students were wearing red arm-bands, and Zosel brought one back to the hospital for Berryman – to his displeasure. Zosel assumed that 'he was not politically where I was at,' but Berryman detailed his own feelings in *Recovery*:

The special trouble was that my students were in crisis themselves, the nation-wide wave of strikes had just hit the University, of my seventy-five kids only one-third had shown up the preceding Thursday and my assistant was lost, he didn't know what to tell them. I had to hear them and tell them myself, the President is a very capable guy but he was handling this particular business all wrong, in fact he was *not* handling it, he had just put students and staff alike on their 'consciences,' what a way to run a vast institution.

'You know, Jim, you're a very affectionate man,' Berryman told him when Zosel returned from his lecture. No one had ever said such a thing to Zosel before, but he was aware that Berryman was also addressing himself. Zosel's actions that day also served to shock Berryman into a new spiritual experience, as *Recovery* relates:

That afternoon as I thought over what had happened I saw that a direct intervention had taken place and I recovered one particular sense of God's being I lost as a child. My father shot himself when I was twelve. I didn't blame God for that, I just lost all personal sense of Him. No doubt about the Creator and Maintainer, and later it became quite clear to me that He made himself available to certain men and women in terms of inspiration – artists, scientists, statesmen, the saints of course, anybody in fact – gave them special power or insight or endurance – I'd felt it myself: some of my best work I can't claim any credit for, it flowed out all by itself, or in fact by His moving. But I couldn't see Him interested in the individual life in the ordinary way. Now I did. [Jim] was his angel if you like – emissary, agent – I've never had any trouble with angels. Or what they call 'miracles' either. I became a different man.

Berryman believed that this intervention enabled him to accept the Second Step of AA – 'Came to believe that a Power greater than ourselves could restore us to sanity' – and wrote of it on 4 June:

Finally you opened my eyes.

My double nature fused in that point of time
three weeks ago day before yesterday.
Now, brooding thro' a history of the early Church,
I identify with everybody, even the heresiarchs
    ['Eleven Addresses to the Lord', No. 6,
                  Love & Fame].

Although, in Dr Mann's opinion, this experience of conversion was not lasting, Berryman did refer to it constantly and devoutly. It might also have contributed to the new responsiveness that Jim Zosel noted in his record: 'P[atien]t *good* progress. Confronts & seems very much in touch with the depth of his problem. Seems less anxious & phoney. Very compassionate man who is leveling with feelings.'

Berryman felt better disposed towards treatment for about the next three weeks, a temporary state which is marked in Zosel's notes. On 19 May he recorded, 'Progress. In touch with deep feelings'. On 27 May, 'P[atien]t making progress in spontaneity & breaking out of illusion.' The trend came to a halt, however, on 5 June: 'P[atien]t progressing but seems to have "drawn the line" as to how far he will go. Gets little insight. Does not see self as insecure, inadequate, anxious or fearful. Physical health is poor. Bodily shaking continues. . . . Lots of "God talk" which seems too pious.'

Marion Mann – who witnessed Berryman's apocalyptic confrontation with Zosel and his consequent burst of co-operation with the group – always felt that he was maintaining a superior attitude. He was usually to be seen sitting by himself in the lounge. One morning, however – probably soon after his conversion-experience – he was experiencing such a sense of euphoria that he came over and kissed her on the forehead: 'That's a token of my celestial love for you.' (On another occasion, he spoke of a book he was planning to write about the unit, in which all the patients were to be animals. Eventually he decided against it.)

Berryman's regression after a period of happy responsiveness was self-destructive. It was noticeable that he would disable himself by a pattern of repeated failures. Whenever things seemed to be going well for him, Dr Mann recalled, 'he would go out of his way to set something up to change that.'

'Keg', then a counsellor-trainee whom Berryman describes in *Recovery* as 'the Knife, most fearsome of confronters', was also present when Zosel confronted Berryman about his exeat. Berryman wrote of him as 'an ally against himself. Bony, with bright eyes, a sharp intellectual teutonic look, a high narrow forehead under brush-hair, . . . Thirty years old maybe, [Berryman's] height (five-ten), leashed.' For his part, 'Keg' felt Berryman's 'super concern' for others in the group. He ached for them to get well, and yet was himself detached from the whole process – 'a spectator of a drama'.

Chris Fall, the ward secretary who had received Berryman into the hospital, herself entered treatment during Berryman's term. Berryman became a sort of father to her, and helped her considerably with her own recovery. He also helped an extremely volatile, explosive Indian patient: where others feared to speak, Berryman confronted the man boldly. Despite his kindness and insight, however, Berryman managed many times to turn the conversation towards the subject of suicide.

One memorable day, Jim Zosel tackled Berryman about a personal habit. During a conversation Berryman would go into a form of trance, his legs locked together, and hum to himself. With the words, 'Let's talk to the hum,' Zosel brought gestalt therapy to bear on the problem. Berryman himself remembered the occasion with awe: 'I have a low tuneless unconscious hum: one awful morning Jim made me put it on a chair in front of me & talk to it, then move the chair, be the hum & talk back – it was hallucinatory. Finally he made me talk to what was *under* the hum.' According to Chris Fall who was present, when Berryman was asked to name the tune he was humming, he knew only that it dated from the time of his father's death – 1926.

On 28 May, Berryman took his Fifth Step with the Reverend William J. Nolan; according to the book, he 'Admitted to God, to ourselves, and to Another Human Being, the Exact nature of Our Wrongs.' The purpose of Step Five is to reduce the burden of moral anxiety and guilt which the patient's new degree of self-awareness has brought into conscious focus. The alcoholic frankly reveals his character.

While he may have lacked a lasting personal faith, Berryman was able to pray for others. Of one fellow-patient, he wrote shortly afterwards:

> Let one day desolate Sherry, fair, thin, tall,
> at 29 today her life the Sahara Desert,
> who has never once enjoyed a significant
>   relation,
> so find His lightning words
>   ['Eleven Addresses to the Lord', No. 7,
>   *Love & Fame*].

Sherry was a bright woman for whom Berryman conceived a special fondness. He decided that he could maintain his own sobriety by caring for her; he would continue in life by gathering people he could help. He even reached a point of wanting to adopt her. While it appeared capricious, his motive was in truth profoundly felt. At about this time, when he read *Please Touch* by Jane Howard, Berryman marked this quotation on page 82: '. . . "You're insecure? Make somebody else secure",' and explained on the end-paper simply: 'me > Sherry'. While there was invariably a strong element of sexual attraction in his relationships with young women (as with another fellow-patient, a capable, kind, and bright woman called Lavonne), and while it was true that for Berryman sexual involvement was a chief form of coping with loneliness, it was also true that he felt a deep sense of altruism. He was impressed with the sublime significance of Step Twelve: 'Having had a spiritual awakening as the result of these steps, we tried to carry this message to alcoholics, and to practice these principles in all our affairs.'

Berryman tended otherwise to be exclusive and reluctant in his relationships in the unit. He was drawn particularly to Betty Peddie, who was not in the same therapy group but occupied a room across the hall from him, and to a man named Brian. He felt that they constituted an elite, but they did not share that sense. The 'Author's Notes' to *Recovery* include a brief account of the connection:

> Liz was a foxy intelligent sumptuous woman, rich, with four splendid girls, a bad but unassuming portrait-painter, a great friend of his. Towards their discharge, a year ago, he had proposed that three of them – [Brian] was the witty snobbish advertising director for the second largest department store in the city – start their own AA group. Incredible? Yet at the time he hadn't understood at all when [Terry Troy], to whom he had mentioned the gorgeous project in two sentences on the wing, had just said, 'Sounds selective to me' and vanished down the corridor towards some meeting.

Betty Peddie felt that Berryman 'tried to be friendly and gregarious, which he wasn't.' He seemed to be too exclusive, arrogant, and stand-offish by nature. On one occasion in the group, he said, 'I'm not worried about what people think of me now, I'm worried about what people will think in 400 years.' Their conversation together consisted mostly of Berryman talking, while she listened. He would talk about himself, trying to impress her with his bragging. At one time he reported Martha's comment that 'My daddy has won all the prizes,' and claimed, 'I've slept with more women than you would believe.' During another conversation, he declared, 'I'm afraid I'm going to kill myself.' He tried always to convey the truth that he was enormously gifted. Betty Peddie's response to Berryman and her feeling of disappointment are perhaps best expressed in a review of *Recovery* that she read privately in group therapy after his death:

When he tried to relate to other people he did make friends, but he couldn't ever be wholehearted about belonging with the rest of us; he was constantly retreating into his uniqueness, but he really thought it was all he had that made him worth anything. So he stayed shut out, and he couldn't make it alone.

When a speaker failed to arrive one day, Berryman was obliged to read something, and he did so grudgingly, 'I get paid a thousand dollars for this sort of thing!' Students came to see him and pay homage, while he worried about what Kate's attitude would be.

Evidence of Berryman's failure to prove his credibility as a recovering alcoholic was shown by his own Step One. Alcoholics Anonymous provides in Step One that 'We admitted that we were powerless over alcohol – that our lives had become unmanageable.' Berryman's First Step, which he took with Dave Olsen, a man commonly known as 'The Big Bear' who helped with the First Step Group, was memorable as one of the best ever. Berryman himself later recalled that 'Last Spring I wrote one which [Dave Olsen] – a severe judge – recently called one of the best he had ever seen,' and was amazed that the man he referred to as 'the savage' could have been deceived by what he came to recognise as a 'merely circumstantial Step.' Berryman recalled in *Recovery*:

I must have conned [Dave Olsen] with my First Step: I don't see how. [Dave] is fond of glaring at some shivering alcoholic who has just recited his sins, leaning forward with his hands on his thighs and elbows out – a brutal type, coarse with suspicion – and booming at him, 'You're a drunken *lying* halfassed bum!' *Or* he leans back, with a tender expression, and says gently: 'In my opinion, you're not an alcoholic, I don't know what you're doing here. If I could drink the way you do – or say you do – Friend, I *would*.' So I don't see how I got away with whatever I got away with.

Here is the text of Berryman's Step One:

Social drinking until 1947 during a long & terrible love affair, my first infidelity to my wife after 5 years of marriage. My mistress drank heavily & I drank w. her. Guilt, murderous & suicidal. Hallucinations one day walking home. Heard voices. 7 years of psychoanalysis & group therapy in N.Y. Walked up & down drunk on a foot-wide parapet 8 stories high. Passes at

women drunk, often successful. Wife left me after 11 yrs of
marriage bec. of drinking. Despair, heavy drinking alone,
jobless, penniless, in N.Y. Lost when blacked-out the most
important professional letter I have ever received. Seduced
students drunk. Made homosexual advances drunk, 4 or 5
times. Antabuse once for a few days, agony on floor after a
beer. Quarrel w. landlord drunk at midnight over the key to my
apartment, he called police, spent the night in jail, news
somehow reached press & radio, forced to resign. Two months
of intense self-analysis-dream-interpretations etc. Remarried. My
chairman told me I had called up a student drunk at midnight &
threatened to kill her. Wife left me bec. of drinking. Gave a public
lecture drunk. Drunk in Calcutta, wandered streets lost all
night, unable to remember my address. Married present wife 8
yrs ago. Many barbiturates & tranquilizers off & on over last 10
yrs. Many hospitalizations. Many alibis for drinking, lying abt.
it. Severe memory-loss, memory distortions. DT's once in
Abbott, lasted hours. Quart of whisky a day for months in
Dublin working hard on a long poem. Dry 4 months 2 years
ago. Wife hiding bottles, myself hiding bottles. Wet bed drunk
in London hotel, manager furious, had to pay for new mattress,
$100. Lectured too weak to stand, had to sit. Lectured badly
prepared. Too ill to give an examination, colleague gave it. Too
ill to lecture one day. Literary work stalled for months. Quart
of whiskey a day for months. Wife desperate, threatened to
leave unless I stopped. Two doctors drove me to Hazelden last
November, 1 week intensive care unit, 5 wks treatment. AA 3
times, bored, made no friends. First drink at Newlbars' party.
Two months' light drinking, hard biographical work. Suddenly
began new poems 9 weeks ago, heavier & heavier drinking
more & more, up to a quart a day. Defecated uncontrollably in a
University corridor, got home unnoticed. Book finished in
outburst of five weeks, most intense work in my whole life exc.
maybe first two months of 1953. My wife said St. Mary's or
else. Came here.

    Worst temptations to drinking:
parties, poetry-readings – refuse both for a year – &
verse-writing: problem won't come up for 18 months or 2
years.

    Replacements for drinking:
work on my Shakespeare biography mornings & afternoons – I
drink v. little when doing scholarly work or writing prose: 2 or
3 drinks a day. Evenings: reading or music or conversation.
Need more social life, tho' not parties.

Absolutely certain my wife will leave me if I start drinking
again; afraid I might then kill myself.
Absolutely certain any more drinking will mean insanity or
suicide, perh. quite soon, 2 or 3 years.
Hopes for sobriety: a reformed marriage, trust in Jim, reliance
on God: outpatient treatment, AA.

Berryman felt that his exposition was sincere, and everyone who
heard him was certainly very moved. What his immediate audience
did not discern, however, was that the schematic qualities and
clarity of the declaration veiled a fundamental delusion. The piece
may have been authentic, but its coherence masked a fundamental
fault. Berryman was working on the level not of feelings, but of
ideas. The statement he recited was a confession of past events
dissociated from his present sensibility. A delusion persists, for
example, in his determination to write more prose because he drank
less – '2 or 3 drinks a day' – while doing so, when it was absolutely
essential for a recovering alcoholic never to drink *at all*. (Similarly,
his efforts to pinpoint the causes of his alcoholism were scarcely
relevant to the present course of treatment.)

During the last week of treatment, Berryman retrenched firmly.
For one reason or another, he was not prepared or perhaps enabled
to cauterise his disease, but only to suck the wound. On 8 June, Jim
Zosel noted, 'P[atien]t not coming on straight with anger & hostility. Will transfer to another group a few days.' Accordingly,
another counsellor tried Berryman in her group – without success:
'Saw him as hostile, deluded and regrouped.'

Berryman was discharged from hospital on 12 June. 'P[atien]t to
be released today,' Jim Zosel wrote. 'Plan to have p[atien]t return
for group for at least 2 wks. Physical health is not such that it may
make sobriety difficult. Needs exercise & rest. P[atien]t seems to
break out into the open & then regroup into hostile, arrogant &
defiant behaviour. Some progress in treatment.' Kate was reported
'to be accepting of program & very cooperative.'

Too often Berryman would project a mask made up ambivalent-
ly of arrogance and pity, aggressiveness and pathos. For a while he
was angry and disappointed with his counsellor because of his sense
of failure, but months later he came to respect and love Zosel. He
certainly felt that he had made a spiritual gain: 'My relation with
Him is quite strong at present.' Physically he was in poor shape: '(I
lost 19 lbs for one minor thing & still can hardly sleep – 3 hrs. a
night): so I don't know. I eat, & walk, & pray, & that's about all.'
Within a week of his discharge from the hospital, however, he
confessed (18 or 19 June), 'I had a "slip" yesterday afternoon: I went

to a bar in St. Paul & drank for ¾ of an hour. Christ!' It became hideously clear to him that all his previous efforts to recover from alcoholism were no more than idle gestures. At least he was now alive to the possibilities of recovery offered by St Mary's Hospital, and by Alcoholics Anonymous.

18
Precarious recovery, 1970-71

As an out-patient Berryman joined Alcoholics Anonymous squad 2 at St Mary's Hospital, whose chairman, Ken Stevens, played the game of 'Wet or Dry' when taking the roll call each Sunday. Berryman liked the game, and would always respond honestly if dramatically; often he would seem about to say 'Wet' but switched to 'Dry', and the group would clap frantically. During the summer Berryman and Kate took a short holiday in Mexico, and Stevens later questioned him about his sobriety during the trip. Berryman had considered two plans – Plan A: Drink; Plan B: Don't Drink – but had decided, as he told the group with his deep, booming, resonant voice, 'Fuck Plan A'. On one occasion, when he answered the roster with 'Wet', he explained, 'You'd drink too if you had an abscessed tooth like mine!' While Stevens, who always felt very protective towards him, tried to rationalise the error, the group as a whole criticised any excuses. When the time came for Berryman himself to lead the meeting one Sunday, he had clearly forgotten to prepare a talk, but after a stunned moment started inappropriately to recite his Fourth Step Inventory (a 'searching and fearless moral inventory', according to treatment handbooks), which would normally be reserved for personal and confidential discussion, not for group rendition. Undaunted, Berryman read his confessions from a paper that he had discovered in his coat pocket, with the result, Stevens recalls, that 'there was snickering and laughing and most of the women in the group were about ready to climb out of the window.'

Stevens found Berryman a poignant, sensitive person painfully aware of the feelings of other people. Once, when Berryman discovered an unknown young woman sobbing quietly in the hall, he inquired and listened to her long sad talk with deep concern, took her name and phone number, and later called her several times. In memory of another girl he had met at another hospital who had subsequently burned to death, Berryman set up an annual poetry contest for junior high school students, judged by himself with cash prizes; he spoke very tenderly of the girl and his project.

After being out of treatment for some months, Berryman had a 'slip', as Stevens recalls.

It was on a Monday afternoon. His A.A. sponsor and I went over to see him. He was seated in his living room surrounded by mounds of books. The whole scene had the appearance of a Castle, moat and walls with John in the middle. We sat on the periphery of the walls and spoke across the moat to the 'defendant'.

He was coherent, sharp and witty but drunk. His sponsor was quite upset and tended to be ponderous and solemn. I took the light approach because I didn't believe that preaching would do any good when he was drinking. (When he was in treatment I had asked him if he was afraid to sober up because he didn't feel he could write as well when he was dry.) He denied this at the time. He apparently remembered this and gleefully showed me some writing he had done in the morning and also some he had done after he had drunk quite heavily and asked me if I could tell the difference. I told him that I couldn't understand one damned thing he wrote, drunk or sober, and he laughed like hell about that. The sponsor was quite upset and told us this was no laughing matter. I knew this but John was funny and in no way was he going to get serious until after he sobered up.

Another time John called me late in the evening and he had been drinking. There was no humor this time; he was grief stricken. He wanted me to know what happened. I was very sympathetic with him as I knew how he felt about it and I encouraged him to start afresh and that all was not lost. He did this and came back nicely.

In October, shortly after beginning another slip, Berryman flew to give a reading and be interviewed on videotape at the State University of New York at Brockport. William Heyen, director of the Brockport Writers' Forum, who was his host for a visit lasting two days, found himself awed and agitated by Berryman, whose arrival late on Wednesday 7 October had been preceded by erratic and inconsequential phone calls and travel delays. Immediately after the visit, Heyen took copious notes from having 'felt a sense of history in his presence':

Beard trimmed, hair not as wild, or high. . . . Charming,
disputatious, dominating, brilliant. . . . 'I won that round' after
destroying someone trying to be friendly. He had a bad foot,
pinched or displaced nerve. Went shoeless. . . . In my easy
chair Friday morning, stretched out straight, he seemed unreal,
his clothes much too big for him, or so it seemed, as though
there were nothing under his clothes. And before the reading he
came out of the bathroom shirtless, all bone. . . . We did get
him to eat: a cup of chicken soup Wed. night; a ham & cheese
sandwich Th. noon; a decent dinner Thurs. night. Constant
bourbon, water, no ice. 'Mr. Heyen, I'm an alcoholic. I'd like
another drink.' I'd say sure. Betrayer, I suppose. He wrote my
wife a poem out, which we'll frame: 'After you went to bed, /
Your tall sweet husband and I talked all night, / until there was
no more to be said' ['John Berryman: A Memoir and an
Interview', *Ohio Review*, Winter 1974].

On Thursday morning they conducted the television interview,
though Berryman followed his own train of talk rather than oblige
Heyen's formal questions. Towards the end, Heyen observed that
mental illness seemed to have afflicted Berryman's generation.

Yes, that's so. To find anything resembling it, you have to look
at two generations, at least that I think of offhand: the English
poets of the nineteenth century – Beddoes, Darley, and so on –
and the Soviet poets just after the Revolution – Mayakovsky
and Yessenin. And now! Well, I don't know. I don't know.
Some people certainly feel that it's the price you pay for an
overdeveloped sensibility. Namely, you know, the door sticks,
as I try to open it, it sticks. Okay, so I have a nervous
breakdown. The guy at the corner of Fifth and Hennepin, the
door sticks, shit, he fixes it and he opens it. No sweat! I've been
in hospital for six months! There is an over-development of
sensibility, okay, otherwise we couldn't draw; just as a really
good carpenter or cabinet maker has a sensitivity, feels
differently about wood from the rest of us. It's the price we pay.
So every now and then we wind up in hospital, where they find
us completely untreatable, and pretty soon they let us go. And
we're loose on the body of society again.

The deluded and saddening complacency he expressed was soon
to be punctured. After another sleepless night, Heyen delivered
Berryman to his plane for New York on the Friday morning. After
an hour with Robert Giroux and another editor, Michael Di Capua,

at El Quixote by the Chelsea Hotel, Berryman took the plane back to Minneapolis that night. In a state of acute alcoholic exhaustion, he went 'out of contact' (to use his own phrase) for some hours and turned up only on the Sunday morning; it is impossible to reconstruct his movements in the interim. Confronted in his living-room by his sponsor and by Kate and others, he was admitted once again for treatment at St Mary's Hospital, where he later reproached himself for being unable to cope with the genuine solicitude of his wife and friends.

The prospect of this treatment he found appalling: 'Hours of conferences, confrontations etc. Hospitals are madhouses. They think I'll be here weeks.' One of the most intractable of his concerns was to talk out endlessly with a psychiatrist what he considered the blight of his life, his father's suicide, and the withdrawn, amnesic condition, as he saw it, of his subsequent schooling at South Kent in Connecticut. On a note-sheet headed '4th Friday, noon', for example, he jotted down his poor bare memories of his father. Unable to discover any 'affecting' recollections beyond those of 'hatred' and 'revenge', he could only revert to a dream from 1954 in which he had smashed his father's genitals. At the bottom of the page he drew on to the question of his oblivious experience of school with this groping note: 'God damn it, *is* the other *grand mystery* . . . relevant or *not*? I should *think* it *must* be.' On another sheet from two days earlier, he had questioned: '*Have seen myself* ruined at South Kent School by: failure to go out for football but can it really have mattered as much as that? Surely *not*. And the bullying? Awful, yes; but adequate to explain *3 or 4 years' ambition-lacuna*?' He reached no satisfactory conclusion, and was to continue anatomising his psychological impediments by reference to those two problems even some weeks after leaving hospital; only during 1971 did he seem to suspend his concern with theories in favour of attending to immediate setbacks. Profligate in making plans, he was to find that his grand, even devout, designs overreached the proof of his ability. The question of what, if anything, had first disturbed his temperament became a dead issue in the face of his inability to go on with the life of writing.

Peter A. Stitt interviewed him at the hospital late in October for the *Paris Review* ('The Art of Poetry', XVI, Winter 1972). The state of Berryman's deludedness during treatment can be seen from this fantastically hubristic answer to the question, 'Where do you go from here?'

> I have a tiny little secret hope that, after a decent period of silence and prose, I will find myself in some almost impossible

life situation and will respond to this with outcries of rage, rage and love, such as the world has never heard before. Like Yeats' great outburst at the end of his life. This comes out of a feeling that endowment is a very small part of achievement. I would rate it about fifteen or twenty percent. Then you have historical luck, personal luck, health, things like that, then you have hard work, sweat. And you have ambition. . . .

But what I was going on to say is that I do strongly feel that among the greatest pieces of luck for high achievement is ordeal. Certain great artists can make out without it. Titian and others, but mostly you need ordeal. My idea is this: the artist is extremely lucky who is presented with the worst possible ordeal that will not actually kill him. At that point, he's in business. Beethoven's deafness, Goya's deafness, Milton's blindness, that kind of thing. And I think that what happens in my poetic work in the future will probably largely depend not on my sitting calmly on my ass as I think, 'Hmm, hmm, a long poem again? Hmm,' but on being knocked in the face, and thrown flat, and given cancer, and all kinds of other things short of senile dementia. At that point, I'm out, but short of that, I don't know. I hope to be nearly crucified.

Although he did not conduct himself, giddy and unsafe, quite as at Brockport three weeks earlier, none the less the extremism of Berryman's expression exactly reiterated what he had said there. By March 1971, when reviewing a transcript of the interview, he acknowledged that his attitude had been deluded.

By the end of his fifth week in hospital, he had written seven poems – 'several of which seem to be beauties,' he reported to a young friend, Victoria, whom he had met at a reading at Vassar. 'The various authorities here agree about my progress & I'll probably be discharged next week – not as *cured* (alcoholism is incurable, progressive, & fatal, it can only be *arrested*) but as recovering; and enter then on the two-year out-patient programme.'

While in hospital he took the notion of becoming a Jew, partly, it would seem, from impatience with the mediation of the Christian church (he had scarcely ever doubted the existence of God, but now felt the fervent wish to appeal directly to Him, and not by virtue of clerical intercession), and partly from a desire to identify more closely with his son, Paul, and with his dead friend, Delmore Schwartz. On 13 November, he jotted the following notes:

To become a Jew – the wonder of my life – it's possible! Rabbi Milgrom is coming at 2:30.

My uneasiness with Xt'y [Christianity] came to a head in Mass . . . this morning. Worship God but where? . . . Left and came to my room and incredibly thought of *becoming a Jew*. Always held it impossible because of inadequate concept of God. Ok since [Jim's] rescue – but hostile to Trinity, dubious of X [Christ], hostile to the Blessed Virgin, anti-Pope, deep sympathy with Church, but *not* for *me*.

As a Jew, he considered, he might be 'alone with God, yet *not* alone, one of many worshippers, like them except in blood (who cares?).' He felt a great affinity with Jewish writings and thought, and for years had respected Jewish friends, writers, metaphysicians, musicians. He had already worked to learn Hebrew, begun a translation of Job, borne in mind a project to compile an anthology of Yiddish poetry, and finally, as he put it, 'resented/liked name "Berryman" *being thought Jewish*'. His inclination did not last long, however, and he professed a regular Catholicism throughout 1971. When he completed *Opus Dei*, a section of his next book *Delusions, Etc.* based on the Offices of the Church, by the next summer, he decided (as he told Eileen): 'I'm giving Silvers [editor of the *New York Review of Books*] first look at, though I doubt if those lucky Jews (I worked hard to become a Jew myself last Fall in hospital, the write-up in my novel [never completed] will kill you laughing) can bear the open Xtianity.'

In advance of the publication of Berryman's next volume of poems, *Love & Fame*, Hayden Carruth published a long, censorious review in the *Nation* (2 November 1970) – 'Love, Art and Money' – to which Berryman reacted strongly: it was the first, and remained the most critically damning notice of the book.

What emerges is not a personality, not an integrated being but only a splotchy muddlement of crude desires. . . . The last poem in the book, which is also the longest, is a religious poem, forthright in its devotional feeling and in some passages almost moving, until in the midst of it we are informed, in a tone half-blustery and half-sneering, that the poet's conversion occurred 'three weeks ago day before yesterday.' He seems to be saying, 'If you believe this you'll believe anything.' In a saint or mystic we might accept that, though not without a strain; we might even celebrate it. But in this boasting, equivocating secularist? What does he take us for?

The review especially hurt Berryman since it doubted the reality of his experience of conversion, which had occurred on a specific memorable day, as he vainly pointed out in an exasperated letter (published in the *Nation* on 30 November): 'when a certain religious event is localized . . . the reason is evidently the feeling with which a lover memorializes the date and place of his first kiss.' Berryman's faith in God seems to have endured through the months until his death.

On 1 December 1970, a few days out of hospital, Berryman wrote to exhort Valerie Trueblood: 'Pitch in. Care. Sweat. *Do* something for somebody (i.e. yourself).' The lesson was equally self-directed: he had returned home from hospital a man chastened, resolved to love and care and never to drink again: 'I feel new – so far, 10 days, okay with no trouble. I'll be in out-patient treatment two years now, then just on maintenance of the severe daily discipline I established in hospital 5 weeks ago & have not since once relaxed. The next drink I take will probably be on my death-bed, if then.' At 7 o'clock that evening, he wrote a poem addressing Emily Dickinson (published as 'Your Birthday in Wisconsin You are 140'), in which one phrase read 'I'm in Wankesha/reading your ditties' and which he significantly changed for publication to 'drinking your ditties'. Berryman was later to proclaim that the new lyric form employed in *Love & Fame* was modelled on a study of Emily Dickinson's; it was appropriate, therefore, that he should at last write her a personal poem. In his copy of *The Complete Poems* he noted that her obscurity was 'not *quite* self-pity', that she 'doesn't expect to *hear*, only to *be heard* & tolerated – or even loved', and that although she sustains a 'plea' for '(pathetic) continued loyalty' from the lover of her poems 'she rejects him'. Emily Dickinson embodied for Berryman several aspects of his own mission, and he could identify with the loss, neglect, and irony of her poems. To Berryman, she was one who sought love and fame, whose poems expressed the velleities and regrets of her own existence, the wistfulness of her own occasions for personal love, as well as her teasing and sometimes harrying relationship with God. A failure in personal relationships, she became more and more a seeker after the knowledge of death, and spent her days winkling cryptic wisdom and irony out of her seclusion. To all these searches – for love, fame, God, and death – Berryman was now very much attuned.

The following day, he took down his edition of *Emily Dickinson, The Mind of the Poet* (Harvard University Press, 1965), by Albert J. Gelpi, which the author sent him in appreciation of his poetry reading at Harvard in March, 1966. He noted on the fly-leaf, 'I find myself at *once* more alert spiritually than years ago on first look,' and read eagerly. On page 5 he underlined the words 'can't stay' in the sentence, 'I can't stay any longer in a world of death.' He was clearly experiencing a chafing sense of impatience with death, not for the fact, but for the knowledge of what follows. On a separate scrap of paper he noted themes from Dickinson's life and poetry – 'love', 'disillusion', 'pain', 'loneliness' – and headed the page with Dickinson's observation on her own father: 'His Heart is pure & terrible & I think no other like he exists.'

Also in December that year, he tore from a newspaper a cutting about the Artful Dodger's relationship to Fagin: 'The important thing', it read, 'is to *be brought up by somebody.*' In Freud's *Civilisation and its Discontents*, which Berryman also read at the time, he marked this passage: 'I could not point to any head in childhood so strong as that for a *father's protection*' (Berryman's emphasis).

Another work he read towards the end of 1970, *Childhood and Society*, by Erik H. Erikson, illustrates Berryman's thinking on a number of heads. He considered, for example, his mother's in-fluence upon him, and marked a quotation appropriate to his feeling: 'For we may be sure that whatever deep "psychic stimulus" may be present in the life of a very young child, it is identical with his mother's *most neurotic conflict.*' In another place he reflected on the facts that he considered himself to have been a 'sissy' at his school, and was certainly an alcoholic later in life: 'An individual feels isolated and barred from the sources of collective strength when he (even though only secretly) *takes on a role considered* especially evil, be it that of drunkard or a killer, a *sissy* or a sucker, or whatever colloquial designation of inferiority may be used *in his group*. . . . We are speaking of three processes, the somatic process, the ego process, and the societal.' At the foot of the page, Berryman recorded his own current feeling of developing altruism: 'Okay. And I have always undervalued the societal which do I now *over*value?'

He began writing a book on alcoholic treatment, which progres-sed from three to four pages one night, interrupted at 1.25 a.m. by 'A Prayer After All', a poem which rehearses his long-lost feeling of love and honour for God and the Virgin Mary:

> and now I suppose I have prayed to You after all
> and Her and I suppose she is the Queen of Heaven
> under Your greater glory, even
> more incomprehensible but forgiving glory
>   [*Delusions, Etc.*].

On 29 December, after one-and-a-half hours' sleep the night before, Berryman attended his encounter group. He realised that his life-style (which he defended in the group) was one of exhaus-

tion followed by drinking. He knew he should 'Cut down working!' Kate Berryman and a friend reminded him that 'You're 20
years older now.' Another told him, 'You're going on *nervous*
energy not *physical* energy,' what Kate called 'drive'. He compared a
remark by another group-member – 'It was *nine months after treatment* before I felt all right physically' – to his physician's prediction
of a year in his own case. Bitterly he tasked himself for having
laughed at other remarks – 'If you were a prima donna, you'd have
to keep in shape' – 'You can't write books underground' – and
determined to 'Relax. Swim a little. Massage.' He even invented a
'Step 13' for himself: 'Avoid *all avoidable nervous & mental effort* for
weeks to come. *Only teach*, & that *minimally*. (God can't help a
nervous wreck: he'll drink, being physically alcoholic.) TAKE IT
EASY!' The year ended with such resolutions: to be good to the
living, and still to come to terms with death.

> Gislebertus: Eve deluded brought down on us evil.
> How now shall we encounter His presence again?
>
> I am not therein unemployed myself
> and Kate is making a little Kate again
> ['Another New Year's Eve', *New York Times*,
> > 1 January 1971]

   The fact that Kate was pregnant again after eight years helped
Berryman to warm towards his family as a whole. He suddenly
realised that, throughout three major treatments for alcoholism, he
had never considered his brother Robert Jefferson – 'one of the 3 or
4 *main* people in my life' – during what are called the 'amends' steps.
Accordingly he wrote him at the end of the year with love and
news, and learning that his brother had lately run into difficulties
and was having to spend his nights as a waiter, Berryman also
sent money, 'a morsel, in gratitude for all the times *you* lent *me*
money.'

> Screw that hundred bucks. Screw this thousand, which I hope
> will get you & Rose through. I never want to see either sum
> again. . . . It was horrible to hear of your feet hurting so from
> waiting on table. That is ridiculous; if you love me, never let it
> happen again. What is a brother for? I have felt with dreadful
> certainty of late that for many years now I have been a very bad
> brother to you, and believe me I mean to change; money is not
> important here, just one of many items, but we have to start
> somewhere. Let's write frequently.

His earnings had in fact peaked at this time in his life; his royalties for 1970 reached nearly 10,500 dollars (just short of 8,000 in 1971), and his gross income for 1971 was almost 31,000 dollars.

During the early part of 1971 – a year in which he fought to maintain his sobriety – Berryman injected into his work fundamental elements of political and social consciousness. He determined to leap beyond what all too often seemed to be a customary egotism. On 23 January, for example, he drafted a poem about the revolutionary and cult figure, Che Guevara. His unfinished elegy ('Che', *Henry's Fate & Other Poems*) is half-hearted and ironic. While acknowledging that megalomania formed no part of Guevara's mission in life, and that his vision was not simply territorial, Berryman believed that the better part – according to Matthew 4:10, which he cites in the poem – is to 'worship the Lord your God, and serve him alone. Then the devil left him and angels appeared and looked after him.' His own confession of self-seeking is paradoxically orthodox: 'to head for what but fearlessness and love'. Believing that men are the necessary objects of redemption through the Son of Man, Berryman could not quite credit the ingenuousness of a revolutionary idealism innocent of power-seeking or self-gratification:

> You sought it all for pure joy, anyway,
> sacrifices, the bit. I'm screwed if I'll praise you;
> enjoy and fear you; you open a hope
> we're not contemptible necessity.

It seemed to Berryman in general that what Henry Adams had declared to be the foremost American traits – 'intelligence, rapidity, and mildness' – had become intolerably undermined. Boredom, especially among his students, appeared prevalent. Aghast at what the media brought home to him of America's international intervention, he believed that his role as a teacher included the task of undeceiving his students. He certainly stripped the scales from his own eyes on 25 January, when he sketched a list of what he called 'the most important revolutions of the 20th C. for us':

Russian
Chinese
Korean   – all leftist
Cuban   & 3½ Asiatic
Vietnamese

and we've tried to *crush them all*, with an undeclared hot war (failure) & the long cold war (continuing) with bitter support in

the Chinese civil war (failed stalemate), with two hot wars . . .
in Asia (stand-offs), with CIA invasion of Cuba (debacle) & the
missile confrontation (success).

Of rightist revolutions, we finally fought the German &
Italian and helped destroy them; but we support the Spanish &
Greek revol'y dictatorships and we have helped *establish dozens*
of others (*42* armed interventions in the *last 10 years*), for
instance in Guatemala (military counter-revolution, June '54).

The anti-British movement in India & Israel we've smiled on,
as ideologically 'okay'. But we turned (with insolent treachery)
on the Egyptian revolution when it proved '*not* okay', Nasser
wanting for his desperate country Russian as well as 'American'
aid.

Domestic revolutions:- *vs. blacks; vs. youth.* Actual killing,
besides brutal oppression often illegal.

What a record! – not quite realized by me till now.

Berryman felt like a man waking to a nightmare. In late February, he was sent a book of poems called *Red Cabbage* (written by a
man named George Decq who had died while serving with the
Special Forces in Vietnam), and presently wrote: 'A poet has been
killed at last in the dirtiest war of all.' He went on to draft some
notes for an essay on 'War Poetry', itemising paintings and poems
on the subject. 'Surely,' he observed, 'Uccello . . . is the greatest
poet of war since Homer.'

At 2 p.m. on 12 March, he wrote in five minutes a poem called
'Lines to Mr Frost', the crux of which was his memory of Frost:

> talking about American power and how
> somehow we've got to be got to give it up –   [*Delusions, Etc.*].

Afterwards, he jotted a note to himself: 'This is what I too hope may
happen, that our power will be removed from us by miracle. But
we cannot count on it. We must renounce. . . . Let us seek ex[am-
ples] of humility, activity, inactivity, courage, wherever we can
come on them. They are rare enough. Our most dangerous delusion is self-righteousness . . . our supreme immediate need, self-
sacrifice.'

On 16 March he drafted a poem for the third anniversary of the
massacre at My Lai 4 entitled 'Three Years After'. The poem was
not reworked, but the draft concludes:

> out of soft night

ghostly flare now on all the filthy cities of America falling
falling falling burning out our ghettos & sin.

Although he was not politically sophisticated, Berryman yet had
occasions for insight beyond the average committed newspaper
reader: he could see indifference glooming the eyes of his students.
He also had a highly developed sensitivity to moral outrage: he was
only too conscious of having been himself the cause of personal
suffering. He argued, not so much for a remission of American
offensiveness in Vietnam, but for a recognition of 'collective honor'.
That the war in Vietnam should end was inarguable for Berryman,
and would prevent further misdeeds, but it could not undo the
continuous shame of those already done. It is the latter aspect – the
continuing guilt of the American people – that spurred Berryman's
political sense.

On Friday, 9 April, he read an article in the *Minneapolis Tribune*
about US investment of large sums of money – $30 million in the
1971 fiscal year – to bolster the Vietnamese police force for the
repression of civil disturbances. 'How', asked John Luce, author of
the article, 'can we expect to promote understanding with the
people of a country when our highest officials publicly brag about
"containing" the war-wounded veterans, the students and the
religious groups?' The following day, Berryman wrote off a letter
(unpublished) to the editor of the *New York Times*, borrowing his
substance largely from Luce's article and concluding emotively:

> This aid of ours, by the way, to the enemies of the progressive
> elements in their country, is six times as great as our aid to
> education in South Vietnam. Surely we *did not know* these
> things. Surely we cannot responsibly continue to support an
> administration which is thus, by a natural, if loathsome,
> sympathetic confirmation, repressing exactly those possibly
> democratic elements that all or some of us wish to encourage.
> Not that any of all this ought to be any of *our* pretentious
> Government's *business*! – not even the education bit, when our
> own schools are at most levels radically unsatisfactory and
> thirty million Americans are right this bright Spring morning
> slowly starving.

The bulk of his letter argued on ideological grounds that each
American citizen should hold himself responsible for American
crimes in Vietnam. Ideologically, the demand was sound; politically, couched in a letter arguing economic practicalities, it was naive,
a projection of Berryman's own indwelling need to take blame

upon himself. He knew he could suffer as all men might suffer, and propounded that the whole people should share the guilt of their representatives, whether politicians or particular soldiers, Nixon or Calley. It was hardly a brief to please the self-righteous, and yet it was just them to whom Berryman preached hardest.

In his personal life, 1971 had opened with Berryman in a ferment of negative feelings. The first poem he wrote on 1 January showed him antagonistic towards those whom he had formerly considered kin to his efforts in art – and hence, as he now saw it, in spirituality, the praise of God:

> O even Mark, great Edmund, fine John Ransom
>
> splinter at my procedures and my ends.
> Surely their spiritual life is not what it might be?
> Surely they are half-full of it?
> Tell them to leave me damned well alone with my insights
>   [Ms. draft of 'Defensio in Extremis', *Delusions, Etc.*].

Such a gesture of defensiveness (directed against Mark Van Doren, Edmund Wilson, and John Crowe Ransom) was far from noble – indeed, as Berryman recorded, Kate 'hated' it – but he did see it as an effort to name, and so to recondition, emotions which he had too long repressed. He began to feel that he should pay more attention to others' feelings; a great effort towards resocialisation was in order. On balance, the first three days of the year seemed 'A *sinister showing*. Be v. v. careful. *Still too busy.*' One sign of his better intentions lay in his adding the word 'Anger' to the list of 'Liabilities' on his Daily Inventory, and 'mildness' to the 'Assets'. He also substituted 'self-indulgence' for the phrase 'Negative Thinking', and opposed it with 'self-denial or do something I don't want to', instead of just 'Positive Thinking'.

On 6 January, however, he penned an ominous lyric, 'Drugs Alcohol Little Sister' (*Delusions, Etc.*), about the poet Georg Trakl. The poem includes a parenthetic nightmare with an impression of ghastly dying – 'ordure & the hiss of souls escaping' – and ends with a direct address in the form of persuasion:

> Trakl, con the male nurse.
> Surmounted by carrion, cry out   and overdose & go.

Berryman, as he himself pointed out in the poem, was born nine days before Trakl committed suicide. His identification with Trakl was forbidding and portentous. Trakl referred constantly in his letters to his drinking, and his sister, to whom he was devoted, shot herself in 1917. He served as a chemist with the Austrian army in Galicia, Poland, and looked after ninety wounded soldiers in a barn. Outside, deserters were hanged from the trees. He was unreasoned by the rabid horror that he witnessed – 'der Menscheit ganzer Jammer'. Berryman quoted Trakl's pregnant phrase 'schwartze Verwesung' – 'black corruption' – in his morbidly importunate poem.

Within twenty-four hours, he churned these thoughts into another poem relating his own perennial obsessiveness with the subject of suicide:

> You gave me not a very able tho' of integrity father,
> joyless at last, Lord, and sometimes I hardly
> (thinking of him) perform my duty to you
> 　　[Ms. draft of 'Overseas Prayer', *Delusions, Etc.*].

The poem concluded, however, with a wish to enjoy a greater contentedness with his lot:

> Ah then I mutter 'Forty-odd years past.
> Do I yet repine?' and go about your business, –
> a fair wind and the honey lights of home
> being all I beg this wind-torn foreign evening.

Many times during this early part of the year, Berryman pondered the state of his relationship to God. The burden of his thought was a submissiveness to God's will, and an eagerness to meet death. But even as he held out open arms, he feared the impediment of his sins. On 9 January, he began reading again *Writings from the Philokalia on Prayer of the Heart*, a collection of writings from the Fathers that 'provides the means of . . . leading a man towards the highest perfection open to him.'

> The most effective form of that art of arts and science of sciences is manifested as the practice of the Prayer of Jesus, to use its traditional name.
> 　The primordial condition and absolute necessity is to know oneself.

What is known as the 'Jesus' Prayer Berryman eventually mentioned in his novel *Recovery*. He craved knowledge of death, principally to resolve his doubts about the three Last Things. He had tended to side with Pascal, making a bet on the reality of God,

Precarious recovery, 1970–71

but what of the likelihood of judgment, and of torment and ecstasy?
The question had become urgent to him throughout the 1960s. He
felt awe before the conciseness of Christ's mind, 'pregnant, resonant', and remembered that, as he himself was now doing,

Justin Martyr studied the words of the Saviour,
finding them short, precise, terrible, & full of refreshment.
I am tickled to learn this   ['Eleven Addresses to the Lord', No. 7].

    Berryman's sense of sin swamped him like a miasma. He read
this sentence in Graham Greene's *The Power and the Glory*, 'It is
astonishing the sense of innocence that goes with sin – only the *hard
and careful* man and the saint are free of it,' and identified himself
with 'the hard and careful man' – certainly not the saint – as being
oppressed with guilt. On another page, he endorsed with the
marginal note 'exactly' Greene's comment that 'It would be enough
to scare us – God's love.' This inner debate about the possibilities of
heaven or hell tormented Berryman, now sober and subject to the
cold calculations of a clear consciousness. His merits might be
minimal, but, as he wrote at about this time, he would not credit
punishment: 'I don't want justice – that will be Hell, which I don't
believe in, because there exist people, even worse than I am, worse
servants, who cannot possibly be damned.'
    The problem of sin and punishment nagged him for days. On 24
January, taking his inspiration from a photograph of Gislebertus's
famous carving of Eve in Autun Cathedral, he wrote 'Gislebertus'
Eve', a poem in which he mulled over his own conviction (in
'Another New Year's Eve') that 'Eve *deluded* brought down on us
Evil'. If Eve, Berryman queried, was 'deluded' into sin, is each man
now responsible for his sinfulness? He found the question imponderable and exasperating:

> So now we see where we are, which is all-over
> we're nowhere, son, and suffering we know it,
> rapt in delusion . . .   [*Delusions, Etc.*].

Being human, he could only concur with Eve that 'I too find it [sin]
delicious.' And yet Berryman had become equally impressed with a
sense of goodness and of the reality of divinity – 'Screw *you*, Satan,
is what I say.' He knew that one should take responsibility for
actions in the area of morals, and not plead delusion. Only God's
mercy might exonerate the wrongdoer, who is guilty as charged.
Berryman levelled that argument against what he took to be
Graham Greene's sense of the inexpiable: 'the problem for Greene is

whether anybody can be damned, considering Mercy, & the answer
is YES – it's even easy!'

Not long since, Berryman had given a talk on Death at the
Newman Center in Minneapolis. His notes for the occasion
observed that 'the supreme human *challenge*' was 'to be daily *now*, as
well as *then*, transcended' – to sense, in other words, the everlasting
in every moment, to be prepared for death at any moment. The end
of creation lay in each individual death. That death, Berryman
noted, is 'incomprehensible, even physically, as erection & voiding.
No agreement on when (as none on beginning of life).' In a poem of
20 January, he took the line of entrusting himself to God:

> Merely sensational let's have today,
> lacking mostly thinking, –
> men's thinking being eighteen-tenths deluded. . . .
>
> Lord of happenings, & little things,
> muster me westward fitter to my end –
> which has got to be Your strange end for me –
> and toughen me effective to the tribes en route
>   ['A Usual Prayer', *Delusions, Etc.*].

It may be the last verse quoted – a request for a thicker skin – to
which Berryman referred when he wrote at the foot of the manuscript simply '*predicting* his letter!'

In late January 1971 he went to Chicago to deliver the annual
William Vaughn Moody lecture at the University. Saul Bellow's
'Foreword' to Berryman's *Recovery* clearly refers specifically to that
visit:

> He had arrived during a sub-zero wave. . . . High-shouldered
> in his thin coat and big Homburg, bearded, he coughed up
> phlegm. He looked decayed. He had been drinking and the
> reading was a disaster. His Princeton mutter, once an
> affectation, had become a vice. People strained to hear a word.
> Except when, following some arbitrary system of dynamics, he
> shouted loudly, we could hear nothing. We left a disappointed,
> bewildered, angry audience. Dignified, he entered a waiting
> car, sat down, and vomited. He passed out in his room at the
> Quadrangle Club and slept through the faculty party given in
> his honor. But in the morning he was full of innocent cheer. He
> was chirping. It had been a great evening. He recalled an
> immense success. His cab came, we hugged each other, and he
> was off for the airport under a frozen sun.

Just before he left for Chicago, he received what he considered a
'venomous' letter from Allen Tate criticising *Love & Fame*. Berryman took the message very badly indeed, but by July, in a letter to
his former wife, Eileen, he attempted to palliate his shock by
dissecting Tate's character, repute, and prejudice:

> twenty minutes before I left for the airport . . . I opened and
> read an unbelievable letter from Tate – I drank for 40 hours, quit
> on the plane back, ran a seminar that afternoon, went into
> hospital for a foot operation (successful) next morning. Poor
> Allen retired, neglected, grandiose in Tennessee, with half a
> dozen lyrics to his credit (not I'm afraid the famous Ode, which
> suffers from characteristic inflation, also what Randall hit in
> Washington as 'lack of charm, feeling, tone of forbidding
> authority') – sweating with unacknowledged jealousy. Mark
> and Conrad [Aiken] confess to me that they too are hurting
> with lack of appreciation – I am bitter about this – but they are
> honest & unenvying. Tate used his hatred of *Love & Fame* as a
> springboard for reading me out of not only the pantheon of art
> but the Book of Life, accused me of every known immaturity
> (he didn't read the irony in the two terms of my title *at all* –
> foreseeing, though not in him, this blindness, I drafted out
> while still in hospital last Fall half a dozen readings of 'Her & It'
> which I'm using as Afterword in the British edition, from
> which also I've deleted some of the worst poems) and took it
> upon himself to explain my life-failure as an artist. It was
> wonderful. Saul, to whom I showed the letter that night (I've
> shown it to no one else and will no doubt destroy it sooner or
> later), cursed and said 'predictable'. Problem complicated by
> hypocrisy. The *Bradstreet* poem was hard enough on Tate, and
> his technical debt to 'Canto Amor' (which he imitated for 15
> years during the few moments he could spare from his grandeur
> for verse composition), but what really did him in morally was
> his public utterances about the first volume of *The Dream Songs*
> while he was despising them to our (mutual) doctor (who only
> told me lately) and no doubt other good friends. Allen is a very
> generous and corrupt man, open-hearted, wily, spiteful. I did
> not write down any of the replies I composed to his letter, only
> sent after some months an engraved card 'You hurt me'
> unsigned. Last week I explained to an insolent British reviewer
> who had compared him to 'a very good pencil sharpener',
> insulting Conrad in passing, Tate's high claims as culture-hero
> (Hart Crane's indebtedness, Cal's, mine 'greater still') and lyric
> poet. I bet he won't like *that*.

When he subsequently honoured Tate with a letter to the *Times Literary Supplement* (published 30 July) his chief motive was to take ironic revenge, but he found additional gratification in relaying Sir Herbert Read's view (given at the National Poetry Festival, Washington, in 1962) that the four American poets then most influential in England were Wallace Stevens, Hart Crane, Robert Lowell, and – Berryman himself. It is an index of how deeply Tate's letter had hurt him that he tried in his letter both to cheer himself by puffing Tate and to make amends, 'Is this a man, really, to be patronised?'

19

Last months, 1971-72

In the spring quarter of 1971 Berryman ran two highly successful courses – 'The Meaning of Life' and 'The Post-Novel: Fiction as Wisdom-work' (which included Greene's *The Power and the Glory*, Lowry's *Under the Volcano*, and Hesse's *Magister Ludi*), and exerted himself even further with four Humanities Forum talks on 'The Major American Poets'. When one student complained that the 'Post-Novel' course was pessimistic, Berryman pronounced that *all* Humanities courses were pessimistic. His own literary standing was credited when Drake University, Iowa, conferred an honorary doctorate on him in mid-May. Among his working drafts for the novel *Recovery* (written that summer), some reflections attributed to Severance, the hero, perhaps express Berryman's own ambivalence towards his distinction. 'He felt like a jackass and he also felt like a *shit*. . . . His honorary degrees burned his shoulder-blades. He felt guilty somewhere behind his eyes, several times a month. On the other hand, he regarded the world and in particular his lazy & blind colleagues with wholesale contempt.'

In consequence of the lavish way he spent himself in teaching and of the intense thinking that he had applied to Christ, he was again tested late in February for fatigue, hypertension, and neurosis. The last fortnight in March he undertook a 'spurt' of writing poetry which, he reported, 'was gleefully accompanied by vomiting/ diarrhoea (insomnia) and I decided that my days of verse-composition were over.' (On 29 March he wrote to Peter Stitt, 'Finished at last yesterday the poem that has made the last 2½ months intolerable, a nine-part affair on the Divine Office, called *Opus Dei*. . . . The finale, Compline, is a rare beauty, inspired.') Then again, for five days from 3 May, he was treated for 'extreme nervous irritability', but without physical findings.

What Berryman himself called the 'religious frenzy' that had agitated him for some months resulted in a spiritual crisis on 20 May. Just before attending a weekend poetry festival at Goddard College in northern Vermont, he spent a night in a hotel in Hartford, Connecticut – 'Wallace Stevens' town' – where he experienced the disturbing sense that Christ was present in his room. At 1.15 in the morning ('dry as a bone, nearly 4 months', he noted) he spent an hour writing a 39-line poem called 'The Facts & Issues' (*Delusions, Etc.*), which explores his current conviction that evil ends with death, and that the good probably perseveres. In a conversational style that accelerates towards hysteria, he chaffs the reader with the ironic view that, although he has been 'Happy to be here / and to have been here', he would prefer such luck to stop short at the grave. At the end he exercises the tone of someone persuading himself of his present happiness in order to mollify Christ.

> Let me be clear about this. It is plain to me
> *Christ* underwent man & treachery & socks
> & lashes, thirst, exhaustion, the bit, for *my* pathetic & disgust-
> ing vices,
> to make this filthy fact of particular, long-after,
> faraway, five-foot-ten & moribund
> human being happy. Well, he has!
> I am so happy I could scream!
> It's *enough*! I can't BEAR ANY MORE
> *Let this be it. I've had it. I can't wait.*

Part of the success of the poem inheres in that combination of banter and terror, what William Meredith has called 'the baffling spectacle of a man fending off torrents of a grace that has become unbearable.' When Meredith, who was to drive Berryman to Goddard College, collected him, Berryman talked about his crisis the night before, 'and said to me [Meredith recalls] what he says in that poem about others, that "You are so much better than I am, so much kinder, that I feel you're saved, and I'm not saved".'

'As we drove toward Vermont,' Meredith remembered, 'he told me that he had telephoned his wife that night and asked her (at 4 a.m. . . . .) to tell him "of any act of pure and costly giving" in his life. "I can't stand any more luck, I can't take any more. Neither heaven nor hell – rest, when it's over."' Among notes made later, Berryman recorded, 'Hartford: > Death, but no suicide-idea,' and wrote in his journal for 27 May, 'At present I don't love him; tho' I feel His exasperation as in Hartford a week ago tonight. Even that's bearable. I admit I thought of suicide.' When he acquired a copy of Simone Weil's *Gravity and Grace* on 2 June, he opened it at random and chanced upon a text which expressed 'exactly my Hartford crisis': the specific passage, whose context suggests there is an alternative to the terrifying prospect that Christ will judge each person on his merits, reads: 'Suffering innocence is the measure.'

The plan was to drive on to Meredith's house at Bread Loaf, Vermont. 'But,' Meredith recalls,

> the aging Mercedes that I affect lost a carburetor on the way, and we stayed at Woodstock that night. His talk was rangy, but returned to religion ('the idiot temptation to try to live the Christian life' is a phrase I remember) and to the disease of alcoholism, of which he felt he had at last been cured. He who would never wear decorations was wearing a rosette: the badge of three months' abstinence, from Alcoholics Anonymous. Walking late in a cold mist, he stopped once on a sedate 19th century street of that handsome town and spoke, in a voice that made windows go up in the quiet night, the legend he had decided on for his tombstone. It was to say simply: John Berryman, 1914–19— ('There's no particular hurry about the last date') and then, very loud: 'FantASTic! FantASTic! Thank Thee, Dear Lord!' . . .
> After lunch the next day, two Goddard students came to drive us the last 60 or 75 miles to Plainfield. At one point in the drive, and I can't remember how he came to the remark, he said, 'You and I are the last of the unreconstructed snobs, Meredith.' Partly it was said to shock the pleasantly reconstructed students, a young man and a young woman. . . . At heart, Berryman was a courtly man, though usually (like most of us) he could act out only a parody of that. The forms of behavior that attracted him were as traditional as the forms of prosody ['In Loving Memory of the Late Author of *The Dream Songs*', Foreword, in Richard Kelly, *John Berryman: A Checklist*, Metuchen, N.J.: Scarecrow Press, 1972].

The Goddard Poetry Festival gathered several poets: Galway Kinnell, Michael Dennis Browne, Marvin Bell, James Tate, Charles Simic, Louise Glück, Geof Hewitt, Ellen Bryant Voigt, and Barry Goldensohn (Meredith attended as Berryman's guest). On the Saturday night Berryman shared a reading with Galway Kinnell. 'I read first,' Kinnell recalls. 'Then he got up and said, "Now here come the lies" – in that rabid self-irony he seemed to have – and read The Dream Songs exquisitely, as if they were the absolute truth.' Berryman's loud, engaging, bombastic speech won everyone that weekend, and his implosive manner of reading poems was so powerful that even Kinnell, a fine poet, seemed overshadowed. (Berryman's public performances had become so renowned that, within just a few days, a top agency, W. Colston Leigh, Inc., contracted with him to arrange readings with high fees.) 'Vermont brings out the worst in me,' Berryman whimsically recorded later. 'As soon as I cross the State line I begin to dedicate poetry readings.' That evening he dedicated his reading to '5 good-looking broads' in the audience, Deborah Malone, Louise Glück, Kathy Ungerer, Loraine Flanders, and his ex-mistress Anita Maximilian Landau. Kinnell recalls: 'On the whole he seemed possessed of tremendous vigor to exist & function at all amidst the sadness that seemed to wrap him.'

Moving on to Washington, DC, he visited friends called Keith and Debbi Fort of Georgetown University. They introduced him to a 22-year-old student, Linda T. Lombardo, who, to his surprise and delight, had published in a campus magazine a sequence of eighteen poems about 'Sadeyes' which drew successfully on the Dream Song style – 'Henry's twin sister,' Berryman called her persona. She was amazed and flattered when he regaled her with encouraging conversation throughout one afternoon, and showed a great respect and familiarity with the works of women poets; he was especially pleased to learn that she had been reading Emily Dickinson, since he himself had lately gone 'back to the old girl' as an exemplar of the unrhymed quatrains that he utilised in *Love & Fame*. Since Linda had applied to study in the Writers' Workshop at the University of Iowa, he wrote her an extremely supportive testimonial to Marvin Bell. 'Berryman influenced me in ways I am only now realizing,' she wrote seven years later, 'but I will always remember him as he was that afternoon – a kind, considerate, very literate man in love with his language.'

In the weeks of sobriety since January he had assiduously trained himself to a renewed concern for others, especially the young. With his daughter Martha in mind he planned to write a fresh, accessible biography of Christ, apt to his recent sense of divine influence. 'Granted, I'm abnormally active; but confirmation & guidance are not even exceptional in my life at present. He's busy too. At present I don't bore him. . . . He is HELPING. I am certainly – pathetically – but not uselessly – doing His will. FACT.' Retiring to bed later than the Forts that night, he noticed quite a full bottle of Kentucky Bourbon open on the kitchen counter, and was relieved to record tersely, 'Simply not interested.'

He called on his mother, who had reported many illnesses and problems over the preceding months, and found her 'in a frightful flap, almost completely desocialized'. Throughout the last weekend of May he attempted to persuade her to leave Washington and retire to Minneapolis, where he and his family could be at hand, and tolerated many hours of contrary conversation with her. Sometimes angry, at other moments nostalgic or remorseful, she rationalised and wavered, and at one point even hurtfully claimed that she had given up her hopes for a career as a philologist in order to bring him into the world – 'and never for one moment regretted it, John.' Finally, on the Sunday afternoon, she weakened and agreed to his proposed course. Back home, he took an extremely expensive brand-new apartment for her just across the road from his own house.

He finished the spring teaching dispiritedly. Plotting an intensive spell of writing, including work on the novel, on *Shakespeare's Reality*, and on the *Life of Christ*, he determined to reduce his teaching load to only one course, 'American Character', in the fall, and then possibly to take leave for the winter and spring quarters. What he called 'the real business' – creative and critical writing – took precedence in his mind over the secondary task of teaching. After 1968 he had made two entirely new false starts on the Shakespeare study, but since abandoning drink he had managed to reach his second chapter. The first chapter, called 'Some Problems: Points of Entry', began with a consideration of cruces from *Richard III* and *All's Well That Ends Well*, ventured to redate both plays, and discussed the public figures whom Shakespeare had known well.

In a long application for a senior fellowship from the National Endowment for the Humanities that he completed in June, Berryman rehearsed in understandably boastful detail his qualifications for support in the field of Shakespearean scholarship. For one consideration, he had at some time read almost every surviving non-Shakespearean play written up to 1611 (after that date, his interest dwindled and stopped at 1614). In addition he had made himself a first-rate textual critic while working in the 1940s on his edition of *King Lear*. Having completed an introduction of 125 pages, he had established the complete text and apparatus criticus, and had progressed with a full commentary as far as Act III, scene vi, when G. I. Duthie wrote to him from Scotland with news that his edition of the play was then being printed. Berryman suspended his own work while waiting to determine if Duthie's obviated it, and had complicated his life with writing more poetry and embarking on his critical biography of Stephen Crane before the belated publication of Duthie's edition gave him substantial grounds for completing his own. They disagreed, for example, about the provenance of the Quarto of *King Lear*, which Duthie called a memorial reconstruction, while Berryman was convinced that shorthand had produced it.

Berryman had taught the New Testament for a number of years, and considered himself competent to analyse the biblical influence in Shakespeare, building on the excellent groundwork done by Noble and De Groot.

> My present sense of the matter, subject to revision, is this: John Shakespeare stuck to the Old Faith, his son after an alternation of Catholic & Protestant schoolmasters settled for C of E and practised it until at some point he lost his faith; at some later point he regained it and 'dyed a Papist' like his friend Ben Jonson. My book does not at all resemble the vulgar butcher's-son-makes-good success story of Jos Q. Adams & other biographers; but it does have a happy ending.

Furthermore, having taught the literature, art, and thought – 'from physiology to folklore to political science to cosmology' – of classical, medieval, and Renaissance periods, he felt well able to assess the furniture of Shakespeare's mind. He had for long applied himself to the art of biography, attending particularly to major careers (such as Beethoven, Luther, and Tolstoy), all of which could enrich his task of writing *Shakespeare's Reality*. During the period of his recovery from alcoholism, Berryman asserted his intellectual sharpness and vigilance, and could barely suppress in his application form a note of slanginess and arrogant impatience. 'Who else', he concluded with a grandiose rhetorical flourish, could claim to be

> at ease in the frightful complexities of Q/F *Troil* & *Othello*, past-master of chronology & theatrical history & dream-analysis, veteran of *Quellen-forschung*, author of 100-odd *Sonnets* called in London the most remarkable love-sequence (in English, that is) since the Elizabethans', and of two major poems exercising broad international influence at once, professional biographer, had submitted to E. K. Chambers (1923, 1930) as fully as . . . Erikson to Freud, made far-reaching discoveries, and can bring to bear, matured, the thought of St Paul & Luther & Castiglione & Montaigne?

Having no doubts at all of his own competence, which the world might have recognised from his publications, he found it humiliating to plead his case. It is relevant to mention here that his novel *Recovery*, a strictly autobiographical work, is in large part a redaction of his own hospital diary. Speedily drafting that work, he became aware at an early stage that Severance, the hero, 'often *unconsciously* thinks of himself in the 3rd person, as I do. Let this stand, when it happens. Maybe even *use* it.' (The same consciousness of himself as a third person had informed the technique of the *Dream Songs*.) Among notes for the novel is an admission which expresses Berryman's own sense of superiority and pride, which disdained to ask for alms: 'He was applying for sobriety, with vehemence. Naturally it hurt. On the rare occasions when he had ever applied for anything – Guggenheim & so on – he sweated. It was beneath his dignity. His position was: let the Universe collect & do his bidding *without being asked.*'

On 5 November he was awarded a senior fellowship. Two of his referees, William Meredith and Ralph Ross, had given him unequivocal support. The third, Mark Van Doren, publicly expressed approval to the committee, but told Berryman his reservations in a more chirpy vein than he had addressed to him for a long time.

> I didn't tell [the National Endowment for the Humanities] what I'll tell you, namely that you will never finish the Sh book. There will always be metal more attractive: poems, novels, a memoir, a collection of pensées – God knows what else. You have this illusion that you are a scholar, but you know damn well you are nothing of the sort, any more than I am. Scholarship is for those with shovels, whereas you're a man of the pen, the wind, the flying horse, the shining angel, the glittering fiend – anything but the manure where scholars have buried the masterpieces of the world. You're for the masterpieces, and you know that nothing else matters one tiny little bit, one pitiful little jot, one tit, one tittle.

Neither alarmed nor disheartened by Van Doren's reservations, Berryman expatiated upon his present state of mind and being with a confidence which portended a staggering later in the year.

> I used to ascribe my lifelong failure to finish *anything* to my 24-year-old alcoholism. But I can't buy that. . . .
> There are three reasons, I believe, for my never having finished anything important except the Sonnets, the Crane, the Bradstreet poem, and The Dream Songs. First is: *some* bone-laziness but mostly DOLDRUMS, proto-despair, great-poets-die-young – or at least unfulfilled like Coleridge &

Co., all that crap. Two: the opposite, fantastic hysterical labour,
accumulation, proliferation. I have seldom known you wrong
about anything but you couldn't be more wrong about me as a
scholar. Mark, I am it, Dr Dryasdust in person. The man I
identify with is Housman, pedantic & remorseless (though with
a lyric style far superior to mine), a really bifurcated personality
– and I mean to deal with him some time. . . . Third is
over-ambitiousness. Part of this is temperamental grandiosity
. . . but more of it – unless of course I am wrong – is legitimate
self-demand on the largest conceivable scale. Presenting myself
with any topic whatever, I require to present, or explain, as the
case may be, *everything*. This sometimes holds matters up for
years – always to advantage (provided they ever get done).
Now what are my chances against these awful vices. Well, the
first has ceased to exist. The second is coming under control;
my pedantry is much less self-indulgent, I drop things once I
have their direction & velocity taped or sufficiently indicated for
my immediate purpose. It's the third that's the problem. I don't
know. I admit I am putting myself through a crash-course this
summer of 20 works I should have mastered as they came out,
besides the very elaborate ongoing novel-related reading,
medical lectures and so on. BUT I am insisting on 10 pp. a week
drafted-typed-revised-retyped; so I don't see how I can go far
astray. I am also studying theology before breakfast and after 1
a.m. and keep up a fancy exercise-programme and spend two
evenings a week at hospital & am catching up on 60–70
unanswered letters . . . and supporting with vivacity &
plus-strokes & money various people, various causes. I can drop
any or all of this at any time, but I find I am getting on with it, I
don't sweat.

What is delusory about his remarks is that they took no stock of the
extent to which, since quitting alcohol, he had become over-excited
by recovering clarity of mind and the ability to order his tasks.
Projecting so many plans and commitments, he mistook a dance of
exaltation for dedicated labour. As he was to realise after July, he no
longer had the competence of perseverance.

In the weeks since being discharged from hospital, he had projected
a book on alcoholic treatment, which would function as a kind of
thanksgiving for his own recovery. By the evening of 24 April he
realised that it should be a novel, with its epitome, one man's
recovery, having macrocosmic implications. 'A lunatic coming
sufficiently to his senses to see where he stands, and slowly with

infinite effort, thro' many failures, with every human & Divine help, moving into the position "sanity". His realization then of the insanity of the society in which he has been living.' In a further note, he added, 'A *great* discovery (staring me in the face for weeks). He got to be resocialized by force, his STRUGGLE with his goddam atomized students.' The novel readily incorporated the extensive notes he had made in the hospital the previous fall, complete with conversations recorded verbatim, and to that extent it is forensic. As a devout recognizance of his own recovery, however, the book took a teleological design in Berryman's mind. 'I see I've got to have Severance (the hero) nearer me,' he noted at an early stage, on the understanding that the novel would be both true to past experience and a profession of faith, its shape being not only artistic but also apostolic. His hero would encounter what he called a 'gradually undeluding experience' of out-patient treatment – the 'real world, people, events, history in short'. Berryman tempted fate by announcing before achieving. The novel sublimated his current experience, but by doing so put him at a precarious remove from it.

Regular, day-to-day progress began early in June, for which his notes provide a running commentary. In significant instances, certain jottings indicate that what might otherwise seem straightforward, if wary, plans and sketches took the form of cajolements.

> The great thing is to *get a draft*. I can use it then if I like, as a mere Proustian outline . . . to *fledge out*. OR, unless it stalls (less than 2 pp. a day average over the week), take it *v.* slow. There is NO hurry.
> Late every evening, or next morning, fine-tooth-comb the morning's stint – deleting, improvising & inserting *free!ly* [*sic*], *watching the reader*. . . . As for expression, be Flaubert-like, but ready like Saul to take a high tone, make wild references, demand, demand.

The composition was agonising, as his diary-notes for Sunday, 6 June, illustrate. He went straight to work on waking at six o'clock that morning, and recorded after a little while:

> The planned '4-hrs' is ridiculous, at least in this planning stage – after 3 days I'd be in hospital.
> *Take it easy!* Let it flow, merely – don't over-plan – simply attend to each morning freshly & wide-open, devoted but inventive. Workt on. Staggered, looking at watch finally, to find only 7 minutes had passed.

WORKED ON. Staggered now to find it only 7:12. Stop!

The next evening, after typing just one page at eleven o'clock, he fell into a hysterical depression, and managed to restore himself only by reading the Bible, which he had made an earnest habit for some weeks.

Because of the spiritual dimension in his own recovery, the writing of *Recovery* took a theopathetic complexion. Providence had granted him a charter; Saul Bellow and Pascal would be tutelary spirits. Yet what his ardour and trusted talent started, the arduousness of undertaking would eventually sap. The fact that he should take his measure of artistic success from a spiritual canon was one sorry portent of eventual unachievement; another, that he was too eager to precipitate his plans in letter-writing. Most notably he asked Saul Bellow for his opinion and possible help as early as 1 July, while laying out this elaborately enthusiastic scheme:

> I myself think it is going to be hot as a pistol, but bitter six-times-over experience had taught me that I cannot write plays, and maybe I can't write a novel either. . . . I am simply, with inconceivable effort and cunning, trying to write a readable story about a guy in real trouble. . . . Four sections . . . I – FIRST DAY, 11 pp; II – THREE WEEKS, about 150 pp. III – WEEKS FOUR FIVE SIX, same length; IV – OUT-PATIENT, maybe a little longer. Encyclopedia data, almost as heavy as Melville's about whaling, sifted into Parts II & III, though I hope better dramatized, and a bloody philosophy of both History & *Existenz*, almost as heavy as Tolstoy's in *War & Peace*, crashing around in Part IV, though I hope better dramatized! though no doubt equally deluded and – alas – similarly tyrannical. 20 to 30 main characters, half a dozen very important indeed, but the book is really about him. . . . I am also excited about where your novel must be by now if all is well. Let's join forces, large & small, as in the winter beginning of 1953 in Princeton, with the Bradstreet blazing and Augie fleecing away. We're promising!

In addition to the novel, for which he recounted his ambitions whimsically to Eileen – 'Of course I am determined to produce the most powerful and shapely work of narrative art since *Don Quixote* – what else' – he planned that two other works should emerge in due course, *The Life of Christ* and *The Blue Book of Poetry*, a 'personalized anthology' (Robert Giroux's description he had happily taken up) which he had considered for some years.

On Sunday, 13 June, Berryman's mother arrived from Washington
to take up residence in her new apartment. That very evening Kate
was admitted to hospital and gave birth to Sarah Rebecca at 9.26,
after only two hours' labour. 'I just gave one mighty push,' she told
him. A few days later, on 24 June, Berryman wrote a short poem
called 'Hello' (*Delusions, Etc.*) celebrating the new child, whom he
had promptly nicknamed 'Biscuit'.

> I thought your mother might powder my knuckles
> gript at one point, with wild eyes on my tie
> 'Don't move!' and then the screams began,
> they wheeled her off, and we are all in business.

In the Father's Room, when a doctor brought him news of the safe
delivery, Berryman experienced a 'spasm of chagrin' (a reaction
reminiscent of, but so much less intense than, those he had felt at
Paul's and Martha's births), but after seeing his child he considered
her a 'pretty little broad' with lynx-like ears.

A week later Robert Giroux flew out from New York to stand as
godfather. The night before the christening he read 25 pages of the
novel while Berryman attended his AA group meeting. Afterwards
'(. . . he & I told stories making Kate & Mother laugh,' Berryman
recorded, '& I began to *sweat*, expecting finally to hear I shouldn't
go on with it). "It's marvellous, John" & "Let's get a draft" &
"What about ten thousand dollars" (advance, that is). Cosmic
relief! After he left at 2 a.m., I felt faint & had to take a pain pill.' The
christening took place next day at the Newman Center, attended by
several friends from Alcoholics Anonymous whom Berryman
looked on with pride and admiration. 'Incredible – I'm used to it.
Everybody & his brother dry through the afternoon, adoring Sarah
& levelling.' His courage was so bolstered by Giroux's generous
faith that he promptly drew up a list of no less than thirteen books
which he hoped to complete within the foreseeable future, and
returned to writing with renewed vigour and confidence. 'I feel sure
I can do this novel, no matter *how* yet.' He was not so self-involved,
however, as to overlook what he considered a poignant insight – a
'piercing look' – into Martha's understandable jealousy. When
rousing her that morning, Kate had called out fondly, 'Where's my
lovey-newt?' 'In the other room,' Martha sulkily answered. 'That
child will break my leather heart,' Berryman wrote in his journal.
None the less he always thrilled to the child, as this verse for her last
birthday showed:

> O my *little* Twiss! but *bigger* Twiss!
>   Having you eight years old
> So suddenly fills me with semi-hysterical bliss:
>   you scrumptious to tickle & enfold!

Some days before Sarah's birth he had been meditating so intensively on his fatherhood that he at once wrote 9 lines of a poem on the subject. That 'Proemio' (as he called it) to 'My 3rd epic', a poem which was to have been entitled *The Children* (an answer to, or at least an analogue of, Lucretius' *De Rerum Naturae*), he extended to 62 lines of introduction before abandoning it. 'This is, undoubtedly, bats,' he wrote at the start, sanguinely facing the prospect of what might have developed into a poem of the scope and density of 'Homage to Mistress Bradstreet' or the *Dream Songs*. 'So what? I'm not harming anyone, even myself.' Among jottings for the new work, which he considered for just over a week, he wrote that he had no special plan for subject or story, but that it would include instructions to his children 'on every subject I feel sufficiently strongly about and either know inside-out or am *wholly* perplext by.' When Kate and the baby arrived home from hospital at noon on 18 June, Berryman had watched Martha's face as she peered into the car: that image, he decided – her eyes ineffably seeking her sister – could furnish his poem's conclusion.

In many of his recent poems Berryman had affirmed his faith in God, but he wavered on the question of an afterlife, often wishing it but sometimes in despair of it, as he wrote, for instance, on 30 June: 'I guess I really don't believe in After-Life (tho' who knows? and Christ says so) and am even happy with that – grateful for what there is – only to leave Martha. – I wept.' In the main he felt that his actions, and especially his writing, enjoyed a special covenant with God, and placed faith in an explicit programme:

What is the meaning of life?
It must lie in *our* performance
of *God's* will, *our* free-will being
one indispensable tool.
1) mate & children
2) work = solve problems (vs. boredom)
     (sleep, eat, excrete; keep warm
     enough or cool enough, dry enough or
     wet enough; wash
3) play (for some – the lucky – = 2)
4) worship; resist temptations
5) *help* (others & *accept help*:

Group, Family, Tribe, Nation
6) confront & survive ordeals
7) *become, thro' independence,* FREE.
He desires us to penetrate the universe ourselves but he has
made both mysterious, & banned access to certain all-important
key problems (for instance, the Resurrection).
8) Forgive: all, including ourselves.

For the summer his AA group contained and supported him; he
proudly earned sobriety pins. At an AA picnic, to everyone's
surprise, he entered a foot race with Kate on his back. He had found
reasons for committing himself to group sobriety as early as the
winter, when he read James Dickey's novel *Deliverance* and identified himself with the following quotations:

Survival depends – well, it depends on *having* to survive. The
kind of life I'm talking about depends on its being the last
chance. The very last of all.

I bound myself with my brain and heart to the others; with
them was the only way I would ever get out.

On one occasion he went with Ken Stevens and three other
members of the group to run an AA meeting for the inmates of the
Minnesota State Prison at Stillwater. Seated between two women
in the back seat of the car, he was in rare form, wearing a brown
Chesterfield and his black Homburg and eating an Eskimo pie. 'He
was enjoying the confection while telling the girls that he felt like a
"perfect shit" for not offering them a bite.' During the meeting at
the prison he gave a stirring talk, and wound up by inviting each
and every prisoner to dinner at his home the day they were released.
(One of them actually took him up on the offer.)
    In mid-July he took Martha, together with his son Paul, for a
brief vacation in Colorado. On 16 July they went up a mountain
called Pike's Peak, which is flanked with Douglas firs, to just below
timberline at a height of about 10,000 feet. In the bus on the way
down Berryman experienced a premonition of his own death, as he
roughed out in a poem the next morning.

I've loved enough for fifteen lives, it's enough,
time one poor heart broke,
I have been strong but I'm not that strong

Among notes for *Recovery* he indicated that the novel should end with his intimation of near death: 'He was perfectly ready. No regrets. He was happier than he had ever been in his life before. Lucky, and he didn't deserve it. He was very, very lucky. Bless everybody. He felt – fine.' That sense of self-surrender he had maintained for some weeks; he had witnessed divine intercession in his life, and many times confirmed his reassurance.

Although sobriety helped to reinforce his standards (Kate Berryman found him much more exacting in work and domestic administration, Boyd Thomes thought him 'less sociable' and 'more withdrawn'), he did not altogether reform. During the year he wrote erotic letters to at least two other women, tending proof of his sexual fantasies. One of them he never met, for she answered an advertisement that he placed in the *New York Review of Books* in June. His notes of self-analysis specify 'FEAR & remorse' as the emotions which helped him to cope with 'Resistance to women', but a poem called 'Man Building Up To A Slip' (written probably in May; Berryman himself thought it of 'v. doubtful' quality) expressed his current urges in terms which clearly associated sexual delinquency with his alcoholism.

> I was faithful to my first wife for five years,
> to my second that short run. I have been faithful,
> two minutes once apart, to my mild third
> the whole nine-year sweet time.

At the end of July he went to stay for some days at the faculty club of the University of California at Berkeley, 'to work on the novel faster alone'. The additional family fuss aroused by the new baby perhaps underscored tensions of longer standing. Berryman had given much thought to Kate's strains in their marriage, with a special view to her earlier life. On a note-sheet headed 'K', for example, he jotted what he regarded as significant problems for her, including the fact that her father had 'failed' as 'caretaker, support'. In consideration of the fact that both her father and he himself suffered from alcoholism, and of the large gap between Kate's age and his, Berryman saw himself as embodying and continuing failure in her eyes: 'her rebellion against > me.' Again, of late months Kate had taken up schoolteaching for a career and to give herself an outlet beyond the home, but Berryman had the impression that she was measuring her success in the job against his: 'constant accusations of my "superiority" etc'.

What might seem an earnest and somber picture of the state of their marriage does have hues of ordinary pleasantness, and it should be mentioned without bathos that, for example, the family took meals together like any regular family; Berryman particularly liked goose for Sunday dinner. Since they shared a quick sense of humour, jokes could always pop their quarrels, as he had set down in his journal for 24 April: 'Yesterday I said "You're nasty & ungrateful" & she laughed! & so did I.'

During his 'slip' at the Brockport Writers' Forum the previous October, however, Berryman had drunkenly and seriously oppugned Kate's wishes and intentions, according to William Heyen's notes.

> His marriage is what he had to have it, a storm, he said. . . . I wanted, Friday morning, to send him to Minneapolis and not New York: he replied: 'No, I will negotiate from a position of strength, not weakness.' The last time he had called her (5 in the morning) her line was busy. He believed she had taken it off the hook. He screamed, even to himself when I left him alone in the living room for a minute: 'She'll get out of the house. Out. I will not live with her.' 'She hates me.' 'She cannot bear my fame.' 'She is waiting for me to die.' He kept telling me that he could not convince her that he loved her. . . . Told me he had been unfaithful only once in his nine years of marriage, but that Kate didn't trust him, hated him, envied him, wanted him dead. In the same breath he admitted he was a masochist, and smiled.

For a decade, in fact, Kate had assembled and maintained Berryman's everyday life, shielding his sickness. She found herself increasingly oppressed by his long disease and constant demands, but what she needed for herself was kindness and consolation. Ungrudgingly subserving him, she had dammed her self-expression and the possibilities of fresh personal fulfilment. Taking up teaching gave her a necessary outside interest. By 1971 she felt emotionally and physically run down, and had to confess to him that from time to time her heart misgave her hopes. Mostly because of his alcoholism and of tensions peculiar to a marriage of unbalanced dependency, their sexual relations had become poor. In the nature of their life together, she must have been forced to adultery, or to leave him, or both. When I asked her about it in 1974, it should be said, she felt that, but for death, the marriage would have lasted.

After one fraught phone-call to California, Berryman wrote to her:

> Very somber. So far as getting on with *Recovery* goes, these last days, I might as well be in the Colosseum with the

lionesses. . . . Waked by two nightmares: first 3 or 4 yippies sabotaged an academic broadcast by me, pillaged my possessions, tied a small fizzing bomb to the middle of my back (I was just burnt thin rods); the second ended with my arriving home unexpectedly to find a decayed Russian aristocrat sleeping in front of my fireplace, you left off somewhere – he had been clipping holes in my Shakespearian notes (I showed them to you, saying 'Nothing to you, is it?') – I showed him out, promising him five years for trespass, but you said 'I invited him in' and 'You'll have to get my coat too' – I embraced you hollow you were and woke in despair. Nothing like peace of mind for the practice of art & life.

I was sympathetic to your 'depression' etc. God knows why. 'I've been in shock for ten years' – I haven't heard such crap since 'You've been drunk for nine years' (the aggressive delusion is succeeded by the defensive delusion . . .). So you are 'coming out of it'. . . . So you don't know whether you love me or not, and expect me to sit here sucking my thumbs and working a novel while you brood out the Grand Enquiry to its ultimate delusion. Not interested. I want you, after levelling with the Group for the first time in your life, to put yourself in the hands of a competent analyst, preferably female. I doubt if it will help. I think you suffer from, among other things, the jealous hatred of the very weak for the decisively strong (yes, dear, that's me), and I hope I am wrong or it is reparable; anyway it can do no harm. That's an order. I want you in treatment before I return.

I don't buy the 'busy every minute' either, in regard to letters. Christ you nurse the baby, cook meals, that's it. I have been waiting with impatience and joy, hearing from you. Don't bother. No doubt I am projecting – and if I am projecting wrongly, go ahead and write, but I see no reason to suppose your letters will be any less threatening than your long-distance conversation (in delayed effect). . . .

I don't believe we are going to make it. I feel intolerably depressed.

What the letter does strongly signify is that Berryman was attempting to adjust his domestic dependency to an extent that might have imperilled the marriage even further.

Deliberating on the chance of unfaithfulness on Kate's part, and on the probability that circumstantial stresses could only lead to a separation, Berryman had to weigh what would have been for him the relatively novel emotions of unforgivingness and jealousy, and

– more important – whether he could manage on his own. He had
noted in January:

> I have often congratulated myself on never having *had* to
> experience that terrible 2nd emotion. But that is a damned lie,
> mere delusion. . . .
>   So I *am* a jealous man. I just can't level with it. Hence the
> spiritual psych- drinking- sweating apprehension over I went
> thro' when I did my Inventory at midnight (nightmare about it
> woke me just now) over my 2 *rages* at K. today. . . . I did then,
> v. hardly, work the first part out, praying.

In one of his most poignantly moving late lyrics, he wrote about
their marriage with valedictory sentiment.

> Immeasurably sad, O long ago
> she ceased her being with mine, mine like a fuse
> sputtering toward a common doom.
> She said in her heart 'I must create my own.'
> I learn this now on a mild & terrible morning.
>
> Too late – too far distrust & guilt & pain
> too late for any return or any beginning
> of any nearness or hope again.
> All desire's blown out of me by loss,
> an aching backward only, dull, of our marvellous
>   love
>   ['Loss', *Henry's Fate & Other Poems, 1967–1972*].

At least one late journal-entry – for 1 October – illustrates his deep
wish to coax his marriage back to full love: 'TRUCE! *look on* each
other's GOOD, & be quiet.'
     Only too conscious of the wear of his marriage, and recognising
at last that his body was too impaired by long illness to give means
to his mind, he found his literary plans guttering by the end of the
summer. Having his mother on hand was a further strain; even as
early as June, during his first days of settling into her apartment, he
had recorded that she was 'driving me crazy projecting – suggested
joining Group!' He tried hard to love her, and would stop off to pay
his respects on his way to work at the university. She recalled for me
that on those occasions he would kiss her with more warmth than
he had exhibited for years. In a letter to a friend written late in
October, he showed how family problems had contributed to

making him feel somewhat jaundiced with divine providence, as a matter of almost gay abandon.

172 pages of a novel since April, and other things, have laid me low, dear friend.

We have a new baby, Sarah Rebecca, five months old. . . . Martha will be nine in a month and I will be 57 next week – as she reminds me daily – and I wonder whether 57 can be as convulsive as 56. They are very beautiful children. My son Paul entered Andover this fall where he is learning Russian. In a moment of phantasy last summer I bought an 8-inch reflecting telescope to scrutinize the glories of God and I am trying to sell it back, partly because the glories of God include my anguish yesterday when my mother . . . told me that 3 doctors have given her '6 months to a year' to live and then discovering that my wife simply didn't believe her at all but thinks that she is anesthetizing me for even new more extravagant over-spending (I moved her & all her possessions out from Washington last June into an apartment across the street that costs far more than our house – etc.)

A page of densely scribbled notes elsewhere records that he resented his mother for helping to set him against Kate, and for her 'icy ingratitude & unreality'. (His own financial extravagance included the fact that he had lately been buying books compulsively, especially expensive volumes on art.)

He had for many years suffered the conviction that his father's suicide had tragically violated his own life. Of late he had to recognise that the theory was simplistic and could not wholly account for the insistence of his self-conflicts and sense of guilt. For one important consideration, his mother had (as he conceded only intermittently over the years) as much influence upon his conduct as any other person, but he had put off admitting the full implications of that fact because to do so avoided further complications: his relationship with her called for exigent handling, and not just the ratiocination that he exercised with regard to his father. She had exploited his feelings for her own private causes, one of which must have been an unconscious wish to take revenge upon her husband. Berryman, the agent of her compensation, became its victim.

Two months later, in the first week of January 1972, he committed suicide. In recent months he had certainly made advances towards penetrating his delusions, the most significant step being his acknowledgment that writing poetry was not a function of his alcoholism (for years he had said, as to Professor Ernest Samuels in 1967, that if he had to give up alcohol, he would kill himself). On 18 August 1971 he wrote categorically:

> So long as I considered myself as merely the medium of (arena for) my powers, sobriety was out of the question: no care for self ('not responsible for yourself' as X said).
> The even deeper delusion that my art *depended* on my drinking, or at least was *connected* with it, could not be attackt directly. Too far down. The cover had to be exploded off. . . .

Since 1968, and especially since being treated for alcoholism in 1969 and again in 1970, he had not been able to maintain his creative energy. In poetry perhaps the biggest challenge of his career had been to find a new style after years of writing *Dream Songs*. He felt that he had achieved it with the lyrics of *Love & Fame*: 'this new work is entirely different,' he told Martin Berg (*Minnesota Daily*, 20 January 1970). 'The poet speaks in his own person, they're not dramatic, they're lyric.' When Berg cited Auden's opinion that 'major poets are the ones who show continual improvement,' Berryman agreed: 'These reformations of material and address and technique are only found in ambitious writers.' But the work had delivered neither the same sort of satisfaction as the *Dream Songs* ('if I keep on writing lyric poems, that's all I'll be doing,' he allowed during the interview that winter, 'I'm going to run out sooner or later'), nor the same critical success.

Since writing *Berryman's Sonnets* (which drew immediately on personal experience) in 1947, his life and work had sustained a singular interanimation. Early in 1971 he had largely transferred his ambitions from poetry to prose; when that writing proved unsuccessful, he began to feel that his life altogether lacked value. Mark Van Doren's breezy efforts to dissuade him from the Shakespearean adventure had, as it turned out, been pertinent and solicitous, since (he later observed to me) 'The relevant fact is that most of his projects in this field were unfinished, whereas he always finished his poems.' Partly in consequence of losing heart for his writing, Berryman suffered a virtual seizure of confidence in his teaching, although ironically he had to a great extent withdrawn from teaching as early as the spring by committing himself to research and writing. Loss of faith in himself mounted to dread of his obligations.

One of Berryman's students that fall, Claudia Hexter, vouches

for the fact that his teaching had actually lost none of its efficacy.
During his classes she noted:

> Almost everything he says is humorous but the humour is
> deadly. Every now and then he will smile at his own cleverness,
> otherwise he is unbearable, so tense and awesome is his manner.
> I always feel in conflict & yet that very feeling spurs me on – I
> think I shake as much as he does by the end of each seminar. He
> is not power-seeking; he is power.

Berryman's journal-notes for 13 December take up the catalogue
of distress after a moment's hopefulness for his novel:

> just try – happy a little, grateful prayers.
> All yesterday, terrible
>
> Continual thoughts of suicide – cowardly, cruel, wicked
>   – beating them off.
> Don't *believe* gun or knife; *won't*.
> Can't make Kate happy (*she* last week in kitchen kissed me . . .
>   'I feel I'm playing some sort of game' but it's *me*
> Smoking – cough makes Martha grind her teeth –
>   terminal illness – death
> . . . .
> money – every sum burns with remorse – books, records . . .
>   – never will read or hear – *house not paid for!*
> 20 lb underweight – bad sleep, bad dreams – OLD – pathetic
> penis shrinks into groin – dread of winter
> Fear of new Chairman, & of winter 62 – nervous facing – notes
> probably hopelessly inadequate, & so few registered for
> Honours proseminar!
> – bad teaching this Fall (let students overtalk, & *deprest*, and
> assigned too few books)
>
> Old guilts continually.
> Religious doubts come up – my Mass bad yesterday – wonder if
> Hell –
> obsessed with Daddy's grave
> *Sloth* – stay in bed . . .
> Martha (frightened by my fears) & baby – thoughts only of
> having to *leave* them!

While Kate was out on an errand with Sarah that morning from

10.30 until noon, Berryman considered going downtown to an
hotel, to kill himself with a knife or a gun: 'took knife up to
bedroom. Prayed. Didn't,' he recorded.

Some time earlier he had stopped work on the novel, but then
started again on 2 November. On 13 December, however, he added
to his journal: '*gave up* novel. Bitter disappointment. Told Kate –
she took it OK.' He had invested too much for emotional stability
in literary success. With hindsight it is possible to see that, as a
surety for recovering from alcoholism with a sort of grim level-
headedness, his writing the novel was a desperate play with failure.
Only the most sane and equable perseverance could have redeemed
the bond. His risk had been foolhardy and exact, a courting of
disaster.

He continued his journal with these remarks: 'gradually depression lifted.

Saw: not punished but rewarded! for forbearance?

Hope. Will go back to *The Lives of Christ* [*sic*].' But such
philosophical resignation was only momentary. As his record of a
dream the next night shows, he was still plagued by guilts sometimes associated with sex.

> *Tuesday*. Last dream: had moved back to somewhere we were 4
> years ago – changed by interim tenants – out to find 4 sex films
> at two cinemas nearby – read reviews of them – titles weird –
> went in, paying only 30 cents I said 'how little! In New York
> and Washington, even *regular* films are. . . .' Teller said '*Sex
> films are 2.50? 3? We can do it because so many come – you're
> the new professor in. . . . ? (he knew – recognized beard?) – sat
> next to woman, put arm around her, breast part visible, 2
> middle lower teeth milky, set *back* in jaw, false? felt her hip

His anxiety had reached such a profound level that he jotted many
notes with the same burden,

> anxiety over novel, verse, and other projects
> doubt of superiors
> isolation in University
> resentment and doubt teaching even

and on 22 November he answered the question whether he had
lately resolved his old sense of boredom through recovering sobriety with a note of ironic desperation in his journal: 'Yes! – for frantic
fear & sloth & projected anxiety ('71).' It was in such a mood that he
added the one word 'SLOTH' to his journal in mid-December,

after completing what he considered a 'bad' poem, 'Dry Eleven Months' (*Henry's Fate & Other Poems*), on 16 December.

> O yes. I've had to give up somewhat here,
> illusion on illusion, big books long laboured, a power
> of working wellness to some, of securing this house,
> the cocktail hour, –
> but I am not without a companion: there's left Fear.
>
> I've tried my self, found guilty on each charge
> my self diseased. That jury poll was easy;
> so was the recommendation, on solid showing
> the assassin had been crazy.
> But so too were judge & jurors. Now I see sitting large
>
> and sane and near an altogether new
> & well advised tribunal. When my ticker stops,
> as thrice this fitful year it has done, & re-starts –
> each while poor spirit drops
> a notch – well, when it quits for good, I'm afraid of you.

The poem is better than Berryman thought it, and, given the state of emotional and moral dereliction that he had reached, conforms to his own prescription that 'Some of the best kind of writing is really transparent. . . . The artist just says what he thinks, or says how he feels. . . . The art comes just in placing, pure syntax.' Such a transparent technique he had angled for in the lyrics of *Love & Fame*, but he had managed an intense clarity of feeling in only one or two subsequent poems such as 'He Resigns' (*Delusions, Etc.*), written on 4 August 1970.

> Age, and the deaths, and the ghosts.
> Her having gone away
> in spirit from me. Hosts
> of regrets come & find me empty.
>
> I don't feel this will change.
> I don't want any thing
> or person, familiar or strange.
> I don't think I will sing
>
> any more just now;
> or ever. I must start
> to sit with a blind brow
> above an empty heart.

Delusions, Etc., the last book of poetry fully prepared by Berryman, is not as unified as his earlier volumes; it presents comparatively little sense of cohesion or necessity of structure, more of a compilation of poems (one or two reserved from earlier years, some others individually accomplished, and a few being poems of poor technical quality). It is possible to see that, even in composing the volume, Berryman had tended to be desultory and uncoordinated, and that he hoped to duplicate the fortune of *Love & Fame*, as we may infer from this letter to a friend:

> writing Offices. . . . I began to 'do' them last months but found you really can't – or I can't – in the world; so started composing – a 'Lauds' then 'Matins' – interrupted then by a political anti-prayer I called 'Interstitial Office' – broken off then by sudden absorption in a scale-poem on Guevara – and I only got back to *Opus Dei* (the 9-poem sequence) day before yesterday, with the opening stanza of 'Prime' and the last 3 for 'Nones' . . . my sacred poems. . . . There are as many more of those now, occupying the same position – Part IV – in my next collection, *Delusions*.

Even when writing to his publisher in the spring of 1971 he had referred to the volume with uncharacteristic caution, '*Delusions* . . . is proceeding with slow confidence.'

Work at last failed to give him any buoyancy. He had been impatient of success, but short of strength for the long discipline his projects required. His proliferating plans signalled a diffusion of energy rather than a galvanisation of manifold capabilities. The *Life of Christ* and the poetry anthology came to nothing. Even his Shakespearean sleuthing suddenly looked invalid. 'I thought *new* disappointments impossible but last night (Thurs.) suddenly doubted if I really *have* a book 'Shakespeare's Reality' at all, despite all these years.'

Feeling morally bankrupt, Berryman began to drink again shortly before his death – but only briefly, since it is evident that he had stopped before the end (his death certificate – under the heading of 'Toxicological Findings' – discovered no evidence of alcohol). On Wednesday, 5 January 1972 he wrote a note for Kate, 'I am a nuisance,' and left the house that evening to attempt suicide, but returned. Instead he wrote a poem in the Dream Song style about the projected act and his present dread.

I didn't. And I didn't. Sharp the Spanish blade
to gash my throat after I'd climbed across
the high railing of the bridge
to tilt out, with the knife in my right hand
to slash me knocked or fainting till I'd fall
unable to keep my skull down but fearless

unless my wife wouldn't let me out of the house,
unless the cops noticed me crossing the campus
up to the bridge
& clappt me in for observation, costing my job –
I'd be now in a cell, costing my job –
well, I missed that;

but here's the terror of tomorrow's lectures
bad in themselves, the students dropping the course,
the Administration hearing
& offering me either a medical leave of absence
or resignation – Kitticat, they can't fire me –
  [*Henry's Fate & Other Poems*].

With the poem still short of a verse, he scored a single line through it and dropped it in the wastepaper basket, where it was discovered after his death.

On the Friday morning he again left the house, telling Kate that he was going to clean things up at his office. 'You won't have to worry about me any more,' he said. After Kate had gone out on some errands she returned to find Boyd Thomes and Arthur Naftalin in the house with the news that Berryman was dead. He had taken the bus to the university and walked onto the west end of the Washington Avenue Bridge high over the Mississippi River. Art Hitman, a university carpenter who was crossing inside the glass-enclosed pedestrian walkway, saw Berryman climb over the north side at about nine o'clock. 'He jumped up on the railing, sat down and quickly leaned forward. He never looked back at all.' (One newspaper, the *Minneapolis Star*, reported a witness who observed that he apparently 'waved goodbye'.) He fell about 100 feet, landing near the second pier of the municipal coal docks and rolling 15 to 20 feet down the embankment. Police identified him from his glasses, which carried his name, and a blank cheque. According to the death certificate, he died at the scene of 'multiple traumatic injuries'.

Berryman may have died in despair of himself, but perhaps not of God. In a class assignment he had marked shortly before his death, one of his students happened to write a poem about a man who commits suicide by leaping from the Washington Avenue Bridge. The student appended a note to the effect that he had lately found his own faith in God, but that – since it was a changing period in his life – 'this may change too, but I hope not.' Berryman simply and sincerely agreed by commenting, 'I hope not.'

His body was taken to the Hanson-Nugent Funeral Home in Minneapolis. Father Robert Hazel had no hesitation in arranging a Catholic burial and conducting services beforehand at St Francis Cabrini Church on Franklin Avenue, where Berryman had attended Mass for some months. Berryman's brother flew out that afternoon; the church was thronged for a service eloquent with music and poetry. Robert Giroux, Berryman's publisher, delivered a simple and moving eulogy, 'He loved music . . . he made such great music,' and read three verses from *Lamentations* ending with the words Berryman had chosen for one of his epigraphs to *77 Dream Songs* – 'I am their Musick.' Several of Berryman's poems were recited. Ken Stevens recalls that 'One particularly affecting moment came when a young black barefoot student strode up the aisle during the Mass, kissed the casket, and departed.'

Berryman is buried in Resurrection Cemetery, Mendota Heights, in St Paul, Minnesota. Although oversensitive and profoundly frightened, he had responded to every challenge in his life like a firework of invention and resourcefulness. The record is one that, despite pervasive wretchedness and shame, gives ample evidence of energy and courage, creative genius, and a deep care for his friends and students. Despite the heavy demands he always made, his close friends remember him with unmitigated love.

Appendix:
a famous forebear:
Robert Glenn Shaver

Born in Tennessee of German ancestry on 18 April 1831, Robert Glenn Shaver moved with his parents to a farm in Arkansas as a young man and qualified to practice law. Although not an original secessionist, at the outbreak of the Civil War he promptly recruited the Seventh Arkansas Infantry for the Confederate army on 16 June 1861, and was elected its colonel. On 6 and 7 April 1862 the army of the Mississippi attacked Sherman and Grant at Pittsburg Landing in the Battle of Shiloh. Early in the engagement, the brigade commander was killed, and Shaver assumed command throughout the battle. Opening the fight, the brigade stormed the first encampment in an action so hard fought that Shaver's regiment, first dubbed the 'Ragged Seventh', won such distinction that General Hardee, the Division Commander, afterwards called it the 'Bloody Seventh'. Shaver had two horses killed under him on the first day, another on the second. Every officer on Colonel Shaver's staff was either wounded or killed; Shaver himself was seriously wounded in the hand and left side by the concussion of an exploding shell, which left him unconscious for several hours and gave him continuous pain for the rest of his life. (In all, he was wounded four times during the Civil War, and had six horses killed under him in action.)

In June 1862 he transferred to the Trans-Mississippi Department, where he later organised the thirty-eighth Arkansas Infantry, and distinguished himself in all the principal battles of the Trans-Mississippi Department. When Little Rock was evacuated in September 1863, Shaver covered the Confederate retreat out of the city southward, and chafed at being forbidden to attack the enemy. Always chagrined in defeat, he earned the sobriquet 'Fighting Bob Shaver'. By late in 1864 he was simultaneously and unanimously elected Colonel both of the thirty-eighth Infantry and of the twenty-seventh, which were consolidated and known thenceforth until the surrender in June 1865 as Shaver's Infantry Regiment. When he surrendered his men to General Herron, his regiment was the last organised force of the Confederacy to lay down arms. After his death in 1915, the *Confederate Veteran* eulogised his military prowess. 'That Colonel Shaver was not killed was not his fault, for he gave the Federals every opportunity on many fields. . . .'

After the war, General Shaver, as he had become, was the commander in Arkansas of the Ku-Klux-Klan, then regarded in the south as a glamorous and chivalrous military organisation. He became so closely associated with the avenging activities of the Ku-Klux-Klan, however, that in due course the Republican government indicted him for murder, treason, robbery and arson. When the militia were sent to arrest him, Shaver went into exile for four years in British Honduras. After he returned to Arkansas, the indictments were unaccountably dropped and he became sheriff of Howard County. Until old age compelled him to retire from active employment, he practiced law in the town of Mena, where he lived with his son, Judge James D. Shaver.

On 10 June 1856, Shaver had married Adelaide Louise Ringgold, the third daughter of Colonel John Ringgold, one of the most prominent citizens of the state of Arkansas. They bore six children, but Mrs Shaver died in October 1889, five years before the birth of Berryman's mother. Martha always deeply regretted that she had no surviving grandmother on either side of the family – 'having been sure that grandmother-that-should-have-been would have loved me dearly,' as she put it.

Although Berryman always resented the South for its racial prejudice and for giving a context to his parents' dire marriage, he often shared his mother's pride in her illustrious grandfather.

Selected bibliography

WORKS BY BERRYMAN

'Acceptance Speech for National Book Award'. New York: The National Book Committee, 1969.

The Arts of Reading (with Ralph Ross and Allen Tate). New York: Thomas Y. Crowell, 1960.

Berryman's Sonnets. New York: Farrar, Straus & Giroux, 1967; London: Faber & Faber, 1968.

Delusions, Etc. New York: Farrar, Straus & Giroux, 1972; London: Faber & Faber, 1972.

The Dispossessed. New York: William Sloane Associates, 1948.

The Dream Songs (complete edition of *77 Dream Songs* and *His Toy, His Dream, His Rest*). New York: Farrar, Straus & Giroux, 1969.

The Freedom of the Poet (essays and stories). New York: Farrar, Straus & Giroux, 1976; London: Faber & Faber, 1977.

Henry's Fate & Other Poems, 1967–1972. New York: Farrar, Straus & Giroux, 1977; London: Faber & Faber, 1978.

His Thought Made Pockets & The Plane Buckt. Pawlet, Vermont: Claude Fredericks, 1958.

His Toy, His Dream, His Rest. New York: Farrar, Straus & Giroux, 1968; London: Faber & Faber, 1969.

Homage to Mistress Bradstreet. New York: Farrar, Straus & Giroux, 1956.

Homage to Mistress Bradstreet and Other Poems. London: Faber & Faber, 1959; New York: Farrar, Straus & Giroux, 1968.

Love & Fame. New York: Farrar, Straus & Giroux, 1970; 2nd edn revised, 1972; London: Faber & Faber, 1971 (contents as for 2nd American edn).

Poems. Norfolk, Connecticut: New Directions, 1942.

Recovery (novel). New York: Farrar, Straus & Giroux, 1973; London: Faber & Faber, 1973.

Selected Poems 1938–1968. London: Faber & Faber, 1972.

77 Dream Songs. New York: Farrar, Straus & Giroux, 1964; London: Faber & Faber, 1964.

Short Poems. New York: Farrar, Straus & Giroux, 1967.
Stephen Crane (critical biography). New York: William Sloane Associates, 1950; rpt New York: Meridian Books, 1962.
'Three and a Half Years at Columbia', in Wesley First (ed.), *University on the Heights*. New York: Doubleday & Co., 1969.
'Thursday Out', *The Noble Savage*, no. 3, May 1961, pp. 186–194; rpt in *The Freedom of the Poet*.

CRITICAL STUDIES

Arpin, Gary Q. *The Poetry of John Berryman*. Port Washington, New York: Kennikat Press, 1978.
Conarroe, Joel. *John Berryman: An Introduction to the Poetry*. New York: Columbia University Press, 1977.
Haffenden, John. *John Berryman: A Critical Commentary*. London: Macmillan Press, 1980; New York: New York University Press, 1980.
Linebarger, J. M. *John Berryman*. Boston: Twayne, 1974.

WORKS OF REFERENCE

Arpin, Gary Q. *John Berryman: A Reference Guide*. Boston, MA: G. K. Hall, 1976 (lists articles and books about Berryman in the period 1935–75, with an abstract of each entry; incomplete, but none the less invaluable).
Kelly, Richard J. *John Berryman: A Checklist*. Metuchen, New Jersey: Scarecrow Press, 1972 (lists works by Berryman, including uncollected poems and recordings, and works about him: reviews, biographical articles, interviews, general critiques and monographs).
Stefanik, Jr, Ernest C. *John Berryman: A Descriptive Bibliography*. University of Pittsburgh Press, 1974 (the standard bibliography, scrupulously edited).

Acknowledgments and notes on sources

My principal source for this book is the John Berryman Papers, a magnificent collection of manuscript materials now owned by the University of Minnesota (but on deposit there during the period of my research). Richard J. Kelly, author of an invaluable bibliographical guide *John Berryman: A Checklist* (Metuchen, New Jersey: Scarecrow Press, 1972), has described the collection as ordered by the university in these terms:

> In all there are approximately thirty-six linear feet of papers, now contained within eighty-seven Hollinger boxes.
>
> The scope of the collection is impressive. It includes the original holographs in pencil, pen, or ballpoint of almost all of the published works along with the various revised holograph and typescript drafts, with and without the poet's hand, proof sheets, and plans for the order of the poems within each work. There are also holographs of unpublished poems, prose (essays, criticism, stories) and of numerous plays in varying states of completion. . . .
>
> Also found in the collection is an enormous amount of material on Shakespeare, only a fraction of which has so far been published. There are various notebooks, other notes and fragments of writing, trial lines, and clippings from newspapers and periodicals which relate to his work. In addition, the collection includes a large amount of diary material (in the form of books, notebooks, and loose papers) and a voluminous correspondence, both of which go back to 1931. There are teaching notes, college papers, texts of speeches, lectures and readings, personal and financial papers . . . booksellers' catalogs, biographical and literary notices, photographs and miscellaneous personal effects ['The Berryman Manuscripts', *John Berryman Studies*, II: i, Winter 1976].

The largest proportion of this book is based on information quoted or gleaned from the John Berryman Papers, and I have accordingly though reluctantly decided not to provide footnotes to each chapter, since the majority of what would amount to thousands of footnotes would point to that unpublished collection (which has been inventoried but not thoroughly itemized) and prove of limited assistance to the reader.

I am pleased to acknowledge my gratitude for help received from many individuals and organisations during my research. I am indebted first and foremost to Kate Donahue (Mrs John Berryman), for generously allowing me access to the John Berryman Papers in their entirety and to Berryman's library, for giving me every possible assistance, for her warm hospitality, and for her forbearance. I am happy in addition to offer my affectionate thanks and best wishes to her daughters, Martha and Sarah, for their delightful company and welcome distractions; thanks also to Robert Jefferson Berryman, John Berryman's brother, for an interview in 1974, for copies of letters, and for his enthusiasm and encouragement.

Dr A. Boyd Thomes and Maris Thomes were unfailingly solicitous throughout my visits to Minneapolis, most generously lodged me for several weeks, and always amazed me with their energy and resourcefulness: it is a great pleasure for me to record my thanks for their friendship. A. G. Mojtabai kindly lodged me during the period of my research in New York City, Anita Landau during a brief visit to Vermont, and Claudia Hexter in Cambridge, Massachusetts: I offer fond gratitude to each of them. I owe a debt of gratitude also to James Laughlin for allowing me to consult his files on John Berryman and for his warm hospitality in Connecticut; to the late Robert Lowell and to his wife, Caroline Blackwood, for a visit to their home in England in May 1972; and to Robert Giroux, Berryman's long-standing friend and publisher, for his first interest and help, for his stern criticism, and for supplying me with photocopies of the John Berryman correspondence at Farrar, Straus & Giroux, New York. I should like to thank all the staff and my fellow-guests at Yaddo for the pleasure of the several weeks I spent in residence during the summer of 1975 (a godsent period which enabled me to make good progress with early drafts of the first chapters of this book), and Elmer L. Andersen for a timely grant-in-aid without which my research would have been curtailed in Minneapolis earlier that year.

I am obliged to Alan Lathrop, Curator of Manuscripts at the University of Minnesota Libraries, and his wife Peggy, and to Richard J. Kelly, Reference Librarian, and his wife Lois, for helping me to survive a long and occasionally dispiriting period of archival research in Minneapolis: their hospitality and moral support meant a very great deal to me.

John Berryman's mother, the late Mrs Martha (Jill) Berryman, granted me an interview in March 1974. An aged woman, her memory was unfortunately frail and often confused, and I have accordingly chosen to rely more on the information contained within an additional batch of letters and papers (including the copious letters on grey paper Berryman wrote home from his boarding school) which she subsequently made available to me. Mrs Berryman's own letters relating to the events and circumstances of the 1910s and 1920s (chapter 2) contain manifest inconsistencies and misconstructions. Leaving aside any judgment of the sincerity of her written observations, I was for the most part able to distil from them a good amount of information and comment (much of which could be checked against other documentary sources) in order to establish the story of Berryman's ancestry, his parents' marriage, and the events of his upbringing. In certain instances where Mrs Berryman's contradictory letters evidently contributed to Berryman's confusion and distress in later years, I have cited those letters as necessary evidence.

The welter of Berryman's dream-transcriptions and analyses, notably in his 'Records of Self-Analysis' and in a volume he provisionally entitled *St. Pancras Braser* (which dates from 1954–5), includes much incidental and often reliable autobiographical information, some of it directly recalling events from his childhood as well as later years. Three of his fragmentary and unpublished stories – 'Little Me', 'Memories of an Old Instructor', and 'Sister' – added colouring as well as some facts to chapter 2. I benefited in addition from the kind assistance of the late Professor Russell Cooper, who undertook to track down for me some newspaper reports and official documents in Florida. The article cited in chapter 2, 'Clearwater Jury holds Tampan took own life', is from the *Tampa Sunday Tribune*, 27 June 1926. Much of my information about the early life of the towns and cities of Oklahoma derives from *Oklahoma: A Guide to the Sooner State*, compiled by workers of the Writers' Program of the Work Projects Administration (Norman: University of Oklahoma Press, 1947). With reference to chapter 2, I should also like to thank the following for their personal responses or documentary assistance: Gladys Callahan; Margaret Casanova, Clerk of the District Court, Washington County Court House; Albert Dahl; Richard Dutcher; Howard Ellingwood; Russell W. Fridley, Minnesota Historical Society; Globe College of Business, Inc., St Paul, Minnesota; Joseph Hipp, Head of the Special Collections Department, Tampa-Hillsborough County Public Library System, Tampa, Florida; Leo Lerman; Lorraine B. McNevin, Supervisor, Courts Division, Pinellas County, Florida; Marjorie Mascuch, School Secretary, P.S. 69 Queens, Jackson Heights, New York; Mrs B. H. Massingale; Mr N. J. Dikeman; Mrs Sam Owen, Public Relations Director, Chickasha Public Library, Chickasha, Oklahoma; Miss Priscilla R. Smith, Assistant Supervisor, Administration Unit, Division of Health, Bureau of Vital Statistics, State of Florida.

My inquiries into Berryman's sorry if successful career at South Kent School (chapter 3) were greatly aided by Dr Charles P. Whittemore, present Senior Master at South Kent, who provided me with relevant copies of the *South Kent Quarterly*, assisted me in identifying Berryman's contributions to the school magazine the *Pigtail*, and helped me to locate many of Berryman's contemporaries, masters and elders. I am indebted to the following for providing information or personal reminiscences: Mrs Samuel S. Bartlett; John Bayley; Aldis Butler; D. Pierre G. Cameron; Richard M. Cuyler; Professor Durand Echeverria; Frank Forester, Jr; The Reverend Alexander Hamilton; The Reverend Theodore F. Jones; Henry Kurtz; and Samuel A. Woodward. Particularly useful articles on the foundation and early life of South Kent School are 'How It Came About', the *South Kent Quarterly*, vol. VII, no. 3, fall 1969, and 'The Story of

South Kent School 1923–1973', the *South Kent Quartlerly*, vol. X, no. 2, winter 1973. Berryman's diary has entries from 1 January 1931 to 10 May 1931; a separate notebook – 'Diary II' – has relevant entries from 16 December 1931 to 5 January 1932.

Chapter 4 is informed by several generous contributors: Dorothy Rockwell Clark; Mrs C. W. Crowe; Roselle Davenport; E. M. Halliday; Mrs C. R. Kroeger; Jean Bennett Lanier; Robert Lax; Jane Atherton Roman; the late Lionel Trilling; the late Mark Van Doren; and Dr Philip D. Wiedel. I am also grateful for help received from the Barnard Alumni Office, Barnard College, New York; Charles P. Hurd, Registrar, Columbia University, New York; Marion Moscato, Alumni Federation of Columbia University, Inc.; and Yvonne Untch, Records Secretary, Office of Associate Alumni, Barnard College, Columbia University, New York.

Mrs Nancy Fraser most generously supplied me with detailed characterisations of Berryman's interests and activities both in Cambridge, England (chapter 5), and in New York City at the end of the 1930s. Chapter 5 is also deeply indebted to Professor Brian Boydell; Gordon Fraser; the late Tony Godwin; Dr George Rylands; Diana Crutchley; Nora David; Lady Rothschild; Professor Andrews Wanning; and Professor Ian Watt.

My knowledge of Detroit and Wayne State University in 1939 (chapter 6) is derived from *A Place of Light: The History of Wayne State University*, by Leslie L. Hanawalt (Detroit: Wayne State University Press, 1968). I am profoundly grateful to Professor and Mrs Hanawalt for their enthusiastic interest in my project, for providing me with copious information about Berryman's colleagues and students at Wayne State University, for resurrecting all the necessary archival documents and letters (Wayne State Liberal Arts College Personnel File; Wayne State English Department Personnel File; and Miles Poetry Files, Wayne State University Archives), and for conducting a telephone interview on my behalf with Calvin Shubow, to whom I also extend thanks. Mrs Florence J. Miller gave generous information about her life with Bhain Campbell in the year before his death, and about their relationship with John Berryman. Chapter 6 also owes much to the kind help of other individuals: Professor John Malcolm Brinnin; Professor Alva Gay; Miss Merle Hoyleman; Michael M. Jacobs; Alexander G. Rose; and Professor George Peck.

For the period from 1940 until 1972 it is not possible for me to make a chapter-by-chapter inventory of sources. Many of Berryman's friends and acquaintances met him at various periods during that span of time (Professor William Meredith, for instance, first encountered him at Princeton in the 1940s and then became a close friend from the early 1960s until the end), and it would be improperly misleading to itemise the help they have given me in terms of discrete episodes. I must therefore fall back on the expedient of presenting a list of names which scarcely does credit to individual generosity, but I offer my warmest thanks to all those who have helped me by granting interviews, by providing letters and other communications, or for obliging me with assistance in many other capacities. Since most of Berryman's own letters are still in private hands, I would also like to thank a good many of those individuals listed below who were able either to lend me their Berryman letters or to provide photocopies for my use:

Makka Abhishaker; Mrs Nancy Jewell Aldrich; A. Alvarez; Mrs Gisela Amberg; Professor Robert Ames; Professor Van Meter Ames and Elisabeth Ames; Professor Chester Anderson; Professor William A. Arrowsmith; James Atlas; Professor Carlos Baker; Howard Bard; William C. Barrett; John Baudhuin; Professor Frederick C. Bargebuhr; Professor Charles G. Bell; Professor Marvin Bell; Pearl Kazin Bell; Saul Bellow; Sondra Bellow; Professor Gerald E. Bentley; Professor Bruce Berlind; Mrs Elisabeth Bettman; Professor Walter Bezanson; Professor Cyril E. Black; Mrs Cornelia Borgerhoff; Mrs Betty Bostetter; Keith Botsford; Professor Bernard Bowron; Frederick Boyden; Christopher Nicholas Brown; Professor Huntington Brown; Professor Michael Dennis Browne; Gertrude Buckman; Carl Frederick Buechner; Catherine Carver; John Ciardi; Anthony Clark; Professor John Clark; Walter Clemons; Dr John I. Coe; Joan Colebrook; Terence Collins; Edward T. Cone; Professor Reginald L. Cook; Jane Cooper; Henri Coulette; Jean V. Cox; Professor Louis O. Coxe; Professor Robert Dana; Lynn Davis; James Delmont; Professor James Dickey; Daniel Donahue; Antal Dorati; Jay Dregni; Meredith Sommers Dregni; Jan Jackson Druck; Professor Richard Eberhart; Mrs Murray Eden; Professor Richard Ellmann; Professor Janet Emig; Professor and Mrs Monroe Engel; Albert R. Erskine; Christine Fall; Dr Francis Fergusson; Professor Robert Fitzgerald; Mr and Mrs J. Keene Fleck; Richard Fleck; Mary Folliet; Professor George H. Ford; Keith and Deborah Fort; Professor Charles Howell Foster; Claude Fredericks; Isabella Gardner; Robert L. Girouard; Nancy Gruchow; Thom Gunn; John Haislip; Charlotte Hall; Mrs John Hansen; Polly Hanson; Elizabeth Hardwick; Curtis Harnack; Dr John A. Haugen; Shirley Eliason Haupt; Dr H. C. Haynes; Judith Healey; Mary Heffernan; Professor Robert B. Heilman; Edward Hoagland; Professor Edwin Honig; Professor Howard C. Horsford; Eric Horsting; Jane Howard; Professor Daniel Hughes; Richard Hugo; Paul Hunter; Michael M. Jacobs; Mrs Mary Jarrell; Carol Johnsen; Professor Donald Justice; Mrs Alice L. Kahler; Ellen Kaplan; Professor Alfred Kazin; Professor Edmund Keeley; Robert V. Keeley; 'Keg'; Patrick Joseph Kelleher; Galway Kinnell; Elizabeth Kray; Anita Maximilian Landau; Natalie le Moine; Judy Lebedoff; Martha Leren; Professor Jacob C. Levenson; Professor Harry Levin; Professor Philip Levine; Daniel Lindley; 'Lise'; Linda T. Lombardo; Professor Lynn Louden; Professor Jack Ludwig; Robert Lundegaard; Father William F. Lynch; Earl J. Lyons; Professor John C. McGalliard; Professor David McKain; Dwight Macdonald; Professor Fred R. MacFadden; Donald Mackie; Elizabeth Mackie; Deborah Malone; Dr George A. Mann, Marion Mann; Professor Leo Marx; Professor William H. Matchett; Dr Donald M. Mayberg; Lars Mazzola; Professor William Meredith; Professor James Merrin; William Merwin; Charles R. Metzger; Professor Josephine Miles; Dr Sherman Miller; Henry Allen Moe; Carole Mohr; Professor Sidney Monas; Professor Samuel Holt Monk; Ruth E. Monson;

Professor John Montague; Charles Monteith; Professor Robert Moore; Professor Malcolm Moos; Professor and Mrs Theodore Morrison; Professor Howard Munford; Professor and Mrs Arthur Naftalin; Professor Howard Nemerov; Sean O'Faolain; the late Professor Anthony Ostroff; Timothy O'Sullivan; Milt Otteson; Professor Robert B. Page; Wyman W. Parker; Deba B. Patnaik; Donald and Betty Peddie; Professor Sergio Perosa; Professor Paul Petrie; William Phillips; Professor Robert M. Philmus; Victoria Pope; Dr Robert Premer; Professor John Crowe Ransom; Shreela Ray; Edwin W. Rickert; Dr Carl R. Rogers; Deborah Rogers; Dr Alvin H. Rosenfeld; Professor Ralph Ross; Harriet Rossetto; Joy C. Roulston; Marlos Rudie; Richard Ryan; Bette Schissel Sack; Professor Ernest Samuels; the late Professor Mark Schorer; Karl Shapiro; Peggy Sherry; Professor Philip Siegelman; Professor Louis Simpson; William Sloane; Barbara Smith; G. Roysce Smith; Professor W. D. Snodgrass; Ken Snyder; Robert S. Speaight; Ernest Stefanik; Wallace Stegner; Professor Arnold Stein; Professor A. Wilber Stevens; Ken Stevens; John W. Sturdevant; Dr Tony Tanner; the late Professor Allen Tate; Caroline Gordon Tate; John Thompson; Ruthven Todd; Blair Torrey; Valerie Trueblood; Mr and Mrs George Tselos; Melvin Tumin; Professor Leonard H. Unger; Kathy Ungerer; the late Professor Mark Van Doren; Professor Jay Vogelbaum; Larry Vonalt; Hal Vursel; Professor Robert Penn Warren; Sarah Appleton Weber; E. R. Weismiller; Professor Theodore H. Weiss; Ray B. West, Jr; Professor Richard Wilbur; Professor O. Meredith Wilson; Dr and Mrs Percy Wood; the late James Wright; Professor E. W. Ziebarth; Beverley Zomber; and Jim Zosel.

I am greatly indebted to the following librarians and officials for their ready assistance: Charles P. Hurd, Registrar, Columbia University, New York; Kenneth A. Lohf, Librarian for Rare Books and Manuscripts, Butler Library, Columbia University; Rodney G. Dennis, Curator of Manuscripts, The Houghton Library, Harvard University; Earle E. Coleman, University Archivist, Princeton University; Margaret McFadden, Assistant Curator for Manuscripts and Archives, Special Collections, The University of Chicago Library; Roy P. Basler, Chief of the Reference Department, Manuscript Division, The Library of Congress; Read Greyer, Administrative Assistant, Recorded Sound Section, Reference Division, Music Division, The Library of Congress; Holly Hall, Head of the Manuscripts Division, Washington University Libraries, St Louis, Missouri; Dr Lola L. Szladits, Curator of the Berg Collection, The New York Public Library; and Austin J. McLean, Chief of the Special Collections Department, Wilson Library, The University of Minnesota Libraries.

With Kate Donahue's consent, the following administrators generously made available Berryman's medical records at their institutions: Dr Daniel J. Anderson (Director), Harold A. Swift (Director of Rehabilitation Services), and Mrs Janice Johnson (Medical Record Practitioner), Hazelden, Center City, Minnesota; and Mrs J. Higgins, Supervisor of Medical Records, St Mary's Extended Care Center, Minneapolis, Minnesota. A valuable book by Vernon E. Johnson, *I'll Quit Tomorrow* (New York:

Harper & Row, 1973) helped me to understand the nature of alcoholism and the treatment that Berryman underwent towards the end of his life.

I should also like to thank Ed Haislet, Executive Director of The Minnesota Alumni Association, whose records enabled me to trace some of Berryman's students and who helped me to reach others through an advertisement in *Alumni News*; and Barbara A. E. Yerich, Research Fellow in the Office of Sponsored Programs, who attempted to find additional funds for me at a particularly lean time. I am grateful too for all the firm and sympathetic assistance I have received from Deborah Rogers, my literary agent, and from my editors: Stephen Brook, who adopted this book for Routledge & Kegan Paul and worked hard to help me cut the final manuscript; and David Godwin, who then took up the task.

All previously unpublished poems, journals, letters, and other writings by John Berryman are published by kind permission of Kate Donahue as Executrix of the Estate of John Berryman. The author and publishers are grateful to Farrar, Straus & Giroux Inc. and Faber & Faber Ltd for permission to quote from *Berryman's Sonnets*, copyright © 1952, 1967 by John Berryman; *Delusions, Etc.*, copyright © 1969, 1971 by John Berryman, copyright © 1972 by the Estate of John Berryman; *The Dream Songs*, copyright © 1959 to 1969 by John Berryman; *The Freedom of the Poet*, copyright © 1972 by John Berryman, copyright © 1973, 1975, 1976 by Kate Berryman; *Henry's Fate & Other Poems, 1967–72*, copyright © 1969 by John Berryman, copyright © 1975 to 1977 by Kate Berryman; *Homage to Mistress Bradstreet*, copyright © 1956 by John Berryman; *Love & Fame*, copyright © 1970 by John Berryman; *Recovery*, copyright © 1973 by the Estate of John Berryman; *Short Poems*, copyright © 1948, 1958, 1964 by John Berryman; *Stephen Crane*, copyright © 1950 by Kate Berryman. Extracts from 'Innocent', 'Elegy, for Alun Lewis' and 'The Cage', which first appeared in *Poetry*, copyright 1950 by the Modern Poetry Association, are reprinted by permission of the Editor of *Poetry*. Robert Lowell's letters are reprinted by courtesy of Frank Bidart, as Executor of the Estate of Robert Lowell. I should also like to acknowledge the following libraries for permitting me to publish letters in their ownership: Berryman's letters to Saul Bellow appear by permission of The Joseph Regenstein Library, The University of Chicago; a letter from John Berryman to Randall Jarrell by permission of the Henry W. and Albert A. Berg Foundation, The New York Public Library, Astor Lenox and Tilden Foundations; letters from John Berryman to Robert Lowell by permission of The Houghton Library; and John Berryman's letters to Mark Van Doren by permission of Columbia University Libraries. Bhain Campbell's letters to John Berryman appear by permission of Mrs Florence J. Miller; a letter from Wallace Stevens by permission of Holly Stevens; letters from Allen Tate by permission of Mrs Helen Tate; and letters from Mark Van Doren by permission of Mrs Dorothy Van Doren.

I am grateful to the editors of the following periodicals, in which early or modified versions of passages from this book first appeared: *The Bennington Review, Critical Quarterly, New Review, Partisan Review, Quarto, Stand*, and *Twentieth Century Literature*.

The author gratefully acknowledges the assistance of the Arts Council of Great Britain.

John Haffenden
Sheffield

Index of works by Berryman

PUBLISHED

A. POETRY

'An Afternoon Visit', 296
'An eye-opener, a nightcap, so it goes', 354
'Another New Year's Eve', 386
'Apollo 8', 145
'Ars Poetica', 71
'Auden Landscape', 126

Berryman's Sonnets, 2; 'events seduced me', 167–83 *passim*; 185; 'mad sonnets', 193–5; 344, 346, 401, 414; Sonnet numbers. **1**, 168–9, **5**, 171, **11**, 173; **13**, 173; **16**, 169, 175; **19**, 171–2; **21**, 175; **25**, 239; **29**, 175; **30**, 176; **38**, 175–6; **39**, 174–5; **49**, 173; **71**, 176–7; **75**, 175; **78**, 178–9; **79**, 179; **83**, 179; **107**, 180; **110**, 180–1; **112**, 180; **113**, 180; **114**, 180; **115**, 180; prefatory sonnet, 183; unpublished sonnet, quoted, 182
'from The Black Book (iii)', 205–6
'Blake', 71
'Boston Common', 136

'Cadenza on Garnette', 61
'The Cage', 214
'Canto Amor', 156, 394
'Che', 387, 418
'The Children: Proemio', 407
'Compline', 396

'Conversation', 108
'Cradle Song' (*Cambridge Review*, May 1974), 88
'Crisis', 75

'Death Ballad', 363
'Defensio in Extremis', 390
Delusions, Etc., 383, 418
'The Disciple', 132
The Dispossessed, 152, 166, 190, 193; critical reception, 196–200; 201, 206, 216; 'The Nervous Songs', 141–2
'The Dispossessed', 193, 197
'Down & Back', 62–4, 66–7
The Dream Songs, 2–3; persona 'Henry' in, 4, 25, 253–4, 327–8; dominated by 'enough feelings' about father, 30–1, 209; JB invents title, 250; 253–4, 270, 273, 305–6; struggles with composition, 309–12, 314–15, 318; 321, 322–8, 331, 337–9, 350–2, 355, 394, 402, 414; Song numbers: **2**, 312; **25**, 318; **34**, 297; **37**, 308; **38**, 308; **40**, 314; **45**, 311; **54**, 268–9; **62**, 309; **63**, 249; **66**, 322; **68**, 315; **70**, 311; **92**, 324–5; **107**, 309; **121**, 332; **145**, 25–6; **149**, 312; **154**, 319; **155**, 318–19; **185**, 324; **186**, 301; **188**, 324; **231**, 300; **235**, 298; **243**, 322; **276**, 339; **278**, 338; **285**, 315; **295**, 341; **297**, 344; **304**, 343–4;

433

General index

437

Bellow, Saul – *contd.*
  404–5; *The Adventures of Augie
  March*, 3, 235, 309, 328, 329, 405;
  Henderson the Rain King, 270, 328;
  Herzog, 3, 328–9, 336; *Seize the
  Day*, 328
Bellow, Sondra, 235, 255, 257–8
Benares, JB visits, 265
Bennett, Jean, 69–70, 92, 132, 134,
  136, 137–8, 341–2
Bennington College, Vermont, 153,
  235, 255
Bentley, Gerald E., 163, 165–6
Berg, Martin, 414
Berlind, Bruce, 164; on JB as
  'Prometheus', 166; 173, 197–8
Berryman, Ann (JB's second wife):
  meeting and marriage, 255–6; birth
  of son, Paul, 257–8, 267, 273;
  troubled marriage and separation,
  274–80; divorce, 281; 283, 301–2,
  325, 335
Berryman, Barbara (first wife of JB's
  brother, Robert Jefferson), 130
Berryman, Eileen (JB's first wife),
  4–5; courtship, work, meeting
  mother-in-law, marriage, 132–9;
  'Broom' and 'Rusty', happiness and
  struggles of the first year, 140–7;
  149, 150; employed at Institute for
  Advanced Study, 153; 'like a bird
  singing', 154; 'overjoyed' at JB's
  success, 156; 'will have a child we
  hope', 157; appendectomy, 157–8;
  160, 165; love and loyalty
  throughout JB's first affair, 168–89;
  191–5; accident and minor
  operation, 201–2; 203, 207–8,
  210–11; Master's degree and work
  in clinical psychology, 215; 219, 222;
  visit to Cincinnati, 224–7; suffers
  from JB's work and *modus vivendi*,
  228; trip to Europe, 229–31;
  separation from JB, 232; 235–6, 252;
  divorce, 256; 383, 394, 405
Berryman, Ethel (first wife of John
  Angus Berryman), 22–3
Berryman, John:
  OUTLINE BIOGRAPHY: birth
  and christening in McAlester,
  Oklahoma, 14–15; childhood in
  Anadarko, 16–19; boarding-school

at Chickasha, Oklahoma, 21–2;
Florida, 22; father's suicide, New
York, 34–6, 52–5; South Kent
School (preparatory), 36–57;
bullied, 21, 37, 45–7; makes suicide
bid, 46–7; Columbia College, New
York, 57–75; wins Euretta J. Kellett
scholarship, 74–5; Clare College,
Cambridge, England, 76–103;
meets W. B. Yeats, 90–1; with
Beatrice, his first fiancée, 92–3;
enters for Harness Prize, 94; visits
Germany, 94–5; wins Oldham
Shakespeare Scholarship, 96; visits
Paris, 101; New York, poetry and
joblessness, 103–11; poetry editor of
the *Nation*, 109–10, 113, 116; visits
Grand Marais, Michigan, 110;
instructor at Wayne University,
Detroit, 110–23; epilepsy, 117–23,
133, 144, 153, 179, 184; publishes
Five Young American Poets, 127–8;
Instructor in English, Harvard
University, 129–43; meeting and
marriage with Eileen Patricia
Mulligan, 132–9; publishes *Poems*,
136–7; job-hunting and short-term
employment, 143–6; Instructor in
English, Princeton University,
146–52; Rockefeller Foundation
research fellowship for research on
Shakespeare, 154–8; commissioned
to write *Stephen Crane*, 157;
publishes 'The Imaginary Jew',
157–8; Associate in Creative
Writing, Princeton University,
160–6; 'seduced, lied, cost agony,
betrayed' during first adultery,
167–95; writes sequence of poems
later published as *Berryman's Sonnets*,
167–80; meets T. S. Eliot, 170–1;
starts heavy drinking, 169; begins
work on 'Homage to Mistress
Bradstreet' and publishes *The
Dispossessed*, 196–200, 206; Resident
Fellow in Creative Writing,
Princeton University, 204; works on
The Black Book, 205–6; awarded
Guarantors Prize and Shelley
Memorial Award, 206; writes and
publishes *Stephen Crane*, 206–11,
215–16; visits Ezra Pound, 212–14;

teaches at University of Washington, 210; awarded Levinson Prize, 215; Alfred Hodder Fellow, Princeton University, 214, 216; brief teaching assignments at the universities of Vermont, Rutgers, and Columbia, and at Bard College, 217; Elliston Professor of Poetry, University of Cincinnati, 224–5; Guggenheim Fellowship, 227–8; trip to Europe, 229–32; separation from Eileen, 232–3; teaches at University of Iowa, 236–41, 242–4; teaches summer school at Harvard University, 241–2; expulsion from Iowa, arrival in Minneapolis, 243–5; becomes a professor of Humanities at the University of Minnesota, 249; begins work on *The Dream Songs*, 250, 252; publishes *Homage to Mistress Bradstreet*, 254–5; awarded Rockefeller fellowship in poetry, and the Harriet Monroe poetry prize, 255; divorced from Eileen, marries Elizabeth Ann Levine, 256; birth of son, Paul, 257; Associate Professor of Interdisciplinary Studies, University of Minnesota, 258; visits Japan, 258–9; lectures in Indiana University, 297, meets Information Service, 259–67; holiday in Spain, 267; disestablishment of Department of Interdisciplinary Studies, 269; publishes *The Arts of Reading*, 272; separation and divorce from Ann, 278–81; visiting professor at University of California, 286–94; teaches summer school at Indiana University, 297; meets and marries Kathleen (Kate) Donahue, 298–301; teaches at Bread Loaf School of English, Middlebury, Vermont, 304–8; visiting professor at Brown University, 310–20; reads at National Poetry Festival, Washington, D.C., 311; birth of elder daughter, Martha, 313; holiday in Rhode Island, 320–3; temporary residence in Washington, D.C., 324; publishes *77 Dream Songs*, 324–8;

wins Russell Loines Award, 333; buys house in Minneapolis, 335; awarded Pulitzer Prize in poetry, 336–7; Guggenheim Fellowship, residence in Dublin, 340–8; receives award from the Academy of American Poets, 343, 345; featured in *Life* magazine, 346–8; visits France, Italy, England and Greece, 348; receives award from the National Endowment for the Arts, 349; publishes *His Toy, His Dream, His Rest*, wins Bollingen Prize and National Book Award, 349–52; appointed Regents' Professor of Humanities, University of Minnesota, 356; treated for alcoholism, 357–77, 381–4; writes poems of *Love & Fame*, 361–3, 370, 372; spiritual conversion, 369–72, 382–4, 388, 390, 403–5; joins Alcoholics Anonymous, takes vacation in Mexico, 378–9; publishes *Love & Fame*, 383–4; begins work on poems of *Delusions, Etc.*, 384–5; wins Senior Fellowship from the National Endowment for the Humanities, 400–2; works on novel, *Recovery*, 403–5; birth of younger daughter, Sarah Rebecca, 406; vacation in Colorado, premonition of death, 408; suicide and funeral, 419–20
ALCOHOLISM, THE RECKONING WITH: 349, 356–9 360–77, 381–2, 384, 385–6, 398, 402–6, 408–9, 410–11, 413–14, 416, 418
APPEARANCE: 36–7, 45, 52–5, 59, 65, 67, 69, 97, 105, 108–9, 114–15, 118, 161, 217, 306, 307, 310, 337–8, 352–3, 355, 379–80, 393
CHARACTERISTICS, INTERESTS, PREOCCUPATIONS: 'Daddy's death . . . blocked my development', 8, 25–6, 29–33, 51, 55–6, 124–5, 179, 182, 184, 191–3, 209–10, 248, 274–5, 277–8, 298, 311, 320, 331, 372, 381, 385, 413, 415; *see also under* Smith, John Allyn (father); dreams, 30, 49, 122, 152, 154, 191, 209–10,

Winter Diary and Other Poems, A (Mark Van Doren), 72
Winters, Yvor, 197–9
Wittenberg, Lester, 42
Women's College of Greensboro, N. Carolina, The, 160
Wood, Nancy, *see* Tate, Nancy
Wood, Percy, 217
Woodward, Samuel A., 39–41, 43
Woolf, Virginia, 84
Worden, James, 200
Words and Poetry (George Rylands), 76
Wright, James, 330, 345
Writings from the Philokalia on Prayer of the Heart, 391

'X' (schoolmate), 46–7

'Y' (schoolmate), 46–7
Yaddo, 105, 110
Yale University, 332
Yeats, W. B., 72, 74, 76, 77, 83; JB's hero-worship and research, 85–7; JB lectures on, and meets, 89–91; poetic influence of, 105; JB writes epitaph on, 108; JB and Ezra Pound discuss, 212–14; 344, 382

Ziebarth, E. W., 356
Zosel, Jim, 367–72, 376, 383